The Captive Republic

Studies in Australian History

Series editors: Alan Gilbert, Patricia Grimshaw and Peter Spearritt

Steven Nicholas (ed.)   *Convict Workers*
Pamela Statham (ed.)   *The Origins of Australia's Capital Cities*
Jeffrey Grey   *A Military History of Australia*
Alastair Davidson   *The Invisible State*
James A. Gillespie   *The Price of Health*
David Neal   *The Rule of Law in a Penal Colony*
Sharon Morgan   *Land Settlement in Early Tasmania*
Audrey Oldfield   *Woman Suffrage in Australia*
Paula J. Byrne   *Criminal Law and Colonial Subject*
Peggy Brock   *Outback Ghettos*
Raelene Frances   *The Politics of Work*
Luke Trainor   *British Imperialism and Australian Nationalism*
Margaret Maynard   *Fashioned from Penury*
Dawn May   *Aboriginal Labour and the Cattle Industry*
Joy Damousi and Marilyn Lake (eds)   *Gender and War*
Michael Roe   *Australia, Britain, and Migration, 1915–1940*
John F. Williams   *The Quarantined Culture*
Nicholas Brown   *Governing Prosperity*
Jan Todd   *Colonial Technology*
Shurlee Swain with Renate Howe   *Single Mothers and Their Children*
Tom Griffiths   *Hunters and Collectors*
Deborah Oxley   *Convict Maids*
Marjorie Theobald   *Knowing Women*

The Captive Republic

A History of Republicanism in Australia 1788–1996

Mark McKenna

Published by the Press Syndicate of the University of Cambridge
The Pitt Building, Trumpington Street, Cambridge CB2 1RP, UK
40 West 20th Street, New York, NY 10011–4211, USA
10 Stamford Road, Oakleigh, Melbourne 3166, Australia

© Mark McKenna 1996
First published 1996

Printed in Australia by Brown Prior Anderson

National Library of Australia cataloguing-in-publication data

McKenna, Mark, 1959– .
The captive republic: a history of republicanism in
Australia 1788–1996.
Bibliography.
Includes index.
1. Republicanism – Australia – History. 2. Australia –
Politics and government. I. Title.
321.860994

Library of Congress cataloguing-in-publication data

McKenna, Mark, 1959– .
The captive republic: a history of republicanism in Australia,
1788–1996 / Mark McKenna.
  p. cm. – (Studies in Australian history)
Includes bibliographical references and index.
1. Republicanism – Australia – History. I. Title. II. Series.
JQ4031.M35   1996
321.8'6'0994–dc20   96–3101

A catalogue record for this book is available from the British Library.

ISBN 0 521 57258 4 Hardback

For Fiona and Siobhán McKenna

There is a deep under-current of republicanism in these colonies, which will some day burst forth and astonish the world.

People's Advocate
11 March 1854

Contents

List of Illustrations	ix
Abbreviations	x
Acknowledgments	xiii
Introduction	1

1	The Piratical Republic 1788–1833	12
	Pigs and Lashes	12
	The Blue Mountains Republic 1819–1827	15
	Shaking Off the Yoke	18
	The Rise of the Native-Born: Horatio Wills and the *Currency Lad*	22
2	The Stockmen's Republic 1833–1848	29
	Canada and Lord Durham	29
	The Invisible Compact	31
	A Civil, Constitutional, and Gentlemanly State of Disgust	33
3	The Last Resort 1848–1856	40
	The Year of Revolution	40
	Another America?	44
	The Coming Event	47
	Bringing Out the Doctor	53
	Convict Scum	56
	Nation or Empire	59
	Redemption from Misrule	63
	Lang Stands Again	67
	Driving a Loyal People to Rebellion	69
4	A Bunyip Aristocracy	73
	Bunyips in the House	74
	The Doctor Returns	79
	The First Sacrifice	86

5	A Victorian Republic	92
	Eureka	97
	The Rebellion	98
	After Eureka	102
6	*Quieta Non Movere* 1856–1880	109
	The Loyalty Play	112
	Reconstructing the Empire	115
	Independence Enough	118
7	A White Man's Republic 1880–1887	121
	The First Stirrings 1880–1886	123
	New Guinea	125
	Sudan	127
	Socialists and Republicans	131
	1887—The Jubilee Year and the Republican Riots	136
8	Nation and Republic 1887–1891	151
	1888—The Centenary Year	160
	The Coffee Palace Republic	166
	Queensland—The Banana Republic	174
	The Republicans of Charters Towers	178
9	The Common Weal—Republicanism and Federation	188
	Commonwealth	191
10	The Imperial *Mardi Gras* 1901–1963	205
11	The End of the Affair 1963–1995	219
	The Legacy of Kerr 1972–1988	226
	The Queen's Australian	229
	Celebration of a Nation	239
	The Dead Duck	241
	The Dead Duck Flies 1990–1995	248
Epilogue		264
Notes		268
Select Bibliography		310
Index		325

Illustrations

John Dunmore Lang's vision of an Australian republic.	2
John Dunmore Lang, 1850.	48
Henry Parkes, 1854.	60
Daniel Deniehy, 1859.	77
David Blair.	106
Bulletin, 27 February 1886: 'The Widow's Mite'.	132
Town and Country Journal, 25 June 1887: 'Meeting of Loyalists'.	143
Bulletin, 2 July 1887: 'Only A Name'.	152
Bulletin, 14 April 1888: 'The Imperial Connection'.	152
Louisa Lawson.	155
Henry Lawson.	155
George Black.	165
William Lane.	176
Frederick Charles Burleigh Vosper.	184
Boomerang, 1 February 1890: 'Australia First'.	189
Bulletin, 4 January 1890: 'A New Leaf'.	202
The Royal Visit and You, 'When you meet the Queen and the Duke'.	208
The Royal Visit and You, 'What dress should you wear at public functions?'.	209
OZ, Christmas and New Year issue, 1966: front cover.	220
Geoffrey Dutton, *c.* 1960s.	225
Donald Horne, *c.* 1970s.	225
Citizens for Democracy, announcement of Republic Day, 11 November 1979.	230
Time Australia, front cover (12 April 1993).	242
Independent Monthly, front cover (March 1992).	242
Sydney Morning Herald, 15 February 1992: 'Citizen Queen'.	247
Australian Republican Movement Launch, 7 July 1991.	247
Paul Keating.	252
Age, 30 March 1993, Nicholson cartoon.	255
Sydney Morning Herald, 1 May 1993, Moir cartoon.	255

Abbreviations

Adelaide Law Review	*ALR*
Australian Bicentennial Authority	ABA
Australian Cultural History	*ACH*
Australian Dictionary of Biography	*ADB*
Australian Financial Review	*AFR*
Australian Historical Studies	*AHS*
Australian Journal of Forensic Science	*AJFS*
Australian Journal of Political Science	*AJPS*
Australian Journal of Politics and History	*AJPH*
Australian Labor Party	ALP
Australian Labour Federation	ALF
Australian Natives Association	ANA
Australian Republican	*AR*
Australian Republican Association	ARA
Australian Republican Movement	ARM
Australian Rhodes Review	*ARR*
Australian Socialist League	ASL
Australian Society for the Study of Labour History	*ASSLH*
Australian Star	*AS*
Australian Workman	*AW*
Australians for Constitutional Monarchy	ACM
Brisbane Courier	*BC*
Canberra Bulletin of Public Administration	*CBPA*
Canberra Historical Journal	*CHJ*
Canberra Times	*CT*
(Catholic) *Freeman's Journal*	*FJ*
Centennial Magazine	*CM*
Charters Towers Times	*CTT*
Citizens for Democracy	CFD
Colonial Office	CO
Commonwealth and Worker's Advocate	*CWA*
Commonwealth of Australia Parliamentary Debates	*CAPD*

Abbreviations xi

Communist Party of Australia	CPA
Communist Review	*CR*
Courier-Mail	*C-M*
Currency Lad	*CL*
Daily Mirror	*DM*
Daily Telegraph	*DT*
Daily Telegraph Mirror	*DTM*
European Economic Community	EEC
Freeman's Journal	*FJ*
Goulburn Herald	*GH*
Herald (Melbourne)	*MH*
Historical Journal	*HJ*
Historical Records of Australia	*HRA*
Historical Records of NSW	*HRNSW*
Historical Studies	*HS*
House of Representatives	H of R
Hobart Town Courier	*HTC*
Illustrated Sydney News	*ISN*
Independent Monthly	*IM*
Inquirer and Commercial News	*ICN*
Journal of Australian Studies	*JAS*
Journal of Commonwealth Political Studies	*JCPS*
Journal of Modern History	*JMH*
Journal of the Bankers' Institute of Australia	*JBIA*
Labor Electoral League	LEL
Labour History	*LH*
Launceston Examiner	*LE*
Law Institute Journal	*LIJ*
Legislative Studies	*LS*
Melbourne Historical Journal	*MHJ*
Melbourne Review	*MR*
Melbourne University Law Review	*MULR*
National Advocate	*NA*
National Australian Convention Debates	*NACD*
National Times	*NT*
New Order	*NO*
Newcastle Herald	*NH*
Newcastle Morning Herald	*NMH*
Nineteenth Century	*NC*
NSW Parliamentary Debates	*NSW PD*
Pacific Historical Review	*PHR*
People's Advocate	*PA*
Political Theory Newsletter	*PTN*

Queensland Parliamentary Debates	QPD
Royal Australian Historical Society Journal	RAHSJ
Royal Historical Society Journal of Queensland	RHSJQ
Senate	S
South Australian Parliamentary Debates	SAPD
South Australian Register	SAR
Sunday Telegraph	ST
Sydney Gazette	SG
Sydney Herald	SH
Sydney Mail	SM
Sydney Morning Herald	SMH
Sydney Quarterly Magazine	SQM
Time Australia	TA
Town and Country Journal	TCJ
United Services Magazine	USM
Victorian Parliamentary Debates	VPD
West Australian	WA
Young Australia	YA

Acknowledgments

The first third of this book began as a PhD thesis in the Department of Political Science at the University of New South Wales in July 1990. Although most of the book was written in 1994–95, at times it seemed as if publication was becoming like the republic – allegedly inevitable but never managing to arrive. There are many people who helped to make the book a reality. Phillipa McGuinness at Cambridge University Press was consistent in her commitment to its publication. Several colleagues and friends were particularly helpful.

To Conal Condren especially, many thanks for your support and advice over the last five years. I am also indebted to Averil Condren, who kindly offered to perform the difficult task of indexing my work. To George Winterton for your continued encouragement and support, many thanks.

To the staff of the Mitchell Library, Brian Murray at the Parliamentary Library in Canberra, David Clune at the New South Wales Parliamentary Library and Wendy Kelly, thanks for service beyond the call of duty.

Thanks also to David Headon, James Warden, Franca Arena, Neville Wran, Tony Pooley, Michael Ward, Donald Horne and Myfanwy Gollan who all assisted with access to sources at various stages.

Finally, I wish to thank Fiona McKenna. This book could not have been completed without your support.

Mark McKenna

Introduction

From the vantage point of the late twentieth century, the history of republicanism in Australia is the history of an imagined destiny. The Australian republic is a two-century-old dream not realised, the captive bird that waits patiently for the door of the cage to open.

The belief that Australia would 'inevitably' become a republic was already planted in 1788 when the First Fleet sailed into Sydney Harbour. After the American War of Independence in 1776 many people in Britain accepted that the colonies in the New World would eventually assert their independence and separate from the parent state. In Australia, a republic was long recognised as the end point of the colonies' political development—an ideal that would be realised when Australia finally matured into an independent nation.[1] For more than two centuries the familiar metaphor of Australia as a child awaiting maturation often carried within it the notion of a republican 'coming of age'. Today we are accustomed to public statements from politicians proclaiming the inevitability of the republic. But if we cast our eyes over the history of republican debate in Australia we begin to understand that the idea of an inevitable republic has been the Achilles' heel of Australian republicans. The inevitable republic may be truth, it may be furphy, but Australians have used it to delay the coming of the republic as much as they have used it to legitimise the republic's arrival. In the 1990s we have come to accept that the republic will come of its own accord—without any struggle and with little involvement on the part of the people. Like detached bystanders, we stand on the shore and wait for the boat to come in.[2]

This book is an attempt to understand the role of republican ideas in Australia's past—a political history based on a selective record of the arguments that have gathered around the word *republic*. It is a history not only of republicans but of the political debate which they have helped to stimulate in the press, parliaments and public meetings of Australia since 1788. To some extent it is also a history which is episodic. Republican debate in Australia has been at its most intense at times of national or political renewal. Throughout the book, I have intentionally focused on

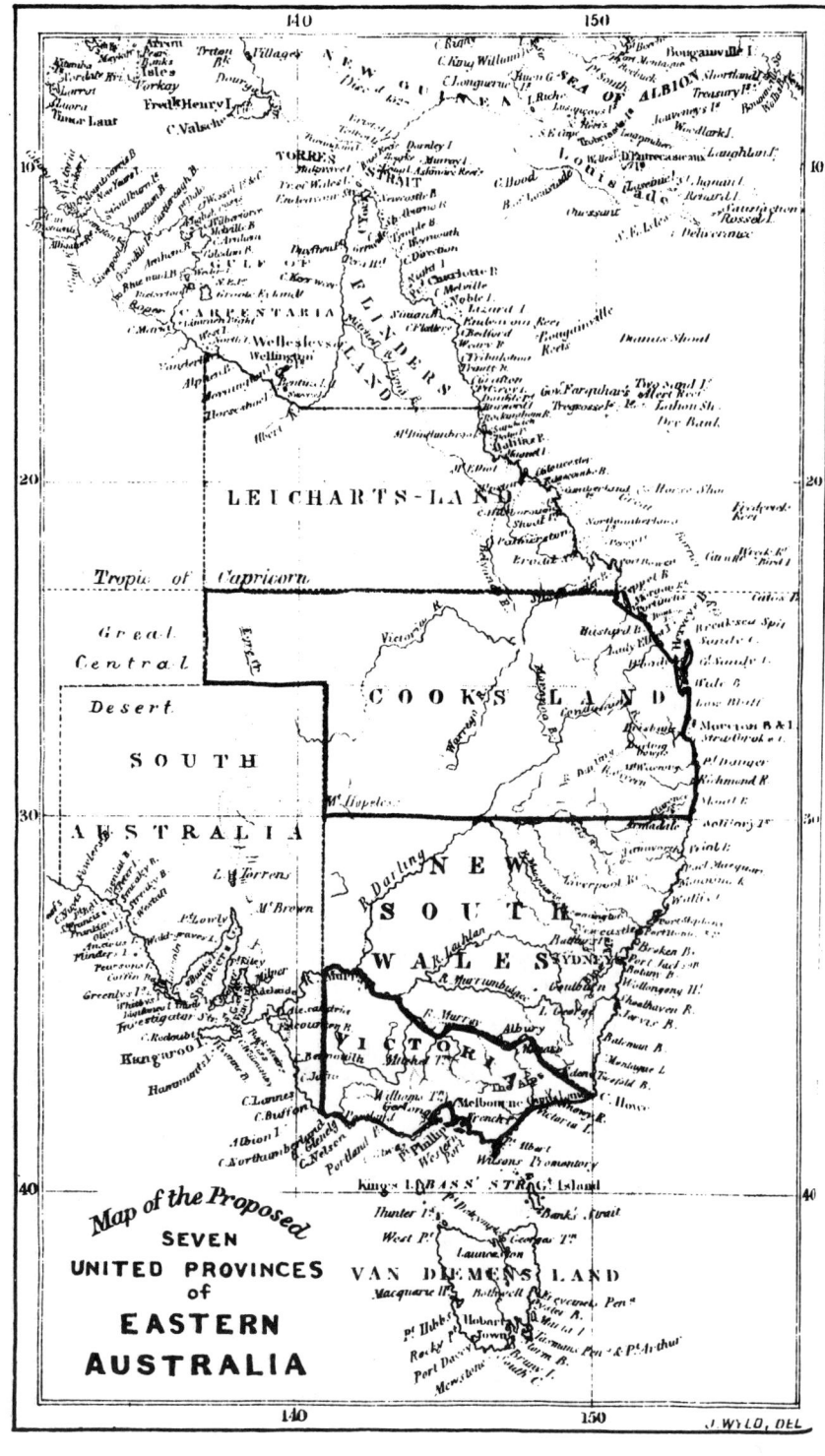

these periods—especially when republican arguments (in one form or another) played a crucial role in the formation of colonial or federal political institutions. Consequently, certain colonies, such as New South Wales, and particular decades, such as 1845–55 and 1880–1901, have received greater attention.

In one sense, it is not surprising that it was the colonies on the eastern mainland which harboured the most explicit forms of nationalist republicanism. In Tasmania, a colony which did not achieve manhood suffrage until 1900, the emergence of a strong working-class political movement was retarded by the legacy of convictism. In Western Australia, the transportation of convicts continued until 1868, while responsible government did not arrive until 1890. In the 1890s, at the height of the labour movement in the eastern colonies, commentators remarked on the rudimentary nature of its development in Western Australia. In South Australia, a colony founded on Protestant virtues and the 'civilising' influence of agriculture, it was faith in land reform, God and British traditions of parliamentary reform which characterised the majority of labour reform movements.[3] When we encounter commitment to republican principles in colonies such as Tasmania and South Australia, it is not in the anti-British mould of the Sydney *Bulletin*. In the chapters that follow, I have tried to write in detail the republican history that has not yet been told, to explain the role played by republicanism in the decades before the granting of responsible government in the 1850s and the Federation of the colonies of 1901. I should add that the book is not a cultural nationalist's tale of republican heroes marching bravely on through an imperial wilderness. Nor is it a history that seeks to nail down any one republican idea as more appropriate or more politically correct. If there are republican traditions in our past they are beholden to no political ideology, party or creed, and they bear as much relevance to the conservative traditions of Australian politics as they do to our radical and socialist traditions. When we think of republicanism today we often imagine a political concept which is anti- (or at least non-) monarchical. We think of severing the last ties with Great Britain—perhaps an Australian president replacing the British monarch as head of state, one final but small step in the realisation of Australia's complete independence.[4] While this may be the meaning which *we* associate with the concept of an Australian republic in the 1990s, we have to be extremely careful not to impose our contemporary sense of the republic on the past.

Lang's vision
This map appeared opposite the title page of John Dunmore Lang's major republican work, *Freedom and Independence for the Golden Lands of Australia*, published in 1852. Lang's vision of an Australian republic excluded the infant colony of Western Australia and split the area north of New South Wales into three separate provinces named in honour of Australian explorers.
(Image Library, State Library of New South Wales.)

Since European settlement began in 1788 republicanism in Australia has represented a diverse range of phenomena trading under one label.

The term 'republic', like the word 'democracy', is a perfect example of the essentially contested concept, a concept about which there can be no precise agreement.[5] In any period, traditional understandings of the republic, such as the 'classical' republic which was based partially on the Aristotelian notion of government as a balance of monarchy, aristocracy and democracy, have coexisted with other more or less democratic notions of the republic. In short, the protean republic and its derivatives—republicanism and republican—have always been labels to be fought over.[6] Writing in *Federalist* Number 39, one of eighty-five papers written by Alexander Hamilton, John Jay and James Madison in 1787–88 to encourage voters in New York State to ratify the American Federal Constitution, James Madison asked the following question: 'What, then, are the distinctive characteristics of the republican form? Were an answer to this question to be sought not by recurring to principles but in the application of the term by political writers to the constitutions of different States, no satisfactory one would ever be found'.[7]

Madison's point is perhaps even more valid today. Although a particular state might carry the title 'republic', the word tells us little about the form of government within that state. This would be true in either a historical or contemporary context. Thus, the monarchical element incorporated in the Venetian republic of the fifteenth century in the form of the elected Doge varied from the form of government found in the Cromwellian republic of the 1650s or the post-revolutionary republics of France in the late eighteenth century. Equally, the form of government found in the modern republic of the United States bears little similarity to the republic of Iraq. In the late twentieth century a president's penchant for military uniform may be a more accurate indicator of the form of government than the appellation 'republic'.

When we turn to the more abstract discussion concerning the 'true' or 'real' principles of republican government we still find considerable room for disagreement. Madison, for example, may have identified the principles of republican government with representative federal democracy, but there were also many Anti-Federalists in late eighteenth-century America who held more democratic notions of republicanism which were traditionally connected with smaller states.[8] This should remind us that 'republican principles' in any period are likely to be contested. In the contemporary republican debate in Australia, for example—at least in the broadsheet press and the academic community—there is an ongoing debate concerning the principles of republican government which may or may not be incorporated into any new or remodelled constitution.[9] Republicans want Australia to become a republic, while monarchists want

Australia to remain a crowned republic.[10] In this light, the Australian republic is 'captive' because of the very fluidity of political language, a notion of political change which is both propelled and impeded by its own historical baggage. Even when participants in the republican debate attempt to locate republican principles in the word's etymology (that is, the Latin *respublica*—the public thing) or 'traditional' republican principles such as popular sovereignty, the rule of law, checks and balances, or the goal of a virtuous citizenry, they are unlikely to agree about the definition of such principles or where, when and how they might be applied.[11] As the American John Adams remarked: 'the word republic, . . . may signify anything, everything or nothing'.[12] Although the word 'republic' has remained the same, its meaning has not. Thus, the history that follows is not the history of a movement or even that of a consistently understood idea.

When I began work on this book in 1990, before the current republican debate began, I expected to write the history of a marginal and somewhat eccentric strand of Australia's political culture which had made little impact on the development of our political institutions. I had read all of the secondary sources on republicanism, what few there were. The majority of historians had tended to dismiss republicanism as a 'flicker' or phantom, the fringe-dweller of a predominantly loyalist and imperial political culture.[13] When republicanism did get a mention, it was usually in association with the Sydney *Bulletin* of the 1880s or John Dunmore Lang's republican lectures in the 1850s. A paragraph or two in general histories, an article occasionally on the 'radical' republicans of the late nineteenth century, but rarely anything more substantial.[14] Republicanism seemed to be the derivative and 'exotic flower' of a minority.[15] In one way, this view was understandable. By relying on the few explicitly republican publications or political movements for source material, and often writing from within a political culture which expressed little discernible interest in a republic, it was only natural for historians to assume that republicanism was of little significance. There was no point in writing the history of an aberration. In part, however, this image of republicanism also stemmed from the way in which republicanism had been perceived as a predominantly anti-British phenomenon. Throughout the book I have attempted to challenge this one-dimensional view of republicanism by acknowledging the hybrid character of republicanism in Australia.

Broadly speaking, there have been four distinct but still overlapping republican experiences in Australian history. The British, the French, the American and the Australian—the latter being a largely derivative variation on the themes of the first three. Perhaps now, in the late twentieth century, we possess a uniquely Australian republican language in the form of patriotic minimalism. To understand the interplay between these republican models it is probably best to begin with the most straightforward—the French.

From the earliest years of the colony, the French Revolution of 1789 evoked images of violence and anarchy. In the minds of the governing classes the French republic and Thomas Paine's *Rights of Man* sparked fears of bloodshed and mob rule. The French model of a republic was seen as a threat to British institutions and the British way of life. Few Australian republicans embraced this revolutionary model of a republic, but the image of a French republic steeped in gore certainly helped to stigmatise the notion of a republic in Australia.[16] This revolutionary republic was kept alive by the revolutions in Europe in 1848, the Easter Rebellion of 1916, the Russian Revolution of 1917 and the many Third World dictatorships which emerged from colonial rule in the twentieth century carrying the title 'republic'. Even in the 1990s it was still possible to find Australians who believed that a republic would mean the end of civil society and gentlemanly behaviour.[17] Traditionally, these fears were also due to the spectre of Irish republicanism. Yet one of the most interesting aspects of the history of republicanism in Australia is that the Irish have left little evidence of their involvement in campaigns for an Australian republic. Only rarely did republicanism slide overtly into separatism, and when it did it was usually at the instigation of colonial governors and politicians. For the most part, Irish settlers kept any republican sentiments focused on their homeland. The majority of republicans who appear throughout the book (especially in the nineteenth century) are English or Scottish-born. Despite the dominance of sectarian concerns in Australia's past, the link between Irish Catholic sectarianism and Australian republicanism has always been more imagined than real.

Closely connected to the French (and English) republican experience was the American. In the Australian colonies the most common understanding of American republicanism was of armed resistance to colonial rule. The American War of Independence in 1776 and the American Constitution of 1787 transformed the image of republican government in the New World. The Americans had demonstrated that a group of British colonies could successfully overthrow British colonial rule and declare their independence. They had shown that republican government could be reconciled with federal government, representative democracy, individualism and free market economics. The American republic—at least rhetorically—had enshrined the principle of popular sovereignty.[18] For some, like John Dunmore Lang in the 1850s, it was a beacon of prosperous, democratic and independent government. For others, it was the alternative Yankee solution should Britain fail to administer the colonies justly. On occasions, republicans in Australia dreamed of a grand Anglo–American empire and cried out for protection from the American

'Eagle'. In the 1880s some Australian republicans shunned the American republic because of its social inequality. The American republic served as both a warning and as a model for change.[19] After the loss of the American colonies, Australian colonists were more easily able to remind the Colonial Office in London of the dangers involved in ignoring colonial grievances. While the American example increased the potency of these threats, it also ensured that they would be less likely to be carried out. Neither the Australian colonists nor the British government desired a repeat of 1776. Yet while Australian republicans may have been inspired by the American example, they rarely viewed the American republic uncritically. Instead, they sought to vary the American model to suit their own environment.[20]

To grasp the English republican model we have to be prepared to accept that the non-monarchical concept of a republic was not the only one present in colonial Australia. We know that the classical notion of republicanism which inspired the medieval Italianate and Dutch republics, Machiavelli and many of the seventeenth-century English Commonwealth men was not necessarily antagonistic to monarchic or aristocratic elements. Anti-monarchical sentiment, at least prior to the French Revolution, was only occasionally a characteristic of republican principles.[21]

If we wish to understand the English republican model we should first ask what particular understanding of the English Constitution was brought to Australia's shores by the early British immigrants. Nineteenth-century England was a society 'steeped in the rhetoric of constitutionalism and the rule of law'.[22] All classes placed great faith in parliamentary and legal processes as the appropriate mechanisms of reform. When conservatives sought the maintenance of existing institutions or liberals or radicals sought reform, all appealed to the English Constitution. These appeals frequently consisted of invocations to the anti-absolutist principles embodied in Magna Carta or the Glorious Revolution of 1688.[23] The right to trial by jury, to be protected from excessive punishment, the right to petition and, above all else, the right to resist arbitrary rule. After 1688 the monarch was restricted to an essentially constitutional role, parliament was sovereign and the old notion of the divine right of kings had been eradicated.[24]

Thanks largely to the work of historians such as J. G. Pocock, we are aware that the language used by Englishmen to protect their Constitution (as outlined in the English Bill of Rights of 1689) relied heavily on classical republican principles.[25] Implicitly, the first of these principles was that 'true' republican government was based on a balance of the threefold order—Kings, Lords and Commons, the classical model of a republic which did not necessarily exclude monarchy. According to Henry Parkes, every

Englishman who arrived in Australia understood the most ideal form of government as a balance between the threefold order. For Pocock, classical republicanism was represented by the articulated desire for balanced government, the separation of powers, civic virtue, and the resistance to arbitrary rule, a tradition of political thought which originated in Ancient Rome, was filtered through Renaissance Florence and enshrined in the Stuart Restoration of 1660 and the Bill of Rights in 1689, before finally providing the foundation for the anti-absolutist arguments of the American revolutionaries in the late eighteenth century.[26] It could embrace or be synonymous with the trappings of proper citizenship status, such as trial by jury. It could be associated with the granting of responsible government. It opposed oppression and tyranny and feared corruption and patronage. It was not principally a doctrine about monarchy but about constitutional rule. Finally, it was neither anti-British nor necessarily anti-monarchical.

Although this language dominated the grievance rhetoric of colonial politics in Australia—especially in the early nineteenth century—it was never referred to as 'republican' by those who used it. More often than not, Australian colonists saw themselves as exiled Britons appealing for citizenship rights under the British Constitution. Their sense of the word 'republic' was overwhelmingly dictated by the modern anti-monarchical concept of republican government as encapsulated in the American and French models. To refer to themselves proudly, actively and openly as 'republican' would have been thought to be anti-British. Yet when they were pressed to explain their understanding of a republic they frequently retreated to the classical model, equating republican government with balanced government, representative democracy, and insisting that their precious English Constitution was essentially a republic in disguise. After the Glorious Revolution in 1688, maintaining the monarchy in Britain was one way of concealing the steady democratisation of the English Constitution—as Lord Balfour admitted in his introduction to Walter Bagehot's *English Constitution*, published in 1867 '[Monarchy] provides the disguise which happily prevents the ordinary Englishman from discovering that he is not living under a monarchy but under a republic'.[27]

The classical republican inheritance of the English model sought to enshrine one form of a republic—not the American or French, but the essentially conservative and disguised English form. Again, we should remember that this pre-modern language of republicanism was not anti-monarchical but anti-tyrannical, a fact which explains why the Australian colonists were frequently able to declare their loyalty to the monarch and, in the same breath, threaten a republic. The threatened republic was the means by which the English Constitution was to be protected and extended to the colonists. Thus, their grievance was never with the monarch—the very person who embodied the principles of balanced government—but with those individual ministers who sullied the Constitution by maintaining unjust policies.

Moreover, the republicanism of key figures such as John Dunmore Lang was not detached from this tradition. Lang's arguments for a republic centred on assertions concerning colonial maturity and American-inspired notions of federal democracy, they did not rest on an antagonism towards monarchy or the British Constitution. Thus, we should not be surprised to find Lang expressing his 'sincere respect and unfeigned attachment' towards the British monarch at the same time as he demands freedom and independence for the Australian colonies. From a contemporary perspective, Lang's loyalty to the throne may appear odd, but in the 1850s it was perfectly consistent with the prevailing doctrines of republicanism in Australia. For those colonists who advocated a republic before 1856, the notion of a republic was often inspired by the English revolutionary experience of the seventeenth century. This language, the language which also inspired many of the American revolutionaries, was not directed against the monarchy. Subsequently, in colonial New South Wales, loyalty to the throne and an expressed support for a republic were not necessarily antithetical. Just as Lang had no qualms about expressing his loyalty, the Sydney crowds who cheered Robert Lowe's threat of republican independence in 1849 had no difficulty marching behind the Union Jack and singing 'God Save the Queen'. This was because republicanism in early colonial Australia was fundamentally different to the republicanism articulated in the late nineteenth and twentieth centuries, a fact which should not surprise us, given that the British monarchy during these years was not a nostalgic, largely theatrical 'other' but the very symbol of the colonists' right to be granted liberal democratic institutions. For the early colonists, the republic was not the cry of anti-British nationalists but more often the protective rhetorical strategy of British loyalists who wished to uphold their right to resist arbitrary rule.

Once we appreciate the enormous variety of republican thought in our past, we are more able to accept that republicanism in its various forms has had considerable impact on the evolution and development of our political institutions. During the first years of my research, when I began to look beyond the radical republican texts of the nineteenth century into the columns of the colonial press, especially during the critical decades before the granting of responsible government in 1856 and Federation in 1901, I found that the theme of a republic had pervaded most political discourse. It was not that I had uncovered any lost republican movement. Rather, I had realised two important aspects of the way in which republican debate had functioned. First, even though self-described republicans were a minority in Australian history, in the context of the debates which led to responsible government and Federation this minority had been the catalyst for a broad debate about the merits of republican government. The explicit debate may have originated from a stump in the Domain but it had ended up in the public culture of pre-Federation Australia. Secondly, I had been surprised by the extent to which the vast majority of colonial reformers between 1830 and the 1880s had successfully relied on the threat of a republic as a bargaining chip in their dealings with the Colonial Office. Such threats had been instrumental in ending the transportation of convicts to the colonies and securing the granting of responsible government.

Following the peaceful attainment of responsible government in 1856, the republicanism which emerged in the late nineteenth century was always going to be different from that which had been expressed before. Whereas republicanism in the early colonial period was most often justified as an antidote for tyranny or as the only means to citizenship and constitutional rule, the Australian nationalist republicanism of the 1880s and 1890s relied on different justifications. In these years, the republic was often justified as cheap and efficient—a predominantly utilitarian and pragmatic argument which also surfaced in England—largely because it was England that bore the cost of the civil list. Equally, Australians justified the republic as a form of autonomy. Essentially, this derived from the axiom of nineteenth-century nationalism that all nations should be self-governing. By the late 1880s republicanism was linked with an aggressive anti-British nationalism together with political philosophies such as socialism and secularism. It was during these years that a belligerent minority managed to provoke a wide-ranging debate on the republic, the breadth of which has not previously been acknowledged. In 1901 the prospect of a republic was effectively quashed by Federation under the Crown, but it was also true that many of those who participated in the Federation debates during the 1890s believed that an Australian republic was inevitable. After 1901 there was a significant lull in republican sentiment. While the reasons for this were varied, by far the most powerful was the fear of foreign invasion and the associated belief that the British connection offered the best possible protection for Australia's white Pacific enclave. White Australia and the British connection were inseparable for the first sixty years of the Federation.

After Governor-General Sir John Kerr dismissed Prime Minister Gough Whitlam in 1975, the idea of a republic was focused on the Office of Governor-General in the Federal Constitution. Rightly or wrongly, Sir John Kerr's action did much to encourage the perception that to become a republic Australia merely had to sever its links with the monarchy and replace the Governor-General with an Australian president. In the 1990s republicans such as George Winterton would argue that Australia was a liberal democratic society which had gradually shed its colonial status to stand as an independent federal republic in which sovereignty resided in the people—in all but one respect: 'The highest symbolic office, the formal headship of state, was occupied by a person deriving authority from birth [or God] but not from the people'.[28]

The patriotic minimalism of Australian republicanism in the 1990s has been carefully focused on the pinhead of State. Ironically, although it grew in part out of the cultural nationalism of post-1960s Australia, it has more in common with English republican inheritance of the nineteenth century. The minimalist republic is the last step in the process which Henry Parkes first put in train almost 150 years ago when he began the fight for responsible government in New South Wales. The substance of the Australian republic will finally be complete without the shadow of the name.

In the 1990s both republicans and monarchists, often unconsciously, rely on 'old' arguments, some articulated as much as 150 years earlier. It is my hope that this book will serve as a useful reference for both sides of the debate. For republicans, it will demonstrate just how widespread has been the belief in the inevitability of an Australian republic. It might also provide a means of self-examination through the critical appraisal of a republican past. Contemporary republicans have notably made little attempt to bring the history of their cause into the public domain.[29] They may be surprised to find that they too have a rich and sophisticated 'heritage' to draw on.

For monarchists, there is an opportunity to examine the Crown's role as a source of appeal in the development of Australia's political institutions. Too often, it seems that the heritage of 'monarchists' is focused solely on the symbolic trappings of monarchy—a somewhat quaint if not antediluvian obsession with imperial nomenclature. But the true strength of the monarchist argument does not lie in the production of letterheads which refer to the Sydney General Post Office as the Royal Exchange, rather it lies in explaining the Crown's role in accommodating liberal democratic institutions in Australia—a role which this book explores. If the Australian republic is to mean more than the induction of a beery, singsong nationalism on the way to the Olympic Games, participants on both sides of the debate bear a responsibility to sustain a high level of public debate. Ultimately, this implies an element of trust in the people—something which the 'republicans' and 'monarchists' of our past never lacked.

Finally, I hope that in some small way this book will help to demonstrate the extraordinarily rich, sophisticated and complex nature of Australia's political and intellectual history. Australia's 'republican' history reminds us that our political institutions have not been 'bestowed' by Britain. They have been shaped by the political philosophies and determination of Australians over the last 200 years.

CHAPTER ONE

The Piratical Republic 1788–1833

Pigs and Lashes

When news of the French Revolution reached the small settlement of Sydney Cove in 1790, Watkin Tench remarked in his diary that the streets of Paris were 'reeking with human blood'.[1] Tench's evocative image foreshadowed the fears of a generation of propertied English men and women. The French Revolution of 1789 and the American War of Independence in 1776 ensured that the popular concept of republicanism carried to Australia in the late eighteenth century would be unequivocally modern.

During the first half century of European settlement, especially in the minds of the governing classes, republicanism was clearly associated with American democratic government, the rejection of British rule and the distinct possibility of revolution. In particular, the image of a bloody republic inspired a vigilant determination on the part of early British administrations to stamp out any hint of republicanism in New South Wales. Writing in Sydney in 1793, Ensign Neil McKellar of the NSW Marine Corps depicted the French Revolution as excessive and unjust.

> The French ... have gone so far as to behead their own king ... tho ours I trust will have nothing to fear; we have liberty enough. I wish with all my heart that the French may be free, tho it is scarce charity to wish them any good after the barbarous unjustifiable manner in which they have treated their unfortunate and innocent king.[2]

Fears of republican revolution in the colony were also exacerbated by the presence of large numbers of convicts. The educated Englishman had always feared the mob, but an Australian republic ruled by convict rabble was almost too hideous to contemplate. In 1807 the English lawyer and politician James Mackintosh suggested that in fifty years, Australia could become an unmixed community of ruffians who would 'shake off the yoke of England, and, placed at a distance which makes them inaccessible to conquest . . . become a republic of pirates, the most formidable that ever roamed the seas'.[3]

Geographical isolation and a convict population proved a heady mix. In a colony which 'afforded the first instance . . . of settlements founded by Englishmen without any constitution whatever'—with no legislature, no municipal government, no avowed political association or party and no independent theatre or press—any opposition to military rule was often characterised as a Jacobin conspiracy.[4]

The first opportunity to gauge the extent of British officialdom's fear of republicanism occurred in 1794 with the arrival in Sydney of the five Scottish martyrs: Gerrald, Palmer, Skirving, Margarot and Muir. Victims of the paranoia that swept through England after the French Revolution, four of the five had been described as 'Jacobins' for their part in supporting fundamental political change at a radical convention in Edinburgh in 1792. The fifth transportee, Thomas Palmer, was sentenced to five years transportation for transcribing and circulating a pamphlet entitled 'An Address To The People'. Only one of the five, Maurice Margarot, managed to sustain his republican principles after arriving in New South Wales. It was Margarot who claimed to have been in Paris in 1789 and to have witnessed the storming of the Bastille.[5] Margarot quickly gained notoriety in New South Wales for his role in the rebellion of Irish convicts at Castle Hill in 1804. Governor King also discovered evidence of Margarot's republican tendencies when he managed to confiscate Margarot's diary. King saw Margarot as the bearer of 'some very elegant republican sentiments', 'let him be where he will, he is a most dangerous character'.[6] Margarot had dared to express his belief that New South Wales would become independent of Britain 'in the course of a few years' yet there is no evidence that Margarot's republicanism surfaced outside his diary entries. The convict rebellion of 1804 was not a republican rebellion and any attempts Margarot may have made to politicise it obviously failed.[7] Instead, King's anxiety was fuelled by the predominantly Irish character of the rebellion.

Of the 2000 Irish convicts transported to New South Wales between 1791 and 1803 over 600 had been convicted of riot and sedition, many during the Irish rebellions of 1798. This glut of Irish rebels perturbed King. His concern about United Irish attempts to unsettle the colony drove him to organise loyal associations, comprising about fifty men, to defend the colony against 'seditious' uprisings. Like Governor Hunter before him, King's fear of 'violent' republicans was typical of English officialdom in the period immediately following the French Revolution.[8] But the possibility of an Irish republican rebellion in these years was extremely remote. There is no evidence that Irish rebels were responsible for the organisation of explicitly republican movements in the early colonial period.

For those convicts who dared to declare their support for republican ideas, there was little mercy. In 1806 Joseph Smallsalts, a convict who had bragged that 'he would be worse than Tom Paine if thwarted' was given 100 lashes for his trouble and sent to hard labour at the Newcastle coal mines. On the journey from Sydney to Newcastle Smallsalts stood in chains with the words 'Thomas Paine' emblazoned on the back of his shirt. Military officials in the colony were familiar with Paine's writings and were in no doubt of their response. 'Read Paine's *Rights of Man*', wrote Ensign McKellar, 'he is a violent republican and tho he says many true things, is oft to lead us too far into republican principles'.[9]

There is one incident in particular which highlights the bogey status of republicanism in New South Wales. In 1795 the English republican John Boston, who had allegedly sailed to Australia toasting the King's damnation, discovered that one of his best sows had been shot by marines in a close belonging to his neighbour, Captain Foveaux. Although Boston's aspirations to become a colonial merchant saw him in economic competition with the officers of the corps, there is little doubt that his republican sympathies contributed to the loss of his sow. At the civil court hearing into the matter, Boston heard Lieutenant McKellar denounce him as a man who had 'publicly drank to the murder of his King [and] to the annihilation of the constitution of his country'. McKellar also explained that the pig was shot 'not in malice or in wantonness' but because it had destroyed the property of Captain Foveaux. 'Fences or fastenings were no security against the levelling practices of this animal, practices which I conclude are carefully and industriously inculcated in every part of the household of its master.' McKellar's use of the word 'levelling' indicates that he saw Boston's pig as a republican. The term 'leveller' had carried strong republican associations in England, especially since the Civil War period in the seventeenth century. In the eyes of Lieutenant McKellar, the insidious pestilence of republicanism was even capable of converting farm animals into an active campaign of subversion. Loyalty to the Crown was the framework within which all political activity took place in New South Wales. Any person (or pig) seen to be stepping outside those boundaries was branded as treasonous. The result was the shooting of Australia's first republican martyr—John Boston's pig.[10]

Considering the expressed antagonism of early British officials to the ideas of Thomas Paine and republicanism generally, it is understandable that the Rum Rebellion of 1809 failed to display any separatist republican sympathies. Although the members of the NSW Marine Corps chose to use armed force against Bligh they subsequently attempted to enlist the forms and rituals of the rule of law to legitimise their actions. Major Johnston later wrote that he was forced to remove Bligh 'rather than permit His Majesty's sacred name to be profaned and dishonoured by deeds of injustice and violence'.[11] Noel McLachlan has insisted that events which followed Bligh's removal did owe something to the rituals of the American Revolution. The rejoicings on the streets of Sydney were fuelled by free alcohol, the burning of effigies of Bligh, cries of 'Liberty!' and 'Tyrant!', a sign outside a pub down near the wharf depicting a highland soldier with sword drawn standing on a snake with liberty handing him her cap, and even evidence of Provost-Marshal Gore referring to the new regime as republican. The Rum Rebellion had managed to borrow the symbolic language of the French and American revolutions while remaining firmly within the bounds of English constitutionalism. When Major Johnston first stated the intentions of the new regime he spoke not of republican ideals but of his intention to 'reduce expenses and improve the quality of the cattle'.[12] The nature of the Rum Rebellion foreshadowed the attitudes and beliefs which would dominate the processes of political change in nineteenth-century Australia. Appeals to British constitutional and legal practice were made by a people who saw themselves as detached British subjects in pursuit of moral and economic improvement. During the first three decades of British settlement in Australia the idea of an Australian republic was predominantly cast as the 'other', the Sword of Damocles which threatened to provide an alternative Yankee solution to colonial political development.

The Blue Mountains Republic   1819–1827

The perception of the Australian colonies as a community separate from Britain developed slowly. For the first thirty years of settlement New South Wales was seen by the Colonial Office as 'a small section of that large dramatic issue of the "State of the Nation"'. A discernible, native political culture did not emerge until the early 1820s. At this time the native-born comprised less than one-fifth of the population, but evidence of republican sentiment appeared in a context which would become increasingly common during the next forty years.[13]

William Wentworth, the native-born 'son of a highway man and a convict woman', was the person responsible for articulating the first demands for political autonomy in New South Wales.[14] In 1819 Wentworth published *A Statistical, Historical, and Political Description of the Colony of NSW*. The 1820 edition carried a small sketch of the settlement at Sydney Cove. It was a romantic image of small seaside farms skirting the placid waters of Sydney Harbour—dotted here and there with trading vessels of mother England at anchor in the cove. Perhaps the sketch represented Wentworth's vision of a New Britannia—a society modelled on the virtues of English commerce and industry, free of the convict stain, possessing all the liberties afforded by the English Constitution. Buoyed by the abundance of the new colony's natural resources Wentworth believed the time had arrived for the colony to be granted trial by jury and a house of assembly. Immediately, he linked the demand for these political reforms to the question of the colony's connection to the motherland.[15]

Despite Wentworth's preparedness to acknowledge the 'impotency and insignificance' of the colony, he was still determined that the Colonial Office should not lull itself 'into a false sense of security'. Wentworth could find no reason for the Colonial Office to refuse his political demands. He believed that Britain already possessed a sufficient number of external enemies without creating additional ones. The terrible lesson of America, said Wentworth, would surely teach Britain to be more cautious with the Australian colonies. Interestingly, Wentworth's appreciation of American power led him to suggest that a repressive English connection might be exchanged for a more liberal connection with the United States.[16] 'Is there no probability, that a perseverance in the present system of injustice and oppression, may on some future occasion, urge the colonists to shake off this intolerable yoke, and throw themselves into the arms of so powerful a protector?'[17] Wentworth was audacious but he was no fool. Like many who dared to threaten separation from Britain in the nineteenth century, his acute awareness of the colony's geographical isolation led him to seek the protection of a greater power.

It was the American paradigm of colonial experience which encouraged Wentworth to threaten the Colonial Office with the prospect of an Australian republic. The loss of the American colonies was an event which framed much of Britain's colonial policy in the early nineteenth century. Mindful of the impact the American Revolution had had in Britain, Wentworth was only too willing to exploit fears of another Boston Tea Party.

Thus, we find Wentworth speaking of a 'thunder cloud of calamity and destruction' if the British failed to yield to emancipist demands.[18] To prove that this was more than an idle threat, Wentworth revealed the military strategy which the young Australian republic would have to employ to stave off the British Army. His strategy was based on one manoeuvre— retreat. 'If the colonists should prudently abandon the defence of the sea coast, and remove with their flocks and herds into the fertile country behind these impregnable passes [the Blue Mountains], what would the force of England, gigantic as it is, profit her?'[19]

Like Johnson's Rasselas in the happy valley, Wentworth imagined his fledgling republic protected by the 'ridges and chasms' of the mountains, isolated from the outside world and safe from attack. Thankfully, this fantasy was never seriously entertained by Wentworth and at no time did he make any attempt to gather public support for the idea. It seems more likely that Wentworth indulged in this hyperbole to make a greater impression on the Colonial Office. He would not be the last Australian to play on British fears of colonial revolution, and like the majority of his fellow reformers, talk of separation was merely a bluff. Wentworth's true political position was made much clearer towards the end of his book:

> I must nevertheless protest against being classed among those who are the sworn enemies of all authority. . . . a band of ruffian levellers who under the specious pretext of salutary reform seek, like the Jacobin revolutionists of France, the subversion of all order, and the substitution in its stead, of a reign of terror, anarchy and rapine . . .[20]

Emerging slowly was an Australian solution to the problem of political reform. Borrow from the example of the American Revolution, even threaten separation if you must, but maintain your faith in the principles of the English Constitution. Like his more conservative opponents, Wentworth was fearful of using the term republic to describe his political demands. The stereotype of the violent anarchic republican reigned supreme. Where Wentworth differed was in his desire for greater democracy. Soon after the publication of his book, Wentworth organised the first of many meetings by emancipists to petition the King for trial by jury and a legislative assembly. At these meetings Wentworth became one of the first political reformers in Australia to seek to disconnect the campaign for representative democracy from the active adoption of the concept of republicanism. Essentially, Wentworth wanted much of the republican baggage without losing his loyalist clothes.

Wentworth's strategy did make sense.[21] The young John Macarthur, for example, saw calls for a wider franchise and an independent press as the work of a minority 'republican party' which was naturally opposed to the 'moral and respectable part of the community'. Macarthur's son, Edward, was so convinced of the republican threat that he worked to set up a colonial militia which would 'inculcate respect for superiors' and 'loyal attachment to the crown'. Fortunately, the formation of a colonial 'Dad's Army' was not needed to steer Wentworth clear of advocating an Australian republic. Throughout the 1820s Wentworth strove to assert his loyalty. While he called for a legislature 'on the same basis as the American colonies', he always did so within the confines of loyalty to the Crown.[22]

Wentworth did not want revolution in the French manner; instead he drew on a skilful mesh of American appeals for political representation to accompany taxation and the traditional political language of English constitutionalism. He called on Australian colonists to demand the extension of the rights and privileges afforded by the English Constitution to New South Wales, without violence and without rancour. Thus, Wentworth's petitions for an independent colonial legislature signalled the beginning of a political struggle which would continue until the

Australian colonies were granted responsible government in 1856.[23] In 1819 when Wentworth worded his first petition to the King, republicans and democrats were synonymous as the bearers of violence and anarchy, while in England the First Reform Act had not yet been passed. By 1856 a significant realignment of the political landscape in both countries would see the concept of representative democracy successfully detached from the necessity of republicanism and separation. The process by which this realignment took place, and the political debates that nurtured it, were fundamentally centred on the nexus of Australia's relationship with Britain. The issue of republicanism was, in its various forms, an integral part of this discussion, and it is this past which has yet to be fully explored by Australian historians.

Shaking Off the Yoke

One of the more significant consequences of Wentworth's demands for trial by jury and a house of assembly in the 1820s was the ushering in of a more diverse political culture in New South Wales. The succession of emancipist remonstrances helped to increase the awareness of the colony's unique condition. When it became clear that British interests did not always coincide with local concerns, demands for greater political autonomy multiplied. The foundations of political culture, an independent press, a local legislature, public meetings and petitions all emerged in the 1820s. In 1824 the first edition of William Wentworth's *Australian* was published carrying a firm declaration to be 'independent yet consistent—free yet not licentious'.[24] Within the next few years the *Sydney Herald* and E. S. Hall's *Monitor* would join the *Australian* to provide a substantial source of independent commentary on political affairs. The tenure of Governor Ralph Darling from 1825 to 1831 therefore marked the first occasion in Australian history where the colonists' grievances could be aired through an independent press. Darling was not a popular Governor and his attempts to restrict the freedom of the press resulted in vigorous political debate. These debates are important for two reasons. First, they represent the earliest example of grievance rhetoric reaching a fever pitch in the colonial press. Secondly, they are the first reliable record of political debates in which it is possible to observe the use of the word 'republic' in New South Wales. When Wentworth and Wardell, the editors of the *Australian*, wrote their first editorial, it was clear that the framework of political debate had yet to be decided. They were pushing the boat out into uncharted waters: 'Whether we be designated radicals or reformers, or Whigs or Tories, or republicans, we shall not the less seek to propitiate [our readers]'.[25] While this description might have suited Wentworth and Wardell, it would not take long for Governor Darling to decide what they were. Darling was fond of labelling all government opposition as republican and Wentworth presented himself as the most likely target.

The most critical period of Darling's administration was 1827. Darling had come under criticism for his handling of the Joseph Sudds affair the previous year. Sudds, a soldier of the 57th regiment, had been convicted of theft. Darling insisted that Sudds be tried in a military court, where he was sentenced to work in chains after being drummed out of his regiment. Sudds' death in custody provoked the press to vilify the Governor for his harsh treatment of the offender. Wentworth even went so far as to accuse Darling of murder. Incensed by the audacity of his critics, Darling immediately passed two bills through the Legislative Council which attempted to place restrictions on the freedom of the press, even providing for libellous and seditious editors to be brought to trial.[26]

In the meantime, less than two months after Sudds' death, a large public meeting in Sydney on 26 January 1827 framed a strongly worded petition to the King and two houses of parliament, demanding trial by jury and a house of assembly. It was at this meeting that Wentworth compared the situation of the colonies to America in 1776, although he stopped short of suggesting that Australia declare its independence from Britain.[27] Darling was disturbed by Wentworth's statements at the meeting, believing that the colony was still not ready for representative institutions. In a confidential despatch to Permanent Under-Secretary Hay he wrote:

> Mr Wentworth speaks, as he wrote when Compiling his book, of the Independence of the Colony, and compares it to the situation formerly of America and the probability of its being driven as America was, to shake off the Yoke. In short, he is anxious to become the 'Man of the People'; and he seems to think the best means of accomplishing this is by insulting the Government.[28]

Darling's despatch was one example of the effort on the part of the governing classes to deny their opponents political legitimacy by raising the republican bogey. But when the crowd applauded Wentworth at the Sydney meeting in January 1827, they signalled their support for greater democracy under the aegis of the British Constitution. It was now simply a question of whether Darling and his allies could discredit these demands by making the republican label stick. When E. S. Hall dared to publish a list of the colonists' grievances in the *Monitor* in March 1827, the *Sydney Gazette* responded with hysteria: 'The *Monitor* . . . has put forth an article that is calculated to engender a spirit of rebellion in the Colony. . . . [We are] running the risk of witnessing our streets deluged with blood, of beholding gibbets in every corner'.[29]

Darling's anxiety intensified in April when it appeared that Justice Francis Forbes would not support his restrictive press legislation on the grounds that it was repugnant to the laws of England. With criticism increasing from the *Monitor* and the *Australian*, Darling was clearly under siege. By late April he seemed genuinely concerned for the future of the colony's relationship with England.

> The situation of this government is becoming so exceedingly embarrassing if not critical . . . America is the grand beacon which Mr Wentworth and the opposition papers have in view and Mr Forbes is an ardent admirer of the institutions of that country and is at heart an American . . . He never conforms to the practice of appearing in court with a wig and I understand as soon as he is seated on the bench he throws off his gown.
>
> . . . I suspect, as it is my duty, that this colony cannot long be preserved to the mother country if the officers of the government are not of opposite principles to those I have instanced.[30]

In this despatch Darling reveals just how closely governing classes in New South Wales associated republicanism with American democracy. Although Darling's plea for 'aristocratic' men was already sounding outdated, his concern for the colony stemmed from a firm belief that a convict society would tend naturally to republican ideas. Regardless of the fact that Wentworth and his supporters had no intention of separating from England, Darling remained unconvinced. If judges were throwing off their wigs and gowns then the republic wasn't far away.

When Darling tried to impose a fourpence stamp duty on the sale of newspapers the *Australian* rebuked him in a language which threatened revolution:

> The Stamp Act is an Act which will . . . engender hostile and deeply inimical sentiments in regard to England . . . What are we to think when a law is proclaimed which breeds universal and unmitigated discontent—discontent bordering on disaffection. The most benignant interpretation . . . is that the legislature . . . knows not how to establish the public weal.[31]

It was this type of rhetoric which unsettled Darling, so much so that the criticism provoked him to announce that the fourpenny Stamp Act would be suspended indefinitely. Although Darling complained that there were too many people at pains 'to show the similarity between NSW and America and to inculcate Yankee principles', on this occasion he only had himself to blame. Introducing a 'Stamp Act' was bound to encourage comparisons with the American Revolution.[32]

When Darling finally departed Sydney in March 1831, the *Monitor* could hardly conceal its elation:

He's off!
The reign of terror ended.[33]

Throughout his term as Governor, Darling had been vilified as a 'tyrant', scoundrel, and monster. At public meetings the emancipists had employed the potentially revolutionary cry of 'no taxation without representation', the *Australian* and the *Monitor* had repeatedly charged Darling's administration with ignorance and corruption and proclaimed their 'universal discontent and disaffection'. They had also called frequently for Darling's removal and compared the political situation of the colony to that which existed prior to the American War of Independence. No wonder Darling perceived his opponents as Americans at heart.[34] Unfortunately, Darling could not appreciate that Wentworth and the emancipists had appropriated much of the oppositional rhetoric of the American Revolution with little intention of carrying their argument to its logical conclusion—separation and republican independence. He was unable to realise that the revolution he confronted was one of loyal, English constitutionalists rather than rabid Yankee republicans.

On 25 January 1828, at the height of discontent with Darling's regime, E. S. Hall, editor of the *Monitor*, explained why Australia was not ready to become an independent republic:

> If England were to withdraw her protecting arm, our situation would be almost as helpless and pitiable, as that of the embryo kangaroo, whom its mother, in her terror to escape from the hunter and in order to lighten her weight and aid her speed, casts out of her bag and leaves to shift for itself.[35]

Hall's quaint native metaphor of an Australian republic as the helpless joey captures the sense of inferiority and weakness with which many political reformers perceived the colony's position. In spite of this, Darling was too preoccupied with the constant references to the American colonies and the imminent rise of the native-born. By the end of Darling's term it is possible that his opponents had been successful in bludgeoning him into the belief that a republic was approaching.

Ironically, although Wentworth and the emancipists shied away from the republican banner, the more Darling insisted on perceiving their intentions as republican, the greater chance there was of their demands being realised without the necessity of republican government. In other words, by playing on the fear of republicanism political reformers would ensure the negation of the republic on the American model.

Throughout the period from 1788 to 1832 republicanism came to the colonial society of New South Wales primarily as an apparition in the minds of the governing classes. Yet at no time during this period did any republican organisation exist in the colony. There was no republican newspaper and no republican agitators, only a distant republican future.

After the American War of Independence, the existence of a New World society isolated in the South Pacific and ruled from afar by the Colonial Office necessitated an understanding of republicanism which involved complete separation from the parent state—a severance of the connection between the Old World and the New. It was this very notion of separation which was to differentiate republicans from democrats in the colony of New South Wales. To be a republican in New South Wales was perceived to entail the risk of losing the sense of being British, and it is for this reason that the idea of an Australian republic first emerged as a second-class option. It was the last resort when the desire to remain British had to be protected by recourse to separation. This is why we can find no evidence of political reformers during this period advocating a republic. Apart from Wentworth's Blue Mountains fantasy in 1819, there was no one willing to advocate separation. Instead, there seemed to be an overwhelming belief that all grievances would eventually be redressed.[36]

While the people of New South Wales embraced the belief that it was the monarch's duty to be the servant of the people, underneath this attitude there was still an undercurrent of fear. Immigration was changing New South Wales from a penal colony to a more diverse society. There were many groups who expected an influential role in the decision-making processes of government. Free settlers, emancipated convicts, pastoralists, lawyers and merchants all had claims to make.[37] It was clear that constitutional reform had to come, and there were still some who thought that if it did not come in time, then the rising native-born would take matters into their own hands. Writing from his prison cell on 8 May 1830 E. S. Hall feared the worst: 'Reflecting on the future, I see nothing but political struggles for a better order of things, which may probably end before my death in a civil commotion ... [I will endeavour] to persuade His Majesty's government ... to change their views and measures ere it be too late'.[38]

The Rise of the Native-Born: Horatio Wills and the *Currency Lad*

> Words are deeds. The words we hear
> May revolutionise or rear
> A mighty state.
>
> Charles Harpur
> 'Words are Deeds'
> (from the *Nevers of Poetry*)[39]

In August 1832 Horatio Wills published the first edition of the *Currency Lad*. The *Currency Lad* was unique in the annals of the colonial press. It was the first newspaper published in the colony which specifically set out to protect the interests of the native-born. In addition, it was the first to openly espouse a form of republicanism—however tentatively. In many ways, the *Currency Lad* was an aberration. Its blatant and sometimes aggressive chauvinism would not be seen again until the emergence of J. F. Archibald's *Bulletin* in the 1880s. The *Currency Lad*'s brief and stormy existence coincided with the passing of the 1832 Reform Act in England and an increasingly vocal campaign in Sydney for trial by jury and a house of assembly.

In a self-consciously gestating political culture, the *Currency Lad*'s brash and outspoken style inevitably earned the ire of the colonial elite. Respect for the power of the written word ensured that Wills' editorials were taken seriously. As if heeding the words of E. S. Hall in 1830, the *Currency Lad* stood as the voice of a native-born population which had come to perceive itself as disfranchised and ignored, yet destined to inherit power.[40]

Wills was born in Sydney in October 1811 to a convict father who died shortly after his birth. Soon after his father's death his mother married George Howe, printer and editor of the *Sydney Gazette*. Wills' youth was spent on the wharves of Sydney and, if rumours are to be believed, living with natives of the South Sea Islands. Yet his most formative experience was the time he spent in the offices of his stepfather's paper. Wills was the model of the native-born intellectual; self-taught, restless and impatient with the continuation of autocratic British rule. His was the articulate voice of a community of men and women who had already begun to develop a sense of their own separate identity in speech, dress, behaviour and attitudes.[41]

The first edition of the *Currency Lad* on 25 August 1832 carried a banner at the very top of its front page. Behind the words 'RISE AUSTRALIA' the crown of the English monarch sat nestled in wildflowers accompanied by corn, wheat, sheep and sacks of grain. In the distance a British merchant vessel, anchored in placid waters, waited to ferry the produce of the granary back home. This was hardly the banner of an anti-British republican but it was definitely the stuff of divided loyalty. The *Currency Lad*'s emblem also carried a slightly amended version of the last two lines of Wentworth's 1823 poem 'Australasia'. 'See, Australasia floats, with flag unfurl'd,/A new Britannia in another world'! In his opening editorial Wills attempted to quash rumours that the journal would be the harbinger of revolution. The farmers on the banks of the Hawkesbury and the Parramatta could rest easy, said Wills, the currency lads were not about to be seen stumbling across the corn fields with 'heads under their arms'.[42]

Within the first month of publication Wills had set the framework within which he hoped to catch the conscience of his King.[43] In the tradition of William Wentworth's *Statistical, Historical, and Political Account of the Colony of NSW* of 1819, he demanded the colonists' birthright as British subjects, and never hesitated to use the threat of rebellion as a cudgel for encouragement.

The first editions of the *Currency Lad* were almost timid in comparison to those published between October 1832 and February 1833. In this short period Wills' language became aggressive and rebellious. To a large extent this change in tone was directly attributable to the passing of the British Reform Act in 1832. Wills' frustration grew steadily as it became clear that the Colonial Office was not about to apply the same principles to New South Wales.

The advances in England filled Wills' heart with optimism. In October 1832, still in a state of exultation, Wills wrote an editorial on the comparative advantages of monarchical and republican government. It was here that he proclaimed that the future destiny of all societies would come to rest on the 'broad and universal wings of republicanism'. 'The names of Grey, of Brougham, of Russell and other reformers', wrote Wills, 'will irradiate the pages of history and the victory gained by Reform—the glorious fourth of June—will be handed down, undimmed and brilliant from generation to generation. The world is fast approaching to republicanism—to cheap and wise government'.[44] It was only when Wills learnt that the Colonial Office had refused the colonists' petition for a house of assembly that his conception of republicanism began to embrace notions of separation and rebellion. Within one month Wills' jubilation had turned to rage. Describing his opponents as 'aristocratical asses' he now turned away from England and looked towards America:

> The question will soon be not between emigrant and emancipist but between the Senate of England and the NATIVES OF NEW SOUTH WALES—between men who have the fate of America before their eyes, and men on whose brow are indelibly traced the stamp of free and determined INDEPENDENCE! ... Look, Australians, to the high salaried foreigners around you! Behold those men lolling in their coaches—rioting in the sweat of your brow while you—yes you, the Sons of the Soil, are doomed to eternal toil—the sport and ridicule of pettifogging worldlings. A House of Assembly would remedy this grievance ... WE WERE NOT MADE FOR SLAVES.[45]

Retrospectively, these words may seem to be nothing more than the mark of a demagogue, but in a colony which had only known a free press for eight years they provoked considerable consternation. Suddenly, we find British authorities described as 'foreigners' and the natives of New

South Wales striving for 'Independence'. The use of the word 'independence' is intriguing. When Wills spoke of republicanism in October he ostensibly rejected any suggestion of independence. Now, in the same breath, Wills brings up the spectre of the American Revolution and Australia's desire for free and determined independence. At once his republicanism entails far more than the advance of representative democracy, it now implies the possibility of separation. Although Wills' words were revolutionary in tone and remarkable in their candour, they failed as an immediate call to arms. The Australian republic still sat in the waiting-room, patiently anticipating the inevitable increase in the 'numerical strength' of the native-born. These subtleties were lost on the government mouthpiece, the *Sydney Gazette*, which quickly attacked Wills' article as 'most dangerous to the best interests of the colony'.[46]

On Anniversary Day 1833 a meeting called to draw up another petition for a house of assembly may have given the farmers some cause to turn in their sleep. The meeting proved rowdy with some participants being accused of 'dangerous and inflammatory language'. The *Sydney Herald* alleged that some speakers at the meeting attempted to give the impression that the Australian colonies were 'on the point of rebelling against the King'—with the 'flame of civil discord raging from one end of NSW to the other'. This sort of hysteria was to be expected from the *Herald*. In the previous year the *Herald* had reported that Thomas Paine's *Rights of Man* had actually been written by two Swiss adventurers who had worked as tutors for English families in France.[47]

While there is some evidence of heckling at the meeting, with certain speakers being hissed by a group of currency lads, there was no indication of open defiance or republican sentiment. The majority of clashes between the native-born and English military during these years were fuelled by the cost or scarcity of alcohol. Perhaps we could lament the fact that the native-born lacked effective leadership to launch a rebellion, but it should be remembered that even if a leader of sufficient calibre did exist his only platform may well have been a plea for more beer.[48] As Manning Clark explains, the native-born's 'public gatherings and ceremonies were not distinguished by any profession of belief'. According to Clark, 'they were not committed to any political or social creed'.[49] In this light, Wills was an exception.

The *Currency Lad* played its role in the commotion which followed the Anniversary Day meeting by publishing a letter which advocated revolution. Written by John Fulton, the Australian-born son of an Irish clergyman, the letter complained of the colonial administration's decision to abolish land grants and charge a purchase price of five shillings per acre. Fulton was also incensed by the recent refusal of the colonists' petition for a house of assembly. The result was an excited and belligerent letter:

> ... To my countrymen I say, *appeal! appeal!* with the firmness of men and in language that cannot be misunderstood. ... Tell them you can abide such injustice no longer, and adopting the language of the American patriot Patrick Henry ... tell them with up lifted arms and your eyes to Heaven. '*For our part, give us liberty or give us death.*' If the British government should show an unjust displeasure at your candid and honest remonstrance, tell the Imperial Senate ... that your next application shall be.********** [REVOLUTION][50]

This threat of revolution demonstrates that rebellious sentiments did exist among certain sections of the native-born in early Australia. But it is still difficult to assess the extent of this sentiment. All available evidence points to the conclusion that Fulton's letter was not representative of the majority of native-born. Public meetings, the available press, and the course of events which flowed from them, carried few examples of Fulton's call for liberty or death. The tone of the letter also suggests that, like Wentworth and Wills, Fulton hoped his threats would make the British yield to the colonists' demands. Whatever Fulton's intentions, his arguments provoked a flurry of criticism from the colony's major newspapers. The *Herald* berated Fulton and implied that he was mad: 'What man in his senses would hold language of independence and open defiance?'[51] The *Australian* concurred, characterising talk of independence as that of the 'fool or a madman', declaring that it never hoped to see the maiden blades of revolution unsheathed in the colony.

> In the first place the colony has not physical strength. In the second place the colonists have not enough of public principle. ... Patronage ridden as this colony is yet there does not exist another more sincerely attached to Great Britain. It is only misgovernment that it complains about—only an unbiased legislature that it seeks. ... Let us never cease petitioning ... till we gain our point fairly.[52]

It is difficult to see any possibility of widespread support for rebellion or the declaration of an independent republic when the *Currency Lad* was the only journal which dared to suggest that petitioning might one day run its course. When calls filled the press for a further meeting to be held due to the 'sweeping' and 'hasty' nature of the previous petition in January, Wills rallied to defend the original petition.[53]

As with Fulton, Wills' attempt to stir his fellow countrymen to action fell on deaf ears. While Wills and Fulton were calling for 'Liberty or Death' their compatriots were busy organising cricket matches between native-born Australians and 'foreigners'. On the same day that Fulton's letter was published in the *Currency Lad*, a letter signed 'Legitimate Australian' brought news of the impending game: 'I have further to state that the

Australians are ready to contend a match of cricket against any body of Europeans in the colony, for any sum, being thoroughly convinced that the boasted superiority of foreigners may be very good in theory but very difficult in practice'.[54] It seemed that superiority at silly leg was more important to the native-born than the framing of a petition for a house of parliament. Perhaps this partially explains Wills' failure to stir his countrymen. In May 1833 the *Currency Lad* ceased publication, despite what Wills insisted was a strong and loyal level of support.[55] In a defiant mood Wills wrote a long letter to the *Australian*, in an attempt to explain the paper's demise:

> Time after time I was remonstrated with on the system of policy which I pursued, . . . Thus, things went on; 'I don't like this and Mr so and so don't like that.' One event followed on the heels of another in quick succession . . . and The *Currency Lad* was blown to the grave! . . . At the very time we were rising daily in circulation we received as it were a tap on the shoulder accompanied with—'thus far shalt thou come and not further!' We shall be explicit. The executor of Mr Howe's Estate thought this journal would be injurious to The *Sydney Gazette*.[56]

Mr Howe was Wills' stepfather and the owner of the *Sydney Gazette*. We know that Wills was forced to rely on a printing press in the *Sydney Gazette* office. Understandably, there were only a handful of presses in the colony, and Wills was indeed fortunate to have had access to one. His explanations for the *Currency Lad*'s demise demonstrate the pressures brought to bear on the radical press during the 1820s and 1830s. Clarion calls for 'Liberty or Death' were too much for the executors of Howe's estate, who were probably more interested in securing a profitable future for the *Gazette*. Indeed, 'Mr so and so' probably put up with the *Currency Lad*'s rebellious editorials only because of the family connection.

After only nine months the *Currency Lad*'s brief existence had come to an abrupt halt. In this short time, the paper had managed to present a radical, nationalist alternative to the conservative press. After the *Currency Lad*, the emergence of the native-born as a political force in the colony could not be denied. To describe Wills as a republican, however, can be misleading unless we understand precisely what his republicanism entailed.

For Horatio Wills, just as it was for Thomas Paine, republicanism was essentially cheap and democratic government, yet unlike Paine, Wills was not anti-monarchical. Wills stated that he had no desire to abolish monarchy by means 'violent and premature'. Monarchy would simply disappear over time as the 'rising tide of republicanism levelled all distinctions with the dust'.[57] Like those who came after him, such as John Dunmore Lang, Wills argued in terms of the inevitable progress of democratic institutions—republicanism was simply part of social and political evolution.

Wills' republicanism also failed to manifest any consistent anti-British sentiment.[58] In this sense Wills was typical of native-born Australians whose notion of citizenship and political participation was heavily reliant on the language of British constitutionalism. If we look closely at the *Currency Lad*'s editorials in early 1833, when Wills had called on several occasions for liberty or death, we can observe the importance of the English inheritance in shaping traditions of political reform in colonial Australia. The following example is typical: 'Let every many who drew his first breath in the "glorious land of freedom" come forward, as his ancestors came forward and claim that freedom which every freeborn Briton holds his birthright. Let not the glorious blood of Hampden be spilled in vain'.[59]

Wills admired the American republic and frequently expressed his view that the fourth of July was indeed a 'glorious day' but his greatest source of inspiration was the English Revolution. The broad wings of republicanism which Wills imagined would one day embrace the world had their origin, not in Paris or Boston, but Westminster. In this sense, Wills' republic was a descendant of the English republic of the seventeenth century. It was Hampden and not Paine who showed Wills the way. Wills' talk of rebellion was an attempt to tap the historical lineage of violent revolt which he believed had arisen to protect the spirit of the English Constitution. Just as Hampden had fought bravely and refused to pay the illegal ship money of Charles I, and the Americans had refused taxation without political representation, so too might Australians rise to assert their rights to a house of assembly. But as Wills well knew, while he toyed with the idea of rebellion the sons of the soil were practising their bowling down at the Hyde Park nets. This is not to suggest that the choice for native-born Australians was between campaigning for a republic and playing cricket, it is simply that the native-born seemed more interested in sport than politics.[60] It was all good and well for Wills to cry 'Liberty or Death' but it would most certainly have been a speedy death if Wills had led the First XI in rebellion.

The broad and universal wings of republicanism which the *Currency Lad* had believed would one day carry Australia were the wings of representative democracy. For Horatio Wills, republicanism would best come to the young colony within the safe bounds of the English connection. Wills had been the first Australian to mould the concept of republicanism to suit the circumstances of the Australian colonies. The next would be John Dunmore Lang, but Australia was to wait another twenty years before Lang would deliver the first of his lectures on the 'coming republic'.

CHAPTER TWO

The Stockmen's Republic   1833–1848

Canada and Lord Durham

When rebellions took place in the Canadian colonies in 1837 the response of the British government signalled a distinct change in imperial policy, one which would have important ramifications for the development of colonial politics in New South Wales. The British response to the Canadian rebellions demonstrated that the Colonial Office had learnt much from its previous experience with the American colonies. If the inevitable destiny of all colonies was complete independence, the Act of Union for Canada passed by the British Parliament in 1840 ensured that this destiny would remain distant.[1]

The first official reply to the Canadian rebellions came in 1839 with the release of Lord Durham's report. Durham proposed a system of government for the Canadian colonies which included ministerial responsibility and the division of domestic and imperial concerns. He intended to concede the control of colonial administration 'to the people themselves'.[2] This admirable concession was to occur without the consequences which had been previously associated with democratisation—separation and republicanism. Although Durham's report referred specifically to Canada, its recommendations had a significant impact on the course of colonial politics in New South Wales. By proposing ministerial responsibility under the Crown, Durham knew he was avoiding the American alternative. He claimed that the granting of responsible government would be the only means of fostering a 'national feeling' throughout the Canadian colonies, 'as would effectively counter balance whatever tendencies may now exist towards separation'.[3]

Durham's use of the words 'national feeling' is intriguing. Essentially, the national feeling which Durham hoped to engender would be one which saw Canadian and British identity as interdependent rather than antithetical. Durham's report contained the bedrock of New World nationalism in the nineteenth century—particularly in Canada and Australia. This form of nationalism was one which entailed an inherent duality. Loyalty was not divided between colony and parent state, for to be loyal to Canada or Australia was also to be loyal to Britain.[4] The meshing of British and colonial identities helped to facilitate a policy of appeasement on the part of the Colonial Office. Together with the Reform Act of 1832, Durham's report and the Act of Union for Canada reinforced the dominant image of the English Constitution in colonial politics as the fount of all liberty.

While Durham's report was by no means immediately taken up by the Colonial Office as a blueprint for colonial development (the Australian colonies were not to receive responsible government until 1856), this did not stop political reformers in Australia from using the Canadian example to support their own demands for constitutional reform. Robert Lowe's *Atlas* illustrated this attitude in 1844: 'The thing has been done in Canada and it can be done here. If self-government be our right, responsible government is incident to that right. We have not ceased to become Englishmen by becoming colonists'.[5]

This type of appeal was not well received in London. In 1844 Colonial Secretary Lord Stanley was irate when he read the petition of the New South Wales Legislative Council which pointed to the Canadian experience. Stanley insisted that the Queen had not entered into any theory or abstract principles concerning colonial government.[6] The convict stain always provided opponents of constitutional reform with a convenient opportunity to argue New South Wales' special status. None the less, the Act of Union for Canada had sent a clear signal that colonial societies could possess a measure of self-government without the dangers of full independence. Herman Merivale, who was later to serve as Permanent Under Secretary in the Colonial Office, recognised this as early as 1841: 'It does not follow as a necessary consequence that the attainment of domestic freedom is inconsistent with a continued dependence on the imperial sovereignty ... Union might be preserved ... long after the sense of necessary dependence is gone'.[7]

Merivale's remarks offered one way to reconcile the competing demands of sovereignty and birthright. The Crown would remain as the sovereign power while the colonists would receive their English birthright without the need for separation. Although many colonial theorists still saw the final destiny of colonial societies as independent and republican, there was now a middle road between dependence and independence. After the Durham report, it was difficult to see the development of circumstances in which an independent, American-style republic would be desirable in New South Wales, especially if the British government adopted a more conciliatory attitude to colonial grievances. The fact that a significant number of people close to colonial affairs in London now believed that colonial societies were naturally more democratic, virtually ensured that there would be little need for a Boston Tea Party in the Australian colonies.

The Invisible Compact

The fifteen years which preceded the granting of responsible government in New South Wales were a crucial period in Australia's political development. It was during these years that the colonists chose between the American model of independent republican government and the maintenance of the imperial connection.

In the two decades between 1830 and 1850, colonial society in New South Wales left behind its image as South Pacific hideaway for convicts and began to take on the appearance of a more open and materialistic society. By the early 1840s the political expectations of new immigrants had begun to impact on colonial anticipations of the imperial relationship, as the *Sydney Morning Herald* made clear in 1844: 'We should have the satisfaction of being ruled like men and not like children—like free British subjects and not like so many felons or slaves'.[8]

We know from Henry Parkes' observations that the British migrants arriving in New South Wales carried with them the 'terms of the threefold order—King, Lords and Commons'. The notion that laws, especially those relating to taxation, should not be passed without the consent of the people was clearly entrenched in the political culture of nineteenth-century England and had been since the seventeenth century.[9]

In a colonial context these ideas often translated into an insistence that the Colonial Office in London not attempt to impose laws without the consent of the colonists. Just as the King and Lords surrendered power gradually to the Commons at home, so too should the imperial power slowly cede greater autonomy to her colonies as the colonies saw fit. In late 1843 the *Sydney Morning Herald* explained its understanding of the obligations held by the Colonial Office: 'The colonial minister . . . should remember that his official powers are held in trust for *both* parties; and that arrogance and oppression . . . are fatal to colonial loyalty and affection'.[10]

This evidence is significant because it demonstrates that by 1840 certain colonists believed that the relation between colony and empire be held for 'mutual advantage'. Put another way, there was an unwritten, yet widely accepted understanding that imperial relations were bound by a compact of trust and consent. The *Herald*'s editorial is ample proof that the days of the master–servant relationship between Empire and colony had now passed. Like the majority of colonists, the *Herald* intended that the Crown remain as the sovereign power in the colony's Constitution, but it also insisted that the Crown be attentive to the colonists' desire to receive their English birthright—a representative house of assembly. Without this 'kind and temperate' treatment, the colonists' consent to the sovereign power of the Crown would be withdrawn. For the colonists, the monarch was the embodiment of principles which held the compact in place, the living symbol of the Constitution. It was the monarch's responsibility to uphold the colonists' right to reject any law which did not have their consent. In part, this explains why political reformers in the 1840s and 1850s frequently distinguished between loyalty to the monarch and loyalty to the colonial governor. One of the most talented and vocal of these reformers was Robert Lowe. An accomplished lawyer and journalist with a gift for oratory, Lowe danced across the political stage aligning himself with various forces at different stages of his career. Through the pages of his paper *Atlas*, Lowe led the campaign for constitutional reform in the early 1840s, but he was also keen to protect the monarch from becoming the object of colonial dissent:

> We owe loyalty to one person—the Queen. . . . We are bound . . . to distinguish between [the Queen and the Governor]. Every mark of respect . . . shown to the governor [is] an insult to the Queen. . . . Be careful on all occasions to distinguish between respect to local functionaries and loyalty to the British Crown.[11]

The only chance for the republican path lay in the failure of the invisible compact between London and Australia. If trust was seen to fail, if consent of the people was not sought, if mutual advantage was found to be wanting, then there would be those who would counsel separation and a republic. The crucial point, however, is that from the outset, separation would always be seen by the majority as the last resort, and more importantly it would usually be entertained to protest the very principles of the English Constitution which the colonists held in such high regard.

Any mention of republicanism in the language of the French or American revolutions still provoked hysteria. In 1842, before news of the new Constitution had reached New South Wales, the Irishman, Henry MacDermott, dared to refer to the 'rights of man' at a public meeting in Sydney. MacDermott accused conservatives, such as James Macarthur, of neglecting the skilled working classes of the colony. Angered by what he saw as the narrow distribution of political power in the colony, he insisted that the indefeasible rights of man entitled all men to the franchise.[12]

MacDermott's use of the phrase 'rights of man' was enough to send the press into a frenzy of anti-republican invective. The *Sydney Herald* claimed that the meeting had been disrupted by Jacobins and the mobocracy. The *Australian* devoted an editorial to MacDermott's crucifixion, warning its readers of the 'infidel' doctrines of Voltaire and Paine and the terrible example of the French republic, a 'nation which got drunk with blood to vomit crime'.[13]

If this was the reaction to one Irishman voicing support for the rights of man, one could imagine the response to anyone with republican sympathies such as Paine. After suffering public humiliation, MacDermott distanced himself from any republican connection. In letters to the *Sydney Herald* he assured the public that he was 'not a leveller Chartist or Robespierre', instead he simply demanded a £10 property franchise and his 'birthright as a British subject'. MacDermott's capitulation still did nothing to stop the press from indulging in its usual hyperbole—portraying his defeat as the 'triumph of royalty over Jacobinism'.[14]

In a fashion which was typical of the ruling-class response to disloyalty in nineteenth-century Australia, James Macarthur and other conservatives who were fearful of losing their leading role in calling for representative institutions, immediately set about calling a second meeting which would erase any hint of revolutionary republicanism. A motion was passed which struck MacDermott's name from the list of petitioners followed by a unanimous vote of support for the 'strengthening and perpetuation' of the connection with Great Britain. It was not enough to defeat and ridicule alleged republicans, public displays of loyalty had to be managed as a performance—a whitewash to cover up any republican stains.[15]

In the years between 1840 and 1856 there would be many occasions when the invisible compact between Australia and England was seen to fail. It was at these moments, when feelings of betrayal were widespread, that the suggestion of an independent republic was often heard. The first of these occurred in 1844 when Governor George Gipps attempted to impose a new set of squatting laws to regulate the sale of land.

A Civil, Constitutional, and Gentlemanly State of Disgust

When the long-awaited new Constitution reached Sydney in November 1842, all hopes of a Canadian-style Constitution were dashed quickly. Lord Stanley's Colonial Office believed that the Australian colonies were not yet ready for fully representative government.

The new Constitution contained provisions for a unicameral legislature of thirty-six members, twelve of whom were to be elected, with high property qualifications effectively denying the possibility of any log-cabin ascendancy. The 1842 Constitution offered neither responsible government nor self-government. Although the Governor no longer sat in Council, he had the right to reject bills, propose amendments or reserve bills for royal assent. The Crown also held the right to disallow any bill within two years of the Governor's assent.[16]

The Constitution quickly became the source of much disaffection in the colony. Stanley had handed down a Constitution in which the executive was not responsible to the legislature. In addition, both nominated and elected members would require a considerable degree of wealth and the new house would have no control over the collection or distribution of revenues. Robert Lowe immediately launched a campaign for responsible government in the *Atlas*: 'This is the colony that's under the governor, that's under the clerk, that's under the Lord, that's under the Commons, who are under the people, who know and care nothing about it'.[17]

In the Legislative Council, John Dunmore Lang moved a motion that the right of Her Majesty's government to nominate one-third of the Council's members was contrary to the Bill of Rights and the fundamental principles of the British Constitution. Lang insisted that the English Constitution rested on the principle that taxes were a voluntary gift and grant of the Commons.[18] Over the next decade, Lang, who had emigrated from Scotland in 1822, would emerge as the most outspoken critic of the Colonial Office. Although Lang had come to Australia like a pilgrim father to establish the Presbyterian Church in New South Wales, he is perhaps even more renowned for his republicanism. Described as a 'fixed and steadfast Scotch type' with a dry sense of humour, Lang was sufficiently enamoured with his own talents to see himself as Australia's Washington-in-waiting, especially after he had visited the United States in 1840 and called on President Van Buren. For Lang, America was a beacon of cheap and sensible republican government. By 1845 both Lowe and Lang had begun to employ the language of revolutionaries. Salvoes such as dictator, despot, oppressor and monster were commonplace.[19] Although the portrayal of the Governor as a medieval ogre was not unusual, there was one issue in particular which served to differentiate the philippic of 1845.

The Act for regulating the Sale of Waste Land belonging to the Crown which accompanied the 1842 Constitution had stipulated that no Crown land be sold for less than £1 per acre, while free land grants were prohibited. When these measures were added to the constitutional specification that revenue from land sales was to remain under the jurisdiction of the Crown, large land holders, squatters and newly arrived immigrants all had cause for complaint. The land issue had always carried the potential to raise colonial grievances to fever pitch. As early as 1839 the *Sydney Herald* had suggested that Australia might have to do without the home government: 'It is clear ... that the home government is becoming an intolerable encumbrance and the colonists ought at once to use every lawful measure to prepare for shaking off its rule at the very earliest possible opportunity'.[20]

Land was to become the first issue in Australian history to spark visions of a plantation-style republic. General dissatisfaction with the 1842 Constitution was exacerbated in 1844 when Governor Gipps attempted to introduce new squatting regulations. Strapped for revenue and led by a zeal to reform the old licence system, Gipps proposed that squatters' rents should be determined according to the amount of land held.[21] Gipps' regulations meant a considerable rent increase for all squatters. The previous system had merely insisted on a flat £10 tax per annum, regardless of the size of the squatters' runs. For years, squatters had been accustomed to claiming land and paying little for it. In the period that followed Gipps' announcement (he intended to introduce the new laws on 1 April 1845) all political activists in the colony were briefly united in their opposition to the proposals. The likes of Lowe and Lang saw Gipps' plans as an opportunity to press home the need for responsible government. Others, such as Wentworth, who only four years earlier had been thwarted by Gipps in an attempt to swindle 20 million acres of New Zealand's South Island from a group of Maori chiefs, had more personal reasons for their dissatisfaction.[22] Opposition extended across a broad spectrum of colonial society. The majority of the press, many members of the newly formed Legislative Council, country storekeepers and squatters, all found reason to protest against the new measures. The Pastoral Association of NSW was formed in Sydney to organise a concerted campaign of resistance and meetings were quickly called in many rural towns.[23]

There is no doubt that the period between April 1844 and mid-1845 witnessed the most systematic and strident opposition to imperial policy yet seen in Australia. The London *Morning Chronicle* described Australia as being in a state of 'indescribable ferment'. In Australia the *Morning Chronicle* claimed the colonial press had become almost as menacing as the Canadian.[24] The author of the most extensive study of this period, Stephen H. Roberts, insists that 'whatever the cause . . . eastern Australia in 1844 was emotionally insane and even sensible pioneers were gripping the stocks of their saddle carbines and openly speaking of rebellion'.[25] Roberts' comments do lead us to ask in what sense the disaffection in the mid-1840s could be said to be republican.

If we begin with the language of the Pastoral Association, we find that the Association's petitions were couched in the usual parlance of English constitutionalism. Never once did the Association threaten separation or independence. At the very first protest meeting held at the Royal Hotel in Sydney, Wentworth directed that resistance should remain passive and constitutional. Some historians have asserted that the language of certain sections of the colonial press, in particular Robert Lowe's *Atlas*, bordered on the seditious. While this may have been true superficially, any careful reading of the *Atlas* demonstrates that Lowe's seditious language was merely tactical. He frequently compared the situation of New South Wales in 1845 to that of the American colonies in 1776, in the hope of forcing the Colonial Office into recognition of his claims.[26]

On other occasions, Lowe spoke of the prospect of a wave of 'successive revolutions', suggesting that 'the folly of denying to Englishmen abroad the rights they enjoy at home' might see the Australian colonies declare their independence and follow the 'honourable' example of America. These were the words of a skilful politician, obviously part of a strategy to gain the attention of the authorities in London. In January 1845 Lowe admitted that the colony was not interested in 'open rebellion'—it was 'only in a civil, constitutional' and 'gentlemanly state of disgust'. Lowe was an opportunist at heart and he had no intention of putting 'the axe to the root of [the] British connection'.[27] Despite Lowe's bluffs and Wentworth's reticence to openly criticise London, there is still some evidence which indicates that a particular republican sentiment did exist among the squatters.

On 19 July 1845 the *Atlas* published a copy of a long letter from John Dunmore Lang to the editor of the *Morning Chronicle* in London. In the letter Lang related several conversations he had had with squatters during his recent travels in rural New South Wales. At the beginning of the letter Lang set out the reasons for the squatters' opposition to Gipps' regulations:

> They regard the imposition of such a tax, on the exclusive authority of the Crown and without the consent of the local legislature as a gross violation of the first principles of the British constitution, . . .
>
> If the Sovereign or his authorised agents abrogate the constitution, it follows, as a matter of course, that the subjects are ipso facto, absolved from their oath or duty of allegiance . . .[28]

In Lang's eyes the Australian republic was the final solution, when all else failed, to protect the English Constitution from the usurpations of Gipps' squatting laws. Eight days after the despatches from Lord Stanley approving the measures had been published in the colony, a magistrate of 'high Tory principles' dropped in to see Lang at his house in Sydney. Lang asked the magistrate to gauge the feelings of his district, 130 miles (209 km) out of Sydney, with regard to the squatting laws:

> 'Why,' he replied with a strong feeling of indignation, 'they think the best thing they could do with Sir George now would be to Bligh him . . . to pack him on board ship and send him off to England.' 'But that' I observed rather drily . . . 'that would imply an insurgent flag and proclaiming a republic.' 'It is the natural and perhaps necessary course of affairs in such a crisis,' replied the magistrate.[29]

Lang goes on to relate details of other conversations held with squatters on his journey, all of which lend weight to the argument that there was considerable disquiet over Gipps' new land tax. According to Lang, one squatter refuted any suggestion that the British military might quash a rebellion. Said the squatter, 'only give me 20 good stockmen and I would defy any regiment in Her Majesty's Service'. Others sang the praises of local horsemen who would protect the infant republic by traversing the land 'with the speed of the wild Arabs of the desert— leaving a conflagration behind them in every suitable locality to envelop their pursuers'.[30] These details were included in a letter Lang had sent to the *Chronicle* in London dated 16 July 1845, a significant date because only nine days earlier he had scrawled a republican fantasy on a piece of paper. In this reverie, Lang naively imagined the 'galling and degrading yoke' being cast off, as Gipps was politely arrested. New South Wales is now 'free to govern ourselves cheaply wisely, and well', he wrote, as 'an independent republic'.[31] Clearly, Lang was in the mood for fiction when he penned his letter to the *Chronicle*. The addition of a few tales of squatters threatening a stockmen's republic would be just the tonic needed to persuade the Colonial Office to change their policy. Despite the obvious licence in Lang's letter, reports of elitist republican sympathies among the squatters can still be substantiated from other sources.

The *Australian* had frequently questioned 'the loyalty of the squatter faction'. It saw Lang's letter as further evidence of what it believed to be 'the treasonous and rebellious principles held by the inhabitants of the bush'. Edward Curr, Victorian squatter and representative of Port Phillip in the Legislative Council, sufficiently doubted the squatters' loyalty to write in a letter to the *Australian* that if the rights of independence continued to be denied to the colonists 'revolution would become an affair of tomorrow'.[32]

One interesting source of support for Lang's anecdotal evidence can be found in the memoirs of the squatter, Christopher P. Hodgson. In 1846 after the criticism of Gipps had subsided, Hodgson, now back in London, published his *Reminiscences of Australia, with Hints on the Squatter's Life*. Hodgson's comments on the intensity of the squatters' feeling in the colony appear to substantiate the evidence of Lang:

> republican spirit exploded, and had not a solitary and salutary clause been inserted, deferring any active operation for 18 months, a scene might have occurred—which too prematurely would have demonstrated to the world, that English hearts and English hands could maintain their rights even at the Antipodes.[33]

While it is true that both supporters and opponents of Gipps' regulations appealed to London, there were many squatters who spoke of resistance.

William Windemeyer, member of the Legislative Council, admitted during a debate in Council in October 1845 that he had heard some squatters talk of their readiness to lead the colony into civil war if they were not successful in persuading the Colonial Office to override Gipps' regulations.[34]

Although we know there was a republican sentiment among the squatters, perhaps the more interesting issue is the nature of this sentiment. There is no evidence to suggest that the squatters were familiar with the lucid arguments of political principle supplied by propagandists such as Lang. Alastair Davidson has pointed out that the Australian colonies of the 1840s were characterised by a culture of possessive individualism. Land and its acquisition was the fundamental basis of this culture. For a brief moment in 1844–45, the squatters 'emerged as leaders of a national popular alliance against the British despots'.[35] The squatters' brand of republicanism bore more in common with a desire to set up a plantation-style republic—a decidedly elitist and anti-democratic vision of a republic which was motivated by the desire to avoid a government tax. Naturally, this is not to imply that the squatters' republicanism was less 'real' or valid than the more democratic republicanism of Wills, only that it was different.

But we should also remember that at no time did the squatters make any attempt to unify and organise disaffection through the formation of a republican organisation. Their republican sympathies entailed no vision of a new society, and after they got their way in 1846 talk of a republic quickly disappeared. The squatters then returned to their role as the bulwark of the English connection. The fact that all evidence of republican sympathies among the squatters is primarily anecdotal indicates that, like Lowe and Lang, their talk of independence was essentially tactical with a good dose of false bravado to prove their rural roots. Like the Anzacs at Gallipoli, who went to war for the adventure of it all—it seemed many squatters hoped for a republic so they could demonstrate their skills on horseback. The republican spirit which 'exploded' in the mid-1840s was mostly conversational boasting, elitist, fearful of open declaration and motivated by hip-pocket sensitivity. Throughout the crisis Gipps had clung tenaciously to his belief in the absolute sovereignty of the Crown—frequently insisting that the granting of freedom and independence was fundamentally incompatible with the continuation of that sovereignty. In 1846 he explained his views in a despatch to Lord Stanley:

> The political position of a British Colony is no unenviable one; to be a member of the British Empire is alone a glorious privilege; but those who enjoy it cannot be allowed to forget that the condition of a Colonist is one to which duties are attached as well as privileges; that men who claim to be Her Majesty's subjects cannot be at the same time Members of an Independent Republic.[36]

This was the view which had prevailed in the Colonial Office since the American Revolution. Yet already there were reformers in Australia who, like Merivale in London, had realised that the granting of limited independence did not necessarily have to entail separation and republican government. If a successful compromise between the theories of absolute sovereignty and birthright could be reached in time, the colonies would have the degree of independence they desired, with the added security of English protection under the Crown. The next decade would prove whether this was possible.

CHAPTER THREE

The Last Resort   1848–1856

> As for John Bull himself, as a moralist and political philosopher—he is proverbially 'slow bellied'. The bare idea of 'moving on' institutionally has to be driven into his hard head as with a sledge hammer.
>
> Charles Harpur[1]

The brief eight-year period which preceded the granting of responsible government to the Australian colonies in 1856 bore witness to one of the most significant political struggles in Australian history. It was during this time that the nature of the political institutions which would carry the colonies to Federation was decided.

Never before had so many threats been made from Australians to sever the connection with Britain as there were between 1848 and 1856. The sources of potential grievance with the mother country were numerous: a Constitution which was widely deemed to be incompatible with the egalitarian and progressive nature of colonial society, the renewal of transportation, draconian regulations on the goldfields, and dissatisfaction with any number of imperial interventions in colonial affairs. If ever there was a time for the idea of separation to find fertile ground these years presented every opportunity.

To date, there has been no extensive analysis of the republican arguments which surfaced in Australia during this period. If we fail to examine the nature of these republican proposals, as well as their opponents, then we also fail to understand the manner in which the colonies attained a limited degree of self-government. It is not possible to understand the Empire which we embraced until we recognise that republicanism, in one form or another, played an important role in the struggle for political liberty in colonial Australia.

The Year of Revolution

When the French King, Louis-Philippe, lost his throne in February 1848, news of the Revolution in Paris spread quickly to Europe's major capital cities. Within weeks, revolution had swept continental Europe; only Belgium and England managed to escape the turmoil. The *Sydney Morning Herald* greeted the news in an excited fashion with a large headline in bold type:

REVOLUTION IN FRANCE!
FLIGHT OF THE KING!
REPUBLICAN GOVERNMENT ESTABLISHED[2]

It is commonly accepted that the European revolutions of 1848 left Australia largely untouched. Superficially, this generalisation is accurate. The Australian colonies did not lurch suddenly into a climate of revolution and there are few examples of political reformers specifically invoking the spirit of 1848. It would be difficult, for example, to sustain any argument which proposed a substantial link between republican rhetoric in Australia and that of the 1848 revolutions. In Sydney, the closest democrats came to invoking the spirit of 1848 was Henry Parkes' depiction of the election of Robert Lowe to the Legislative Council in July 1848 as the 'birth-day of Australian democracy', part of the ineluctable wave of democracy that was sweeping the civilised world.[3] The 1848 revolutions did see a small number of Irish rebels as well as English and Scottish Chartists transported to Australia. Some of these transportees held republican sympathies yet there is little evidence that they carried these principles with them to Australia. The 10 000 German immigrants who came to Australia between 1847 and 1851 also contained a number of men and women who had been present in Frankfurt in 1848, yet, apart from one or two exceptions, they made no attempt to transplant this spirit of revolution in any active or concerted manner.[4] Angus McKay, who had taken over the editorship of the *Atlas* in 1848, complained that the European revolutions had had little effect in Australia:

> While Europe is striking off the fetters which despotism has forged for the people, and the voice of the people is scattering to the winds the divine right of princes and such obsolete humbugs, we who dwell under a government more despotic and more oppressive than any in the world do not make the least manifestation of sympathy with the general movement of progress.[5]

Despite McKay's lament, it would be wrong to imagine Sydney in the late 1840s as a city untouched by the spirit of democratic reform. At this time Sydney was a town still small enough to retain a village-like atmosphere. In a society just breaking free of the shackles of convictism, poets, artists, intellectuals, and political reformers found a natural community of interest. One of the focal points of intellectual debate in Sydney in 1850 was the parlour of a small shop at 20 Hunter Street—only a short walk from John Dunmore Lang's home at the Australia College in Jamison Street. In 1888 David Blair, the Presbyterian preacher, political journalist and one-time disciple of John Dunmore Lang, looked back on his first visit to number 20 Hunter Street:

A few months after my arrival in Sydney, in 1850, I was walking along Hunter Street in company with Dr Lang. He stopped suddenly before a little shop, the window of which was filled with children's toys and said, 'Come in here; I want to introduce you to somebody.' Stepping into the shop, we found a young man of about 30, as I judged, and of strikingly remarkable appearance, with his coat off, engaged in the task of unpacking a case of toys. The introductions were exchanged, and at once the Doctor and the remarkable shopkeeper fell to talking politics. I had not listened for many minutes before I felt myself impressed with the conviction that here were two real statesmen of Nature's own making.[6]

The remarkable shopkeeper who so impressed Blair was none other than Henry Parkes. Parkes had arrived in Sydney in 1839 from Birmingham. An ivory-turner by trade but a politician by instinct, Parkes was now ready to realise his talent as a political journalist and orator. In his own words, Parkes' 'Ivory Manufactory and Toy Warehouse' in Hunter Street was a place where his small 'group of friends privately discussed every question that arose'. The Hunter Street parlour was the drop-in centre for Sydney's radical intellectuals, among them many of the men who would play an important role in formulating the democratic proposals for the colony's new Constitution: E. J. Hawksely, Daniel Deniehy, David Blair, Angus McKay and, of course, Henry Parkes.

These men were also in touch with a wider community of artists and poets who held more utopian visions of Australia's future, such as the native-born poet Charles Harpur or the young painter Adelaide Ironside.[7] For those who came to sit in the back of Parkes' shop to discuss politics, surrounded by toys and bric-à-brac, it was a time of optimism, intellectual curiosity and dreaming; a time when the colony's readiness for a more independent and democratic Constitution fired the ambition and imagination of Sydney's political reformers.

Six months after Robert Lowe was elected as the people's candidate in the elections for the Legislative Council, a small group of Sydney democrats formed the Constitutional Association—among their members, the young Henry Parkes. Led by Parkes, E. J. Hawksely and Angus McKay, the movement's platform was Chartist, and concentrated on the campaign for the extension of the franchise. To proselytise its views it supported the publication of a weekly journal, the *People's Advocate*, under Hawksely's editorship.[8]

The Constitutional Association, formed by democrats, did not wish to describe itself as republican. At the inaugural meeting of the Association in January 1849 the revolutionary republic was broached and quickly buried. Speaking in favour of extending the franchise, Dr Isaac Aaron mentioned that universal suffrage had been 'wrung from the hands of a tyrannical government in France'. As he did so, a voice in the audience cried out 'Long Live The Republic!' and Aaron replied that 'he did not wish to see a republic—only fair and good government for the people'.[9] Parkes stated that their opponents often 'pointed to the excesses of Paris and Frankfurt', and 'how it had dyed the hands of the people in blood'. Even at this stage of his career Parkes was aware that revolution could serve as 'an argument in favour of universal suffrage'. Yet reading the early editions of the *People's Advocate* in 1848 and 1849 it is easy to understand how its platform might be construed as republican. Its motto was a quotation from Lamartine, while the first editorial boldly declared that all power sprang from the people. Inspired by the revolutions in Europe it believed that the wave of democracy spreading through the Old World would soon visit Australia.[10] Despite these sympathies the *People's Advocate* did not advocate an Australian republic until John Dunmore Lang delivered his 'Coming Event' lectures in April 1850. Like its editor, who roamed the streets of Sydney wearing a cabbage-tree hat which sported a tricolour ribbon, the *Advocate* felt free to borrow the republican imagery of continental Europe while remaining within the bounds of traditional Chartist appeals to the English Constitution.[11] On 14 July 1849 Hawksely published an article on the newly declared French Republic: 'Monarchists as we are here at home, and loyal ones too, our cry for France is "Vive la Republique"'.[12]

Hawksely probably did not realise it at the time, but it was this fundamental faith in the capacity of the English Constitution to deliver reform which would ensure the Australian colonies avoided the necessity of separation. Throughout the late 1840s the *People's Advocate* petitioned the Crown for manhood suffrage, vote by ballot, equal electoral districts and more frequent elections. Francis Cunningham, Chartist and co-founder of the *People's Advocate*, reflected the views of many democrats in Australia in his short-lived journal *Citizen*. Although Cunningham praised the heroes of the Paris Revolution of 1830, his revolutionary fervour quickly evaporated when it came to the question of political reform in Australia:

> Far be it from us to wish that any portion of the dominions of our beloved Queen should ... become the arena of civil strife ... thanks to the sound principles of British laws we possess as our inalienable birthright, freedom of opinion and liberty of speech ... We ... possess the happy privilege of attaining redress for our grievances and protection to our interests, by ... the means of peaceful, legal, and constitutional, ... assertion of our rights.[13]

These words throw light on the peculiar ambivalence of democrat platforms in the mid-nineteenth century. The mandatory invocation to the republican heroes of Europe came more from a desire to scare the Colonial

Office than any solidarity with the bloodied hands of their brothers-in-arms. The real aim was the democratisation of the English Constitution in as civil and gentlemanly a fashion as possible. They believed that the English Constitution, which they cherished dearly, would deliver them from the rivers of blood which flowed in the capitals of Europe.

Charles Harpur, who appealed not to the European revolutionaries but to Milton and Marvell, displayed all the reticence of the landed classes of England when he remarked that the French had moved far too quickly towards republican government. Democrat and republican he may have been, but with a particular inherited political language which was not necessarily shared in its entirety by other republicans or democrats.[14] Many democrats wanted democratic government but no part of a republic. Others may have agreed on the republic but disagreed about the means by which it should be achieved, its structure, or its timing. In any event, there were few reformers whose stance was not dependent on the English government granting responsible government, few who espoused a fully independent republic as the only form of government in which democracy would flourish.

In the eight years which followed the publication of the first issue of the *People's Advocate*, the discussion of an Australian republic would surface more frequently than it had in the previous sixty years. By 1856 there would be evidence of an innovative, and not necessarily anti-monarchical, republican language in Australian political culture. Yet the nature of this language was shifting, elusive, and ambiguous. The first issue to bring these factors into play was Earl Grey's Order in Council of 1848 which provided for the renewal of transportation to the Australian colonies.

Another America?

In pouring rain at Circular Quay on 14 June 1849 thousands of people cheered when Robert Lowe stood on a makeshift platform and told the crowd that their protest against the renewal of transportation would be the first step towards Australian independence. There was nothing new about Lowe's vision of the colonies as another America in the South Pacific, but never before had this republican destiny been accompanied by the degree of public discontent which was associated with the issue of transportation. The time was ripe for an Antipodean tea party and Lowe was only too willing to exploit the circumstances.

Moves to abolish transportation had been afoot in both England and Australia since the Molesworth Committee had handed down its highly critical report of the system in 1838. Transportation of convicts to New South Wales ceased with the arrival of the *Eden* in November 1840. In 1846 the

British government suspended transportation to Van Diemen's Land for two years.[15] Despite the reassurances of Earl Grey (who became Colonial Secretary in 1847) that transportation would not be resumed, the pressure on prisons in England resulted in the hatching of several schemes to send convicts to Australia. Gladstone naively attempted to start a new penal colony in northern Australia which ended in starvation and misery in 1847. When Grey secured an Order in Council to renew the transportation of convicts to New South Wales and Van Diemen's Land in 1848, he not only broke his promise not to ship convicts but also reneged on an earlier commitment to match each convict with one free immigrant.[16]

Although support for Grey's intentions could be found among the squatters and urban shop owners, the news provoked almost universal condemnation, especially in Sydney and Melbourne.[17] The 'moral filth' and pestilence of convicts disembarking at Sydney Cove was an affront to the *petit-bourgeois* morality of colonial society. In the mid-nineteenth century, convicts occupied a position in public discourse which has much in common with the 'immigrant' in modern industrial societies. They were the scapegoats for crime, disease and moral decay, the lepers of colonial society, the skeleton in the closet, the stain which blotted the pages of the colony's history. The intensity of public feeling on the issue was so great that the Legislative Council declined to accede to Grey's proposal.[18] The Constitutional Association was quick to seize the moment, clearly hoping to link its demands for more responsible government to the transportation issue while the public's mood for agitation was strong. Parkes and other members quickly set about organising protest meetings, and there were hopes that the transportation movement might be the catalyst of 'the first national movement in Australian history'.[19] Between March and June the Association worked towards the launch of a mass protest meeting on the day of the arrival of the convict ship *Hashemy*. Lowe, who considered the platform of the Constitutional Association too radical, spoke of the possible dismemberment of the Empire if the issue was not resolved.[20] Both Parkes and Lowe were to play pivotal roles in the demonstrations of 1849.

When the day finally arrived, crowds marched along George and Macquarie Streets towards the Quay, shops closed down and soldiers stood with their bayonets fixed, guarding Government House. Despite the rain the crowd numbered around 5000, by far the largest demonstration Sydney had seen. In front of a drenched crowd in need of some inspiring words, Lowe delivered the appropriate performance:

> The stately presence of their city, the beautiful waters of their harbour, were this day again polluted with the presence of a floating hell—a convict ship (*Immense cheers*) . . .

Let them send across the Pacific their emphatic declaration that they would not be slaves—that they would be free. Let them exercise the right that every English subject had to assert his freedom. He could see from the meeting the time was not far distant when they would assert their freedom not by words alone. As in America, oppression was the parent of independence, so would it be in the colony . . . So sure as the seed will grow into the plant, and the plant to the tree, in all times, and in all nations, so will injustice and tyranny ripen into rebellion, and rebellion into independence.[21]

Much has been made of this speech. Noel McLachlan has claimed that New South Wales was 'on the verge of an anti-rattlesnake revolution', and interprets Lowe's words as 'the most powerful invocation of revolution ever heard in Australia'. Ruth Knight, Lowe's biographer, is carried away by Lowe's oratory, insisting that he was attempting to lead a 'quasi revolution'. Robert Hughes also allows licence to run free with his comment that Lowe saw the meeting as a 'prelude to an Australian republic'.[22]

Clearly, there is a need for a more balanced perspective. Lowe, as we have learnt already, was a self-confessed prevaricator. His talk of rebellion and independence was merely tactical, just as it had been in the pages of the *Atlas*. It is difficult to imagine how a man who found the mild platform of the Constitutional Association radical, and later voted against the Second Reform bill in England in 1867, would seriously entertain the thought of an Australian republic. Sensing the mood of the crowd, Lowe merely played the role which the script demanded.

As for the suggestion that the crowd's cheering was evidence of their support for Australian independence—we should not be so gullible. While Pythonesque images of a crowd cheering for its own extermination come to mind, there is no evidence that independence was seriously contemplated.[23] The convicts were not stopped from disembarking, and even when thousands of the crowd were barred from entering the gates of Government House after marching through driving rain, a deputation to see Fitzroy was quietly organised and the crowd remained calm. The slightest hint of disorder would only have vindicated the claims of their opponents that they were convict rabble. To achieve political legitimacy and deny the inevitable barbs of disloyalty, the possibility of openly adopting the label 'republican' was effectively blocked. Perhaps this is why not one emancipist or native-born citizen spoke on 14 June.[24] Although Lowe's bluff of revolution is frequently quoted, a far more important speech made by Henry Parkes at a second meeting on 18 June is often overlooked. Parkes made a point of specifically denying any talk of republicanism:

> . . . He did not agree with the allusions which had been made to America . . . As a community we possessed little of the stern and sturdy spirit of the old

American colonists ... It would be wise and well to cherish a feeling of true loyalty towards Great Britain.[25]

The man who had proclaimed in 1841 that 'Money! Money! Money!' would be his watchword for the future, probably spoke for the majority of colonists in Sydney and Melbourne when he rejected the need for separation and independence. As a businessman, Parkes was well aware that separation would risk the possibility of the British government placing large export duties on goods sent to Australia. This, combined with his pessimistic view of Australian character, was enough to encourage Parkes to steer clear of the word 'republic'.[26]

As the convicts continued to arrive over the next three years, many doubted that the British government was listening to the colonists' petitions. With resentment to transportation capable of reaching fever pitch, it was still feasible that a stubborn Colonial Office could provoke a more brazen and proudly republican spirit in Australia. One only had to look at the reaction to the arrival of convicts in Melbourne to realise that resistance to transportation was deeply entrenched. Protesters in the Port Phillip District were so vehement in their opposition they successfully persuaded La Trobe to send all convict ships attempting to berth on to Sydney. The *Argus* reported a large meeting held at Queen's Theatre in Melbourne on Monday 20 August 1849, which was attended by more than 1500 people. While speakers delivered the usual pleas of loyalty, they also made it clear that independence was a definite alternative if transportation continued. One man exhorted the audience to believe that the British government was driving them into rebellion. Others insisted that separation from Great Britain and a 'solemn declaration of independence' were 'the only alternative'. There was even the suggestion that 'rifles and muskets' would be the only appropriate reply to Grey's intransigence.[27] Rhetorically at least, it seemed that the door had not been completely closed on an independent Australian republic. Much would depend on the response of the British government.

The Coming Event

> Doctor Lang, like a bold bad boy, would kick up a row in the house, smash the plates and dishes, burn his mother's crutch, put the cat's tail in the rat trap, throw the fat in the fire and then run away to sea.[28]

If Australians wished to erect a republican hall of fame, a large part of the pantheon would be devoted to one man. John Dunmore Lang was the greatest in a long line of flawed republican heroes in Australia. Possessing

Lang
John Dunmore Lang in 1850 about the time of the 'Coming Event' lectures. The struggle between Lang and Parkes, one of the greatest stories in pre-Federation Australia, captured the spirit of the debate on Australian independence which would continue until the late twentieth century.
(Portrait by Charles Rodius, 1850, crayon, Image Library, State Library of New South Wales.)

abundant wit, intelligence, and astonishing reserves of energy, Lang was the person most responsible for forcing the issue of an Australian republic into the mainstream of political discussion in the 1850s. In the space of two years Lang delivered lectures, speeches and publications at a frantic pace. His importance stems as much from the eloquence of his republican arguments, which are still echoed in the romantic nationalism of late twentieth-century republicans such as Thomas Keneally, as it does from his role as the founder of Presbyterianism in Australia. In the words of Daniel Deniehy, John Dunmore Lang towered above his contemporaries 'like a cathedral dome above a city'.[29]

Lang had come to the attention of the colonial authorities while living in London between 1847 and 1849. His outspoken columns in the *British Banner*, and his persistent efforts to initiate an immigrant assistance scheme to the colonies, earned him instant recognition in the halls of the Colonial Office. Irritated by the lack of support for his immigration scheme, and what Lang perceived to be discrimination against Presbyterian ministers in the allocation of assisted clerical passages to Australia, he wrote an open letter to Earl Grey in November 1849. The letter demanded Grey's impeachment and threatened the authorities with the possibility of a United States of Australia. Lang, with his usual humility, implied that the future republic would need to look no further to find its first president—John Dunmore Lang.[30]

Embittered by his experiences in England and inspired by the principles of the Chartist movement and his earlier travels in the American republic, Lang returned to Australia in March 1850 and prepared to launch his campaign for the future independence of Australia.[31] In April 1850 Lang delivered a series of three lectures entitled 'The Coming Event' or the 'United Provinces Of Australia'. These lectures, which were later published in pamphlet form, constitute the first comprehensive argument for an Australian republic. Even before Lang gave the lectures, the Constitutional Association had disbanded due to internal divisions and lack of public interest. Now, with public anger rising over the transportation issue and the lack of responsible government, there was a definite opportunity for Lang's republican platform to gain a foothold in New South Wales. As the *Hobart Town Courier* remarked, the mere discussion of such questions implied the possibility of separation.[32] The circumstances for Lang's call for independence could hardly have been better.

In front of large and enthusiastic audiences, Lang announced that the time had arrived for the declaration of a federal Australian republic.[33] He rested his argument on three broad principles—inevitability, national invigoration and the political, economic, and social advantages which would flow to both the mother country and the colonies after separation. Lang's vision of the coming Australian republic was one which relied on the racial and cultural superiority of British immigrants, a *petit-bourgeois* utopia of yeoman farmers industriously tilling the soil in a white Pacific enclave. His determinist sense of history led him to portray the future republic as a logical consequence of immutable historical processes— 'some day or other [the colonies] would become sovereign and independent communities'. If the birth of a nation was a process similar to the birth of an individual, then its inevitable maturation would lead to eventual separation. Lang championed independence as a natural and inherent right, indefeasible and indestructible. A republic was the only practicable and natural government for a New World society such as Australia. The colonies lacked the 'requisite traditions' for any other form of government.[34]

To lead the native youth of the colony to the head of the civilised world ('instead of being the very tail of it') Lang proposed the formation of an Australian League—a 'great political league' with branches in every colony. The greatest applause was reserved for Lang's projection of the League as the seed of 'one people, having common interests, . . . the nucleus . . . of *one Great Australian Nation*'. Interestingly, this romantic vision of nationhood was not accompanied by any antagonism towards monarchy. Lang portrayed himself as both loyalist and republican, expressing his 'sincere respect and unfeigned attachment' for Queen Victoria.[35]

Lang was determined to avoid the tag of 'seditious republican'. In his attempt to portray loyalty and republicanism as compatible, he threw down a direct challenge to all those who relied on the traditional juxtaposition of the two terms. His chances of success would hinge on his ability to successfully argue that republicanism and loyalty were natural bedfellows. Lang argued that the desire for separation did not need to be motivated by anti-British sentiment. To bolster this proposition he relied on the third principle, the belief that Britain would support and welcome Australian separation. Unlike the majority of colonists, Lang claimed that separation would actually benefit Australia and Britain.[36]

The effect of Lang's association with Cobden and Bright and the ideas of the Manchester School is not difficult to identify. Quoting Thomas Babbington Macaulay, who Lang referred to as the 'greatest historical and political writer of our age', and the unidentified support of parties of the highest standing in London, Lang suggested that England was now fully prepared for Australian independence.[37] At times, he sounded like an agent for British trade, shrewdly arguing that separation would effectively be performing a service to the British economy. If Lang was to be believed, there would be much dancing in the streets of London if the Australian republic was declared.

The infant colony's greatest fear in the 1850s was its vulnerability to foreign invasion, something which talk of separation was bound to exacerbate. Lang tried to avoid this pitfall by arguing that Australian security would not be endangered but enhanced after separation from England. With characteristic humour, he amused his audience with examples of hypothetical invasions. Would the colonies, he asked, be attacked by the Negro nations of southern Africa, the Spanish republics of South America or China, Burma or Japan? Lang's answer had the crowd in fits of laughter: 'Why, none of these formidable people know where Australia lies: they would never be able to find us out! We have therefore to look for our enemies ... in the other Hemisphere'.[38]

Thus, it was only through England's involvement in war with France, Russia, or America that the Australian colonies would have cause to fear an attack. With separation and the complete freedom and independence attained after the declaration of a federal Australian republic, the new nation would actually find itself in a more secure position, free from any possible entanglement in imperial wars. If such ideas were condemned in twentieth-century Australia they were considered equally barmy in the autumn of 1850. Lang was to struggle desperately but unsuccessfully to gather support for these ideas over the next four years. The cheering which had greeted his republican lectures in April still belied the difficulty in establishing any firm bank of support for his cause. One of the men who carried the ability to muster this support was among the audience at Lang's second lecture on 16 April. Since the collapse of the Constitutional Association, Henry Parkes had been eager to form a political organisation which would effectively campaign for democratic reform and an end to transportation. Like the majority of those present on 16 April, Parkes was carried away by Lang's oratory. Clearly inspired by what he had heard, Parkes immediately wrote to Lang on the following day:

> ... I send my name as *one* ready to enrol himself in the League for the entire 'Freedom and Independence' of this—the land of my children's birth. I would suggest that no time should be lost—there are men enough prepared for the struggle, though, as you appear well to know, not among the dunghill aristocracy of Botany Bay ... A meeting might be got together on any Monday—why not again before the Government [House] gates?—where 8 or 10 thousand resolute British Australians should organise the League.[39]

Potentially at least, Parkes was probably the most talented political campaigner in New South Wales, and his support was crucial. If Lang could manage to bring Parkes into his republican fold then other democrats would surely follow. Only three days after Parkes pledged his commitment to Lang, E. J. Hawksely endorsed Lang's views on independence in the *People's Advocate*, calling on the people to rise with 'a voice of thunder' and demand their liberty and independence.[40]

Lang now had the backing of the colony's leading radical journal and its most competent political strategist. The stage was set for a stirring inaugural meeting of the Australian League. On 26 April at the Australia College in Sydney, a small group of men gathered to form the Australian League. Parkes' dreams of '8 or 10 thousand' people gathering at the gates of Government House were bitterly disappointed. The heady reception Lang had received only one week earlier had not guaranteed the commitment of the people to a participatory role. James Wiltshire, native-born businessman and ex-mayor of Sydney, chaired a meeting attended by between 20 and 100 people. As well as Wiltshire and Parkes, David Blair, the young democrat who had been mesmerised by Lang's articles in the *British Banner*, was present to hear the objects of the League declared.[41] The League's platform contained the seeds of a grand plan for republican agitation. Lectures, pamphlets, delegates in London, and a firm commitment to the political education of the people were to be the backbone of the republic of the United Provinces of Australia. The emphasis was on independent self-government, freedom from the convict stain, and the racial purity of British immigrants. The platform was inspiring enough, the pity was that there were so few present to hear it.

Two weeks later Lang travelled to Melbourne to deliver his republican lectures, and did so in front of what the *Argus* described as a 'very numerous audience'.[42] A similar pattern of events soon followed. Lang's calls for a republic were greeted with rapturous applause, a provisional committee of the Australian League was formed, and within weeks of Lang's departure the League had folded and none of its initial five members was interested or able enough to sustain its existence. Why then, was Lang's idea of an Australian republic well received initially by audiences in both Sydney and Melbourne, yet unable to muster any substantial support when it came to the formation of a political organisation?

The first and most obvious answer is that in any political culture it is possible to find evidence of crowds cheering for radical proposals, cheers which are not necessarily indicative of a popular will for the formation of political structures to work towards the realisation of such proposals. It is quite feasible that the crowds attending Lang's lectures reacted with enthusiasm because Lang provided them with an expedient outlet for the expression of their anger with the colonial authorities. In any case, the gap between cheering and political participation is great. We can also appreciate that the political culture of a colony accustomed to authoritarian rule was not yet familiar with the processes of political participation. The *People's Advocate* was devastated by the lack of interest in the Australian League and blamed the spread of a rampant materialism.[43]

While apathy was another factor which contributed to the failure of the Australian League, there was also the scandal which constantly dogged its driving force—J. D. Lang. One day after his successful lecture at the Protestant Hall in Melbourne, Lang was arrested and imprisoned. Robert Wilkinson, a man who had sailed to Australia on one of Lang's immigrant ships, the *Clifton*, alleged that he was owed £719 by Lang. Meanwhile, the *Sydney Morning Herald* had begun a vitriolic campaign against Lang, targeting him as a swindler and charlatan. According to the *Herald*, Lang had collected money from immigrants on the basis that they would immediately receive land grants upon arrival in Sydney. After eleven days in gaol Lang was released. He had been saved by the grace of Wilkinson and the fund-raising capabilities of the Presbyterian church, but his reputation had still been tarnished. Immediately, Lang attempted to win a vote of public confidence by standing as a candidate for the vacant Legislative Council seat of Port Phillip but was soundly defeated.[44] When he returned to Sydney much of the attention he might well have devoted to the Australian League was diverted into mounting a defence of his reputation.

Writing in 1888 David Blair looked back on Lang as a man who 'seemed to have no sense at all of . . . pecuniary liability'. Blair knew that Lang's 'total want of magnanimity' and poor financial sense fatally wounded any chance of him becoming a great statesman. Lang's personality left him open to constant criticism from the conservative press. The Melbourne *Herald* denounced him as a 'disappointed demagogue and red republican'. The *Sydney Morning Herald* preferred more colourful barbs, describing him as an 'arrogant, intolerant and scheming charlatan'. There is no doubt that these attacks harmed Lang's public standing and also, in turn, his attempts to launch a republican league.[45]

If Lang's financial debts were not enough to attract public condemnation, he also had to deal with conservative opposition to his republican campaign. The *Sydney Morning Herald* chose to ignore his ideas, offering scant coverage of his three lectures. Those papers which did take the trouble to address his proposals were often critical. The *Geelong Advertiser* labelled Lang a 'red republican' in too much of a hurry to 'leave the parental roof'. Lang's ideas also drew a concerned response from colonial governors. In Tasmania, Governor Denison wrote to Edward Deas Thomson, Colonial Secretary of New South Wales, fearful that 'a noisy liar like Lang could do an infinity of harm'.[46] By the middle of 1850 John Dunmore Lang was probably the most renowned political reformer in the Australian colonies. He had attracted the censure of the Colonial Office, several colonial governors, and the majority of the colonial press. Lang was now a red republican with more than his fair share of opposition.

Bringing Out the Doctor

> June 1850: 'An election for Sydney happened to fall just then. It was necessary, in the first place, that the battle for popular rights should be fought; and, in the second place, that Dr Lang should go into the Council to defend his character

and reputation against his many and bitter merciless enemies there. At a conference held in the little shop in Hunter Street, it was resolved to bring out the Doctor for the vacancy.[47]

This is how David Blair described the decision to stand J. D. Lang as a candidate for an unexpected vacancy in the Legislative Council in June 1850. After delivering the first public lectures in the colony which advocated an Australian republic, being imprisoned in Melbourne and returning to controversy in Sydney, Lang now engaged himself in a brave attempt to test the level of his public support.

For Lang's fellow reformers, such as Parkes and Blair, the resolution to 'bring out the Doctor' would provide a useful litmus test of the Sydney electorate's readiness for democratic reform. At this point, Parkes was still a reliable ally of Lang and he immediately set about organising a successful campaign committee.

Lang was to become the first uncloseted republican to be elected to an Australian parliament at a time when his public reputation was under constant attack. This quite remarkable achievement, and the debates surrounding it, reveal much about the interplay of forces which would eventually determine Australia's relationship with Britain for the remainder of the nineteenth century.

On the day of Lang's victory, a day of 'public calamity' according to the *Sydney Morning Herald*, he leaned from a window on the first floor of the Star Hotel in George Street and thanked his supporters gathered on the street below. In a jubilant mood, Lang told the crowd that his election represented the struggle for three principles—the extension of the franchise, equal representation, and the rejection of transportation.[48] As we know, these principles were an integral part of Lang's republican platform which he had outlined in the 'Coming Event' lectures. In this sense, Lang did not deny his republicanism in his victory speech, he merely omitted any mention of separation. The people who had voted for Lang, and later walked to hear his speech at the Star Hotel, were obviously aware of his republican views, indeed some of them may well have been in attendance at the republican lectures in April. Once we recognise the most important aspect of republicanism in 1850 was the introduction of a more democratic form of government, we can appreciate that Lang's election was in many ways a tentative endorsement of his republican views.

On Tuesday 30 July, the day Lang was to take his seat in the new Council, between 2000 and 3000 of his supporters marched along Macquarie Street from Circular Quay to Parliament House. There, they were quickly joined by another 5000 or 6000 people. Almost 10 000 people then cheered on Lang as he walked up the steps of Parliament House.[49] This was the high point of Lang's popularity, the brief and heady climax of the successful working relationship between Lang and Parkes. But it would not last for long.

Henry Parkes had previously acknowledged the strategic advantage of campaigning for a republican without mentioning the 'r' word. But one week before the election he had already begun to distance himself from Lang's republicanism—the republicanism of separation. Parkes wrote to the electors of Sydney through the columns of the *Representative*: 'The members of this committee . . . have for the most part no connexion nor personal acquaintance with Dr Lang, neither do they identify themselves with some of his public acts now under discussion: nor do they agree with his expressed opinions on many points of considerable importance'.[50]

It is not difficult to ascertain what Parkes meant with his evasive conclusion. This was the beginning of Parkes' departure from Lang, less than three months after he had pledged Lang his total support. Even though Parkes had led the singing of 'Auld Lang's Syne' at the official celebrations for Lang's victory, he must have known then that he would not be on Lang's side for long.[51]

In the meantime, Lang made no attempt to hide his republican views once he was elected. His fellow councillors wasted no time in attacking his public advocacy of republicanism. On 13 August, the second day of the Council's sitting, Councillor Terence Murray focused on Lang's support for separation: 'it was quite plain the honourable and reverend member had but one object in view . . . to sever this colony from the parent state'.[52]

This was exactly the type of criticism which would have encouraged Parkes to back away from Lang's republicanism. The conservative members of Council shrewdly focused on the one aspect of Lang's campaign which was the most vulnerable to attack. By concentrating on the issue of separation they could easily imply that Lang was disloyal.[53] It is probable that the only way Parkes could see around these accusations was to avoid the republican tag altogether. Lang, on the other hand, staunchly defended his views in the Council. Lang's reply to Murray was proof that republicanism was very much part of his life as a Councillor: '. . . He [Dr Lang] held it to be a principle of undisputed truth, that when a colony arrived at maturity, when it was able to support itself, it ought at once to be free from its dependence on the parent state. This was just what Mr Gladstone had advocated'.[54]

This speech demonstrates that Lang was willing to defend his republican views in parliament and that, when pressured, his republicanism was just as reliant on gathering Australian support as it was on gaining the sanction of the British authorities. None the less, it is untenable to suggest that Lang's election in July 1850 did not demonstrate that a considerable amount of sympathy existed among his supporters for his republican platform. Lang made no secret of his views on the matter.

David Blair supported this conclusion in 1888 when he rejected the claim of Rusden's *History of Australia* that the general community scarcely sympathised with Dr Lang. Instead, said Blair, 'if the political status of the people had been only one degree more advanced than it actually was, a popular rising would have been provoked which would have resulted in the forcible expulsion of the Governor'. In the last months of 1850 Lang accelerated his campaign to republicanise popular discontent in New South Wales. The Anti-Transportation Movement presented him with the appropriate foil and the public mood was bordering on hostile.[55]

Convict Scum

> Up Australians! Hark, the trumpet
> Calls you to a holy fight!
> Round the evergreen—your standard
> Gather, and as *one* unite![56]

Between the months of July and October 1850 there were occasions when talk of rebellion in the Australian colonies was often heard. The transportation issue had aroused the ire of a broad cross-section of citizens, especially in Sydney and Melbourne. When a despatch which Fitzroy had sent to Grey after the Circular Quay meeting in June was published in the Sydney press, the extent of public anger was revealed. Arrogantly, Fitzroy described the demonstrators who had stood so patiently in torrents of rain at the Quay as 'the mob of Sydney', 'the lower orders of the population'. Immediately, Parkes and Hawksely organised a mass protest meeting which was attended by almost 8000 people. Being referred to as the mob's representative offended Parkes' aspirations to bourgeois respectability, and more than anything else, it was this insult which encouraged him to make the most revolutionary speech of his career. Quoting Byron, Parkes told the audience that it was only in 'native swords and native ranks' that the colonists would find the courage to resist the unjust policy of Earl Grey.[57]

While Parkes relied on poetic allusions, Lang drew parallels between Fitzroy's despatch and the correspondence of Charles I—a correspondence which had revealed the King's disdain for parliament. In a fiery speech Lang continued his push for a republic, telling the crowd that like the citizens of Paris, they were the soul and intellect of the nation, and that the time had come to stand up to the handful of squatters who stood in their path.[58] When the George Street grocer, Richard Peek, addressed the crowd he went even further than Lang:

If they did not obtain responsible government he would not say that a resort to physical force ought always to be condemned. No one blamed the Americans for having armed in defence of their liberties; and the case of the two countries, would not, under these circumstances, be dissimilar.[59]

Here we witness the emergence of the republican issue in the context of the defence of the perceived principles of the English Constitution, as in America in 1776. The relationship between the colony and the mother country was continually being called into question, primarily because the colonists felt that the privileges of the Constitution were denied them. Even conservatives such as William Wentworth had presented the Colonial Office with a list of grievances.[60] It seemed that there was no section of colonial society which did not have cause for complaint. The distance between England and Australia meant long delays in communication, which could obviously prove crucial at times of crisis. So long as Earl Grey's recalcitrance continued many in the colony became concerned during the last months of 1850 that Parkes and Lang would incite the Sydney mob to rebellion. During a Legislative Council debate on whether the Council should foot the bill for a continued British military presence in the colony, William Wentworth spoke of his concern for the colony's future stability:

> The mob of Sydney, under the wild and seditious doctrines which had been instilled into them, had become ripe for any violence, any outrage, . . . and like the mob of France, would soon form itself into a compact body whose will should set all law and order at defiance.[61]

Wentworth's alarm appeared to be well-founded when a meeting called for 16 September to establish a formal organisation to work towards the cessation of transportation attracted a crowd of between 6000 and 10 000 people. The protesters marched to Barrack Square behind a banner which displayed the Union Jack. In front of them a citizens' band played 'God Save the Queen'. One of the first speeches the crowd heard was from John Dunmore Lang. After telling tales about convicts molesting women and children, Lang had the crowd ready to lock up their sons and daughters. But he soon turned to the crux of the matter: 'How far were they prepared to go rather than allow this colony to be made a penal settlement once more?' With the crowd primed to agree with any answer, he told them his solution:

> Much as he honoured and loved that glorious flag of England which had braved, for upwards of a thousand years, the battle and the breeze, he would

not hesitate for a moment in assisting his fellow colonists to pull it down and to hoist the flag of freedom and independence in its stead. (great cheering!) For his own part, if such an alternative were forced upon him, he would not hesitate for a moment between no convicts or an Australian republic. (loud applause!)[62]

There it was, a straightforward choice. No convicts or an Australian republic. The crowd who had sung 'God Save the Queen' and marched behind the Union Jack now applauded the introduction of an Australian republic. This would probably seem surprising to Australians of the late twentieth century, but in the context of colonial politics in the 1850s it was a perfectly understandable reaction. The people who cheered Lang's call for a republic did so because they felt their loyalty to the Queen and England had been betrayed by Earl Grey and Governor Fitzroy. Their threat of a republic was made to protect their right to be afforded the privileges of the British Constitution. The republic which beckoned was a direct result of their allegiance to the Constitution and Crown of England. They were loyalists first and republicans second, a gathering of extremely reluctant rebels. Unlike many of the republicans of the 1880s and 1990s their republicanism was not driven by an opposition to British culture and institutions. Rather, it was motivated by a desire to protect their British heritage, a desire to be more British than the British authorities would allow them to become.

Meanwhile, the *People's Advocate* joined Lang's calls for a republic. 'If the transportation issue were left unresolved,' wrote the *Advocate*, 'there could not be the slightest doubt our connection with Great Britain would be jeopardised'.[63] Unfortunately for Lang and the *People's Advocate*, the very issue which they hoped to ride to independence was already being steered into safer waters. The formation in September of the NSW Association for preventing the revival of transportation, led by liberals such as Charles Cowper and Thomas Mort, signalled the flight of the protest movement into more moderate waters.[64] Although people such as Lang and Parkes were still on the committee they were vastly outnumbered by the colonial bourgeoisie. Lang's republican voices would still be heard, but in future they would be forced to emerge from a much more marginal position.

On 1 October the NSW Legislative Council passed a resolution which called for Grey's Order in Council to be revoked. Colonial politicians still preferred to cling tenaciously to their faith in the capacity of the British parliament to redress grievances. In spite of the fact that the Anti-Transportation Movement had been commandeered by colonial liberals, there were other issues which would encourage an erosion of public patience. Throughout 1851 and 1852, calls for a republic would feed not only off the transportation issue but the continued reluctance of the Russell ministry to grant the colonies responsible government. In October news reached the colony of the Australian Colonies Government Act of 1850 which had been passed by the British parliament. The Act made provision for the formation of the new colony of Victoria and lowered the property qualification for members of parliament from £20 to £10. The most contentious aspect of the Act was its failure to provide for an increased percentage of elected members. Although the new Legislative Council was to increase in size from thirty-six to forty-eight members, the ratio of two-thirds elected members to one-third nominated remained unchanged. Any suggestion of ministerial responsibility was negated by the continuation of imperial control over land and revenues. The Governor and Executive remained independent of the legislature, while the final bone of contention was the provision which allowed for the old Legislative Council to be the architects of the new electoral boundaries. Those who had hoped for real constitutional reform would have been disappointed by Russell's statement in the House of Commons in which he suggested that the colonies were not ready for independence.[65]

This attitude typified the mood of the Colonial Office under Grey. Grey's wild schemes of a federated Australia which had been hatched in 1849 and greeted with such hostility in the colonies, revealed his preference for the maintenance of imperial control. Grey and Russell remained unmoved by the opinions of colonial reformers such as Gladstone and Cobden. In their eyes, the Australian colonies were not yet ready for freedom and independence.[66] So long as these attitudes reigned in London there was always a chance that resentment would intensify in the colonies.

Nation or Empire

In the new year of 1851 the two men who had done most to initiate debate on Australia's relationship with the mother country were already showing signs of parting ways. In April 1850 Henry Parkes and John Dunmore Lang had both pledged to work for the entire freedom and independence of the colonies. By the end of 1851 they would offer radically different proposals for the political development of the Australian colonies.

On 28 December 1850 Parkes began publication of the *Empire*, a new weekly journal of news, politics and commerce. Four days later, on what Lang romantically described as 'the first day of the latter half of the nineteenth century', Lang published the first edition of his own weekly newspaper—the *Press*.[67] The title of Parkes' journal was indicative of the

Parkes
Henry Parkes in 1854. Shrewd, ambitious and pragmatic in his attitude to political reform, Parkes probably did more than any other individual in nineteenth-century Australia to keep John Dunmore Lang's dream of an Australian republic at bay.
(Image Library, State Library of New South Wales.)

direction which his views were taking. Parkes' vision of Australia's future was of an infant British society staking its place in the global Empire, a babe too fragile for complete independence. Lang, on the other hand, saw republican independence as the necessary catalyst for the invigoration of colonial society into a more mature and confident community.[68]

To date there has been little attempt to examine the relationship between Parkes and Lang and the reasons behind their parting. There is no doubt that Parkes' metamorphosis from radical republican to guardian of Empire deprived Lang's republican movement of much-needed support. Parkes' skill as a political tactician, orator, and publicist, would be sorely missed. To understand the reasons for Parkes' change of heart is to appreciate the process by which Lang and his republican views became marginalised in colonial politics.

We have already seen that Parkes had begun to back away from any public support of Lang's republican views during the campaign for Lang's election to the Legislative Council in July 1850. Parkes knew that the criticism which the term attracted was too much of a political liability. When faced with criticism, Lang's instinct was to fight; Parkes, on the other hand, was more willing to soften his principles for political expediency. In many ways, these political temperaments reflected the different personalities of the two men: one impetuous, brash and outspoken, the other cautious, calculating, and eager to please.

A. W. Martin has correctly identified one factor which influenced Parkes' departure from Lang.[69] Parkes' association with colonial liberals such as Charles Cowper in the summer of 1850–51 saw him on an equal footing with men who were far more wealthy and conservative than he was. It was obvious to Parkes that any pretensions he may have had to political legitimacy in the eyes of the colonial bourgeoisie would not be facilitated by brandishing a republican sword. Yet Parkes was not only influenced by liberals like Cowper but also by his peers such as David Blair. More than any political reformer, Blair had been a confidant of Lang, both friend and comrade since he had followed Lang to Australia in 1850, leaving everything to follow his mentor. Although Blair had been one of the founding members of the Australian League, the time he spent with Parkes on the small journal, the *Representative*, proved crucial to the development of both men's understanding of republicanism. The barrage of criticism which was levelled at Lang for his wayward conduct and republican tirades convinced Blair that it would be best to avoid supporting Lang's views on independence. When Blair delivered his lecture on Australia at the Australia College in 1850 he had already learnt to skip around the word 'republic': 'Without independence, no colony, no nation can prosper. Mark! I do not speak of Australia as connected or disconnected with Great Britain. . . . I simply assert that the people must be independent . . . before this colony ever can prosper'.[70]

To ensure the success of their predominantly Chartist platform, both Blair and Parkes knew that linking separatist republicanism to their cause would be fatal. Thus, as early as 1850 they had begun to contemplate alternative definitions of 'independence'. It was this kind of diplomacy which Parkes began to cultivate in the columns of the *Empire*. When he learnt that sections of the English press had perceived Lang's election in July as evidence of popular support for an Australian republic he publicly distanced himself from Lang for the first time. In no time at all, Parkes' editorials on the question of the colony's relations with England bore more similarity to those of the *Sydney Morning Herald* than to the ideas of Lang. It must have made Parkes squirm with envy to read the flattering tone of the English press towards Lang. The *Morning Chronicle* thought Lang's election was a sign that 'republicanism had been taken up warmly by a considerable number of inhabitants' in the colonies. Other papers depicted Lang as Australia's John Wilkes. Lang was credited with being elected as representative of 'the metropolitan constituency of NSW', after devoting himself to 'bringing about a separation between the Australian colonies and the mother country'. The London *Daily News* concluded that his 'supporters must wish for such a consummation and the rest must at least look forward to it without dislike or dismay'.[71] Such talk stirred the *Sydney Morning Herald* into a hostile attack on the viability of independence for the Australian colonies: 'The colonists are not such blockheads as to hold the British nation responsible for the blunders of an individual. ... These colonies, whatever their inclination may be, have not yet acquired sufficient strength to be independent'.[72]

Parkes joined the anti-Lang crusade, strongly criticising the same man he had fought so hard for in the July election: 'He is neither the Wilkes, the Washington, the Franklin, the Francis, nor even the Papineau of Australia, and we hereby caution all English journalists against the appropriation of such tempting but fallacious epithets when writing of Dr Lang'. Parkes probably harboured his own dreams of becoming the Washington of the Australian colonies and his dreams of grandeur were not to be thwarted by the nagging attention of a republican blowfly like Lang. Parkes also appeared to have decided that Lang lacked the temperament to lead the movement for responsible government: 'Hero worship is not a virtue which we Australians cultivate extensively and even if it were, the Doctor is not the model hero which we should all willingly fall down and worship'.[73]

Although Parkes was most probably jealous of Lang, he had also concluded that the struggle for democracy would not be achieved through the advocacy of Lang's republicanism but through petitioning the Crown. By focusing on English birthright without challenging the absolute sovereignty of the Crown, it would be much more difficult for the opponents of democracy to make their revolutionary barbs stick. Forget republicanism, and the accusations of socialism and communism which Lang's 'Coming Event' lectures had attracted in 1850 would vanish. The claim for political legitimacy would be so much easier. Parkes now became the champion of a major strand of republicanism in Australian political thought. He became an 'inevitablist':

There is nothing bad and unseemly in entertaining the idea of separation—nay—it is rather a truly English piece of wisdom to look at the event as a prospective certainty . . . the idea of Australian independence has germinated and it cannot be destroyed . . . but we should not anticipate the season of the ripened corn . . . England with all thy faults, we love thee still.[74]

Parkes had learnt the first lesson of the inevitability club. Claiming that the republic was inevitable allowed one to escape criticism and provided an opportunity for delaying the formulation of a clear policy on the issue to succeeding generations. When a correspondent with the republican pseudonym 'Tiberius Gracchus' wrote to the *Empire* arguing for the introduction of a republic in April 1851, Parkes was so concerned his readers might mistake these views for his own, that he added a disclaimer below: 'Our correspondent, whose manly spirit we have had other occasions to admire, must excuse in expressing our unqualified dissent from his notions of Australian independence.—ED. E.'[75]

Parkes' position was now firmly in place. The Australian republic sat patiently in the waiting-room. When the debasing influences of convictism had subsided, a second generation of more 'manly' Australians would open the door. Parkes and Lang now held two conflicting visions of Australian political development. Ostensibly, both men proclaimed their loyalty to England, yet the stuff of which this loyalty was made was not identical. Lang admired English institutions and was proud that the Australian colonies had sprung from such a noble past, but his admiration was never fawning; instead, he saw Australia as an independent community ready to deal with England on equal terms. For Parkes, England was the Minerva to be worshipped, the lost Mecca from which Australia had been set adrift, the metropolitan superior powering the light of civilisation for a provincial colony far away. Lang's vision was optimistic, romantic, independent and nationalist, while Parkes' was cautious, pragmatic and dependent. These were the stars around which much of the republican debate would circle until Federation in 1901—Crown or country, nation or Empire, monarch or president. Parkes and Lang were now on different paths.

Redemption from Misrule

When the Australasian League was officially formed in Melbourne on 15 February 1851 it seemed that the colonies were entering a new period of co-operation. The parochialism which had hitherto characterised inter-colonial relations was briefly set aside. For the first time, the colonies had come together to form a national organisation for the purpose of ending transportation.[76] But the Australasian League was not to be the seed of independence. Although some sections of the press saw the League's formation as the first step towards Federation or 'a declaration of independence', its existence owed more to the affront convicts presented to bourgeois morality. Led by members of parliament, the League represented the material aspirations of what was fast becoming a predominantly free immigrant society.[77] Writing forty years later, Henry Parkes neatly summarised the League's position:

> The Anti-Transportation cause fell largely into the hands of the new men supported by the free immigrant working classes and the movement was directed against the popular leaders of the past ... Most of the merchants and shopkeepers and the whole artisan body [gave their support] ... [On the other side] were the large country employers [and] ... the great officials who held their appointments direct from imperial authority in England.[78]

Lang was very much aware that it was the artisan class which would be integral to any successful push for his Australian republic. He clearly saw the anti-transportation issue as a Trojan horse. Writing in the *Press*, he urged the members of the League to be prepared for revolution if the Colonial Office should prove unresponsive.[79]

At a public meeting held at Circular Quay on 31 March for the purpose of formally dissolving the NSW Anti-Transportation Movement, Lang stepped forward to play the role which the British press had bestowed on him. Mindful of the American and French revolutions, Australia's Wilkes encouraged League members to adopt his Declaration of Rights as part of their platform. The Declaration was lengthy, and began by pointing out that the Queen held sovereignty for the 'welfare and protection' of the colonists, reminding the Colonial Office that the royal prerogative did not extend to the imposition of measures to which the majority of colonists disapproved. The section which caused the most uproar, however, was Lang's conclusion, which directly threatened rebellion.[80]

While the liberals at the head of Australasian League would have found the mere mention of a 'Declaration of Rights' worrying enough, they were in no mood to counsel revolution. John West, who later wrote in his *History of Tasmania* that it was at this time that the League was in danger of being led astray, stood at the meeting to reject Lang's declaration.[81] Although Hawksely seconded Lang's motion, after pressure from West, Campbell, Wright and others, Lang was forced to withdraw his motion. The first attempt to republicanise the League thus failed dismally. Lang also faced the ridicule of the *Sydney Morning Herald*, a journal which he colourfully described as a 'filthy animal'—which like an 'American skunk delights to eject such foetid matter ever and anon'. Like the majority of League members, the *Herald* believed that any talk of separation or republicanism would seriously prejudice the League's cause.[82] While this was clearly the most popular position, the continuation of the crisis over transportation was beginning to encourage republican murmurs in quarters not directly associated with John Dunmore Lang.

Throughout March and April, a series of letter writers and guest columnists argued passionately for an Australian republic in the pages of the *Empire*. Adopting pseudonyms drawn from the Roman Republic, such as Tiberius Gracchus and Publicola, they presented miniature republican manifestos with regularity.[83] Even before Lang's Declaration of Rights was placed before the public, Charles Adam Corbyn (alias Tiberius Gracchus) argued for an Australian republic, free of British or American influence:

> Is this country forever to continue a part of the British Empire? Or is it to be free, self governed and independent? ... The sooner we become free the better ... Then may we have a constitution of our own choosing instead of the villainous wretched abortion with which we have been favoured ... Then may we live in liberty, equality and fraternity and not under the 'stars and stripes' ... but under our own national banner.[84]

It was not difficult to see that separatist and nationalist republicanism lay close to the surface of colonial politics under a cloak of platitudinous loyalty. As the number of grievances increased, and their existence became more deeply felt, there was every chance that Lang's ideas would become more attractive.

In March, Fitzroy must have trembled when he read the details of the new electoral boundaries in the Legislative Council. A gerrymander had ensured the squatters greater representation than the populous Sydney metropolitan area. Immediately, the measure was condemned by the Sydney press and public dissatisfaction with the Constitution sharpened.[85]

With the transportation and constitutional debates now running along an increasingly volatile path, the *Sydney Morning Herald* announced the discovery of an 'extensive goldfield in the Wellington district of NSW'. After the discovery of gold in both New South Wales and Victoria by July, the colonies stood on the verge of a decade of rapid population growth. Lang rejoiced in the anticipation that Australia would now achieve nationhood and full independence.[86] Writing in the *Press*, he could hardly conceal his excitement: 'The announcement of this wonderful discovery in our land is tantamount to an authoritative proclamation ... that Australia henceforth shall be free ... It is now a matter of certainty that Australia will henceforth be free through the resistless influence of her coming democracy'.[87]

So inspired was Lang, he presented a futuristic piece on Australia in 1871. Lang imagined himself as the English immigrant, Jabez Porterfield, who writes a letter to his friend back home in England after arriving in Sydney: The letter is addressed to Dear Fred, under the title 'AUSTRALIA, TWENTY YEARS HENCE' and headed 'Sydney NSW, 1 April 1871'. It begins:

> After a very favourable run of rather more than four days, from the City of Hereweare, Leichardstland, per the Steamship Leviathan we reached this magnificent capital of the Seven United Provinces of Australia ...
>
> ... The progress of the country ... has been incomparably more rapid since the Treaty of Independence than ever it was before ... now the Australian Ambassador takes his place in Paris, in Washington, and in St. Petersburgh, as well as in London with the oldest courts in Europe ... It has ... been proposed to make the neighbouring city of Parramatta the capital of NSW, while Sydney will be the capital of the Australian Empire.[88]

While Lang dreamed of a white republican empire, Governor Fitzroy looked forward to the gold rush with trepidation. Fearing social dislocation, anarchy and revolution, many conservatives placed pressure on Fitzroy and La Trobe to call for immediate reinforcements from England. Fitzroy was acutely aware of the popular appeal agitators like Lang could muster, especially if a flood of free immigrants stoked the fires of disaffection. The existence of substantial grievances with the Colonial Office created a situation which was potentially explosive, or as Lang described it: the authorities were 'smoking their legislative pipes over ... a barrel of gun powder'.[89] Fitzroy only had to read the resolutions passed at a meeting of the Australasian League at the York Street Circus on 29 July to realise that the political stability of the colony was at risk. With Lang locked in Parramatta gaol for defamation, League members took it upon themselves to point out the gravity of the situation:

> Your Majesty's petitioners ... will not disguise ... their persuasion that what was lately but a grievance is rapidly ripening into a quarrel, and their opinion that the continuance of transportation, in opposition to the united resolve of the Australasia leagued together against it, will peril the connexion of these colonies with Great Britain, ...[90]

Here was a threat of separation from the colony's leading liberals without the provocation of red republicans like Lang. These words must have made Fitzroy decidedly uncomfortable, for on this occasion he could not accuse the authors of belonging to the lower classes or the mob, these were men of property and wealth. Two days after the York Street meeting, Fitzroy wrote to Grey: 'the continued agitation of the transportation question is doing much mischief and giving a very great advantage to the at present small and uninfluential party who are advocating republican principles under the leading of Dr Lang'.[91] Fitzroy was obviously concerned that talk of separation might spread if transportation did not cease at once. The activities of certain members of the Legislative Council during this time also reveal that Fitzroy was not the only concerned person. In July several Council members organised a meeting at the Royal Hotel to discuss the possibility of an appropriate antidote to the 'r' word which had been heard around Sydney. In a somewhat gauche manner, councillors proposed that the government of New South Wales purchase a gold diadem for Her Majesty as a sign of the colony's deep loyalty to the Crown. Other members thought a diadem too costly, and suggested sending 'a pair of colonial blankets' instead. Gilbert Wright sounded a note of reason when he pointed out that the meeting was not representative of public feeling, 'many of whom would not have supported sending gifts to the Queen at a time when Grey was tormenting the colony'. Lang thought the whole meeting farcical and referred to it as a gathering of 'flunkies'. In the *Press*, a poem from 'J. G.' of Bathurst described the loyalists as 'members of the Great Merino Ram and Kiss the Royal Thumb Club'.[92]

The number of disgruntled voices was increasing, and in the middle of 1851 there was little sign of Grey or the Colonial Office giving way. In the large urban areas there were signs that patience was wearing thin. In Tasmania, John West's *Launceston Examiner* voiced its concern in language which was becoming increasingly common:

> In one word, the colonists want local self-government in all its shades and nothing less, will or ought to satisfy them. If this be denied or tardily conceded it is not difficult to indicate the inevitable result. It may now tingle the ears of some to tell it, but if they are spared ten years the sound will be welcome. The issue will be an Australian republic.[93]

It remained to be seen whether those who threatened a republic would find the will and courage to set about the process of separation and independence.

Lang Stands Again

When Fitzroy sent his despatch to Grey in July he was aware that Lang would be standing as a candidate in the September elections for the new Legislative Council. Whereas Parkes had kept the lid on Lang's republicanism the previous year, on this occasion Lang decided it was time to risk his election on an open declaration of republican principles. On 18 August, still imprisoned in Parramatta gaol, he wrote an open letter to the electors of Sydney which was published in the *People's Advocate*. Although he admitted that the issue of a republic was not likely to come before the new Council, he did not see this as an obstacle. When a million British freemen stood demanding their independence, said Lang, a 'gagged and fettered' Council was hardly likely to stand in their way.[94]

Throughout the campaign, Lang's opponents consistently took up the challenge and defended the maintenance of the British connection. Speaking on nomination day in September, John Weekes reminded the audience that 'the tie between the colony and the mother country . . . will be a golden link . . . Great Britain cannot afford to lose her only gold country'. There is no question that Lang's republicanism was very much part of the campaign. On the same day Wentworth claimed that 'Chartists, Socialists, Communists and Republicans' were posing a threat to the social order. Predictably, as Lang later observed, he then pointed to the American and French revolutions as model examples of the consequences of mob republican rule.[95] The discovery of gold, and the unusual intensity of the colony's grievances, had ensured that speakers at all political meetings were forced to declare their support or disapproval of Lang's republican campaign.

When the votes were counted on 17 September Lang was declared the first elected. Lang's 1191 votes had topped the poll—176 more than the next candidate, John Lamb, and 200 more than his arch-rival, William Wentworth.[96] The three members for the Sydney metropolitan area were now elected and the candidate with the most votes was the republican. When he gave his victory speech in front of 4000 people at Macquarie Place, Lang declared that those who had voted for him had given their assent to his republican platform:

> Now he (Dr Lang) had thought fit to risk his election by laying down this principle [the colonies' right to independence] very prominently in his address to the electors, for he was convinced it was a right and a true principle . . . To this principle by their act of yesterday they had yielded their assent. (Cheers!)[97]

While it is true that two-thirds of the electorate voted against Lang, it must be remembered that the voter turn-out was extremely poor. Obviously, there were significant numbers of people in Sydney who were broadly supportive of Lang's republican views. When Lang toured the goldfields at Sofala and Turon only weeks after his election, his popularity demonstrated that support also existed outside Sydney among the diggers. At Sofala, an enormous open-air meeting greeted him as a hero, Australia's Washington in waiting: 'You are the apostle of the independence of Australia and this will be the foundation of your future fame'.[98]

By December, Fitzroy not only had Lang's popularity to contend with but an increasingly impatient Legislative Council. The Council's latest list of grievances was accompanied by an interesting caveat which stated that 'the authority of the local executive' would be difficult to maintain if urgent matters continued to be deferred to an 'inexperienced, remote, and irresponsible department in London'.[99] This alone was enough to convince Fitzroy that something needed to be done. When he despatched the Council's petition to Grey, he warned that the failure to grant concessions would endanger the imperial connection. When conservatives such as James Macarthur were putting their signatures to petitions which warned of separation, Fitzroy knew the situation was serious. At the end of 1851 it was not uncommon to hear speakers at public meetings claim that 'the sooner the connexion was dissolved the better'.[100] There was not one section of the political spectrum which had not at least threatened to take up the option of separation.

In the eyes of the *San Francisco Herald*, the Australian colonies were 'ready to be revolutionised', 'the bold and hearty feeling of self reliance amongst the people', being 'strongly indicative of a republican principle' at the heart of the community. Astutely, the editors of this American paper recognised from afar that the crucial factor was the determination of the colonists 'to assert by deeds the boldness of their language'.[101]

Driving a Loyal People to Rebellion

By 1852 Earl Grey's determination to continue the transportation of convicts to the colonies had encouraged the development of an indigenous political culture in New South Wales, Victoria and Tasmania. Metropolitan, derivative, and relatively small in numerical terms, this new political activity was directly related to the continued irritation of colonial grievances. The public meeting and the petition had emerged as the legitimate vehicles of colonial protest.

After the discovery of gold in 1851 many political leaders in the colonies believed the end of transportation to be a formality. Earl Grey had announced his intention to end transportation in 1850, and it was widely assumed that the peaceful remonstrances of the Australasian League would force Grey to yield. In April 1852 these hopes were shattered when news of correspondence which had taken place between Grey and one of the League's delegates in London was published in Sydney. Grey had revealed privately that he intended to continue transportation to Van Diemen's Land and Moreton Bay. By the end of the year, public meetings had been organised by the League in Hobart, Melbourne, and Sydney condemning Grey's 'unjust and iniquitous' policies. The news forced many opponents of transportation to question the effectiveness of their methods of protest. In all three colonies, the possibility of separation was canvassed with regularity. Just how much of this was hollow threat seems to be a critical question.

It is important to remember that much of the disaffection which surfaced in 1852 occurred without the presence of the colony's most vocal republican—J. D. Lang. At a time when the receptiveness of the colonists to Lang's republican ideas might well have been at its peak, Lang was forced to resign his seat in the Legislative Council and depart with some haste to England.[102] The sudden absence of Lang's leadership and political skills proved fatal to his cause. He was the only high-profile republican with a proven ability to attract public sympathy. His dreams of a grand republican league would have had far greater chance of success in 1852, if only he had been there to promote them. As it was, Lang left for England in February, taking much of the chances for 'Freedom and Independence' with him. At the public meeting organised by the Australasian League on 6 April at the York Street Circus, the unexpected arrival of Grey's correspondence with John King (the League's delegate in London) caused the meeting to adopt a revolutionary tone. It was at meetings such as these that Lang's mettle was sorely missed.

The cautious liberals who had previously rejected the option of separation now courted it as a desirable alternative. Cowper spoke of the need to resort to 'other means' while John Lamb insisted that 'the time for petitioning had passed': 'The case of these colonies was a deplorable and unhappy one. Much as they might wish . . . to preserve their connexion with the Crown of Great Britain . . . under a policy like this . . . the hour of separation, bitter and angry separation must sooner or later arrive'.[103] Speaker after speaker vented his anger by relying on language which manifested the spirit of the anti-tyrannical arguments typical of English constitutionalism. Archdeacon McEnroe confessed that he had always thought a constitutional government would alleviate grievances, but that lately he had grown sick of repeating himself. As the Roman schoolmaster noted, he said, 'Constant repetition of the same lesson would weary the hardiest scholar—it was no use to talk anymore, the question was,—what were they to do; . . . the sooner they took a hint from their friends across the Pacific and cut the painter, "the better"'. Gilbert Wright reminded the audience that 'to submit would be to approve themselves to use the language of John Milton—the lowermost, the most defected, the most underfoot of vassals'. Even the *Sydney Morning Herald* joined the bandwagon, claiming that if the League's protests were not heard in London, it would be 'farewell to Australian loyalty'. Yet not one speaker was brave enough to claim responsibility for initiating separation. Instead, it was the Queen's advisers who were to blame. As McEnroe said, 'If they were compelled by misgovernment to separate themselves from England, on England would rest the tremendous responsibility'.[104] Their remonstrances made no attempt to insist on a positive or pre-emptive declaration of independence—as Lang might have done. Instead they prayed for deliverance, for redemption from misrule. Parkes' remark at a League meeting in June, where he claimed that there was a 'higher loyalty than that to any earthly monarch', was in fact a stern warning to the Colonial Office to profit from the fate of Caesar and Brutus, Charles I and Cromwell and America and George III.[105] Parkes' 'higher loyalty' was not a loyalty to any separate Australian nation but to English constitutionalism. Like all of the League members who threatened separation throughout 1852, Parkes did so to protect his English birthright.

The unutterable republic was in every way a republic in the tradition of 1649. Like their ancestors, League members saw the republic as the last refuge of freedom and justice and they differed from John Dunmore Lang in several respects. First, they never used the word 'republican' to describe themselves. Although their political language (English constitutionalism) drew heavily on the English republican language of the seventeenth century they usually referred to this inheritance as 'English'. Their sense of 'republicanism' as an active agent in the New World was dominated by the American and French revolutions. Secondly, their threats of separation were essentially a source of great sorrow; while for Lang, the advocacy of a republic was cause for pride, independence and nationality. Just as the majority of anti-transportation protesters prayed for deliverance lest they be forced to turn to republicanism, Lang demanded deliverance and the rightful independence that a republic would bring.[106] Of course, there were still those, like Daniel Deniehy and Gilbert Wright, who stood somewhere between the colonial liberals and Lang. They were more willing to emphasise that it was 'the duty' of the colonists to take up arms and resist transportation if the English government did not yield. Deniehy, who was barely twenty-two years of age, showed the seeds of his later nationalism with his references to British manhood and his pride in being a 'son of the soil'. At the meeting on 30 June he was the only speaker to talk of an 'Anglo–American' tradition of resistance to tyranny, which if unable to release itself by constitutional means was bound to cry 'Up with the barricades and invoke the God of battle'. Like Parkes, he stressed that this tradition was not the language of wanton defiance or disloyalty, but thoroughly British—'the language of free men'. Born in Sydney in 1828, the son of Irish convicts, Deniehy had visited Ireland during his teens while on a European sojourn with his family, attending the public speeches of the Irish Liberator, Daniel O'Connell.[107] While this experience was undoubtedly important in Deniehy's intellectual development, it would be a mistake to ground Deniehy's republicanism in a simple Irish–nationalist cast.

Deniehy's Irish background may have been influential in his politicisation and romantic nationalism, but like Lang, Blair and Harpur his republican speeches were most likely to draw on the Anglo–American republican heritage of Cromwell, Hampden and Washington.[108] Deniehy was familiar with this inheritance, which was why he always maintained that the American Revolution had been fought to protect the English Constitution, not to reject it. His republican vision had its roots in this selfsame tradition. Aside from Deniehy, it was Parkes who uttered the most telling statement of the League's motivations for threatening separation. He protested against its language being represented as that of wanton defiance, as Deniehy had done before him, and declared that if the colonists were forced to choose 'between the British connexion *in name* and an unsullied British character *in fact*, they would choose the latter.[109]

In Melbourne and Hobart, Anti-Transportation meetings in 1852 revealed a similar language of dissent. There were the usual declarations of loyalty, followed by complaints, followed by threats.[110] In Tasmania, petitions and remonstrances became increasingly angry, while in Melbourne, protesters focused on the possibility of immigrant convicts from Tasmania, pouring across Bass Strait to pollute Victorian society. Yet, as Alderman Johnson of the new Victorian Legislative Council explained at a meeting in April, if Grey persisted 'in inundating the Australian colonies through the medium of Van Diemen's Land with the outpourings of British crime' it would 'rapidly wean the affections of the colonists from the parent state ... and must inevitably drive them to seek refuge from such heartless tyranny and oppression in national independence'. In Victoria and Tasmania, just as in New South Wales, separation was the refuge of disappointed loyalists.[111]

When the *Sydney Morning Herald* examined the two Anti-Transportation meetings of April 1852 in Sydney and Melbourne which had witnessed so many threats of separation, it seemed surprised at the extent of public disapproval which the transportation issue had aroused:

> Two great communities, without concert ... were simultaneously struck, for the first time since their existence began, with a feeling of incipient disaffection to the mother country. ... Both had the courage to warn the lordly despot against carrying his rough usage too far. May he take the warning before it be too late.[112]

As time passed, it seemed that the colonists would never decide that it was too late. Their natural inclination was to prayer, not rebellion.

CHAPTER FOUR
A Bunyip Aristocracy

> If the imperial Government shall continue to pour her criminals upon any part of the shores of the States confederated for this purpose a constitutional reason for separation from the parent country will have been established . . .
> *Hobart Town Courier*, 27 January 1853[1]

With the fall of Lord John Russell's government in May 1852, the man who had been the focus of much disaffection in the Australian colonies was finally removed from office. By the time Sir John Pakington replaced Earl Grey as Colonial Secretary the attitude of the Colonial Office had become far more conciliatory.[2]

The discovery of gold in Australia immediately turned the spotlight of the British press on the colonies. The majority of papers supported the colonists in their calls for an end to transportation and the extension of responsible government. Robert Lowe, now back in London and writing regular columns for *The Times*, was one of the most vocal advocates of change. With the swearing-in of Stanley's ministry, the British government finally seemed ready to embrace the views of colonial reformers such as Gladstone and Cobden.[3] When Pakington formally ended transportation to Van Diemen's Land on 14 December 1852, he signalled that future colonial policy would be governed by the colonists themselves—not by Downing Street. 'We find . . . that there is a . . . strong repugnance in Van Diemen's Land and . . . adjacent colonies to the further reception of convicts . . . Her Majesty's government have therefore felt it their duty . . . to comply with a wish so generally and so forcibly expressed by Her subjects.'[4]

The spirit of Pakington's despatch would be embraced even more fervently by the Duke of Newcastle, who succeeded Pakington as Colonial Secretary after the collapse of Stanley's government in December 1852. There seemed little doubt that the decision to end transportation had been encouraged by the many threats of separation received by the Colonial Office during the previous three years. We know that Pakington had referred specifically to reports which had stated that 'the formation of a republican government' in New South Wales was being contemplated. Warned by newspaper clippings he had received from the British Consul at Philadelphia in September which linked the imminent arrival of Americans in Australia with the rise of 'Freedom, Liberty and Republicanism', Pakington immediately sent copies of the Philadelphia despatch to colonial governors. Although Fitzroy and La Trobe both stressed the overwhelming loyalty of the Australian population in their replies, Pakington had not received this advice when he decided to put an end to transportation in December. Repeated threats of separation—a South Pacific re-run of the Yankee solution—had played their part in Pakington's decision.[5]

When the *Sydney Morning Herald* looked back on the transportation crisis in December 1853, it admitted that the colonies had been 'in imminent danger of suffering a sudden and violent severance from England'. Separation and an independent republic would have been the only alternative if Pakington had continued in the vein of Earl Grey.[6] More importantly, the transportation question was the only political issue which carried the potential to unite the colonies and force them to declare their independence.

When news reached Australia that transportation had ended, large public celebrations rejoiced in the triumph of a 'bloodless revolution'. The change of policy in England had become the revolution.[7] The final capitulation of the Colonial Office would serve as a constant reminder to Australians that their grievances could always be redressed by constitutional means. The end of transportation boosted public faith in the glorious Constitution. This could only mean that the imperial nationalism espoused by the likes of Henry Parkes would henceforth appear as the 'natural' path for the colonies to follow. Conversely, the more independent and republican nationalism embraced by John Dunmore Lang, which insisted on separation, would be seen as radical and unnecessary, until it finally reached the stage of warranting no further discussion. In this way, the cessation of transportation was an important contributor to the process of marginalising positive, separatist and nationalist republicanism in Australian political life. Australians would continue to look to heaven and London instead of taking matters into their own hands. When Lang returned to Sydney in 1853 the 'genius of English freedom' had stolen much of his thunder. With the thorn of transportation removed, Lang's supporters would be forced to rely on other grievances to sustain their demands for independence. The most obvious place to begin was the public disquiet surrounding the proposed Constitution for New South Wales.

Bunyips in the House

> Tell Mr Wentworth and his supporters ... that you do not demand a Republican Form of government but your own old and cherished British Liberty.[8]

As soon as word reached the Australian colonies in early 1853 that the British government was willing to grant responsible government, the battle to mould the character of Australia's first representative institutions began. Before leaving office in December 1852 Pakington had already indicated that the right to design the Constitution would rest with the incumbent Legislative Council. In August 1853 Pakington's successor, the Duke of Newcastle, confirmed this policy in a despatch which advised Governor Fitzroy to prepare the colonies for the introduction of responsible government.[9] The only substantial difference was Newcastle's support for an elected upper house, a stance which typified his more liberal attitude to colonial affairs. Unlike Pakington, whose caution led him to advocate a nominated upper house, Newcastle saw colonial societies as naturally democratic and had no fear of a fully democratic bicameral system.

Whatever the advice from London, the Legislative Council of New South Wales, under the leadership of William Wentworth, seemed determined to replicate the Old World in the New. On 29 July 1853 the Council's select committee on the new Constitution put its proposals before the public. The committee's proposals represented a naive attempt to impose a caste system on the Australian colonies. Foolishly, Wentworth suggested a colonial peerage similar to the House of Lords which would provide a natural buffer to the excesses of democracy.

Wentworth's Constitution was to be the rock of his New Britannia, that same Britannia 'with flag unfurl'd' of which he had written in 1823. What he failed to understand was that his dreams of colonial Lords romping on Sunday morning fox hunts at Vaucluse House were sadly out of touch with the spirit of the age. As John Hirst has pointed out, many of Britain's leading politicians already believed that elected upper houses were more appropriate for colonial constitutions. 'From Britain itself came the word that the threefold order of King Lords and Commons' was no longer necessary for Britishness—'the old country had declared that the new could be different'. It was also true that by the time of Russell's 1854 Reform Act, Britain was moving slowly towards democracy.[10] The steady democratisation of the English Constitution undermined Wentworth's proposals, making them appear archaic and inappropriate. Wentworth's Constitution was the last breath of the old conservatism in New South Wales which had stereotyped all democratic tendencies as wild republicanism. Over the next two years, political reformers in New South Wales would demonstrate that the gradual introduction of democracy did not necessitate anarchy or revolution, nor a denial of British heritage. In the Legislative Council, Wentworth's attempts to label his opponents as red republicans would fail, while the democrats' success in disengaging democracy from the republican bogey would help to ensure the success of their campaign.

Gradually, Lang's republicanism was being denied political utility. The challenge for republicans like Deniehy and Lang was to gild the opposition to Wentworth's bill into a cry for republican independence. This was the only chance of sidestepping the demise of their cause. Australian democracy would either be legitimised by the British Constitution or a declaration of Australian independence.

When Wentworth's proposals were made public, it was clear that the ensuing political debate would be fiercely contested. The *People's Advocate* greeted the news with an interesting suggestion:

> Why should we humbug ourselves about Mr Wentworth's hereditary convict Lordships and Dukedoms? Let us discard all connexion with the whole of the wretched rickety jimcrackery of his Constitootion [sic], as he calls it, and spit upon it as we would upon a loathsome toad or other foul creeping slimy reptile.[11]

The most damning and effective criticism of Wentworth's Constitution came from the young Daniel Deniehy. Speaking at a public meeting in Sydney on 25 August Deniehy brilliantly lampooned what he called 'these harlequin aristocrats, these Botany Bay magnificos, these Australian Mandarins ..., a bunyip aristocracy'. The howls of laughter which greeted these words were a clear indication to Wentworth that the language of Australian politics was more democratic than he cared to admit. The aristocracy which Deniehy envisaged for Australia was not the colonial peerage suggested by Wentworth but an aristocracy of talent and merit—or as Deniehy described it, 'God's aristocracy'.[12] This was an image of an Australian meritocracy similar to that expressed in the republican ideology of the United States. Deniehy had no intention of balancing class interests in his republic.

Charles Harpur found more room for ridicule in the pages of the *Empire*. Harpur suggested that the only way to elect Wentworth's House of Lords would be to select the men with the largest noses and receding foreheads, 'the upper facial type of the great mass of the British aristocracy'.[13] While Deniehy and Harpur embraced an openly republican language in their opposition to the bill, the most organised and vocal dissent came from the more conservative opponents such as Henry Parkes. At an open-air meeting held in the government grounds adjacent to Circular Quay on 5 September, Parkes told a large crowd that their opposition to Wentworth's bill was not republican:

> He was born in the heart of Old England, within a few hours' walk of the spot where Shakespeare was born, where some of the noblest associations of English history were fresh in the hearts of even the rural population; ... He spurned the attempt to fix upon him any advocacy of republican government.

Deniehy
Daniel Deniehy, appropriately remembered in this classical image, was the most prominent of Australian-born republicans in the early colonial period. Born the son of an Irish convict, Deniehy's life bore testament to his belief in an aristocracy of merit. Articulate, witty, and erudite, Deniehy's commitment to an Australian republic was driven by his faith in the uniqueness of Australian national identity.
(Bronze medallion by W. Lorando Jones, 1859, Image Library, State Library of New South Wales.)

> He was sincerely attached to his native country and her institutions . . . He did not want a 'Yankee Constitution' any more than Mr Wentworth.[14]

This emotional speech was typical of Parkes' determination to distance himself from Lang's republicanism. He knew full well that the men who backed Wentworth in the Legislative Council would depict the constitutional debate as a choice between a conservative British Constitution and cutting the painter for a Yankee republic. Consequently, Parkes strove to portray his opposition to the bill as a defence of the 'true principles of the English Constitution'.[15]

In the Legislative Council, members perceived their role as an historic opportunity to 'choose a form of government'.[16] In doing so, they referred to classical authors such as Aristotle and Cicero, Milton, Locke, as well as Hume and the American and Canadian Constitutions. Debate on republican government was very much part of these discussions and from the outset it was presented as the alternative, radical and unBritish option. 'We came here to be English', said Councillor Marsh, 'and English we will be in spite of those Yankee notions now agitated and maintained in certain quarters'.[17] Macarthur managed to work himself into a frenzy, insisting that he would rather choose death than allow a republic: 'I believe the measure we now propose to be the nearest possible approach to the mixed form of the British Constitution. . . . I believe it will be a barrier against republicanism and democracy . . . Ours is the glorious monarchy of England and we will maintain it to the death . . .'.[18]

When Darvall suggested that Australia would inevitably become a republic, a succession of speeches followed from the whiskered aspirants to Wentworth's House of Lords, relegating any mention of an Australian republic to all but distant generations. Some went so far as to claim that Darvall had breached his oath of loyalty to the Queen. As the debates continued, it became clear that many of the councillors were more interested in denouncing republicanism than discussing the details of Wentworth's bill. Wentworth was most critical of Lang's attempts to persuade the English authorities that the colonies were 'desirous' of republicanism.[19] Yet for all this denunciation, the people who stood patiently outside in Macquarie Street were not about to storm the palace gates.

The prominence of the republican bogey in the Constitution debates of 1853 is not difficult to explain. In the first place, the majority of councillors were either ignorant or dismissive of the changes which had taken place at home in England. Their perception of the English Constitution was rooted more in the eighteenth century than 1853. Fearing that greater democracy would lead to separation, they were forced to deny any inkling of republicanism. These two threats to social stability and English culture were synonymous and indivisible. Finally, they hoped to defeat the opponents of Wentworth's bill by throwing as much republican mud as possible. Conscious of their role in history they wished to bequeath a thoroughly loyal legacy to their descendants. It was for these reasons that the *Sydney Morning Herald* proclaimed the debates as a significant victory for those forces loyal to England:

> The mere suspicion of republicanism was scouted; the slightest insinuation of republican tendencies was repelled and disavowed; and the sole aim and

object of the deliberations of the House was to achieve 'the closest analogy to the British Constitution which the circumstances of the colony would allow'.[20]

Despite the *Herald*'s cocky tone, those who openly embraced a republic were not to be scouted yet. John Dunmore Lang was on his way back from England, determined to see the entire freedom and independence of the colonies.

The Doctor Returns

John Dunmore Lang returned to Australia convinced that the whole fabric of British power in the colonies rested on a rotten foundation, in defiance of the ordinance of God and the rights of man.[21] Lang disembarked at Circular Quay with recently published copies of *Freedom and Independence for the Golden Lands of Australia*. This was Lang's *tour de force*—more comprehensive and incisive than the 'Coming Event' lectures, *Freedom and Independence for the Golden Lands of Australia* was, he believed, in every respect the work of a genius. With his usual lack of modesty, Lang proclaimed the work as 'the first and only in the English language in which the rights of colonies and colonists have ever been stated and vindicated in the light of both reason and history'.[22] Lang hoped that *Freedom and Independence* would have as great an impact on the Australian political scene as the publication of Thomas Paine's *Common Sense* had had in the United States in 1776.

Freedom and Independence certainly reveals why Lang was such a unique republican.[23] Unlike many of his supporters and occasional sympathisers, Lang was proudly republican—there was no attempt to employ euphemisms or back away from the term. *Freedom and Independence* demonstrated Lang's resolve to legitimise republicanism in Australian politics:

> As to the charge, that the Australian colonists, who ... earnestly desire their entire political freedom and national independence, are somewhat tinctured with republicanism, I fear it must be admitted. The fact is, there is no other form of government either practicable or possible in a British colony obtaining its freedom and independence than that of a republic.[24]

There was much in the book which must have struck a chord with Henry Parkes—especially Lang's suggestion that Australian republican government would be built on the pillars of universal suffrage, federalism and representative democracy.[25] But perhaps the most interesting facet of *Freedom and Independence* is the extent to which many of Lang's arguments prefigure those of late twentieth-century republicans, such as

Thomas Keneally and Donald Horne. Lang was the first republican in Australian history to suggest that the British connection constituted a form of psychological dependence. For Lang, monarchical allegiance and political independence were incompatible: 'Under the universal government of God, there cannot possibly be two inconsistent and incompatible rights, . . . the right to obedience or allegiance on the one part, is clearly inconsistent and incompatible with the right to freedom and independence on the other'.[26]

Lang's presentation of the issue as a choice between the polarised options of republican independence and the sovereignty of the Crown was actually out of step with the perceptions of most colonists. As Lang well knew, he would encounter opposition from 'public functionaries, government officials, squatters, merchants, professional men', and the large bulk of the population who displayed a 'positive indifference' towards political participation.[27] While Lang could easily have attracted popular support with his Chartist platform alone, it was his dogged insistence on republican government, separation and military independence which ensured his political isolation. Despite the reluctance of the colonists to countenance voluntary separation, *Freedom and Independence* had still stamped Lang as the colony's most capable political theorist.

Lang was the only intellectual in nineteenth-century Australia to publish a detailed blueprint of republican government. Drawing on a wide range of historical and political sources, from the classical scholars of Greece and Rome to the modern theorists of republican France and the United States, Lang linked the introduction of republican government with a comprehensive vision of democratic government. In *Freedom and Independence* Lang took the trouble to go beyond broad generalisations about independence, and provide a thoughtful discussion on matters such as the Constitution of the lower and upper houses, the electoral system, payment of members, parliamentary terms, trade, land reform and defence. The breadth and detail of this vision have not yet been matched. Compared to *Freedom and Independence* the republicanism of the 1880s and 1990s would seem shallow.

When the arguments which Lang had put forward in *Freedom and Independence* reached the colonial press, it was immediately clear that Lang was on his own. As one poem published in the *Sydney Morning Herald* quipped, 'While ye're makin Constitutions Dunny's plannin revolutions'. The *Illustrated Sydney News* depicted Lang's proposals as 'wanton, preposterous, ridiculous . . . the ravings of a fiend gone mad'. Any republic would necessitate violent 'amputation' of the connection with the mother country, independence 'baptised in blood'.[28] Predictably, the press overlooked the most substantial part of Lang's work and concentrated on the issue of separation, equating republicanism with anarchy and revolution. It seemed that Lang would never manage to disconnect the image of a republic from revolution so long as the majority of the press kept harping on this theme. While the cries of 'red republican' from the conservative press were to be expected, Lang had hoped to attract the support of colonial democrats. Unfortunately, these hopes were dashed when Henry Parkes launched a series of attacks on Lang's republicanism in the *Empire*.[29]

In December 1853 Parkes' arguments had taken on a far more formidable and sophisticated allure than his earlier efforts in 1851. On 19 November, Parkes devoted an entire editorial to the issue of republicanism. Largely written in response to the *Herald*'s allegations that every opponent of Wentworth's bill was a republican, the editorial outlines many of the principles which characterised Parkes' attitude to imperial relations throughout his political career.

REPUBLICANISM

The bugbear of Republicanism is again sought to be raised to frighten the sober politicians of New South Wales out of their righteous demands.

. . . The word 'republic', as everybody ought to know, does not convey any necessary distinction between one form of constitution and another. Every constitution is in reality a republic. There is just as much a republic in England as there is in the United States, the only difference being, that in the one case the word is not used, and in the other it is. Surely no one will be so obtuse as not to perceive that there is an immensely greater difference between the ancient Republics of Greece and Rome, and that of the American system, than there is between that system and the British theory. The essence of the thing does not consist in the distinction between the throne of monarchy and the presidential chair; nor even between the status of our hereditary rulers according to the English system, and that of a president periodically elected. It is absurd, after the doctrine established in 1688, to pretend that it does. . . .

As to the other characteristics of the two systems, popular power and right is the prevailing doctrine both in the old empire and the new . . . the tendency in England is precisely that which is here dreaded and impugned under the terrible name of Republicanism.

. . . We avow that we do not care by what name the popular principle is designated—the name is a shadow, and we merely want the substance. Let us disabuse ourselves of the stigma, and perhaps we shall cease to be thrown into convulsions.[30]

One of the strongest features of Parkes' editorial is its sophistication. Instead of attacking republicans with the rhetorical language reminiscent of those in the Legislative Council, Parkes relied on historical analysis to destigmatise the republican bogey until it seemed irrelevant to Australia's political future. Put simply, Parkes perceived the republican scare as little more than an imbecilic fear of words—much ado about nothing. His argument rested on an almost surgical exposition of the word's etymology. Cleverly, he distinguished between the pure republicanism of the ancients and the modern application of the term—which he saw as so varied that it provided no indication of constitutional practice. The pivotal moment in history for Parkes was 1688. Parkes saw the principles enshrined in the Glorious Revolution as the essence of modern English and American government. Once the monarch's rule was dependent on the consent of the governed, the seeds of the disguised republic were sown. The superficial differences between monarch and president provided no guide to the respective politics of England and America—and there was even evidence to suggest that America was more of a monarchy than England, as the *Sydney Morning Herald* realised in September: 'The fact is patent to everybody. Individually, the President . . . exercises great power—greater far than the Queen of England'.[31]

By exposing the ambiguities and inconsistencies of the term, Parkes argued that republicanism was a benign concept. Honest enough to admit that what was dreaded under the terrible name of republicanism in Australia was nothing more than what was already happening in England, Parkes revealed republicanism as the very spirit of the age—'the popular principle'.[32] It was this understanding of the English Constitution which would be the death knell of the republicanism championed by John Dunmore Lang. According to Parkes, if republicanism was little more than the extension of representative democracy, then there seemed little point in declaring national independence when most of this could be had under the aegis of the Crown. After all, for Parkes, the nation was both British and Australian. It was only Parkes' conclusion which saw him play the politician and attempt to deceive his readers. By claiming falsely that he did not care about the name given to the popular principle, Parkes failed to acknowledge the one component of republicanism in an Australian context which would always preclude him from describing himself as a republican—separation. Parkes had no desire to separate from Britain and consequently cared deeply about which word was used to describe reformers in Australia. In this respect, Parkes avoided recognition of the one aspect of Lang's republicanism which might have afforded it some distinction.

Throughout the summer of 1853 Parkes hid his disapproval of separation behind the cloak of inevitabilism. On 5 December, after defending opponents of Wentworth's bill against charges that they were the spiritual descendants of the American revolutionaries, Parkes spoke of independence as something which would be achieved 'at length'. The task for the meantime was simply to establish a 'sound preparatory state of political existence'. One week later, he devoted another editorial to Lang's republicanism and again insisted that independence would come 'sooner or later', Dr Lang's proposals were 'impracticable' and bound to precipitate the colonies into a nation before their time.[33] Parkes thought Lang's scheme of an Australian League a 'piece of madness' and made short shrift of Lang's appeals to England to grant the colonies their independence: 'The mind of this country is not ripe for revolution and it would need to be overripe for the bloodless revolution that has been shadowed forth to us'.[34]

These were the words of a shrewd politician who held an already transparent ambition to be lauded as an imperial statesman. Parkes might have genuinely believed that independence was a distant certainty, but his relegation of the issue to a future *'sine die'* also served as an expedient delaying tactic. By becoming an inevitabilist, Parkes was able to put himself forward as the moderate alternative to separationists like Lang. In addition to their political differences, the two men were now at loggerheads in other ways. Parkes' association with the wealthier colonial liberals had encouraged him to develop a healthy respect for the pound. He admitted being upset by what he referred to as Lang's contempt for the wealthy members of society.[35] Since Lang's departure Parkes had worked hard to organise the opposition to Wentworth's Constitution bill and his stature as a political reformer had grown immeasurably. He must have resented Lang's sudden reappearance on the political scene. Lang's weighty tome, *Freedom and Independence*, would also have caused a degree of envy. Soon after Lang's return Parkes had published several letters from the democrat, John Robertson, in the *Empire*. Robertson criticised the Constitution Committee for its handling of the debate on the new Constitution and urged Lang to provide a more radical and effective leadership. Criticism of this nature must have irked Parkes. Robertson had labelled the committee as 'puny, sickly and contemptible', then Lang chipped in by calling it 'utterly insipid and worthless'.[36] These arguments over political strategy had previously been far more courteous, and Parkes was aware of Lang's ambition to lead a successful republican crusade against Wentworth's bill. Both men saw themselves as future leaders and Parkes was not about to sit idly by while Lang stole the limelight. Instead, he rejected Lang's talk of separation and offered prayers to England, prayers from a lost fragment of British civilisation cruelly isolated in the South Pacific:

> We are not only separated by the immense distance of sea, but broken off from the parent stock by the cumbrous action of the Constitution which endeavours to extend its protecting branches to the ends of the earth. Hence, whenever any grievance is severely felt in a colony, we see honest men of all ranks and of all shades of opinion, almost unconsciously to themselves, evolving the idea of separation as the *dernier ressort*.[37]

While Parkes prayed for deliverance from the terrifying option of the *dernier ressort*, Lang was busily working to form a national league which would place separation as the *premier ressort*. After reading Parkes' denunciation of the republican option he quickly wrote to the *Empire* and took Parkes to task. Tired of the endless petitioning of the last decade, Lang insisted that the only way of redressing colonial grievances was to 'agitate at once for entire freedom and independence'. He then went about firing a few personal barbs at Parkes. He accused Parkes of being more interested in the commercial viability of the *Empire* than the nascent independence of his adopted land. Parkes, said Lang, was more concerned with his 'own honour and glory', a nineteenth-century jellyback who simply 'trimmed the head of his sails to suit the actual breeze'. Upset by Parkes' accusation that his drive for republican independence was motivated purely by a desire to get even with the colonial authorities, Lang criticised Parkes for his soft approach to the dung hill aristocracy of Botany Bay and threatened to move an amendment at the next meeting of the Constitution Committee which would advocate separation.[38] Lang finished his letter by suggesting that he and Parkes should 'shake and make-up'. 'After all' said Lang, they fought 'under the same liberal banner'. Surely the 'good cause of the future' demanded a truce be struck. Unfortunately, Parkes was in no mood for reconciliation—the issue of separation was too big a hurdle. In his letter, Lang had bragged that he had the necessary enthusiasm to lead the colonies to independence:

> What man, either in modern or ancient times has ever been good for anything, either for this world or the next, who has not been an enthusiast. The man who has got possession of any peculiar idea, whatever it may be, as a motive power for society, must hold that idea . . . with the grasp of death. It must have an all pervading and over-mastering influence over his own mental character. He must have a firm and unshaken faith in it. He must regard it as the polestar of his country, as the hope of long oppressed and deeply wronged humanity.[39]

These were hardly the words of a minimalist. Lang was not the progenitor of the pragmatic republicanism of the 1990s. As if to show that he had the ability to live up to his words, he immediately set about working towards a reformed Australian League. Naively, he dreamt of a League 10 000 strong—'a snowball that would become a mountain'. The League would succeed in setting free 'a noble bird of right royal plumage'—the Australian republic.[40] To gather public support for the League Lang delivered three 'Anatomical Lectures' at the York Street Circus in January 1854.[41]

When the inaugural meeting of the reformed League was held in the hall of the Australia College on Australia Day 1854 only thirty people bothered to attend. Lang must have been bitterly disappointed. Although he had predicted inauspicious beginnings for the League, nothing could have prepared him for this. He had imagined Australia as 'a young man just starting into life' ready to set up his splendid new shop—'number 1 in Pacific Ocean'.[42] Yet for all these allusions to commercial prosperity, when the doors were opened the shop floor was empty. Chairman Richard Driver asked those in attendance not to be discouraged as many great schemes had 'humble beginnings'. Lang bravely rose to read the League's platform which he had written for the thousands he had hoped would march under its banner. Like Driver before him, he excused the poor attendance, suggesting that the anniversary celebrations had kept many away.[43]

Lang must have known that if the promise of a harbour regatta and a belly full of beer had been sufficient to distract his republican brothers, then there was little hope for his dreams of a League 10 000 strong. If the reasons given by Driver and Lang for the poor attendance at the meeting were accurate, the only hope for an Australian republic would be for the British authorities to introduce prohibition! Perhaps this is why Lang included 'the political education of the citizenry' as one of the objects of the League. This was consistent with the civic humanism Lang had espoused in *Freedom and Independence*, the republic would open up 'honourable ambition' in every form and the cause of education morals and religion would advance and prosper.[44] Lang believed that apathy was one of his biggest obstacles. The only newspaper to support Lang was the *People's Advocate*, which seemed to adopt Lang as some kind of guru after the publication of *Freedom and Independence*. With increasing verve, the *People's Advocate* called for complete independence, 'gloriously stigmatised by the name of the Australian republic'. Mimicking Lang, Hawksely foresaw the onset of a 'glorious series of colonial republics', 'free from British allegiance or responsibility'. Editorials entitled 'Freedom and Independence' were not uncommon, and Hawksely made every effort to portray Lang's League as the 'only remedy for colonial grievances'.[45] But aside from the *People's Advocate*, Lang's only articulate support came from Daniel Deniehy.

At a subsequent meeting of the Australian League in March Deniehy delivered an outstanding lecture before another poor audience. Like Lang, he praised the progressive colonialism of the ancient Greeks before stressing the far-reaching effects which independence would bring to the Australian colonies. For Deniehy, the republic was the panacea for all ills, just as it was for Lang, and in some respects for Keneally, 150 years later:

> [With independence] Government [would be] entirely identified with place and people, the growth of national character, the full development of the country's physical resources, the necessity that would ensue of making the best of everything around us and so converting the country really into a home, . . . While Australia remained a mere British colony or a dependency of any state, [this] was impossible.[46]

Deniehy's visionary eloquence was a cry in the wilderness. Despite the continued loyalty of the *People's Advocate* only a small group of men joined Lang's League and by the end of 1854 the Australian League was non-existent. Words had not been enough to set Lang's noble bird free. Without the spectre of convict vermin it seemed difficult to organise any popular political movements in New South Wales, as the fate of Parkes' Constitution Committee had already demonstrated.

In the *Empire*, Parkes' anger turned to pity. He saw Lang as Australia's 'modern Sisyphus'. 'Every time a stone rolls back upon his labour he resumes his task as cheerfully and hopelessly as before.' He lamented that Australia's native sons were unable to fathom Lang's love of country and the 'true motives of this extraordinary man'.[47] While Parkes' concern was most probably genuine, it was far easier for him to pour out the tributes now that the tide was beginning to turn against Lang. As Parkes admitted, Britain was finally awakening to find a new sympathy 'for the cause of good government in the colonies' and the time for Lang's republican overtures had passed:

> Great Britain may be a republic in point of fact, the Queen perpetual president and the Parliament a senate and House of Representatives but John Bull will never believe in anything but Queen Lords and Commons and a great democratic engine of forty Lang power will not cudgel the idea out of him.[48]

Essentially, Parkes was asserting the preference of his countrymen for the mixed Constitution over the modern, independent republic. It was simply that the former went under the euphemism of 'the Constitution' while the latter—advocated by Lang—would always be seen as the antithesis of this Constitution, no matter how hard Lang tried to educate the public otherwise. With Parkes composing the Kyrie, the *Sydney Morning Herald* completed the Gloria in the Requiem for Lang's republic:

> the oft preached republicanism of feeling which has been supposed to characterise colonies as a matter of course, does really not exist in Australia. . . . We have not a jot, not a shadow of that democratic habit of mind which is the great and distinguishing characteristic of American society, . . .[49]

By 1854, with Lang's plans for an Australian League in tatters and responsible government nigh, the possibilities of Lang igniting a republican movement seemed remote. Still, surrounded by dirge and ridicule, Lang was intent on persisting with his Sisyphean task. He would be given one last opportunity in May 1854.

The First Sacrifice

The Crimean War afforded the Australian colonies their first opportunity to express loyalty and devotion to a motherland under threat. If there was any set of circumstances tailor-made to suffocate Lang's campaign, it was the climate of hysterical fealty encouraged by an imperial war. At a time when Lang's republican campaign was already faltering, the news of war in Europe sounded the call for Empire and England and turned the eyes of the Australian people towards the Dardanelles. The public meeting called on 22 May in Sydney was an important moment in the colony's history. John Darvall recognised the import of the occasion: 'It was very seldom indeed that any subject should call the citizens together which should unite all grades and classes of society, from the highest to the lowest, from the youngest to the oldest, in one common bond . . .'[50] As with all imperial festivals, their function was as much to praise God, Queen and country as it was to condemn the enemy, and republicans were certainly in the latter category. Darvall wasted no time:

> He was sure there was not a man among them who would talk of 'cutting the painter' . . . (Uproarious cheers, clapping of hands, waving of hats!) No man now, . . . would speak of such a thing, but would wait for quieter times when separation, if required, might gracefully take place. He believed the struggle would be a short one; but it might be that it would involve the invasion of Port Jackson.[51]

Darvall's plea was naturally a very thinly veiled reference to Lang. The thought that Lang would dare to mention separation at a time of crisis for the motherland filled him with embarrassment. His request for Lang to wait for quieter times was typical of anti-republican rhetoric in the nineteenth century. Quieter times, of course, might never arrive and imperial conflicts would continue to submerge any talk of Australian independence. If the Russians were coming (or the Germans, the Japanese, the French, the Chinese or Portuguese pirates) then how was it possible to talk of separation when the protection of mother England was most needed? The fact that Fort Denison was later constructed as Australia's first line of defence against the Tsarist fleet is evidence enough that Darvall was not alone in his fears. Talk of invasion also allowed speakers at the meeting to dust off their swords and indulge in belligerent fantasies of colonial brigades routing the Russians at Rushcutters Bay. Major Thomas Mitchell, who was by now a rather crusty old explorer, suggested he would lead a boarding steamer against any Russian frigate. 'With pike in hand and a firm and steady band of Australians at his back', Mitchell imagined himself as Australia's first military hero (perhaps warranting a statue in the Domain).[52] It was not difficult to see that there might not have been so many willing diggers if the enemy had been slightly closer. Mitchell may well have died before the Russians managed to find Port Jackson.

Other speakers followed Mitchell's lead, dreaming of a harbour dotted with Russian frigates that had somehow been waylaid on their way to the Crimea. Then, into this war-mongering madness came a solitary voice of reason. Lang took the podium amidst a clamour of hisses and cheers. To demonstrate to the crowd that he was not a Romanov, he offered the mandatory declaration of loyalty to the Queen but before long his words had the meeting in uproar:

> He objected to the address, in the first instance, on the ground that they were an isolated colony and not in any way mixed up in the disputes pending between the mother country and Russia. (Groans and hisses mingled with cheers!). . . . He did not pretend to say whether this war was a righteous one or not. It might or might not be, but that was a question with which they had nothing whatever to do. [Cries of Yes, we have!][53]

After more than five minutes of turmoil, Lang was finally allowed to complete his speech. The crowd's reaction only seemed to further his resolve. In mocking tone he asked the audience what rational reason there was for a puny colony like New South Wales to declare war on 65 million people? Determined to assert Australia's self-interest, he then linked the issue of the Crimean War to an Australian Declaration of Independence. This was too much for Parkes, who claimed that he was sickened by the abominable doctrine that the adversity of the parent country afforded the most fitting opportunity for redressing grievances. Whereas Lang viewed Australia's interests as separate from Great Britain, Parkes saw them as synonymous:

> The reverend gentleman had said it was no question of ours whether England went to war or not. What, and are we no longer Englishmen? Does the mere distance from our native country separate us from all those sympathies of association, that love for our native soil, and veneration for those free institutions under which we were born.[54]

There was no doubting Parkes' allegiance to his native soil—the soil of England. Parkes could just have easily been voicing the sentiments of certain Australian Prime Ministers who came after him — Hughes, Bruce or Menzies—for it was this brand of imperial nationalism which would dominate Australian public culture well into the twentieth century.

After the meeting of 22 May the fanatical tide of loyalty that had been whipped up by the Crimean War all but buried Lang's republican campaign. It seemed that his dreams of an independent Australian republic with separate interests from Great Britain were now destroyed.[55]

Although Lang managed to gain a narrow majority in the August elections for the Legislative Council seat of Stanley in Moreton Bay, he discovered that the conservative press no longer saw his republicanism as a danger. Lang's opponent in the election had tried hard to make republicanism an issue in the campaign but the *Moreton Bay Courier* was not interested. Instead, it suggested to its readers that they vote for Lang. According to the *Courier*, Lang's support for a republic was identified with the promotion of popular democratic reforms—therefore, voters should vote for the republican candidate and keep the colonies within the British Empire. By voting for the republican they would ensure that the Colonial Office would yield to colonial demands for responsible government, thereby 'mollifying public discontent' and postponing separation.[56] Lang's republicanism was now seen as harmless, so much so that papers like the *Moreton Bay Courier* were prepared to toy with it. Even before Lang's election, Daniel Deniehy had written to Lang expressing his concern for 'the cause of Australian republicanism'. Deniehy had been disheartened by the events at the York Street Circus in May, and could not hide his disappointment with the grovelling tone of the speakers—especially Parkes:

> ... *Our cause*—the cause of Australian Republicanism, would scarcely have been benefited by [the recent farcical scenes at the York Street Circus] ... From Mr Parkes the Republicans of New South Wales may expect little aid or sympathy ... Mr Parkes has too much not of the English man *in* but of 'Englishmanism' *about* him, to do otherwise than he did. The distinction is subtle, but no one can better perceive it than yourself ... help he will not give ... he is no common man.[57]

Deniehy's observations were perceptive but they also revealed that he was a recent convert to Lang's cause. His assessment of Parkes demonstrates an intuitive understanding of Parkes' motives and correctly identifies Parkes' pivotal role in the demise of Lang's republican campaign. He was aware that the York Street meeting heralded the end, or at the very least the postponement, of republican independence in Australia. Over the next few months the response of the colonists to the war in the Crimea demonstrated just how 'desperately loyal' Australian society had become. The contribution of New South Wales to the war effort—a startling £60 000—easily eclipsed that of any other British colony.[58]

Another effect of the war was that it diverted attention away from the British government's long delay in granting the colonies responsible government. The Legislative Council had passed Wentworth's bill back in December 1853. It was not until May 1855, however, that the British parliament could find time to debate the bill. After vigorous debate it was finally decided, under the leadership of Lord John Russell, to provide the colony with a nominated upper house and a fully elected lower house.

Wentworth's controversial proposal that the Constitution not be amended without a two-thirds majority was also defeated.[59] News reached Sydney in December 1855 that the colony of New South Wales had finally been granted a degree of self-government. The Constitution, with its nominated upper house, property qualifications for members and voters and blatant gerrymandering, was hardly democratic but it did afford the colony much greater independence.[60]

In the middle of June 1854 the *People's Advocate* could still manage to continue the fight which Lang and Deniehy now acknowledged to be lost. Under editorial headlines such as 'Advance Australia' the *Advocate* bravely persisted with a staunchly republican campaign:

> The independence of the Australian colonies is not a mere abstract idea. It is as certainly approaching as is the dawn of tomorrow's sun . . .
> If we are not prepared for our freedom now, we cannot expect to be so a century hence . . . we are prepared for the event and the sooner it arrives the better.[61]

These words were now a lone voice of dissent. The independence that arrived in the form of the new Constitution would shatter the *Advocate*'s morale to the point of despair. After campaigning since 1848 for responsible government and complete independence from England since 1850, the *People's Advocate* was suddenly confronted with a Constitution which was but a mere shadow of the vision it had held for seven years. By 1855 there seemed to be little cause for optimism: 'How long shall we submit heaven only knows. . . . Everything tends to shew that chains are being now forged to bind us still faster . . . We have talked and written so long upon this matter that we are almost tired of recurring to the subject'.[62]

The pages of the *People's Advocate* in 1856 bore scant mention of Lang's republic and less than two years later the paper was defunct. Lang, Deniehy, Harpur and Adelaide Ironside continued to cling to their dreams of a republic. Deniehy, from his room on the top floor of Mandeleson's Hotel in Goulburn, wrote a column for the *Goulburn Herald*. Harpur penned the odd sympathetic line from his farmhouse in Singleton, Ironside wrote Keatsian odes to Lang and Australian independence, while Lang published a revised edition of *Freedom and Independence* in 1857; but none of this was sufficient to have an impact on the course of political life in New South Wales. Instead, like bunkered patricians privy to an enlightened philosophy, they corresponded between themselves and confessed their republican sympathies as if articulating the dream of an after-life.[63]

Daniel Deniehy, plagued by alcoholism and loneliness, wrote sanguinely of leading a van of republican opposition in the New South

Wales Legislative Assembly which would 'scatter dismay in the camp of the Philistines'.[64] Deniehy's van was never sighted. Of all those who gladly embraced republicanism, it was only John Dunmore Lang who had been able to muster significant pockets of public support and by 1854 even he had tired of speaking on the matter. The York Street rally in May had effectively been his last hurrah.

At the same time, Lang was beset with yet another public scandal. This time it was his son George who, having inherited his father's skill for financial management, was charged with embezzling funds from the Bank of New South Wales in Ballarat.[65] Even if one discounts the personal problems Lang had always succeeded in overcoming on previous occasions, he must have known that the tide had turned. The colony's most long-standing grievances had finally been redressed by the British government. Although Lang and Hawksely were unhappy with the new Constitution, most colonists rejoiced at its arrival or chose to express no opinion at all. It seemed that Parkes had been right after all. The Constitution which arrived in 1855 provided the people of New South Wales with 'republicanism enough' without the shadow of the word. The excessive displays of loyalty during the Crimean War also demonstrated that even if Lang had been correct in his assertion that the British government would grant the colonies their independence, the colonists would have most likely refused it.[66] Their sense of isolation and inferiority was far too strong to contemplate separation. But perhaps the final word on the republican campaign of John Dunmore Lang should be left to the man most responsible for its defeat:

> Dr Lang is quite right in his abstract principle, but quite wrong in his mode of applying it . . . Such a government as he proposes to establish here could only be achieved by a revolution; and a revolution in time of great material prosperity is a phenomenon of which, profound historian as he is, we think he will be unable to show an example . . . It is not probable that a sudden severance of these colonies from the mother country will ever take place; . . . We think freedom and independence may be achieved without disintegration, and we had rather agitate for possibilities than lose our time in chasing a phantom.[67]

The battle between Parkes and Lang was now over. By 1856 Australians had rejected John Dunmore Lang's dream of a republic—at least for the time being. The cautious approach of the man who had been born 'just a few hours walk from the spot where Shakespeare was born' had proved too much for Lang. Henry Parkes had won the day.

CHAPTER FIVE
A Victorian Republic

> A large population is gathering, thinking men and men of action are coming. Government should be the liberty of the virtuous and intelligent will of the people—not the patrimony of effete politicians.
>
> Letter from the Bendigo goldfields to *Argus*, 23 October 1852

If the virtues of independence were to be exalted in the Australian colonies, then the most fertile ground was surely the colony of Victoria. Separated from New South Wales in 1851 and buoyed by the discovery of gold in the same year, Victoria was at the forefront of social change in Australia. With the gold rush came an overwhelming tide of free immigrants from Europe, China and America, and it was this young, skilled, itinerant, and predominantly literate population, which also carried the potential for political dissent.[1] Aspirations of material prosperity were bound to clash with a governmental structure more suited to a penal colony. The influx of gold-lust immigrants encouraged the perception that Victorian society would now diverge from the English model, as the *Argus* explained in 1852:

> The broad distinctive features of English social life are almost lost in a colony . . . The character of society is rapidly assuming the American type . . . Personal independence in speech and act, self assertion, lack of conventional distinctions and an all absorbing pursuit of wealth as almost the only object of existence . . .[2]

Whereas men in Sydney, such as Parkes and Wentworth, were intent on duplicating the English model, in Melbourne there was a much more independent and 'Victorian' outlook. As David Blair remarked shortly after he had moved from Sydney to Melbourne in 1850 'over head and ears in love', Sydney was a city immersed in the 'stillness of intellectual death' while Melbourne seemed to be a city 'with abounding vitality in every department of human activity'.[3] Politically, this atmosphere of intellectual curiosity resulted in a milieu which would have been receptive to notions of independence and democracy. The best account of the climate which prevailed in Melbourne is probably provided by James Smith, who arrived there in 1854 and was later to work as the Victorian Parliamentary Librarian:

> The years I speak of were years of political excitement and turbulence. Among the new-comers were combative Chartists from Glasgow, Clerkenwell, and

Chelsea, brim-full of schemes for the reformation of mankind in general and of the people of Victoria in particular; . . . Many of them had been . . . in the revolutionary movements which had agitated Europe in 1848. You met men who had fought in the streets of Paris; political refugees from Frankfurt, Berlin, Vienna, and BudaPesth, and Carbonari from Italy. Mostly young, ardent, enthusiastic, and animated by more or less Utopian visions . . .[4]

What had been a predominantly British population before 1851 was now suddenly multicultural. Chinese, Germans, Americans, Irish, Italians, French, and a 'few score' negroes from the West Indies and the United States had joined the flood of British immigrants who had come to the Victorian goldfields in search of wealth. In the ten-year period between 1851 and 1861 Victoria's population increased by over 700 per cent—from approximately 80 000 to more than 540 000.[5] While it would be tempting to portray the bars and cafes of Melbourne in the 1850s as some kind of republican left bank, we should remember that only one-tenth of those immigrants who became diggers were not of British origin. The overwhelming majority of 'the diggings community' were committed to traditional British institutions—especially the monarchy and the principles of responsible government. Still, in the midst of so much social upheaval, there were many like the Victorian Governor La Trobe in 1853, who feared that the 'democratic spirit' brought by the new immigrants would eventually 'loosen the bonds of attachment to the parent state'.[6]

In the six-year period between 1850 and 1856 there would be three particular grievances which would encourage talk of an independent Victorian republic: convict transportation, taxes on the goldfields, and the delay in the arrival of responsible government. Although these grievances also applied in New South Wales, they were more keenly felt in Victoria.

When the Victorian Legislative Council came to debate the new Constitution bill in the summer of 1854, there was a broad consensus that the Council should take particular care to avoid the introduction of any provision which might sow the seeds for future grievances similar to those which 'led the people of America to separate from the parent state'.[7] Unlike the debates which surrounded Wentworth's Constitution bill in New South Wales, the Victorian debates at least appear to pay some lip service to the 'spirit of the age'. All councillors were mindful of the fact that the discovery of gold had resulted in an influx of men and women who were aware of their political rights. When councillors came to discuss the appropriate wording of an oath of allegiance for future members of parliament, it was agreed that the oath should not contain any reference to Victoria being 'dependent on or belonging to the United Kingdom'.[8] While separation was, in the words of one member, 'beyond the lives of any of us here now', members also sent a clear signal to London that Victoria was a colony with certain interests which were separate from those of Britain. The Victorian Legislative Council's support for a fully elected bicameral system and the extension of the franchise to all miners who had held licences for twelve months or more, certainly made Wentworth's Constitution seem reactionary by comparison. Equally, it is important to remember that the election of members to the Victorian Upper House on a restricted franchise for ten-year terms, ensured that the Legislative Council would remain a 'well-nigh impregnable bastion of pastoral wealth'.[9]

In 1854 it was not so much the Council's proposal for a new Constitution which provoked public outrage but the interminable delay to its assent. Although the Constitution was sent to England in March 1854 it was not returned approved for another eighteen months, and it was during this period that tensions in Victoria rose to fever pitch. In this short space of time 35 000 immigrants arrived on the goldfields. In 1853 Governor La Trobe had only narrowly managed to avert a full-scale rebellion over licence fees on the diggings at Bendigo.[10]

Victoria's first major 'republican' scare occurred in October 1854 when news broke that the Colonial Secretary, Sir George Grey, had instructed the new Governor, Charles Hotham, to immediately release all Tasmanians imprisoned under the Convict's Prevention Act of 1852. If there was any issue likely to incite talk of rebellion in Victoria it was the prospect of the 'pestilence' and 'moral filth' of another convict plague, especially at a time when the goldfields were seething with discontent. Immediately, a public meeting was called in Melbourne on 23 October 1854. The meeting was unusually large—official estimates placed the crowd somewhere in the vicinity of 10 000, perhaps the largest in the colony's history.[11] It was at this meeting that many threats of separation were made. One historian, Noel McLachlan, has even suggested that Victoria could easily have become a republic if Governor Hotham had gone ahead and implemented Grey's instructions.[12]

The man who was responsible for the most dramatic republican threat at the meeting was none other than David Blair. After his arrival in Melbourne in late 1851 Blair had quickly gained notoriety as secretary of the Melbourne Branch of the Australasian League and co-editor of the *Argus*. Together with fellow Scot, Ebenezer Syme, Blair used the editorial columns of the *Argus* to demand a 'Grand Charter of Australian independence'.[13] The *Argus* had a wide circulation, and more than any other paper, between 1852 and 1854 it led the campaign for responsible government and an end to convictism. Syme and Blair were not afraid to threaten an 'Australian 4th of July', and it was precisely this type of revolutionary allusion which struck fear into the heart of Governor La Trobe in 1853; so much so that La Trobe sent a long despatch to the Colonial Office which included copies of the *Argus*, a paper which he referred to as the 'propagandist of republicanism and freedom'.[14] While La Trobe's description of the *Argus* as 'republican' was probably more indicative of his conservative perspective than anything else, Blair had learnt much from his time with John Dunmore Lang in Sydney, and when he stepped forward at the Melbourne meeting in October 1854 he delivered a speech which could easily have been construed as republican in the eyes of La Trobe:

> We ask for freedom, and they give us slavery! We ask for virtue, and they give us vice. We ask for free citizens, and they send us convicts . . . In doing this England herself is severing the connection, and she must take the consequences . . . If England will not deal honourably . . . her dependent states must take their own welfare into their own hands.[15]

The truth was that Blair had more in common with Parkes than Lang. Blair was the reluctant rebel, praying for the British government to save Australia from its fourth of July—holding the guillotine while at the same time kneeling at the altar of the English Constitution. Blair's speech was consistent with his columns in the *Argus* and John West's *Launceston Examiner*, a paper which the *Argus* quoted frequently. His first preference was always for the English connection and if the bluster of 'separation' had ever become a reality in Victoria in 1854, it would have been because a loyal people had been driven to desperation to save the principles of the English Constitution.[16]

The crucial question seems to be in which way Blair's rhetoric could be said to be republican, and whether it followed in the tradition of much of the public protest over transportation in the 1850s—that is, simply using separation as a cudgel without any realistic prospect of it being carried out. When we look at the other speeches made at the meeting the answer is not difficult to find. The meeting's final petition to the Queen gave some indication: 'Your petitioners feel that the carrying out of Sir George Grey's suggestions will render the royal prerogative odious to the colonists and . . . endanger the connexion existing between this colony and the parent state'.[17]

The Melbourne press continued the theme, the *Argus* in particular depicted the situation with some amusing imagery: 'Not even the Queen has the right to seize us by the throat, demand our purse and proceed to tickle our carotid artery with the point of a large knife'.[18]

The October meeting was not so much about the possibility of an independent Victorian republic but the insistence that the principles of the Glorious Revolution of 1688 be adhered to. Speakers devoted much more of their time to demonstrating that the function of the royal prerogative was meaningless without the consent of the people. Threats of separation were simply a poker-face addendum to the central strategy—to show that any rejection by the British government of Victoria's right to intern Tasmanian convicts was unconstitutional on the grounds that it infringed royal prerogative. The speech of Thomas Michie is perhaps more indicative of the protesters' motives than that of Blair:

> Where are we to fix a limitation to the prerogative? The answer must be, that prerogative is not and cannot be anything inconsistent with the interests, the security or the happiness of the people ... If the prerogative is to be prescribed for us ... by our owners—as we might call them, what mere cant it was for them to talk about the glorious revolution. That revolution was an assertion of the people in opposition to the royal prerogative when it militated against the lives and property of the people. That was justly styled a glorious revolution, and it was one that made kings feel very uncomfortable—and why? Because it taught that all power—even the power of kings—existed for the people and not the people for them.[19]

Supporting Michie, the following speaker, Mr Langlands, reminded Governor Hotham that the proposal for a new Victorian Constitution, to which he had given his assent, rested on the sovereignty of the people. Almost every speaker asserted that the people were the only true source of political power.

When they spoke of separation it was used as a stimulant, to alert the British government to the fact that the principles of 1688 should also apply in the Australian colonies. The protesters' grievance was not with the monarch, who was the embodiment of these principles, but those who falsely claimed to rule in her name, the evil doers such as 'Grey and the gaoler governor of the convict island'.[20] It is true that Hotham did write of his fears that the colonists would separate if he refused to sign the bill to prevent the further influx of convicts.[21] But Hotham's concern should not necessarily be taken as an accurate assessment of what might have happened. Threats are not enough to spark revolution. More important things are required—arms, organisation, platforms, strategies and luck. Australia was not another America. The Victorian protesters never once attempted to organise a revolutionary council or draw up a declaration of independence and it is not difficult to see why. They never intended to take matters into their own hands, only to ensure Hotham's compliance by making their threats of separation sound convincing. The editorial columns of the *Age* reflected the depth of allegiance to Britain in Victoria:

> The tie of too many warmly cherished associations unites us whose claims would never be forgotten unless forfeited by harsh and unnatural treatment ... Is separation to be the watchword? and will it be our lot ... to bear through

the world the turbulent and restless messenger of republicanism? or rather will England be true to herself?[22]

The independent republic of Victoria was still an uncomfortable thought for the *Age*: too turbulent, too restless and too frightening. Less than one month later, when news of the Eureka rebellion reached Melbourne, there were many who feared that the republic was on its way after all, marching like a Napoleonic army towards the city.[23]

Eureka

> Every Australian who honours the men who have sacrificed their lives for their country, should adopt their faith, and swear allegiance to republicanism.[24]

It did not take long for the Eureka rebellion to be appropriated as a symbol of positive, nationalist republicanism in Australia. Examples of heroic rebellion were few in Australian history and Eureka provided a much-needed boost to the flagging hopes of many Australian nationalists—especially in the late nineteenth century. Although Eureka was not a republican rebellion, its subsequent function as a symbol of independence is what makes it important. Before looking at the rebellion itself, I first want to show that Eureka was already perceived in a republican context before it took place. It was, in every sense, destined to be republican.

As soon as gold was discovered in the Australian colonies a wave of anxiety swept through the British corridors of power. Fears of a 'digger democracy' were evident as early as 1851 with Fitzroy and La Trobe's apprehensive reaction to the gold discoveries. The imposition of licence fees for miners represented a determination on the authorities' part to avoid the inevitable anarchy and social decay that had been forecast. The goldfields were frequently depicted as a working model of democratic and republican ideals. The *Argus*, for example, claimed that the goldfields were the closest approach 'to the ideal of republican equality' that had ever existed in Australia. The *Ballarat Times* had also portrayed the resistance of the diggers in Bendigo in 1853 as the 'birth of an Australian nation'.[25] A rebellion such as Eureka was bound to attract the republican tag, regardless of its circumstances.

In addition to these expectations of independence, the large numbers of Americans on the goldfields also encouraged prophecies of a republican future for Victoria. Certainly, many of the Americans who arrived at this time believed that the Australian colonies would eventually follow in the footsteps of the United States and become a republic.[26] The Order of the Lone Star, an American organisation formed specifically for the purpose of exporting the principles of freedom and republicanism, alerted William Peter, the British Consul at Philadelphia, to the dangers of a large influx of Americans. When the Consul sent his despatch to Australian Governors in August 1852 he feared that many Americans on their way to Australia were members or sympathisers of the order: 'Hundreds if not thousands of adventurers are either now or will soon embark from various parts of the United States for Australia—most of them bent on extending the area of Freedom, and in aiding their fellow men in the pursuit of Liberty and Republicanism'.[27]

Fitzroy correctly attributed the Consul's alarm to earlier reports about republicanism in Australia, which had been inspired by Lang and published in London newspapers. He seemed relatively ignorant of the Order of the Lone Star, and not overly perturbed by the threat posed by American immigrants. La Trobe, on the other hand, who was much closer to the front, did admit that 'some danger might be appreciated from any large influx of Americans into these colonies'.[28]

The presence of the Americans, combined with large numbers of continental Europeans and Irish, also helped to foster the impression that any future conflict between diggers and the authorities would inevitably involve republican overtures.[29] In addition, the subsequent delay in the arrival of responsible government and the public uproar over the Convict's Prevention Bill, only weeks before the rebellion, ensured that the word 'republic' featured commonly in political discussion. Hence, the cheeky advertisements placed in the *Argus*: 'Wanted!—a governor, apply to the people of Victoria'. The *Age* seemed obsessed with the issue of separation after only its first day on the news stands, fearing that the events of 1854 would only strengthen the hands of those desirous of separation.[30] Only weeks before the Eureka rebellion it warned that separation was a distinct possibility in Victoria: 'The cry of separation is already heard . . . The people have no voice in the councils, the government is an institution of mere surveillance . . . and colonial demands are yielded or refused at the dictation of rulers in whom the colonists have no faith . . .'[31]

In a political climate where there was so much talk of separation and any number of idle threats of rebellion, Eureka was a psychological barrier finally broken. Even before blood had stained the wattle it was destined to be perceived as republican blood.

The Rebellion

It is indisputable that there was an element of republicanism present on the Victorian goldfields. At times this so-called republicanism meant little more than the desire for responsible government and an extension of the principles of the English Constitution. At other times it may have meant separation from the parent state, or simply a somewhat confused resentment of British rule, a word bandied about to signal an opposite state of affairs to that which prevailed. For all its various meanings, it almost always entailed the notion of Victorian (as opposed to Australian) self-government.

Although there was no republican movement as such, the 'r' word was often traded in association with the diggers' grievances. At Bendigo in 1853 we know that there were miners who preached of the 'evils of English tyranny and the virtues of republicanism'.[32] In Ballarat, at the meetings which led to the formation of the Ballarat Reform League, the Englishman, George Black, and his associate, Frederick Vern, breathed the fire of 'red republicanism'. Rafaello Carboni, an Italian republican involved in the Eureka rebellion, is also said to have spoken of himself as a defender of the rights of man—'a descendant of the Gracchi'. It is almost certain, as Noel McLachlan asserts, that 'every field had its republicans'.[33]

Yet we have to search hard to find any indication of sincere republican sentiment, whether it be at Eureka or in the more general protest movement of the diggers. When a small number of diggers (perhaps as few as 150) were attacked by government forces in a pre-dawn raid on Sunday 3 December 1854 it took little more than ten minutes before the Eureka 'rebellion' was routed. The diggers had not even launched a pre-emptive strike, instead they were roused from their sleep in a vain attempt to defend their poorly armed stockade. Thirty diggers lost their lives in a battle which they never stood any chance of winning.[34] The tensions that had existed on the goldfields for more than two years had finally been brought to a head in a tragic anti-climax. Eureka was the result of the entrenched social and political divisions on the goldfields. Antagonism between diggers and police, and resentment over draconian government regulations on the diggings, particularly in relation to the heavy-handed imposition of licence fees, saw a brave rump of diggers take up arms when they could see no other way out.[35] But these men, who would later be lauded as heroes, had no revolutionary aims or intent, indeed it is not even certain that they would have initiated an armed rebellion if left alone.[36]

Eureka, after all, was only a minority expression of a much wider strategy on the diggers' part. Only around 15 per cent of diggers at Ballarat supported the stockade. The majority were led by the predominantly Chartist platform of the Ballarat Reform League.[37] On 11 November, three weeks before Eureka, over 10 000 miners gathered at Bakery Hill, Ballarat, and lent their support to the proposals of the Reform League. Although the editor of the *Ballarat Times*, Henry Seekamp, had described the League as the 'germ of Australian independence', the final platform to which the miners gave their assent was distinctly moderate: 1 Full and fair representation; 2 Manhood suffrage; 3 No property qualifications for members of parliament; 4 Payment of members; 5 Short parliamentary terms.[38]

This Chartist platform was not in any way augmented by a desire for separation or a republic. In fact, the League's platform went out of its way to distance itself from these options:

> taxation without representation is tyranny . . . it is the object of the League to place the power in the hands of responsible representatives of the people to frame wholesome laws and carry on an honest government. . . . it is not the wish of the League to effect an immediate separation of this Colony from the parent country, if equal laws and equal rights are dealt out to the whole free community; . . .[39]

This was little different from the remonstrance of the protesters in Melbourne only one month earlier. English constitutionalists first, Australian nationalists a distant second—1688-ers, rather than 1848-ers. While some of the diggers may have been sympathetic to a more confrontationist strategy, the majority of men who resorted to arms on 11 November had little interest in a Victorian republic.[40]

We do know that one of the leaders of the stockade, Alfred Black, drew up a 'long', 'flowery' and 'verbose' 'declaration of independence' on the Friday evening, less than two days before the attack on the stockade. From the available evidence, it seems that a largely 'incoherent and bombastic' declaration of independence was drawn up in Black's tent late on Friday. Writing in 1855 Rafaello Carboni saw the declaration as a minor issue and he was most probably correct.[41] At the very best the declaration was signed by a minority of miners and was ill-considered and hastily drawn up. Any other suggestion that Eureka was influenced by republican sentiment usually revolves around statements attributed to the leader of the Eureka Stockade, Irish-born Peter Lalor, and the large number of Irish diggers involved. Lalor was alleged by one eyewitness, H. R. Nicholls, to have stated that he was for 'Independence—plump and plain'.[42] While this may or may not be true (given the rivalry that existed between Lalor and Nicholls), Lalor did write a letter to the *Argus* on 10 April 1855 in which he explained what he meant by 'independence': 'I looked around me. I saw brave and honest men who had come thousands of miles to labor for independence. I knew that hundreds were in great poverty who would possess wealth and happiness if allowed to cultivate the wilderness which surrounded us'.[43]

Lalor's struggle for independence at Eureka was a desire for economic autonomy, the removal of an unjust tax and freedom from government interference.⁴⁴ Considering Lalor's political ambitions, it was obviously in his interest after Eureka to deny that he was a Chartist, communist or republican. In any case, a few words about independence do not add up to much. Even H. R. Nicholls admitted in his 'Reminiscences of the Eureka Stockade' that the Eureka rebellion 'did not take the form of one for independence'.⁴⁵ Rafaello Carboni, the eccentric Italian, wrote in his *Eureka Stockade* that the diggers' grievances were centred on the removal of the licence fees first and foremost, followed by some 'yabber yabber about not being represented in the Legislative Council'. As one American digger on the goldfields is reported to have remarked: 'Folks here are republican enough in their ideas though they do not wish you to think so'.⁴⁶ From the time of the troubles in Bendigo in 1853 it was clear that nationalist and separatist republicanism was not part of the diggers' agenda.

The presence of large numbers of Irish at Eureka may prove that the Irish were more prone to take up arms than any other ethnic group on the diggings, but it would be wrong to think of Eureka as an 'Irish' rebellion—and there is no evidence that the Irish diggers at Eureka carried any grand republican strategy up their sleeves.⁴⁷ Like the Americans, who were conspicuously quiet by the time of Eureka, the Irish may have spouted some rebellious words but they showed no sign of formulating these sentiments into any political statement.⁴⁸ Despite the heroic rebellion which took place on Eureka Sunday, the bulk of the diggers' protest fell within the tradition of political protest that had already been well established in the colonies—strongly worded petitions to the Queen advocating the extension of the principles of the English Constitution. The statement framed by J. Basson Humffray and C. F. Nilhols after the rebellion (essentially as a plea to Hotham to grant a general amnesty to those diggers still imprisoned) reveals the sentiment of the majority of the diggers in Victoria. It perceived the military assault on the Eureka Stockade as an 'unconstitutional attack' and was signed by over 4500 miners:

> The diggers of Ballarat were attacked by a military body under the command of civil officers, for the production of licence-papers, and, if they refused to be arrested, deliberately shot at.
> ... The diggers did not take up arms against British rule, but against the *mis*-rule of those who were paid to administer the law properly; and however foolish their conduct might be, it was an ungenerous libel on the part of one of the military officers to designate *outraged British subjects* as 'foreign anarchists and armed ruffians'.⁴⁹

This evidence is far more important than trying to guess the contents of Black's declaration of independence. A few republican threats muttered in a tent do not quite stand up against a document signed by so many diggers. Naturally, this is not to suggest that Eureka itself was a Chartist rebellion, but the petition does reveal that the majority of diggers wished to be seen (and probably saw themselves) as English constitutionalists rather than Australian nationalists. This might explain why, even at Eureka, the miners constantly referred to Hotham's remarks that 'all power stemmed from the people'. The diggers were not bent on separating from Great Britain but on asserting the principle that 'reciprocity exists between the government and the governed'.[50] Only afterwards did the Eureka Stockade become an expression of Australian nationalism.

After Eureka

When the news of the rebellion at Eureka reached Melbourne the colonial press quickly prepared a revolutionary republican straitjacket. British troops and police had clashed with the diggers and over thirty lives had been lost. Regardless of the fact that Eureka was not about British rule *per se*, so much as it was concerned with British misrule, the juxtaposition of an unBritish rebellion with an allegedly non-violent 'British' tradition of protest was too easy to make. The bourgeois press quickly stamped Eureka as an 'unBritish error', perpetrated by foreigners advocating 'balderdash' about the rights of man.[51] It was clear that the most influential groups in colonial society were determined to push the rebellion into Thomas Paine's corner. By doing so, they helped to ensure that republicanism in Australia would be frequently associated with anti-British sentiment. Interestingly, this process was also facilitated by those who supported the actions of the diggers, as well as their critics. For many democrats, the shedding of blood at Eureka afforded an opportunity to press their claims for responsible government more strongly. For those with dreams of a unified and independent Australia, Eureka was the heroic act for which they had been waiting: 'Blood has been shed! A number of Australians have been killed for defending a new faith . . . This birth in blood of a new nation will not, cannot die. . . . Australia must have martyrs'.[52]

It did not seem to matter that many of the Eureka martyrs were not Australian, nor that they had given little thought to the idea of an Australian nation, they were now going to be conscripted to serve the cause regardless of their motivations. When the *Age* correspondent reported from the Commission of Enquiry into Eureka at Bendigo he played the Eureka card as the forerunner of an independent republic: 'If they refuse to listen, United Australia will hold them responsible for the consequences, and the next movement will be . . . for separation and independence. The men of

Ballarat have not died in vain'. Very quickly, Eureka had become the violent warning of a future 'unBritish' republic. The *Argus* editorial of 5 January made the choice clear: 'Great Britain must now give up forever her right to intermeddle in our local politics or she must prepare herself for giving up the Australian colonies themselves'.[53]

For the more conservative press, portraying Eureka as a republican rebellion was a means of reasserting the value of the British connection and portraying separation as the consequence of violence. The *Freeman's Journal* reacted condescendingly:

> The insurgents . . . seemed to think they had nothing to do but to hoist a Flag with 'five stars', in the vain hope of securing the aid and co-operation of the five Australian colonies in their futile and whimsical attempt at shaking off allegiance to Great Britain and in setting up an Australian republic . . .[54]

The Victorian government only reinforced the perception of Eureka as a republican rebellion through its language of prosecution during the trials of the Eureka rebels. The official public notice which offered £400 for the arrest of Lalor and Black described the accused as guilty of 'treasonable and seditious language, and inciting men to take up arms . . . to make war against our sovereign lady the Queen'.[55] As much as republicans like Lang had fought to disconnect republicanism from notions of disloyalty, the weight of the French and American revolutions proved too great. Fighting the redcoats and mounted police at Eureka was an image which repeatedly brought these images to the surface.

In Melbourne, fear of a diggers' army marching on the city gripped the people throughout December, with some believing that there was a possibility of revolution.[56] This anxiety brought out the essentially conservative character of the people. The *Age* appealed for calm and insisted that its sympathy for the diggers extended 'no further than the limit of constitutional agitation'. With military forces still on the goldfields, shopkeepers in Melbourne met to form a 'Dad's Army' to defend the city, while Hotham despatched an urgent message to Denison in Tasmania requesting additional troops.[57] On 6 December 6000 people gathered in a vacant block adjacent to St Paul's Church on Swanston Street to discuss the ramifications of the rebellion. In preparation, the authorities had dispersed special undercover constables throughout the crowd to identify seditious protesters.[58] Not surprisingly, these extreme measures proved unnecessary as the tone of the meeting was anything but revolutionary. Those who spoke made it abundantly clear that they would persist with 'peaceful agitation' until their grievances were redressed.[59] Tactfully, they pledged their support for the diggers' grievances but condemned the act of rebellion. All speakers valued the protective umbrella of the imperial connection and contributed the customary exhortations to the glorious principles of the Constitution. Copies of a new Constitution were distributed at the meeting but this was no desire for a radical 'utopian republic of heroic citizen soldiers'.[60] In fact, the Constitution contained provisions for a standing army, anathema to classic notions of the heroic citizen soldier, and it did so to protect the property of the citizens of Melbourne from republican insurgents. Rather than taking up arms for an independent republic the meeting was more interested in defending shopfronts and houses.

Aside from the Swanston Street meeting, there were still reports of Eureka inspiring a republican spirit within Melbourne. In January 1855 the *Empire*'s Victorian correspondent reported on the mood in the public houses and parlours of Melbourne:

> The future independence of Australia is no longer a mere dream of Dr Lang's ... but is a cherished aspiration of thousands in Victoria ... The blood spilt will be the seed of free and noble thoughts and actions. Every great extension of political freedom and development of national independence in the world has received a bloody baptism ... I am quite satisfied that I do not exaggerate the general feeling in Melbourne ... [the city has manifested] a spirit of sympathy with armed resistance to authority and with revolutionary and republican views ... [Wealthy merchants ... young men of intelligence and those in the public house parlours speak of Australian independence] ... The leaders at Ballarat are spoken of as noble fellows. [At one performance by Monsieur Coulon at the Bourke Street Theatre ... the Marseillaise was sung and greeted with contagious and enthusiastic applause, exceeded only by that which greeted God Save the Queen.] ... Independence is no longer the bugbear that it was, the idea we laughed at before we regard now with serious earnestness.[61]

The *Age* thought that the correspondent's report bore no 'revolutionary bias' and described it as 'unimpeachable'.[62] Even if we accept the *Empire* correspondent's assessment of the public mood as accurate, it is still problematic. Just as the Marseillaise is an infinitely more stirring song than 'God Save the Queen' after a few drinks, we should remember that most of those in the public houses who spoke of republicanism and separation had probably taken up more beer than arms. It is all good and well to speak of rebellion under a cloud of ale—alcohol has a knack of making the impossible seem possible. The words 'Australian independence' could be heard in the public house parlours of Melbourne but they were never once seriously entertained by those who gathered on the streets. As far as the enthusiastic reaction to the Marseillaise is concerned, what else would we expect 'Monsieur Coulon' to sing after his performance? The applause was more likely due to Coulon's sterling act than any desire for an

Australian republic. With these things in mind, it is hard to see any evidence that the republican spirit escaped the confines of the public houses and cafes of Melbourne. What cannot be doubted, however, is that the Eureka rebellion kept the discussion of republicanism and separation prominent.

In March a debate took place at the Temperance Hall in Melbourne on the question 'Is separation from the mother country practicable at the present time?'. While most of those present agreed that republican government was 'the purest form of government on earth', they also believed that Victoria was not yet ready for complete independence.[63] This type of sentiment was to prove typical of the majority who pressed for constitutional reform in the months after the Eureka rebellion. The most interesting example of fiery rhetoric after Eureka came from a recent arrival on the news stands—the Melbourne *Age*. The columns of the *Age* in 1855 provide a window to the different understandings of republicanism in the Australian colonies, and throw considerable light on the true nature of reformist movements in Victoria during the mid-1850s.[64]

In May 1855, still waiting on confirmation of a new Constitution from the British government, an impatient *Age* began to propose independence as the only remedy. Frustrated with the Constitution's delay and annoyed by what it perceived as England's ignorance of colonial affairs, it had arrived at the conclusion that Victoria would be no worse situated as an independent colony. Editorials encouraged readers to shake off the colonial system and suggested that the time had come for Victorians to take the business entirely into their own hands.[65] Superficially, these sentiments might be construed as a campaign for republican independence, yet it is also important to understand the specific characteristics of the republican independence which was being proposed.

First, it comes as no surprise to learn that David Blair and Ebenezer Syme were now employed as co-editors of the *Age*. From the outset their involvement should make us sceptical of any attempt to label the *Age* as an advocate of the separatist and nationalist republicanism espoused by the likes of John Dunmore Lang. In an editorial on 21 March entitled 'Who is the republican?', the *Age* set out to answer criticisms from New South Wales that the people of Victoria were given to 'republican bias'.[66]

The desire of the *Age* to be 'let alone' with the true British inheritance was no call for a new Australian nation, instead it was the selfsame call of the English protectorate and the American Revolution—the call for the extension of the principles of the English Constitution and fair and just representation. Why else would the *Age* later quote Cromwell's criticisms of the Rump of the Long Parliament? Precisely because Cromwell's condemnation of the parliament, violently dissolved in 1652, was just as true when applied to the Victorian parliament of 1855. As the *Age* explained:

Blair
David Blair, seen here towards the end of his life, was one of the leading agitators for responsible government during the 1850s. Like Henry Parkes, he believed republican government to be compatible with continued allegiance to the Crown.
(*Antipodean*, 1893, Image Library, State Library of New South Wales.)

> In 1855 the lives of some of our governing classes are still 'scandalous', they engross all the places of 'honor and profit' they 'delay business' they 'perpetuate themselves' they meddle in private matters they are 'unjust', 'proud', 'ambitious', 'self-seeking' and unless there be some power to check them it will be impossible to prevent our ruin.[67]

It was the inheritance of Cromwell, Hampden, Milton and Blake which the *Age* strove to protect and inculcate in Victoria. In the same way that the Lord Protector of the English Commonwealth had 'saved the country' in 1652, the *Age* feared that the people of Victoria would also be called upon to save the true spirit of the Constitution in 1855.

Even more important was the fact that the *Age* did not perceive its opposition to misrule in Victoria as republican but 'English'. Instead, it employed the term 'republican' to refer to those who were opposed to the inheritance which it strove to protect. Thus, it was Governor Hotham who was the republican and not the *Age*, the people of Melbourne or the miners at Ballarat. It seemed that the word 'republican' was a term no individual or group wanted to claim as their own in Victoria during the 1850s. The American miner was probably correct in his judgement that although the people were republican enough in spirit they certainly had no wish to be referred to as republican. The public culture of loyalty successfully washed 'republicans' into the five o'clock swill. The term 'republic', it seemed, could not be dissociated from the spectre of separation and revolution. The only answer therefore was to redefine loyalty in a colonial context—allowing scope for independence without including the dangers of republicanism and separation. This was precisely what the *Age* did in May 1855: 'We unhesitatingly confess that our loyalty is strictly colonial, not imperial. And wherein lies the difference? An acute reader will ask. Why, here; we are loyal to the British Crown, but not to British absolutism'.[68]

Here again we witness the duality in the dominant strain of nationalism in Australia. The loyalty of the *Age* was to an almost independent Australian Britannia, that vision of Australian Britons held by Parkes and Menzies—free of heavy-handed interference from London but retaining the monarchical connection as the symbolic embodiment of the people's legitimacy to govern and the protector of an exiled Anglo-Saxon culture.

For the *Age*, the republic of John Dunmore Lang and Daniel Deniehy was the *dernier ressort* just as it was for David Blair's *Argus* in 1852. To say that the *Age* fought for national and republican independence would be misleading. In August 1855 the *Age* devoted an editorial to the term 'republic' which left no doubt that the Victorian 'republic' of Blair and Syme was not the same as John Dunmore Lang's in New South Wales.[69]

A LESSON IN POLITICAL DEFINITIONS

The inauguration of the Victorian Republic need not be long postponed. Whether directly advocated, or merely hinted at, through the press, at public meetings, or in private conversation, it is generally received with enthusiasm . . .

. . . A Republic may . . . have various ideas attached to it, according to circumstances. In this colony . . . from the nature of our relation to England, it has become synonymous with national independence. This is almost the only meaning we attach to it when we use it ourselves, and we observe the same in others. A Victorian Republic indicates Victorian self-government. We shall have the reality under the New Constitution; and having that, the name is of little consequence. We may add, what may appear a paradox, that, in our opinion, we shall have more of the reality without the name than with it.[70]

The republic fought for by Blair and Syme through the pages of the *Argus* and the *Age* was simply a limited form of self-government. By the time the new Constitution arrived in Victoria in late 1855 it was no longer necessary to threaten separation. Blair and Syme, the radicals of the early 1850s, would soon be sitting in the new Legislative Assembly.[71]

After the onset of responsible government in the Australian colonies, successfully attained under the aegis of the Crown, much of the democratic element of republicanism had been subsumed by the English Constitution and its extension to the colonies. There had been no need for a revolution, no need for separation and, for most colonists, the new Constitution had brought independence enough. Thus, the *Age* rejoiced in the arrival of the disguised republic—the reality without the name, the substance without the shadow. Republicanism in Australia would now frequently appear as a hollow shell of anti-monarchical jibes focused primarily on the crimson thread. The majority of those in the labour movement who later took up the republican cause would inherit the legacy of the Eureka martyrs and rely more on an anti-British mythology. In the late nineteenth century Australian republicans would brandish their swords with little idea of what their future republic would look like. The malleability of the English Constitution and the belated compliance of the Colonial Office in the 1850s encouraged future republicans to rest their arguments on cultural nationalism rather than political or constitutional grounds. Unlike the United States, the introduction of responsible government in the Australian colonies was not legitimised by a declaration of independence, instead, the wellspring of Australian democracy would be identified with the English Constitution and the British sovereign.

If 'Australian democracy was born at Eureka', its birth was parallelled by the emergence of another myth equally as powerful—the myth that that democracy was somehow 'granted' or bestowed by the British government without any struggle on the part of Australian colonists. The first myth denied the fact that many of the democratic reforms which followed in Victoria after Eureka were already on their way. The second myth gave all the kudos for the birth of Australian democracy to the British and the glorious Constitution, forgetting that Australians had fought tenaciously to have these principles extended to them.

CHAPTER SIX

Quieta Non Movere 1856–1880

> Quieta non movere should be the maxim of Australia ... Let us look on in silence ... the time for action has not yet arrived.
>
> *Age*, 2 July 1870

After the granting of responsible government in 1856, the Australian colonies stood on the verge of a period of economic prosperity which would last for more than three decades. The grievances which had been the source of so much discontent in the colonies had finally been removed. At the same time, the connection with the mother country was about to be fortified by an ever-increasing traffic in goods, capital and immigrants.[1]

Although the new Legislative Councils in the colonies were to encounter some strident opposition over their tardy treatment of the land issue, for the most part, the years between 1856 and 1880 were the time of what Noel McLachlan has called 'the peaceful pursuit of plenty'.[2] Admittedly, the squatters and colonial bourgeoisie still wielded undue influence in the upper houses of Victoria and New South Wales, but the bulk of the population paid little attention to this unequal distribution of power. After all, compared to the conditions which the majority of immigrants had left behind in the Old World, by the mid-1850s the Australian colonies were very much the vision splendid. Images of a penal colony gave way to tales of economic prosperity. If the earlier years of discontent had not been enough to force the colonies to separate, it seemed unlikely that an Australian republic would emerge from the seeds of the workingman's paradise.

In 1857, when the Victorian government tabled legislation which attempted to leave the squatters' domination of the land intact, certain 'highly respectable' colonists and recently arrived immigrants formed a 'Land Convention'. The choice of the title 'Convention' was an indication of what was to follow. Determined to defeat the government's bill and unlock the land, Convention delegates borrowed freely from the symbolic language of revolutionary republicanism. Their banner depicted 'a flash of lightning passing through a Southern Cross'—inscribed 'vox populi'. In 1858 the Convention organised a torchlight procession along Bourke Street to Parliament House when parliament did not meet their demands. The crowd sang 'Yankee Doodle and the Marseillaise as well as Rule Britannia' and cheered for liberty, equality and fraternity. As Geoffrey Serle has observed, the Convention's programme and strategy may have been extreme but it was still 'well within the centuries-old tradition of agrarian protest'.[3]

The tactics of the Land Convention were consistent with previous political campaigns in the early colonial period. Employ the language of revolutionary republicanism, organise, petition, threaten and cajole, then hope that this quite dramatic strategy would achieve the required result—the acquiescence of the authorities. One month after the Bourke Street march, the bill to unlock the land was passed. Once again, the image of a revolutionary republic had played an important role in achieving political reform.[4] So far as grievances with the Colonial Office were concerned, after the granting of responsible government it was clear that any republican reverberations in the positive, separatist mould had been effectively mollified. It was not that republicans had gone into hiding, both Deniehy and Lang, for example, continued to cling to their republican views. It was simply that the opportunity for launching their republican campaigns had all but disappeared. The absence of colonial grievances meant that the reluctant republican threats which had so dominated grievance rhetoric in the first half of the nineteenth century were no longer required. The appeals which had invoked the heroes of the English Revolution before threatening a republic were now put aside. By the 1860s Old World fears of the French revolutionary model of republicanism erupting in Australia also subsided. In their place, the American paradigm remained secure, although now predominantly attached to the notion of republican inevitability and visions of Australian grandeur in the South Pacific. Increasingly, talk of republicanism and separation became intertwined with the next stage of the colonies' political development—Federation.

Advocates of Federation, such as the Irish immigrant Charles Gavan Duffy, believed that the application of the word 'Australia' to describe the colonies could not occur until 'there was some federal connexion' between the colonies.[5] Duffy worked tirelessly between 1856 and 1870 for Federation, to little avail. The colonies were not interested in union, and as Duffy himself remarked in 1870, he had single-handedly led and organised the federal movement for twenty years but 'the flowers gathered from so much seed made but a scanty bouquet'.[6] Predictably, Duffy was wary of connecting the move for Federation with republicanism. Like Parkes before him, who had claimed that republican overtones would prejudice the colonies' chances of attaining self-government, Duffy steered clear of any open declaration of support for an independent federal republic.[7] Although the concept of non-republican Federation had been in evidence long before the Confederation of Canada in 1867, there were still many colonists who believed that separation would, *ipso facto*, be part of any federation. Mention of federalism was also bound to encourage analogies with the federal republic of the United States. Yet for the majority of colonists the time was not yet ripe to move towards Federation.[8] Instead, they showed far more enthusiasm in bickering over issues such as tariffs, trade, communication, postal regulations and railway tracks. Public debate on the Federation issue in the period 1856–1880 was most often initiated in London.

Between 1856 and 1870, there was a prevailing opinion in the Colonial Office that the possession of colonies placed an intolerable burden on the mother country's resources and retarded the natural progression of colonial societies towards independence. The *Sydney Mail* explained the trend in October 1869: 'The tendency in many influential quarters [in England] appears to be towards provoking the colonists to claim their independence ... The doctrines announced by Mr Cobden have evidently sunk deep into the hearts of the people'.[9]

It was the popularity of the ideas expressed by the Manchester School which led Duffy to write to Lang in June 1870: 'The Colonial Office in later times seems to be quite in accord with you as to Australian Independence. They are ready to shake hands and part and a little impatient perhaps that we delay so long'.[10]

While there was no doubting the mood in London, the Australian colonists reacted with petulance and anxiety to suggestions that they might be forced to fend for themselves. The publication of Goldwin Smith's articles on colonial emancipation in the *London Daily News* during the winter of 1861–62 provoked a nervous response from the colonial press in Australia and immediate condemnation from the small group of ex-colonists who had gathered to represent the interests of the colonies in London. Smith's proposals were not unique. The difference on this occasion was that the Colonial Office was open to persuasion.[11] When news of Smith's scheme reached Sydney the *Sydney Morning Herald* promptly declared that it had no desire to be part of a 'new and experimental republic'. After all, said the *Herald*, 'when a colonist stood in the streets of Milan or Morocco and cried out "I am a New South Welshman"—where would be the magic of this sound?, where the prestige of this name?'.[12] Well before Federation, the basic core of the arguments which would characterise anti-republican rhetoric in Australia until the end of the twentieth century was set in place. By and large, this strategy consisted of stressing the fundamental similarity between existing constitutional status and any change to a republic. Differences were merely nominal, cosmetic or ceremonial. Then, to ensure that republicans didn't become too downhearted, the inevitability card was played: 'We have never doubted Australian independence is among the things to come. It is certain that any hurry in the liberation so fondly predicted is utterly unnecessary and must be mischievous'.[13]

Independence—surely, a republic—most definitely, but never now—that was always too soon. This still seemed to be the most expedient way of keeping positive, separatist republicanism off the political agenda. While there was little evidence of any support for republicanism between 1856 and 1880, the occasion of the first royal visit to the Australian colonies in 1868 certainly proved that fear of the dreaded 'r' word had not subsided.[14]

The Loyalty Play

On 21 January 1868 *Galatea*, the ship carrying Prince Alfred, Queen Victoria's second son, docked at Circular Quay. Ashore, colonial members of parliament stood under an enormous triumphal arch nervously waiting for the Prince to disembark. Among them was Henry Parkes, the man who had attended the great Chartist demonstrations of the 1830s in Birmingham as a young ivory-turner, and who now stood on an imperial stage as Colonial Secretary, clad in blue and gold court dress with sword and cocked hat.[15]

In the three months which followed, Parkes would extract great delight from his association with royalty. As he wrote to his wife, Clarinda, he was overwhelmed by the thought that a humble couple who had married in Edgbaston 'would live to dine with Princes and be led in by Earls'.[16] When the Irishman, Henry James O'Farrell, attempted to assassinate Prince Alfred at Clontarf beach in March 1868, it was Parkes who anointed himself as the chief conductor of a wave of sectarian hatred and loyalty, 'almost run mad'.[17]

For a colony so intent on demonstrating its loyalty, O'Farrell's act came as a shock. Immediately, the *Sydney Morning Herald* insisted that the assassination attempt had 'no connexion in any way whatsoever, however remote, with anything Australian'.[18] It was not difficult to imagine which ethnic group would shoulder the blame. Irish Catholics bore the brunt of community outrage—especially as O'Farrell was alleged by Parkes to have acted as part of a Fenian conspiracy.[19] Although a New South Wales Parliamentary Committee later found that there was no evidence to support this allegation, during the months of March and April, Parkes did his utmost to inflame sectarian divisions, demanding quite absurd declarations of loyalty from the New South Wales parliament. The document which most accurately captured the mood of the community was the Treason Felony Act, passed by parliament on 18 March, only six days after the assassination attempt. Orchestrated by the two men who had shown such a fondness for imperial pageantry at Circular Quay, Premier James Martin and Henry Parkes, the bill was hurriedly passed by parliament to ensure 'the better security of the Crown', and explicitly provided for the 'suppression and punishment of seditious practices'. The debate which accompanied the bill's passing reveals the manner in which republicanism was swept up in an overwhelming tide of sectarian bitterness. After O'Farrell's actions at Clontarf it was easier for colonial authorities to associate republicanism with the spectre of an Irish Catholic rebellion, or in the words of one member of parliament—'those who sucked disloyalty with their mother's milk'.[20] More important than any real connection between the Irish in Australia and a campaign for an Australian republic is the fact that the assassination attempt helped to cement the connection in the public imagination.

In the manner of the best burlesque theatre, New South Wales parliament passed an Act which provided for the arrest and imprisonment of all those who used language disrespectful to the Queen—including those who failed to drink a toast to the Queen at public occasions. Naturally this raised a particular difficulty for the police who were to enforce the new laws—how to tell the difference between teetotallers and republicans. Premier Martin attempted to dispel any doubts:

> We are not talking about drinking . . . When a toast is proposed a person may rise or not just as he thinks proper. But what we propose to deal with is factiously refusing to drink the Queen's health or other loyal toast. A person must not factiously avow that he refused the toast because he does not like the sovereign . . . but of course a man may drink or not as he pleases.[21]

One can just imagine a policeman approaching an individual who failed to toast the Queen at official occasions and politely enquiring: 'Excuse me, Sir! but are you not drinking because you factiously refuse to drink the Queen's health?'. The farce was sustained by members' fears that by passing the bill the parliament would be making a *de facto* admission that pockets of disloyalty existed in the colony.[22] Some members were so anxious about implications of disloyalty that they became hysterical. There was no doubt, however, that republicans were one of the prime targets of the legislation, as Martin explained: 'The language is sufficiently large to include any attempts at deposing the Queen, establishing a republic, or putting down the courts of law, or any designs which may exist here or elsewhere for any such persons as those'.[23]

Republicans were again so far outside the acceptable boundaries of the political spectrum that they had become potential criminals. The Treason Felony Act helped to sustain the popular association of republicanism with anarchy and moral decay. John Dunmore Lang, unable to place his hatred of Rome aside for the republican cause, voted in support of the bill, despite W. E. Forster's reminder that the bill's terms of reference were so far-reaching that Lang's previous republicanism would have placed him in 'circumstances of danger'.[24] Even the British government thought the Treason Felony Act excessive, withholding royal assent for the bill. Unfortunately, this news arrived in the colonies too late to avert the senseless arrest of many Irish immigrants. On one occasion an elderly Dublin man was arrested at Gundagai racecourse for yelling 'Hurrah for the Green!'. Wisely, the judge who presided over the case accepted the man's explanation that he had actually been barracking for a jockey dressed in green and dismissed the charge.[25]

From a republican perspective the turmoil which accompanied Alfred's visit was important, primarily for two reasons. First, the royal tour was a fundamental step in facilitating the process by which British heritage in Australia was reduced to the person of the monarch. After 1868 it would be paramount for members of the royal family to make regular pilgrimages to the colonies. As the personification of home, culture and Empire, their presence was a boost to the faithful and an integral part of imperial propaganda. The monarch and her heirs were now established as the most sacred icons in colonial public culture.

Secondly, the assassination attempt, and the fanatical displays of loyalty which followed in its wake, did much to reinforce the familiar juxtaposition of monarchy/loyalty/stability and republic/disloyalty/Irish in Australia. The difference about the polarity of the republican issue after 1868 was that sectarianism and Irish rebellion had largely filled the shoes previously occupied by the 'rights of man' and the French Revolution. Whereas republicans were once assumed to be sympathisers of the tricolour or American democrats eager to transport the revolution, they were now seen as Irish and Catholic.[26] Consequently, it was common to see leading colonial journals casting a cold eye on reports of Catholic disloyalty. The *Albury Banner*, for example, was most upset in 1870 when the *Sydney Morning Herald* reported that certain scholars at a convent school in Albury had not risen from their seat during the singing of 'God Save the Queen'.[27]

Increasingly, republicanism would become connected in the public imagination with a failure to conform with the rituals of a dominant imperial culture. Republicans were less likely to be seen as the bearers of democracy, instead they became people who refused to drink toasts, sing anthems, wave Union Jacks, or pause in silence in front of the Queen's portrait in the foyer. Just as British heritage was bowdlerised and trivialised through its reduction to the pageantry of monarchy, republicanism seemed condemned to equally superficial preoccupations. With the granting of responsible government a large part of the issue of democratic representation had disappeared from the context of the colonies' relations with Empire. In this sense, the nature and function of debate on republicanism was about to undergo a fundamental change: from a wide-ranging, sophisticated and literate debate on responsible government, imperial policy and colonial independence to a frequently shallow and superficial fixation with the public rituals of monarchy. By the time Henry James O'Farrell fired his bullets at Prince Alfred in 1868 one of the most erudite phases of republican debate in Australia was well and truly over.

The loyalty play during Alfred's visit would be staged with increasing fervour during each successive 'royal visit', culminating in the royal tour of the young Queen Elizabeth in 1954. Despite the importance of the royal visit and the public displays of fealty, Australians could still see the humour in it all. More than one year after the attempt on Alfred's life, the Melbourne lawyer, A. C. Michie, delivered a lecture entitled 'Loyalty, royalty and the Prince's visits' to a large audience in the Princess Theatre in Melbourne. In a lecture brimming with wit and candour, Michie lampooned the events of the previous year:

> How comes it that a simple, gentlemanly, unaffected young man, possessing the one mysterious advantage of Royal birth, should drive a reflecting sober people frantic with the desire to gaze upon him? ... Is it equally intelligible that we should throng and crowd together, and almost choke each other with dust, raise triumphal arches and make gold trowels, and pawn our pianos and go into general convulsions on account of one whose preeminence consists of the accident of rank alone?[28]

The Melbourne audience laughed at these words. They enjoyed the speech of a man who proclaimed republican government 'as the best form of government that human ingenuity has ever invented'. Yet their support was, at best, academic. Despite their ability to acknowledge the droll nature of colonial loyalty they were not willing to take up Michie's call for 'intellect and integrity' to rule over rank and title.[29] Unknown to all those present that evening, a new age of imperial rivalry in Europe was about to spark an important change in British attitudes towards the colonies. The audience may well have laughed just as heartily if Michie were to have told them that Australians would be kissing the toes of royalty for a century to come.

Reconstructing the Empire

> The problem which British publicists are discussing is how to keep together a number of colonies all enjoying independence.[30]

In July 1870 delegates from New South Wales, Victoria, South Australia and Tasmania gathered at an Inter-Colonial Conference in Melbourne. There were two issues which dominated the agenda—the possibility of a Customs Union for the Australian colonies, and the issue of the colonies' defence. The Franco-Prussian war of 1870–71 had intensified a long-standing concern in London that the British government could no longer afford to station troops in far-flung corners of the Empire.[31] While the final withdrawal of British troops from Australian soil had been expected since the early 1860s, and even welcomed, fear of invasion did much to concentrate the minds of the Conference delegates on the vulnerability of the colonies' defence. Mr Barrow MLC, a Tasmanian delegate, moved that the Conference urge the Queen to draw up a treaty with other European powers, thereby ensuring the neutrality of the Australian colonies in the event of war in Europe. Victoria's Chief Secretary, Sir James McCulloch, demanded that delegates petition the Queen to secure written assurance that Her Majesty's imperial government would provide for the 'protection of the coast line of Australia'. It seemed that Australian colonists feared being left without British protection or being embroiled unnecessarily in wars of Britain's making. In many ways, the Conference represented the climax of a decade of persistent fears that the British government was about to force separation on the colonies. Writing to John Dunmore Lang from London, Duffy saw the withdrawal of the British troops as confirmation of the British government's desire to 'free the mother country from all responsibility for the colonies and hasten the break up of the Empire'.[32] A similar interpretation of events motivated Charles Cowper at the Melbourne Conference: 'The Federation and separation of the colonies from the mother country would [not] make much difference. She would say "Good-by, God Bless You, now go and do for yourselves"'.[33]

Concern over colonial defence had been prominent ever since an American ship arrived in Port Jackson in 1853 with the news that the French had annexed New Caledonia. After the outbreak of the Crimean War and the Franco-Prussian war, there was no shortage of potential aggressors. Fictional accounts of invasions proved extremely popular with colonial readers.[34]

Republican debate was steadily shifting from a local to a more global context. Whenever republicanism was raised it was bound to be associated with a wide range of issues which had previously been more peripheral to the debate.[35] By the early 1870s republicanism was no longer purely a matter for Victorians, gold-diggers or New South Welshmen. Instead, it was an issue which necessitated a discussion of imperial conflict in Europe and the attendant risks in the South Pacific, the defence of the colonies and their possible Federation, the relative merits of free trade and protection, immigration, sectarian divisions and the usual issues of loyalty and identity. Although these issues had appeared in the context of republican debate in the 1850s they were brought into much sharper focus in the late nineteenth century.

As the concept of an Australian nation began to enter political debate in the colonies, the concept of Empire also began to cast its net wider. The fears of many colonists in the two years that followed the withdrawal of imperial troops that the British government would impose separation and independence on the colonies were soon placated by a sharp change of attitude in London. By the time Disraeli's government took office in 1874 the views which had dominated the Colonial Office since the early 1860s were in abeyance. Previously it had been thought desirable that colonies should be cast off from the imperial parent. Now, a new age of imperial rivalry and militarism in Europe had encouraged the British government to see its colonial possessions as a source of prestige. The global empire, the cult of race, and the glory of conquest were to take precedence over the emergence of infantile nationalism in Australia. Even before he took office, Disraeli signalled the shift in British opinion in a famous speech to the House of Commons in 1872:

> Well, what has been the result of this attempt, during the reign of Liberalism, for the disintegration of the Empire? It has entirely failed. But how has it failed? Through the sympathy of the Colonies for the Mother Country. They have decided that the Empire shall not be destroyed; and in my opinion no Minister in this country will do his duty who neglects any opportunity of reconstructing as much as possible our Colonial Empire.[36]

This was to be the temper of British colonial policy for many years to come. London, the metropolitan heartland of Empire, dispensing an imperial culture which would be joyfully received by the provincial hinterland. The greater the distance from home the greater the loyalty of the Empire's quarries. It did not take long for the spirit of Disraeli's speech to have an impact on the political scene in the Australian colonies. Whereas many colonial politicians had previously been sceptical of Federation, the newfound determination of the British government to hold tight the bonds of Empire now made it easier for them to imagine Federation under the Crown. Indeed, many would go even further and fantasise about a grand scheme of Imperial Federation. As Parkes wrote to Gladstone in 1874: 'Any new national importance that could be given to [the] young states would tend to bind them more firmly to Great Britain'.[37] It seemed that a way had been found for the colonies to advance to the next stage of their political development without the need for a republic. This was certainly the implication of the *Sydney Morning Herald*'s observations on Sir Hercules Robinson's pro-Federation speech at Albury in 1877:

> A few years ago [a speedy separation and independence of Australia] . . . was the favoured policy in official circles. Now a change has taken place . . . The

conservative party, with considerable tact has boldly announced that it is in favour of maintaining the integrity of the Empire ... If Australia is to remain British its communications with Downing Street would be very much simplified by the colonies being federated.[38]

For conservatives, secure in the knowledge that the British government no longer desired separation, Federation now became a means of ensuring the continued unity of the Empire. The ramifications of this development were substantial. Once again, well before debate on Federation had begun in earnest, the possibility of an independent Australian republic had become less likely because of London's flexibility and capacity for compromise.

By the 1870s it was clear that the British government would encourage the union of the Australian colonies under the aegis of the Crown. The person of the monarch was the instrument through which the 'colonial' connection and the priorities of Empire would be maintained.

Independence Enough

While the British government was doing its best to ensure the maintenance of imperial ties, the efforts of Victorian Attorney-General, George Higinbotham, in 1869 proved to be a further boost to the concept of limited independence under the Crown. Higinbotham demonstrated that the connection between colony and Empire could still survive despite the right of colonial legislatures to complete independence in administering domestic affairs.

The philosophy of the Manchester School had been partially founded on the assumption that the maintenance of imperial ties was not commensurate with colonial independence. Higinbotham, however, assiduously went about defining the limits of colonial independence while at the same time insisting that the links with the Crown remain. Throughout the 1860s, when the Victorian Parliament had lurched from one constitutional crisis to the next and with the two houses constantly in a state of deadlock, Higinbotham struggled to define a more autonomous, democratic and participatory model of responsible government.[39] Through the likes of Higinbotham, David Syme and Charles Pearson, Victorian liberalism projected an ideal of citizenship within the 'civilising mission' of Empire.[40] In 1869 Higinbotham successfully passed resolutions in the Victorian Parliament which asserted that, with regard to domestic issues, the colonial governor—like the English sovereign—could act only on the advice of his responsible ministers. In other words, according to Higinbotham, the Secretary of State for the Colonies had no business issuing instructions to colonial governors in matters which did not concern the Empire. Although he explicitly expressed the colony's desire to leave all powers relating to foreign affairs in the hands of the British government, he also insisted on the complete autonomy of the colonial legislature with regard to local concerns. Higinbotham's resolutions were to prove instrumental in asserting the notion of independence under the Crown, the very principle which was to guide the Federation of the colonies in 1901. Their acceptance only served to undercut the possibility of a republican appeal on the grounds of legislative independence. Higinbotham was not interested in severing the imperial connection, merely in placing relations on a more equal footing.[41]

One year after Higinbotham's resolutions were passed in the Victorian parliament, Queen Victoria formally surrendered the monarch's prerogative of the control of the British armed forces. Gladstone's cabinet had thus ensured the complete superiority of parliament. The *Age* saw this as further evidence of the virtues of British government as 'a nominal monarchy but a real republic'.[42] The more that the British Constitution was perceived as a disguised republic, the easier it was for similar assessments to be made about colonial legislatures. Higinbotham's belief that responsible government had bestowed a system of government on the colonies in every way parallel to that which operated at home in England, kept the door open for all those who favoured the maintenance of imperial ties to repeat the selfsame defence of the status quo which Parkes had used in the 1850s. Namely, that the inherited British political institutions possessed by the colonies represented the substance of republican government without the shadow of its name.

It was this argument, that of the disguised republic, which would form the nucleus of anti-republican rhetoric in Australia for more than a century to come. When David Blair wrote the introduction to Henry Parkes' collection of speeches in 1876, he explained why the colonies were already self-governing republics:

> The future of the Australian colonies is now, in fact, quite independent of their continued allegiance to the Crown of England. They are separate, independent, and self-governing republics, to the full extent that they would be such if their common connexion with Great Britain were entirely severed ... The simple truth is that the British supremacy here—in so far as it affects the internal development of the several colonies, the growth of a sentiment of Australian nationality, or the republican freedom and simplicity of our institutions—has ceased to be anything more than nominal ...[43]

The cogency of Blair's argument would continue to appeal to colonial societies which identified more strongly with London than they did with one another. It seemed that Gladstone had been right all along. Britain had little desire to limit colonial self-government and by adopting such a strategy they would only foster a more loyal colonial population.[44] Although the colonies were still very much interested in constitutional issues, as the Victorian crises in the 1860s demonstrate, there was never any suggestion of severing links with the Crown.[45] It was difficult to see support gathering for separation when there seemed to be little to struggle against.

Even before the publication of the *Bulletin* in the 1880s it was clear that if republican debate appeared in the latter part of the nineteenth century, it would be markedly different from the debate which had emerged in the early 1850s. Finding it more difficult to appeal for a republic on the grounds of representative democracy or legislative independence, republicans would inevitably be forced to focus their attack on the public culture of British imperialism. Motivated largely by socialist philosophies, republicans would target their arrows at British imperialism's most pivotal and visible symbol—the British monarchy. At the same time, the image of a previously taciturn Queen Victoria was about to be refashioned by the British press into that of a loving and caring mother of Empire.[46] Consequently, it was Victoria Regina, the plump and ageing Venus of a British race spread so gloriously across the globe, who would bear the brunt of republican condemnation in the 1880s.

Together with a contempt for the trappings of monarchy, republicans would also immerse themselves in the struggle between labour and capital. Indeed, on many occasions, the idea of an Australian republic would appear almost as an afterthought or postscript to the more central programme of socialist reform. Intermingling with these concerns would be the most powerful ideas of the age—race, nation and Empire. Writing in 1855 Daniel Deniehy prefigured this aspect of the late nineteenth-century republican debate when he maintained that the important questions were 'whether Australia is for the Australians' and 'whether the Australian and English nationality are henceforth to be identical'.[47]

Australians who supported a republic in the late nineteenth century would often turn away from constitutional arguments and look instead towards Australian 'identity' as the wellspring of the republic.

CHAPTER SEVEN

A White Man's Republic   1880–1887

> We want Australia not the world . . . We want to throttle the British connection that is as a bandage upon our limbs, not to throttle anything else whether British, German, Dutch or French . . . We don't want another Rome or another England. We only want an Australia, a new nation, a glorious republic, a free state, a country from which injustice shall be banished and in which every citizen shall do his duty and injure none other while protected from injury to himself.
> *Boomerang*, 7 April 1888, p. 3

The republicanism which surfaced in the Australian colonies in the last decades of the nineteenth century went far beyond the pages of the Sydney *Bulletin*. Until now, the most common image of republicans in the 1880s and 1890s has been that of a small group of Sydney bohemians inhabiting the outer reaches of colonial politics. Led by the likes of Henry Lawson and J. F. Archibald's *Bulletin*, this motley crew of 'radical nationalists' is supposed to have inspired a brief flowering of republicanism before Australia lapsed into a century of imperial loyalty.[1]

The history of republicanism during the 1880s and 1890s is a more elusive story. Far from being the whim of a few soap-box activists on Sundays at the Domain, the issue of a republic was raised in all colonies, classes and cultures. It was an integral part of colonial politics, consistently hovering over many discussions concerning the colonies' relationship with Britain. In every sense, the issue of an independent Australian republic was an important part of political culture in pre-Federation Australia.

Instead of perceiving republicanism as the fringe-dweller of Australian history or the river running underground,[2] it is more appropriate to see republicanism in the 1880s and 1890s as a varied political phenomenon which shared many beliefs and values in common with the more dominant imperial culture. In other words, we should see republicanism in these years not as an island unto itself but as one of the many interchangeable and ill-defined labels used by those who opposed the status quo. At the same time we should not forget that republicans were not entirely detached from mainstream attitudes and beliefs. While it is true that the republicanism of the *Bulletin* was both sexist and racist by today's standards, these attitudes were also common to those who favoured the maintenance of the imperial connection. Racism and sexism were not the exclusive domain of republicans—the concept of Empire was just as dependent on notions of Anglo-Saxon superiority as the *Bulletin*'s republic. In a similar way, although the *Bulletin* may have mocked the British aristocracy it never denied the virtues of 'British blood, grit and force'.[3] Republicans were always enamoured with their own carefully selected showcase of British political and cultural traditions.

One of the most interesting aspects of republicanism in the 1880s and 1890s is its diversity. Throughout the twenty-year period which preceded Federation there were more than fifteen republican organisations and over twenty newspapers or journals published which were sympathetic to the republican cause.[4] Republicans were just as likely to be found in Charters Towers, Brisbane or Wagga as in the streets of Sydney. In addition, we are not confronted with a simple dichotomy of imperialists and republicans, loyalists and rebels or conservatives and radicals. Instead, we find a rich and shifting range of political ideologies and allegiances. Loyalty, nationalism, and the colonial *heimat* were rarely one-dimensional. Republicans, like many of their imperial opponents, more often carried the burden of a dual allegiance to both motherland and adopted land. Citizens of all colonies lived in societies which incorporated several layers of loyalty. Motherland, adopted land, Empire, Queen, colony and nation, all competed for the people's allegiance.

For many imperialists, such as Sir Charles Berry, Victorian Agent-General in London, the Australian nation was a concept which could exist comfortably within that great Commonwealth of Nations—the British Empire.[5] Those loyal to Queen, God, and country still projected their hope for an Australian nation safe within the arms of the British Empire. The *Daily Telegraph* referred to citizens of the Antipodes as 'independent Australian Britons'. When workers in Victoria celebrated one of the great achievements of Australian labour—the eight-hour day—they marched down the main streets to the tune of 'God Save the Queen'. The 1880s were a time when labels such as 'nationalist', 'loyalist', 'radical' and 'republican' could be applied across class and ethnic boundaries. It was not uncommon for leading colonial politicians who favoured the maintenance of the imperial connection (such as George Higinbotham and Alfred Deakin) to reject offers of knighthood.[6] Belief in an egalitarian Australian nation was not always accompanied by republican nationalism, nor was it necessarily antagonistic to loyalty to the Crown. Consequently, the politics of allegiance were not polarised, rather, as always, they were characterised by a strong sense of duality. Thus, when we seek to understand the republicanism articulated in this period, we should not expect to find a great number of detailed republican platforms and strategies. More often than not, republicans tended to be clear about their desire for a separate and identifiably independent Australian republic, but somewhat vague and confused about the exact shape this republic would take.

Essentially, they were clearer about what they wished to reject than what they wanted to construct.

We need only turn to one of Australia's greatest mythological characters, Ned Kelly, to witness the mix of Old World hatreds and New World dreaming which combined to produce an extremely belligerent but ultimately shallow form of republicanism. In 1880 Kelly wrote the Jerilderie letter, something of a last testament, in which he carefully detailed a decade of injustice at the hands of those 'big, ugly, fat necked, wombat headed big bellied magpie legged narrow hipped splay footed sons of Irish Bailiffs or english landlords . . . better known as the officers of Justice or Victorian police'. The Kelly gang's hatred of the Victorian police and their refusal to forget the pressure and tyranny of the English yoke in the 'old Erin's isle',[7] naturally led the gang to advocate republicanism. But when Joe Byrne scribbled his republican dreams in a small exercise book at one of the Kelly gang meetings, he spoke not of an Australian republic, but of the 'republic of North East Victoria'. There was no doubt that the Kelly's republic was 'the symbol of an anti-British political system'. But there was little idea about the specific constitutional character of that republic beyond the 'quaint mock legalistic language' of Byrne's draft.[8] Like the Sydney *Bulletin*, the gang's republicanism was driven more by the hatred of British authority. In addition, Kelly's republican sentiments were focused primarily on Ireland. His somewhat provincial republican dreams for north-eastern Victoria were more of an aside. The Jerilderie letter was no republican manifesto, but it did provide sufficient detail on Ned Kelly's plans for the Victorian police: 'I would have scattered their blood and brains like rain, I would manure the Eleven Mile with their bloated carcasses and yet remember there is not one drop of murderous blood in my veins'.[9]

Kelly's uniqueness probably lies in his claim to being one of the few republicans in Australian history who would have been prepared to take up arms for the struggle. Yet, in another way he is the least interesting of republicans and the least typical. His simplistic, aggressive and shallow rhetoric may fit the mould of the stereotypical republican hero but there were few republican heroes in Australia. Unlike Kelly, Australian republicans were politically active individuals who eschewed violence. They drew on a wide range of European and American political traditions, and the story of their role in Australian political culture is an exploration of the intellectual history of pre-Federation Australia.

The First Stirrings   1880–1886

In 1881 the non-Aboriginal population of the Australian colonies was almost 2.5 million, and over 60 per cent of this figure were native-born.[10] For republicans of the early nineteenth century, such as Horatio Wills and

Daniel Deniehy, the inevitable majority of the native-born was the foundation of the future republic. Now, with this majority attained, there was little sign that the native-born were about to launch a campaign for republican independence. Instead, there was the stirring of Australian national sentiment as something distinct, if not necessarily detached, from Britain. On 25 April 1872 the Australian Natives Association (ANA) opened its doors to all native white Australian men of good repute.[11] Although the Association had formed one year earlier in Victoria, the launch of a national body was specifically intended to act as a catalyst for the cultivation of national sentiment and the Federation of a white Australian nation. In a society where allegations of disloyalty were still powerful enough to derail any political or social movement, the Association trod meekly on the issue of an Australian republic.[12] In the words of Charles Blackton, the Association 'gave to Britain voluntarily an allegiance which they refused as an obligation'. While the ANA was rarely republican, it did serve to stimulate public debate on political matters from a new perspective of national (as opposed to colonial) interest. The concept of advancing a 'national ideal' was just as much a part of the ANA's programme as it was for the Sydney republicans. The difference, however, was that the ANA's largely 'self-reliant' and 'egalitarian' vision of Australian independence under the Crown was to prove more influential and more effective.[13]

The 1880s was also a time when catchphrases such as 'Australia for the Australians' became increasingly prominent in public debate. As the *Daily Telegraph* remarked in 1888: 'It is only lately that the words "national" and "nationality" have been applied to the public life of Australia'. G. W. Meudell's article 'Australia for the Australians', published in 1882, applied a crude form of social Darwinism to argue for the emergence of an independent Australian nation inhabited by racially superior Antipodean natives.[14] Like the ANA of which he was a member, and the *Bulletin*, which would later adopt the title of Meudell's article as its masthead, Meudell constructed an ideal stereotype of the white Australian male which would lead Australia to independence. The belief that an Australian republic would simply beach itself as a well-muscled, meat-eating male, was consequently present long before Archibald's *Bulletin*. In 1874 the writer Marcus Clarke imagined the future republic of Australia lying south of the Tropic of Capricorn with its intellectual capital in Victoria and a 'fashionable and luxurious capital on the shore of Sydney Harbour'. Clarke also described the citizens of the future republic:

> The inhabitants of this republic are easily described ... The boys will be tall and slender—like cornstalks ... The Australians will be a fretful, clever, perverse irritable race. The climate breeds a desire for out-of-door exercise.

Men will transact their business under verandahs, and make appointments at the corners of streets ... The Australasians will be large meat eaters ... The present custom of drinking alcohol to excess ... will continue.[15]

Clarke's republic of men, a kind of cornstalk Utopia, was to be a popular theme with republicans in the 1880s and 1890s. By the early 1880s visions of Australian independence based on the racial purity of the native-born male were commonplace.[16]

But although there was now a clear majority of native-born in the colonies, economically speaking the colonies' livelihood was still linked with Britain. Together with a predominantly British stream of migrants, over 70 per cent of colonial imports came from Britain, nearly 80 per cent of colonial exports were sent to Britain, and all overseas borrowing took place in London. Considering the fact that the colonies had maintained defiantly separate paths of development, the chances of a republican federation looked fairly slim in the early 1880s.[17]

New Guinea

On 4 April 1883 the Queensland government, led by Thomas McIlwraith, raised the Union Jack at Port Moresby and declared that it had annexed Papua New Guinea and surrounding islands in the name of the Queen. Convinced that Bismarck had similar intentions, McIlwraith implored the British to endorse his government's action. In July British Colonial Secretary, Lord Derby, sent a prompt and unambiguous reply. Under no circumstances would the British government approve McIlwraith's move. Derby pointed out that colonial governments had no authority to act on behalf of Her Majesty's government and rejected the suggestion that Germany was preying on New Guinea. He reminded Queensland that the natives of New Guinea had certainly given 'no sign of a desire that their land should be occupied by white men', nor had they indicated their desire to provide Queensland with a coloured labour force, something which Derby insisted the indigenous inhabitants would 'not willingly accept'.[18]

Eighteen months later, Derby's hypocrisy was exposed when the British government raised the Union Jack at Port Moresby to claim the south-east coast of New Guinea ten days before Germany annexed north-east New Guinea and the Bismarck Archipelago.[19] Yet even before Germany invaded there was considerable disquiet in the Australian colonies over Britain's refusal to support Queensland's annexation. McIlwraith's audacity and Derby's firm response brought the associated issues of Federation, defence, imperial policy and Australian security to the fore. There was no sudden outburst of republicanism, but in a manner not dissimilar to the Anti-Transportation debates thirty years earlier, the New Guinea crisis made it more acceptable for discussion of separation to occur and it was the starting point of a ten-year period which would see Australians question the value of the imperial connection more than ever before.[20] McIlwraith himself acknowledged the change wrought in colonial attitudes towards the Empire when he addressed the Queensland parliament in October 1884: 'It is only in the last 12 months that I have seen it really considered whether the Australian colonies would be better off as part of the British Empire or as a federated nation by themselves . . .'[21]

The fact that every colony had supported Queensland's action in New Guinea meant that it was possible to imagine the colonies forming a united front in opposition.[22] This naturally gave rise to unusually frank statements from members of parliament and colonial premiers. Victorian Premier, James Service, was responsible for several agitated memorandums after it became clear that the British government was not willing to support Queensland's move. Equally concerned about French activity in the New Hebrides, Service cabled the Agent-General in July 1883: 'England must act promptly and firmly . . . Intense indignation here. If France is allowed to make New Hebrides cesspit for convicts consider this as crisis in Australian history'.[23]

When the Germans finally annexed north-eastern New Guinea in November 1884 Service spoke of the 'bitterness of feeling' which was being created between Britain and her Australian colonies—a bitterness which he claimed would 'not die out for a generation'. Colonial politicians and the press were beginning to ask whether the British connection was still necessary if it merely facilitated the exposure of the colonies to the hazard of a 'foreign menace'. At an Intercolonial Convention held in Sydney in December 1883 delegates framed a strongly worded set of resolutions expressing concern for the safety and well-being of the colonies should German and French activity in the South Pacific continue to go unchecked. This Conference also witnessed the first steps towards Federation, when delegates proposed the formation of a Federal Council to deal with 'naval defence and Australia's relations with the Pacific Islands'.[24]

It would be fair to say that between the years of 1883 and 1887 dissatisfaction with imperial foreign policy was acute. Yet although colonial grievances had rarely been this intense, it would be wrong to exaggerate the extent of republican threats or to misrepresent their true intention. While it is true that talk of separation and independence had increased dramatically, it is equally true that an overwhelming majority of colonists still desired the maintenance of the imperial connection. When threats of separation did occur they were most often shouted down in a volley of loyalist abuse.[25] In fact, the political strategies employed were little different from the tactics used by the Australasian League in the 1850s. Colonial leaders threatened separation in the hope of forcing Great Britain to change its policy in the South Pacific. Separation was the wild card used to exert influence on British colonial policy—a kind of take-your-bat-and-go-home diplomacy which was repeatedly used with great effect despite the awareness on both sides that no one really wanted the game to end. But there were signs of change. There seemed to be a steadily increasing number of separationists, such as Meudell, Buchanan, and McIlwraith on occasions, who were not bluffing. Even Sir Henry Parkes admitted that the interests of the Australian communities were increasingly coming into conflict with those of the Empire.[26] The New Guinea crisis and the scare over the French presence in the New Hebrides had demonstrated that the Australian colonies held interests which could be perceived as national rather than colonial. It was from this point that the material conditions necessary for promoting an Australian republic came into being, thus laying the foundation for the emergence of a strong republican sentiment in the late 1880s.

Sudan

On 3 March 1885 Australia despatched its first sacrificial ship to an imperial war. When New South Wales' Acting Premier, William Bede Dalley, learnt of the death of the British General, Charles Gordon, in Khartoum, he was overcome by a desire to demonstrate the colony's willingness to assist Britain in her hour of need. Despite the fact that England did not require Australian help, as Dalley himself admitted, he took the extraordinary liberty of pledging the immediate despatch of a contingent of 500 men together with ten 16-pound guns without seeking the sanction of parliament.[27] Three weeks later, the streets of Sydney were festooned with streamers and flags in a nineteenth-century version of the ticker-tape parade. On this occasion, however, the men who marched down Oxford Street from Victoria Barracks towards Hyde Park had become heroes even before putting bat to ball. By the time they reached the corner of College Street, the flowers, ribbons and rice thrown by the swelling crowd carpeted the path before them. In the words of the *Sydney Morning Herald*'s reporter: 'they marched on with a swinging step to the well worn tune of "The Girl I Left Behind Me", as women ran from the crowd to plant kisses on their cheeks'.[28] Some weeks later, as they disembarked at the hot, salt-encrusted Red Sea outpost of Suakin, these same men must have marvelled at the long arm of their Premier's foreign policy. The palpable and painful reality was that the war in Sudan had nothing to do with the Australian colonies. The British had not expected Australian assistance and were even uncertain whether they should accept the Australian offer.[29] In defiance of all reason, Dalley and his delirious public had sent Australian men more than 10 000 kilometres to fight the Arabs in Sudan. As the republican David Buchanan told the New South Wales parliament: 'The whole country lashed into madness and imbecility, blockheads going on to the platform and offering money and this that and the other thing, while one glance of a sensible rational mind would at once reduce their commotion to an absurdity'.[30]

Buchanan, a Scottish Chartist who first entered New South Wales parliament in 1862, was one of the few members to provide an alternative viewpoint in the debates which surround the despatch of the Sudan contingent. Speaking in much the same manner as his fellow countryman John Dunmore Lang might have done, he reminded parliament that the Arabs in Sudan were fighting for their liberty. Australian soldiers, said Buchanan, should feel nothing but shame for fighting a people who had never once harmed Australians. Finally, he suggested that the only remedy to ensure the colonies' security was to separate from Great Britain, thereby protecting Australia from any further embroilment in imperial wars.[31] Aside from Buchanan, it was largely a chorus of 'Wish Me Luck as You Wave Me Goodbye'. After the formation of the Patriotic Fund to support the expedition there were at least fourteen meetings convened in the Sydney metropolitan area to support the war effort as well as many in rural towns such as Albury, Windsor, Singleton and Grafton. When Edmund Barton told those present at a Sudan 'rally' in Sydney that the enterprise went to the heart of the great English nation, and with it 'whether we want to consider ourselves English or not', he diagnosed the colony's affliction correctly.[32] There was a manifest uneasiness about the nature and future of the relationship with Britain—especially in relation to defence and foreign policy. When one considers the enormous amount of suspicion and fear created by the German annexation of New Guinea and the French presence in the New Hebrides, it is not surprising that the colony of New South Wales snatched at the chance of sending troops to aid the mother country. The nature and place of the war were irrelevant. What mattered was that the colony could demonstrate her loyalty with blood sacrifice. As one speaker in the New South Wales parliament explained: it was 'sacrifice alone, suffering, death if necessary' that bound Australians to the mother country.[33]

The despatch of troops was a bargaining chip, a blood-stained handkerchief which would hopefully divert the ill-directed course of imperial policy in the South Pacific. The public displays of loyalty during the Sudan episode were representative of the pathological insecurity of the Australian colonies. David Buchanan's allegations that any opposition to the despatch of the contingent (especially republican opposition) was effectively quashed at public meetings, is evidence enough of the prevailing paranoia regarding disloyalty.[34] While the Sudan episode provided the opportunity for the anxiety over the British connection to be deluged in a torrent of imperial loyalty, it failed to stamp out the doubt that had clearly been rising since 1883. The next few years were to prove that the colonial loyalty displayed in 1885 was not quite as unanimous as the soldiers who marched down Oxford Street might have believed.

There was no surer sign that the relationship between the colonies and Britain was undergoing a process of redefinition than the formation of the Imperial Federation League in London in 1884. When a branch of the League formed in Melbourne one year later, speakers at the inaugural meeting left no doubt about the choice facing the Australian colonies. As the Reverend Dr James Moorhouse explained: 'We must either separate from England in order to escape Imperial dangers, or federate with England to gain Imperial privileges'.[35]

The new age of colonialism had encouraged the proliferation of a bloc mentality in foreign policy and there were many conservatives in London and Australia who favoured the Federation of the Australian colonies within the protective umbrella of a wider Imperial Federation.[36] Throughout the 1880s and early 1890s the debate on Australian Federation would often be depicted as a polarised battle between the two extremes of republican and Imperial Federation.

Writing in the *Liberator*, in 1889 Joseph Symes offered a typical example: 'Australia must be first federated then a republic will be easily established. Imperial Federation must be scouted as a hateful device of the enemy . . . its object is to transfer the government of these colonies to London and destroy all self-government amongst the Australians'.[37]

There were colonists who subscribed to the theory of Imperial Federation simply to stave off separation, just as there were many attracted to republicanism in the hope of avoiding Imperial Federation. That there was to be no overwhelming enthusiasm for either of these two options in the Australian colonies suggests that the indifferent middle ground of late nineteenth-century Australian politics was a muddied pool of divided loyalties.[38]

In 1884 the New South Wales democrat and member of parliament, E. W. O'Sullivan, formed the Democratic Alliance, a relatively small and short-lived political organisation which aimed to protect the interests of the labouring classes. Writing in the group's newspaper the *Democrat*, O'Sullivan published an article entitled 'The coming republic' in early 1884. If nothing else, this was a fascinating fusion of imperialism and democratic republicanism. O'Sullivan dreamed of a grand Anglo-American republic, a Roman fantasy of a federal republic so mighty that Australians could rest assured that 'no foreign foe would ever violate her shores'.[39]

One week before the Alliance was formed, a large anti-immigration meeting was called by O'Sullivan and colleagues in Sydney. At the end of the meeting, when 'three cheers were called for the Queen', a disturbance was caused by one of the speakers protesting and shouting that he was a republican. Immediately, a quick response was delivered by a man who announced himself as an Australian (the would-be republican being an Englishman) that they would have nothing to do with that sort of thing and the remark was cheered to the echo, the man who had protested receiving a volley of groans and hisses.[40] The amusing irony of an Australian loyalist shouting down an English republican was one indication that the most vocal republicans of the 1880s were 'new chums' rather than native-born Australians. But within the frequent discussion of topics such as Federation, protection versus free trade, and colonial defence, there were signs that the monochromatic 'Englishness' of the community was being challenged on several fronts.

In 1886 A. S. Bailes, a member of the Victorian Legislative Assembly, managed to upset parliament and most of his electorate at Bendigo when he stated that a republic was imminent. Speaking during a debate on the proposed plans for the Melbourne Exhibition of 1888, Bailes came up with an idea not dissimilar to that expressed by ex-Prime Minister Bob Hawke in 1992—when the Queen 'ceased to live', monarchy should be 'extinguished' and Australia become a republic. For this rather innocuous gesture Bailes was challenged to a sword duel by one member of parliament and forced to make a public apology.[41] Then, to wipe away the stain of disloyalty, a public meeting was called at Sandhurst Town Hall to denounce Bailes and proclaim the electorate's true feelings towards the Crown. The result was a loyalist show trial which went horribly wrong. Instead of the loyal atmosphere the authorities might have hoped for, the meeting was disrupted by 'hundreds of youths and young men' who booed and hissed while the audience attempted to sing 'God Save the Queen'. So great was the uproar that the mayor was forced to flee to the balcony of the Town Hall in the hope that the speakers would receive a fair hearing. A crowd of 2000 people then gathered in the square below—many booing mention of the Prince of Wales and cheering for Bailes. Remarkably, the resolutions declaring the people's 'unwavering devotion and loyalty to the throne of the Empire' were still carried, mainly because no one could hear them when they were read out.[42]

Gilbert and Sullivan would have given anything for a script like this. One would be forgiven for thinking Bailes was about to lead a revolution. The farce was so obvious that the *Age* devoted an editorial to the embarrassing 'sycophancy' of Victoria's 'zealous colonial loyalists'. As the *Age* pointed out, it was almost as if members of the royal family were supposed to be exempt from criticism, something which the *Age* said had caused considerable mirth among society journals in England. This kind of exaggerated colonial loyalty—of the 'gushing kind'—would only result in a 'feeling of repugnance' among young Australians which might prove injurious to the 'peace and unity of the Empire'.[43] In this sense, the *Age* was probably correct. The Bailes fiasco, with its show trial atmosphere, was reminiscent of Parkes' loyalty march in 1868, and it would not be the only example in the 1880s. It seemed that the more absurd loyalist reactions to republican murmurs became, there was every likelihood that the republicanism which they sought to quash would attract more attention. At the very least, the issue of colonial loyalty was, by 1886, very much in the spotlight. The uproar at the Sandhurst meeting was evidence of the growing divisions in the community. In Tasmania, at the opening of the first Federal Council meeting in Hobart in the same year, Tasmania's Premier Adye Douglas stunned the audience by advocating separation. Douglas told the gathering of colonial officials that the time had come when Australia no longer needed to be attached to a 'little bit of an island in the Northern Hemisphere'.[44] This was a sure sign that sympathy for republican nationalism was not limited to the young men at Bendigo. The emergence of an organised republican movement was close at hand.

Socialists and Republicans

> Certainly, our decayed monarchs should be pensioned off. We should have a hospital for them or a sort of zoological garden where these worn out old humbugs may be preserved.[45]

In the brief seven-year period between 1887 and 1893 republican sentiment would surface in the colonies in a manner which would not be seen again until the late twentieth century. These years were a time when the fundamental bases of institutional and social practice were open to question, a time when both state and nation were challenged to renaissance.

In New South Wales parliament the faction system which had dominated political negotiation for the previous thirty years gave way to the first political parties. The frequent debates on free trade and protection in the parliament were themselves an indication of the wider contest between insular nation and interdependent Empire. Outside parliament, public meetings at the Domain began to attract large crowds to political debates. John Docker has described the 1880s and 1890s as 'apocalyptic times', dominated by an impending *fin de siècle* crisis. Utopia, dystopia, republicanism, socialism, anarchism and atheism—in the late nineteenth century there was a time when they all seemed inevitable.[46]

In many respects, the proliferation of new ideas was a function of

The Widow's Mite.
"Her Majesty the Queen has contributed £500 (!) to the fund for the relief of the unemployed."—(Reuter cablegram.)
"Queen Victoria is the richest woman in Europe. Her accumulated savings are known to exceed five millions sterling."(?)—(English paper.)

'The widow's mite'
Much of the republican animosity towards the monarchy in the 1880s and 1890s focused on the issue of the Queen's wealth. The monarch was often seen as the major obstacle to social equality.
('The widow's mite' by Phil May, *Bulletin*, 27 February 1886, Image Library, State Library of New South Wales.)

economic and social change. Colonial societies were becoming increasingly urbanised, especially in New South Wales and Victoria where more than half the population lived in cities or towns. Almost 75 per cent of men were wage earners, and the shift from a predominantly pastoral and commercial society to a predominantly industrial commercial society was well underway.[47] As colonial economies moved towards the economy characteristic of modern industrial societies in Europe, similar patterns of social inequality and class rivalry developed in Australia.

The appearance of various republican movements in New South Wales, Victoria and Queensland between 1887 and 1893 was associated closely with the clash between labour and capital. As the swelling labouring classes looked for solutions to social dislocation, unequal distribution of wealth and the need for collective and institutional structures with which to negotiate with the capitalist class, they turned to the theories of European and American socialists. Especially in Sydney, an alternative political culture, led largely by a literate and self-educated artisan class, many of them 'refugees from London's declining trades', eagerly debated the various political ideologies which would deliver the New World utopia for the coming century. Looking back on the intellectual climate of the 1880s and 1890s in Sydney, republican George Black described these years as a time of 'mental upheaval' and 'intellectual readjustment': 'We studied night and day all the political economic and philosophical treatises . . . and subjected to close scrutiny every new scheme for the regeneration of mankind'.[48]

It was from this cauldron of predominantly derivative socialist philosophies that the first republican leagues were born. Like the word 'republican', socialism was understood in various ways. On certain occasions it implied the collective ownership of the land and means of production, distribution, and exchange, as it did for the English socialist league of William Morris and its Australian counterpart, the Australian Socialist League. At other times, it meant a single Joh Bjelke-Petersen-style tax on unimproved land values which would miraculously result in an equal distribution of wealth, a classless society and a new sense of community. Sometimes it represented authoritarian state socialism, and sometimes it was anti-authoritarian and anarchist. Finally, it could simply express a platitudinous desire to be 'mates'—as it did for the Riverina *Hummer* in 1892.[49] But whatever its 'meaning' the doctrines of socialism were establishing the key terms of political debate—capital versus labour.

In its various guises socialism was frequently the bedfellow of republicanism, and the distinctions between the two were often quite arbitrary. Theoretically, at least, republican government was the logical conclusion for all those who subscribed to socialist philosophies. After all, monarchy was the very bastion of the class-ridden society which socialists sought to obliterate. All those who attended public lectures, read newspapers or engaged in reformist political activity of some kind were exposed to a common diet of literature. A glance at any of the pages advertising books, pamphlets or journals in the republican or socialist press reveals that there was a mutual bank of potential influence.[50] The writings of the American socialists, Henry George, Edward Bellamy and Laurence Grönlund, were particularly popular together with works in the free thinking, deist tradition of English radicalism, such as Morrison Davidson's *Book of Kings*, Max Nordau's *Conventional Lies* and Paine's *Rights of Man*. Populist and utopian, all of these works bore a strong distaste for monarchy, aristocracy and the social inequalities of capitalism. Morrison Davidson's *Book of Kings*, originally published in London in 1872, was widely quoted in the *Bulletin*, the *Radical* and the *Republican*. Davidson's book typified the philosophy of the republican movements in England during the 1870s. His history of the monarchy in Britain presented a colourful if somewhat repetitive tale of the monarchy as 'plunderers, imbeciles, tyrants, scoundrels, torturers, adulterers, bigots and debauched, crooked, self-willed, heartless liars'.[51] The *Bulletin*'s depiction of monarchy was not dissimilar: 'The Royal family exists to play baccarat and lay foundation stones, and make dreary speeches at dreary institutes ... to yawn vacuously over addresses from bumpkin corporations and to be fat and stupid and unutterably dreary'.[52]

In the colonies, this view of monarchy was one which was not exclusively republican but common to a broad cross-section of political reformers, many of whom would not necessarily have referred to themselves as 'republicans'. Criticising monarchy for its opulence was a common feature of working-class politics in Australia, just as it was in England. To understand the republicanism of the 1880s and 1890s we must appreciate that republican sympathies did not always translate into an active campaign for republican independence. Republicanism was merely one of several highly derivative 'isms' which competed for the allegiance of political reformers, manifesting itself in a fluid and largely minority political culture in which philosophical boundaries were difficult to discern. The question which springs immediately to mind is why certain political reformers chose to enclose their programme of reform within the dream of an Australian republic. There is no simple answer, but much can be explained by the convenient sense of occasion provided by historical circumstance. The Queen's Jubilee year and the celebration of the centenary of settlement in 1888 would alone provide sufficient provocation for republicanism to take centre stage. For a short time, the *fin de siècle* utopia would become an Australian republic.

The *Bulletin*, which had been sceptical of the institution of monarchy since its inception and consistently resistant to the prospect of Imperial Federation, was by 1887 beginning to evince a more belligerent and impatient form of nationalist rhetoric. Widely circulated, and with a large and informed readership, it was the *Bulletin* under the editorship of J. F. Archibald which, according to Henry Lawson, fostered a purely 'Australian school of Art and Literature' and through its encouragement of Australian writers, became synonymous with the 'spirit of Australia'.[53] In 1887 the *Bulletin* spoke often of Australia's need to attain its 'freedom and manhood', but by its own admission 'the idea of national independence' was still 'vague and undefined'. Beyond 'a determination to break away from the vicious traditions and mischievous institutions of the old world', the *Bulletin* had little idea of what form the future Australian nation might take. It spent most of its time vilifying the Chinese or the pretensions of the English aristocracy otherwise known as those 'inflated boobys' 'Sir Tom or Sir Dick'.[54]

The *Bulletin*'s representation of political life as a struggle between evil capitalists and virtuous workers was reminiscent of the same English journals it quoted so frequently. Archibald, for example, had clearly been influenced by the proletarian *Reynolds News* during his stay in London. English republicans of the 1870s, such as Charles Bradlaugh, became the pin-up boys of republicans in Australia.[55] Bradlaugh espoused an essentially populist form of republicanism not dissimilar to that found in Morrison Davidson's *Book of Kings*. The dominant thesis was straightforward: monarchy and the privileged pillars of society which it protected—the civil list, the House of Lords and the aristocracy—were fat with wealth, corrupt and resistant to democratic reform. Monarchy, being the most public and visible symbol of class inequality, shouldered most of the blame for economic inequality. Consequently, this form of republicanism involved a vituperative assault on the public cost of monarchy with all-too-easy juxtapositions of a 100-kg monarch and the spartan virtue of the working male.[56]

Similar philosophies were evident in Australian political movements of the 1880s such as the Australian Socialist League, which was formed in Sydney in May 1887 and contained many members of later republican organisations. Members of these groups were sharply divided over both theoretical and practical issues. Some, such as the Melbourne Anarchists, were more doctrinaire and did not perceive monarchy or the imperial connection as the main threat to Australian labour.[57] Others, like the Australian Socialist League, were republican but more internationalist than nationalist.[58] Yet, in spite of these differences, there was a common distaste for monarchy and imperial ritual. While these movements were not significant in terms of membership, many of their beliefs were discussed in the pages of the *Bulletin*, the *Radical* in Newcastle, the *Liberator* in Melbourne and the *Boomerang* in Brisbane, as well as in countless numbers of public debates and meetings. It was this intellectual milieu—which John

Docker has described as the 'bourgeois public sphere'—which captivated the nineteen-year-old Henry Lawson in 1887 in Sydney.[59]

The 'radical and free thought' lectures to which Lawson and so many others were exposed in the early 1880s, as well as Archibald's *Bulletin*, were the wellspring of the republicans' populist message—Labour over Capital! New World over Old! Australia for the Australians!

1887—The Jubilee Year and the Republican Riots

> The droughts of the early eighties, coming with the pleuro, the rabbits, crop and vine diseases and other troubles, burst a lot of us round there. Some old selectors did pick-and-shovel work in the city, or drove drays, while their wives took in washing. I worked for sub-contractors in coach-factories, painting; tramped the cities in search of work; saw the haggard little group in front of the board outside the *Herald* office at 4 o'clock in the morning, striking matches to run down the 'Wanted' columns; saw the slums and the poor—and wished that I could write, or paint.
>
> I heard Tommy Walker, and Collins, and the rest of 'em, and, of course, a host of Yankee free-thought and socialistic lecturers. I wore the green in fancy, gathered at the rising of the moon, charged for the fair land of Poland, and dreamed of dying on the barricades to the roar of the Marseillaise—for the Young Australian Republic. Then came the unexpected and inexplicable outburst of popular feeling (or madness)—called then the Republican riots—in '87, when the Sydney crowd carried a disloyal amendment on the Queen's Jubilee, and cheered, at the Town Hall, for an 'Australian Republic'. And I had to write then—or burst. The *Bulletin* saved me from bursting.[60]

This was how Henry Lawson described the republicanism of 1887, the year when Sydney played host to an embarrassing series of 'republican riots' during the public celebrations for Queen Victoria's Jubilee.

The Jubilee celebrations epitomised the metamorphosis of Queen Victoria from shy, retiring monarch to matriarch of the British Empire. The streets of Sydney and Melbourne were festooned with lamps, illuminations and banners. Public transport was painted in red, white and blue. Buildings, statues, parks, parades and countless speeches were devoted to the glory of Queen Victoria.[61]

On Tuesday 31 May 1887 a meeting was held in Sydney, attended largely by politicians and businessmen, to consider methods of celebrating the Queen's Jubilee. 'Thirty gentlemen' subscribed £370 and decided that a public meeting should be held on the following Friday 3 June at Sydney Town Hall to discuss the matter further.[62]

When this meeting was convened it attracted an interesting audience. The *Sydney Morning Herald* described the majority of the 150 persons present as 'democrats' while the *Daily Telegraph* referred to them as emanating from the 'comparative obscurity of the School of Arts debating society'.[63] To everyone's surprise, the meeting had been hijacked by those antagonistic to the Jubilee. Chief among the rebels was the thirty-year-old Thomas Walker, the Lancashire-born secularist and republican whose brilliant lectures were to inspire Henry and Louisa Lawson, and the republican trade unionist John Norton who was later to edit the *Truth*.

When a fairly innocuous motion was moved that a fete should be given to the Sunday school children of Sydney to celebrate Queen Victoria's fifty years on the throne, it was overwhelmingly rejected. Instead, 'in an orderly fashion', a resolution was passed which declared that, in the opinion of the meeting, 'the proposal to impress upon the children of this colony the value of the Jubilee Year of the Sovereign is unwise and calculated to injure the democratic spirit of the colony'. A startled Mayor Riley wasted no time in closing the meeting lest even more embarrassing resolutions be passed.[64] This premeditated coup by the city's nondescript 'democrats' shocked the conservative press. While the *Bulletin* praised the meeting's outcome as 'one of the most important in the history of the people', the *Herald* and *Telegraph* blamed the 'sluggish apathy' of the city's loyal majority for failing to attend.[65] Although the word 'republic' had not been mentioned at the meeting, the *Telegraph* was in no doubt as to the source of the trouble: 'The gushing travellers who write ecstatic books about the loyalty of the Australian colonies ignore a great deal ... The fact is that there is a very strong anti-Imperialist and republican sentiment growing in this community'.[66] Republican sentiment indeed, but still ill-defined and focused predominantly on a rejection of the Jubilee. It was still nothing more than stirring.

The *Sydney Morning Herald* on the other hand was more spiteful and bent on atoning for the embarrassment which the meeting would cause the colonies in London: 'the matter must not be allowed to rest. The citizens of Sydney will scarcely be prepared to let this record go forth as the will and action of the colony. Immediate steps should be taken to neutralise the effect of last night's meeting'.[67]

And so they were. As with the Bailes fiasco in Victoria, the sin had been committed and now it had to be eradicated from public memory. Immediately a second meeting was called for Friday 10 June, again at the Sydney Town Hall. When the *Brisbane Courier* heard the news of the first Sydney meeting it passed a comment which unfortunately went unheeded in Sydney. The great majority of colonists were loyal, said the *Courier*, but this loyalty was 'passive rather than active'. There was little real 'enthusiasm over the business' but disloyalty would only be encouraged if the 'inflated phraseology' of public addresses continued to be out of keeping with the more sober 'sentiments of the majority'.[68] The

Courier's assessment was probably correct. If the republicans in Sydney were a radical minority then so were the gushing loyalists. The bulk of the community appeared to be moved by neither extreme. None the less, by the time of the second meeting they were preparing for a violent clash.

Aware that the democrats, republicans, socialists, secularists and free-thought rabble would again try to hijack proceedings, organisers of the second meeting decided to indulge in some dirty pool. They issued personal invitation cards to those persons deemed 'suitable' to attend. Holders of the cards were specifically instructed to appear at the Druitt Street entrance of the Town Hall no later than 7.15 p.m. (the meeting had been advertised in the press for 8 p.m.). The idea was cunning, fill the Town Hall with loyalists, then when the doors opened at 7.30 p.m. there would be hardly any room for the general public. The colonial elite had little confidence in the loyalty of the 'lower' classes and their fears would soon be justified. By mid-afternoon on Friday the attempt to deceive the public had failed. One whisper about the invitation cards and the bush telegraph did the rest. As soon as the republicans got wind of the plan they began to forge their own invitation cards. Led by John Norton they quickly printed circulars which were passed around the city:

> Dear Sir,
> The toadies and office seekers will roll up in great force on this occasion to endeavour to reverse the grand decision of last Friday night. The honour and independence of our country demand your attendance and that of your friends on this occasion. Let nothing short of death prevent your getting an early seat. Pass this circular round.[69]

Much to the chagrin of the authorities Norton's scheme proved extremely successful. The Druitt Street gates were opened at 7 p.m. but the false invitation cards were not discovered until 7.30 p.m. Many dissenters had managed to gain entrance. As soon as the forgeries were revealed extra police were quickly stationed at the gates while agitated committee men frantically tried to inspect tickets. Norton himself managed to get inside on several occasions before the commencement of the meeting only to be 'ejected' by police. A large crowd had gathered outside the Town Hall since well before 7 p.m. and their mood had become steadily more volatile, so much so that the noise of the crowd could be heard inside the hall.

When the gates were opened shortly after 7.30 p.m. 'a tremendous rush of excited men and youths ensued'. Inside, rows of chairs had been placed as close to the platform as possible. On the platform there were 'several ladies' and 'a number of leading colonists' including Sir Alfred Stephen, the Lieutenant-Governor and Sir Frederick Darley, the Chief Justice—or in the words of the *Bulletin*, 'all the Sir Williams, Sir Georges,

Sir Henrys, Sir Thomases and Sir Albans capable of being raked together in Sydney—the big fish who had come out for a swim'.[70] Very quickly the Town Hall was packed with somewhere between 2000 and 3000 people while thousands more waited outside, unable to gain admittance. The *Sydney Morning Herald* described the events that followed:

> Standing room was unobtainable in the aisles or galleries, and the walls and niches were lined with men and youths. The police, . . . aided by the Town Hall assistants in a body, kept what amount of good order it was possible to obtain, but beyond checking an occasional hand-to-hand fight at the outset, they were powerless from the force of overwhelming numbers.
>
> At 8 o'clock, the Mayor, whose voice was drowned by groans, hisses, cat-calls, and loud cheering, made an ineffectual attempt to declare the meeting opened . . . after the lapse of about an hour, during which an incessant and deafening roar was kept up, the Mayor remarked that the hall was not large enough to hold the meeting, and that he would consequently adjourn it until Wednesday afternoon next, at the Exhibition Building, Prince Alfred Park . . . Before the Mayor took this action a scene of a rather lively character took place. One of the leaders of the New South Wales Secular Association was urged on the platform, but immediately pushed off. This move was resented by some of his followers, and a rough and tumble wrestling match ensued. Fighting at this juncture broke out in all directions. The press table was rushed, and the chairs, table, and reporters were swept bodily away—the latter being forced to beat a hurried retreat to the platform. Their places having been immediately filled, a mob crept upon the table, and with sticks, umbrellas, and fists held their posts, until they were either knocked or dragged to the floor. In the lulls between violent discussion and party groans and counter cheers, voices in several quarters were heard to interject, 'Three cheers for the Queen,' and others, 'Three cheers for liberty. Englishmen, and their offspring', each call being the signal for fresh uproar and additional free-fights. Every now and then the enthusiastic loyalists on the platform burst forth with a verse of the National Anthem to which a chorus of groans and hisses was supplied by many in the body of the hall.
>
> Those on the platform were the leading citizens of Sydney, including members of both Houses of the Legislature, aldermen,—clergymen, magistrates, barristers, bankers, merchants, etc. So great was the disturbance that Mr Foebery was driven to the necessity of calling in the major portion of the police on street patrol, and it was only by this means that the hall was cleared . . . and many of the more rowdy were forcibly ejected.
>
> A meeting of citizens was subsequently held in the Mayor's reception rooms, under the presidency of his worship the Mayor.[71]

The *Herald* omitted to say that amidst the confusion there were continued cheers for 'separation', an Australian republic and the Australian people. In fact, in the half-hour that it took for the meeting to close there were repeated and 'resounding' cheers for a republic. Norton in particular, had managed to give the demonstrations a nationalist republican edge. The demonstrators had succeeded in forcing the 'toadies' they despised to abandon the meeting. In a state of shock, thirty or so dignitaries, led by Mayor Riley and Premier Henry Parkes, immediately adjourned to the Mayor's room above the vestibule for the purposes of holding an 'indignation meeting'.[72] Predictable volleys of abuse and florid protestations of loyalty then ensued. Mayor Riley spoke as 'an Australian' and expressed his 'outrage' and embarrassment at the disorder precipitated by 'the enemy'. Other speakers, in particular the Chief Justice Sir Frederick Darley, called for the republican threat to be stamped out by closing public theatres to all those who held objectionable ideas. Speaker after speaker confessed their 'disgust' and 'sadness', yet as always, it was Henry Parkes who rose to deliver the most resounding denunciation of republicanism. Parkes now had forty years of experience to draw on. The arguments he had used with such great effect during the Anti-Transportation debates in the 1850s had not been forgotten and on this occasion he was no longer an aspiring politician but Premier of New South Wales. His speech was vindictive but masterly:

> These persons would rebel tomorrow against a Republican form of government, just as much as they profess to rebel against a monarchical form of government. They are, in fact, enemies of society. (Loud cheers). They are the professors of lawlessness and of hatred of everyone and everything that is higher and better than themselves. (Cheers) . . . We must do something more than talk. (Renewed cheers) . . . we must unite as one man—shoulder to shoulder—as a loyal British people, and we must not rest until we have given the lie to these scandalous proceedings as representing even a considerable multitude of the law abiding people of this country.[73]

This was Parkes at his best. Holed up in the vestibule with thirty 'indignant' gentlemen while crowds milled outside the Town Hall gates, Parkes retained all the arrogance of a despot. Like his colleagues, Parkes believed that the thousands outside constituted a 'minority' while the loyalist rump that had taken flight represented the majority. This was an indication of just how far Parkes had moved away from the ideas of the young democrat who had eagerly offered his support to John Dunmore Lang in the early 1850s. Not only did he reject republicanism, he asserted that the demonstrators were not even worthy of the label 'republican'. This theme was also picked up by the colonial press. Demonstrators were curiously described as rowdy ruffians, 'larrikins', 'criminals', 'wild beasts', 'anarchists', 'enemies of society', 'a howling mob', 'blackguards from the slums', 'a troop of wild Indians' or 'slinking furtive wretches'.[74] The *Brisbane Courier*, like the *Argus* in Melbourne, identified the source of Sydney disloyalty: '. . . Sydney, . . . was for over two generations the refuse heap of

Great Britain . . . The Sydney larrikin is a more degraded and brutal wretch than even his repulsive fellows in other Australian capitals'.[75]

Blaming Sydney's convict past may have reassured the people of Brisbane and Melbourne that similar embarrassment could not befall their own cities, but it did little to identify the true source of discontent. Parkes was well aware that the working classes of Sydney were being led to republican and secularist philosophies by the likes of Thomas Walker and John Norton, and he was not the only one to show concern. Leading members of the Sydney clergy had repeatedly lobbied Parkes to close all public theatres on Sundays in an effort to curb the spread of secularist and republican lectures. On the Saturday morning after the Town Hall meeting, Parkes, still reeling from the events of the previous evening, met with a delegation from the Ministers Union. It was after this meeting that Parkes took the extraordinary step in his capacity as Premier of closing all public theatres on Sundays. The fact that Parkes acted less than twenty-four hours after the Town Hall meeting, before the matter could even be discussed in parliament, showed just how determined he was to retaliate quickly. Forced to rely on an outdated Act passed during the reign of George III which bore somewhat tenuous relevance to the case in hand, Parkes had taken a draconian stand.[76] The news travelled quickly through the city on the Saturday evening and by Sunday police constables had been ordered to stand guard outside theatres in case crowds should try to force their way inside. When Walker and Norton saw that the Theatre Royal was under guard they adjourned to the pedestal at the top of King Street:

> The crowd swelled rapidly till it filled the whole space from Macquarie Street to St. James Church and extended around the other side of the pedestal towards Hyde Park . . . The assemblage might be estimated . . . at about 6,000 . . . At about 20 minutes past 7 a cart was driven in near to the pedestal and took up a position from which several speakers addressed the meeting.[77]

With such a large and sympathetic crowd, it appeared to be the perfect opportunity for the gains of Friday night's meeting to be consolidated by launching a campaign for republican independence based on an appeal to the fundamental liberty of freedom of speech. Yet there was no mention of republicanism. Those who spoke at the meeting and those who formed a deputation to see Parkes on the following day made it clear that they were intent only on ensuring the withdrawal of Parkes' declaration. Norton, referring to himself not as a republican but as a 'trade unionist', stressed that the people would object in a constitutional manner, while Walker claimed that although he himself was a republican he knew just as many loyalists that were opposed to Parkes' edict.[78]

It seemed that the earlier cheers for an Australian republic had suddenly become irrelevant or else too politically divisive to risk losing the support of the loyalists who also opposed Parkes. Faced with a reactionary law, Friday night's rebellious republicans became Sunday's constitutionalists. The following Friday, Walker organised a deputation of 'citizens' whose task it was to ask the Governor to cable the Queen the following message:

> That we the citizens of Sydney deeply regret that this Jubilee year of Her Majesty's reign should be sullied by the action of the Colonial Secretary in closing the theatres on Sunday against the people, a suppression of the right of free speech and an infringement of the liberty of the people.[79]

While Walker's avoidance of the word 'republic' was politically expedient, there was something wonderfully ironic about a group of citizens, dutifully petitioning the Queen to come to their aid when only days before many of them had cried out against her. Unwittingly, they had participated in a process which was to remain one of the fundamental reasons for the irrelevance of separatist republicanism in Australia. Republicans were constitutionalists at heart and for the majority of Australians the Queen was not the symbol of oppression but of basic human freedoms, and she became even more so after the Jubilee.[80]

Much of the opposition which Parkes faced in the press and in parliament was based on the assumption that he had sullied the very principles of the English Constitution which the Queen embodied. In his attempt to thwart a supposedly disloyal minority Parkes had only succeeded in forcing many loyalists to side with the alleged republicans. The general consensus in the press, despite the fact that Parkes had support inside the parliament, seemed to be that the measure was hasty, unnecessary, intolerant and potentially inflammatory.[81] As the *Telegraph* observed, 'the dual division' entertained by Parkes and other 'reactionary orators' between 'loyalists' and 'disloyalists' or 'Christians' and 'infidels' was entirely misguided. In reality the community held sympathy for neither 'class of extremists'. Instead, they cared simply for 'the principles of intellectual freedom'.[82]

The stage was set for an enthralling battle on the occasion of the third meeting, and during all this time the schoolchildren of Sydney remained blissfully unaware of just how hard their representatives had been working to secure a picnic on their behalf. The resolve of Parkes and his indignant loyalists had only hardened after the disastrous meeting at the Town Hall. They promptly decided that an attempt would be made to hold a third meeting at the Royal Exhibition building at Prince Alfred Park on Wednesday 15 June. In the days leading up to the meeting the city was abuzz with rumours of impending violence and disorder. There seemed

The Recent great Public Meeting of Loyalists, held in the Exhibition Building, Prince Alfred Park, Sydney.
(See Letterpress on another Page.)
1. Precautions. 2. The Rush at the Door. 3. The Gallery. 4. Lord and Lady Carrington on the Platform. 5. Shifting a Republican. 6. A would-be Speaker.

Meeting of loyalists
During the so-called republican riots in Sydney in 1887, republicans were frequently denied the right to free speech. If they did manage to get past the front door at loyalist rallies, they soon found themselves at the exit if they dared to speak out.
(*Town and Country Journal*, 25 June 1887, Image Library, State Library of New South Wales.)

to be a definite fear that the meeting would once again be overrun by those disloyal to the Queen. To reduce the risk of another display of disloyalty the especially-appointed organising committee cleverly arranged for Lord and Lady Carrington to be in attendance. An earlier public meeting which Lady Carrington was due to attend for charity was cancelled and merged with the meeting at the Exhibition Centre. The committee hoped the broad popularity of the Governor and his wife would discourage any plans to disrupt the meeting.[83]

When the day finally arrived it soon became apparent that the public 'meeting' had become a public 'rally' of loyalists backed up by police, standover men and military force. The committee had left nothing to chance. Determined to stamp out any hint of disloyalty or republicanism they had a battle plan drawn up as if they were about to go to war. Dividing the building into six sections, they placed large numbers of various loyalist organisations—including 'a contingent of hair-oiled dudes from the Primrose League'—in each compartment.[84] In addition, uniformed police were placed at every entrance and exit while plain-clothed police mixed among the crowd. At Hyde Park Barracks, troops loaded their guns and waited for the call to arms. As the *Bulletin* described the scene, it seemed that the city was in a state of siege:

> Every available engine of cunning and violence was called into requisition by the promoters and the press to make the disgraceful orgie of that Wednesday night a decided success. The Orangemen of Sydney were massed in hundreds and were admitted *by password* long before the doors were thrown open to the public; 400 footballers, wearing heavy boots, rolled up at the call of a youthful softgoodsman, and were placed where they might kick to the best advantage on behalf of the good cause; the University, an aristocratic institution run by a well-paid crowd of imported English Tories, sent 150 rowdy youths to the scene of action; the Primrose League gathered a hollow-chested battalion badly off for brains, and its cultured members rubbed against a gang of professional prize-fighters, who had mustered to slog for the British Crown; almost the entire police and detective force of Sydney, too, was pressed into the service, as were also the men of the Naval Brigade and Naval Reserve, the Volunteer Artillery, the Sydney Lancers, and a large number of blue-jackets from the British men-of-war in the Harbour. More than 3,000 soldiers, sailors, pugilists and bullies of all descriptions were collected to silence opposition and assail those whose 'loyalty' was suspected, and yet each successive speaker asked his audience to believe that the Australian party, against whom all these preparations were made, were only an insignificant handful of malcontents, so few in number as to be not worth notice.[85]

The *Sydney Morning Herald* referred to these measures as 'precautions' but the massing of so much loyalist muscle and firepower was more symptomatic of colonial psychosis than the threat posed by the republican 'enemy'. The rally had become a vehicle for the major institutions in the city (and anyone who wished to join them) to vent their anger after the embarrassment of the previous two meetings. Loyalty was declared by stamping a military boot on to an allegedly minority republican face. As usual, Henry Parkes led the charge:

> We meet here tonight to wipe out a burning disgrace ... and to tread disloyalty into dust. [We assert] the loyalty of this people and our devotion to the throne and person of the Queen and to the laws and institutions of the Empire—This meeting is a noble response to the riotous disgraceful and scandalous insults that have been cast upon the city—and it says in triumphant tones that we will not submit to the clique of seditious and cowardly tyrants ... [who] would rob us of all liberty of speech.[86]

While Parkes spoke about liberty of speech, John Norton tried on several occasions to gain admission to the platform but was denied access. Even Norton's written amendment, which he had succeeded in giving to the chairman of the meeting after much difficulty, was not read to the audience. At the same time, several 'republicans' were forcibly removed from the meeting by police. It seemed that freedom of speech was not to be granted to republicans. Although the city's leading papers portrayed the meeting as an enormous success, the proceedings were still characterised by a reasonable degree of disorder which the *Herald* described as 'alarming'. When a banner was raised by a group in front of the platform which called on the meeting to support the establishment of a fund for the colony's destitute women, the crowd suddenly became 'disorganised'—people rushed the platform and fought in 'hand-to-hand combat'. Civilians and police were involved in a general 'melee' which extended along the front of the platform. So intense was the struggle that the chairman's cedar table and several chairs were completely smashed. During all this time the band dutifully played 'Rule Britannia' and 'God Bless the Prince of Wales'. The meeting continued in this manner until the arrival of Lord and Lady Carrington. Then, like a classroom of recalcitrant schoolboys suddenly coming to attention, the crowd came to order.[87]

It was clear the press had failed to acknowledge that there was still a considerable element of dissent—despite the mustering of all the King's men. Loyalty had not been spontaneously displayed, instead it had been contrived, almost at gunpoint. Speaking in the Legislative Assembly on the following day, George Dibbs offered an accurate assessment of the meeting:

> We have loyalty run mad just at present and there is a great deal of lip loyalty ...

> What did we find last night at the public meeting? Loyalty enforced at the point of the bayonet! ... We found the building packed, and ruled over by the military, and by an organised body of loyal Orangemen who were hunted up for nights and days by a minister of the Crown. ... thirty or forty others were [also] there to punch the heads of her Majesty's subjects ... who dared to open their mouths to speak.[88]

Unfortunately, this kind of honesty was sadly lacking in the colony's press. The *Sydney Morning Herald* preferred to use euphemisms such as 'good humoured scrimmage' to describe the disorder at the meeting. The *Daily Telegraph* claimed the meeting had been 'a victory for law and order and the rights of free speech'—proof that 'the Walkers, Nortons and Joneses' ... 'so ridiculously anxious to cut the painter [had] completely miscalculated the community'. The *Town and Country Journal* omitted any mention of dissent and devoted more time to 'Sydney Jubilee fashions'.[89] As the *Bulletin* rightly explained, the Sydney dailies fabricated 'a glowing and wholly false account of the affair'. There seemed to be an almost manic determination on the part of the press to suppress the truth about the meeting and prove that 'the heart of Australia still beats true to her mother England'. Time and time again papers stressed that the meeting had scouted 'the Dead Sea apple of republicanism', repudiating 'everything disloyal'. Doctored cables were quickly sent off to London so that the desired reply would alleviate any sense of guilt. Eventually, the London correspondents cabled the message that Sydney longed to hear: 'Her Majesty has expressed her gratification at the result of the recent royalist meeting at the Sydney Exhibition building'.[90]

While the rally was perhaps the largest public gathering in Sydney's history, somewhere in the vicinity of 20 000 people, it is doubtful that the majority were as fanatically loyal as the papers supposed.[91] As the loyalist *Sydney Mail* admitted:

> The great mass of colonists live their little life thinking seldom of kings and queens, and as seldom of any government except their own. They hear from time to time of such subjects as Imperial federation and national defence but such matters have little or no interest for them. Topics like these, Australian colonists are content to leave to the newspapers. But little as the average colonist troubles himself about the British connection he has no wish to see the connection severed.[92]

By the end of the Jubilee celebrations, if the average colonist did advocate separation, that voice would either be drowned in a torrent of loyalist propaganda or be pushed outside the normal boundaries of political life. The action of the 'republicans' in Sydney during the Jubilee, and the response of the authorities, demonstrated the manner in which much anti-monarchical sentiment had been suppressed by the upper-class monopoly of public meetings and a press which was eager to omit certain realities.[93] Parkes' absurd request in parliament for an expression of loyalty from the house—one which was eventually carried—was also framed in such a way as to exclude the possibility of a republic. Parkes read the motion only one day after the third meeting. The show trial atmosphere of the previous day had clearly not been enough. Parkes asked the parliament to declare its 'unalterable attachment . . . to the laws and institutions of the British Empire'.[94] The most appropriate reply came from Henry Copeland:

> If we are to assert 'unalterable' attachment to the laws and institutions of the Empire, what are we here for? Hardly a session passes that we do not enact laws antagonistic to the laws of the British Empire. I need only refer . . . to our divorce laws, vote by ballot, and manhood suffrage.[95]

Parkes' pretext for the loyalty motion was based on the embarrassing events of the first two meetings and the existence of a pamphlet published by the Melbourne secularist and editor of the *Liberator*, Joseph Symes. Parkes alleged the pamphlet had been passed around at the second meeting and contained the most 'gross, brutal' and 'indecent' attack on the Queen. So 'vile' was the attack that Parkes was forced to protect the loyal ears of the house from its contents. As George Dibbs remarked, why the house should work itself into such a frenzy over one pamphlet published in Melbourne of all places was a mystery. Other members taunted Parkes with accusations that he was creating 'another Treason Felony affair'. When Parkes was pressed as to why he had not prosecuted Symes, he replied in an annoyed fashion, 'he is in Melbourne we cannot prosecute him'. The comedy continued with Parkes then insisting that the house be subjected to a lengthy oration on the virtues of Queen Victoria's reign. Even members who supported Parkes' motion were heard to cry out 'No', 'We know all that!'—'Go home and read it!'[96] But Parkes carried on regardless. One week later, he announced that the government would not grant permission for lectures to be held in public theatres on Sundays, especially those against Christianity or in 'favour of republicanism'. This was a measure meant to satisfy political pressure exerted by conservatives and the clergy, rather than any serious obstacle to republicans or secularists. Yet it was Parkes more than any other politician who had once again played the role of *oberführer*—the grand conductor of asinine expressions of loyalty and spiteful attacks on republicans.[97]

The 'white heat' of loyalty also carried on outside parliament. After hearing of the fracas in Sydney, rural towns cabled declarations of loyalty, signed by hundreds of citizens.[98] The Adelaide *Advertiser* remarked after the celebrations that the colony was recovering from 'an attack of Jubilee on the brain'—'We have had Jubilee for breakfast, lunch and dinner, it has been with us waking and sleeping'. One letter writer to the *Sydney Morning Herald* pointed out that if crowds of between 30 and 60 000 regularly attended cricket matches in the Domain then a prayer meeting for the Queen might attract similar crowds to Hyde Park. Churches devoted masses and prayers to the Queen while others talked of a law which would force all citizens to wear badges to proclaim their loyalty. Meanwhile the press continually extended the boundaries of hyperbole with blandishments such as this one from the *Illustrated Sydney News*: 'Her Majesty the Queen, we all firmly believe, is at the apex, so to speak, of the pyramid of her sex'. The chorus of praise for Victoria seemed resounding. Even the Irish Catholic *Freeman's Journal*, which had been critical of the whitewashed public celebrations, distanced itself from the sentiments expressed at the first two meetings.[99] If ever there was any doubt that republicanism in the 1880s was not instigated by an ethnic enclave of Irish republicans, a glance through the pages of the *Freeman's Journal* will suffice. For the *Freeman's Journal* Irish home rule and Catholicism mattered more than any dream of an Australian republic. Publicly at least, the Catholic clergy often paid their dues to the Crown—one example being Cardinal Moran's sermon on the occasion of the Queen's Jubilee. On that day, Irish Catholics joined a church parade to celebrate Victoria's reign and Moran left no doubt in the minds of his congregation that loyalty to the monarch was an essential duty for all Catholics in the colony:

> We cannot be faithful . . . to God unless we show to the temporal ruler the loyalty honour and obedience which are his due . . . It is your duty not only to be loyal to your sovereign but to be the assertors of that loyalty and if needs be, to become with your very lives a bulwark, a rampart around the throne . . . every best interest of this colony—its peace and liberty, and prosperity—are all linked with fealty to the throne.[100]

While Moran was hardly likely to advocate a republic from the pulpit, the sermon does indicate the manner in which loyalist indoctrination touched all segments of the community, even those groups who were traditionally seen as the most resistant. But throughout all of the Jubilee festivities, meetings and speeches in June, it remained abundantly clear that there was a growing public debate on republicanism which had been fostered more by the over-reaction of the ruling elite than any groundswell of republican sentiment. By the end of June the events in Sydney had encouraged newspaper editorials, public lectures, illustrations and many letters to the editor on the respective merits of republican and monarchical systems of government. The debate ranged across the colony of New South Wales and could also be found in Melbourne, Hobart, Brisbane and Adelaide.[101] The clash of Sydney's larrikins and rabid loyalists had ignited the imagination of all colonists. Loyalty, the republic, Federation and Australia's future suddenly dominated public debate. As the *Newcastle Morning Herald* observed, 'republic or monarchy' was 'a subject which even the most ardent loyalist must admit is receiving ... frequent discussion in the lecture hall, on the platform and in the columns of the public press'. Although much of the debate focused on theoretical distinctions or on the issue of cost, for many colonists there was an undeniable feeling that the time had arrived 'when the colony ought to sever its connection with England' and 'manage its own affairs'.[102]

At the end of June, however, there was still a lack of any cohesive republican philosophy. Despite the cheers for a republic at the second meeting there was little evidence that the events of June were specifically republican. Indeed, it could be argued that the so-called republicans of June were simply intent on highlighting the disparity between the poor and destitute of the colony and the lavish celebrations for the Jubilee. Beyond the usual barbs about the Queen being 'an obese old woman fond of whisky' there was little structure or thought given to the resistance. The banner raised at the final meeting had not been for a republic but was instead a plea for economic justice for the colony's destitute women. Just as the Newcastle *Radical* suggested that it was not so much a matter of 'God Save the Queen' but 'God Save the Working Classes' many of the so-called 'republican' riots were 'republican' simply because it was the monarch who happened to bear the brunt of anti-loyalist sentiment. The primary motivation of the June rebels had always been to focus attention on the colony's needy and working classes. This explains why much of the 'republicanism' of the next twelve months focused on the issue of cost.[103]

The criticisms of Sir Alfred Stephen in the New South Wales Legislative Council were pertinent:

> I heard voices in that large assembly [the Town Hall meeting] desiring and suggesting cheers for a republic. What republic? The republic of NSW with these two insignificant men at the head of it, or is it a republic of the united colonies? ... The brawlers little considered the nonsense they were talking.[104]

While reports of the meeting showed that there were many cheers for a republic—what's in a cheer after all? No philosophical outline, no plan, no political programme, only sentiment.[105] True, republican *sentiment* had surfaced, and the matter had begun to dominate public debate but there was still no movement, and no answers for the arguments that awaited any such movement. Sir Alfred Stephen continued:

> In America, . . . there was undeniably injustice against which the people rose in revolt—the same principle for which Hampden rose, and became, by his resistance to illegality and tyranny, immortalised as a patriot . . . Where is here the oppression? Where is the injustice of which they have to complain? What circumstances, in the name of heaven, have given rise to the question of a republic here? . . . [We the people in effect] actually govern in her [the Queen's] name.[106]

By July, republicans would attempt to provide an answer.

CHAPTER EIGHT

Nation and Republic 1887–1891

> The Jubilee is viewed with as much coolness by the public in Australia as it is in the mother country. The fact is, and it must be apparent to every observant person, that republican ideas are rapidly spreading throughout the length and breadth of the British Empire.
> *Inquirer and Commercial News*, Perth, 11 May 1887

By mid-1887 republicanism was suddenly back on the political agenda after an absence of more than thirty-five years. Yet this 'republicanism' was not the republicanism of the 1850s. Unlike the earlier debates of the 1850s, the emergence of republican sentiment during the year of the Queen's Jubilee was not related so much to grievances with the Colonial Office as it was to issues such as loyalty, nationalism and inequality of wealth. Mention of the words 'Australian republic' in the 1880s and 1890s was a cry for a unique cultural and national identity, much more so than in the decade before the granting of responsible government. The turmoil of the 'republican riots' in June had crystallised a previously disparate and ill-directed opposition into a nationalist and republican movement. This movement, united more by sentiment than organisation, championed a new language of political dissent. Led by J. F. Archibald and the *Bulletin*, it began to filter a traditional socialist critique of monarchy through an aggressive nationalist perspective. The struggle was now not only between labour and capital or the city's destitute and an affluent monarch, but between the Australian and the British. The new democratic land of the Australian native, striving to assert his 'manhood' through independence, and the old corrupt land of the British imperialist.

Within three weeks of the final Jubilee meeting in Sydney there was a republican union, a republican journal and a defiantly republican *Bulletin*, writing what was to become the quintessential definition of its political nationalism:

> By the term Australian we mean not those who have been merely born in Australia. All white men who come to these shores—with a clean record—and who leave behind them the memory of the class distinctions and the religious differences of the old world: all men who place the happiness, the prosperity, the advancement of their adopted country before the interests of Imperialism, are Australian . . . Australian and Republican are synonymous. No nigger, no

'Only a name' and 'The imperial connection'

The *Bulletin*'s promotion of nationalist republicanism was often motivated by fear and racism. Above, we see Queen Victoria ridiculed through the equation of her title with those meted out to Aboriginal Australians by colonial whites, while below, Australian independence is seen as a means of stopping further Chinese immigration.

('Only a name' by Phil May, *Bulletin*, 2 July 1887; 'The imperial connection . . .', *Bulletin,* 14 April 1888, Image Library, State Library of New South Wales.)

Chinaman, no lascar, no kanaka, no purveyor of cheap coloured labour, is an Australian.[1]

This racist, isolationist, protectionist and 'masculine' republic became, for a short time, the most expedient flag to fly for the *Bulletin* and those who were sympathetic to its ideals, although not all republicans would consistently display the same degree of chauvinism as the *Bulletin*. In every colony, the constant comparison of monarchical and republican forms of government at a time when the colonies were witnessing the birth of national sentiment meant that the issue of a republic had to be publicly endorsed or rejected whenever the occasion demanded. Only one day after the *Bulletin* editorial, the Australian National Union was launched in Adelaide to 'stimulate a national patriotic feeling amongst Australians of all classes and creeds', and promote a unity of feeling among all the colonies of Australia. Predominantly conservative, the union was still more 'radical' than the *Bulletin* in its definition of an Australian. It insisted that members had to be born in Australia or to have arrived before the age of five years and resided in Australia for at least twenty-one years. The Union's inaugural meeting at the Adelaide Town Hall saw several speakers go to extreme lengths to reject any suggestion that the Union was feeling its way towards 'independent nationality and an Australian republic'.

The importance of these events in Adelaide is that they again demonstrate the manner in which the nationalist flower was not the exclusive property of the Sydney *Bulletin* or its republican supporters. An 'Australian patriotism' which sought to assert Australian national interest without 'weakening the ties to the mother country' was emerging at the same time as the *Bulletin*'s republican nationalism.[2] In Victoria, bodies such as the ANA projected similar sentiments, while in New South Wales it was perfectly natural for members of parliament to join with American citizens in Sydney to celebrate the American Declaration of Independence on 4 July. 'Natural' because for loyalists like William Bede Dalley and Alfred Stephen the American Revolution was the just overthrow of monarchical tyranny, the people's last line of defence, a situation which they believed would never come to pass in Australia where the monarch was effectively benign.[3] Consequently, when those present spoke of Australia following in the footsteps of American greatness, they did so without any thought that an Australian nation would be separated from Great Britain.

Back in Sydney, a nineteen-year-old Henry Lawson felt that he had to 'write or burst' after the 'inexplicable outburst of popular feeling' in June. Like his publicist and mentor, J. F. Archibald, the events of June fired a strong republicanism in Lawson:

> One wet night I was coming home through Hyde Park from working late on a job at Paddington. Rain and wind and swept boughs and sickly gaslights on the wet asphalt; and poles and scaffolding about in preparation for the Jubilee celebrations. I had sent a couple of attempts on the subject to the *Bulletin*, and had got encouragement in Answers to Correspondents. And now the idea of 'Sons of the South' or 'Song of the Republic' came. I wrote it and screwed up courage to go down to the *Bulletin* after hours, intending to drop the thing into the letter box, but, just as I was about to do so, . . . the door opened suddenly and a haggard woman stood there. And I shoved the thing into her hand and got away round the corner, feeling something like a person who had been nearly caught on the premises under suspicious circumstances . . .[4]

Lawson would not see 'Song of the Republic' published until October mainly because Archibald thought it too good to waste. The poem called on the 'Sons of the south' to rise up and choose between the 'old dead tree and the young tree green'.[5] But while Lawson wrote in vainglorious tone of an Australian republic led by men, it was a woman who was responsible for instigating Australia's first republican journal.

Louisa Lawson, Henry's mother, had come to Sydney from Mudgee with her family in the early 1880s. Independent and intellectually curious, it was Louisa who first made contact with Sydney's radical intelligentsia. Living in an old-fashioned double-fronted cottage at 138 Phillip Street, Louisa introduced her family to free thought, republicanism, secularism and socialism. The same intellectual independence that encouraged Louisa to abandon institutionalised religion also led her to advocate a republic and champion the rights of women.[6] When George Black brought Thomas Walker's zealous twenty-five-year-old secretary William Keep around to Phillip Street in late June, the idea for a republican journal was born. Keep had had republican connections in London where he had worked as a draper's assistant and a printer's apprentice. Now, as a young man who worked as a van proprietor in the Sydney suburb of St Peters, he was keen to devote himself to the struggle for an Australian republic. Louisa, Keep and Walker significantly chose the date of 4 July for the first edition of the *Republican*. Walker's republicanism had developed during the years he spent in the United States as a journalist, and the American War of Independence was an event he was only too pleased to commemorate by launching a republican journal, especially after the fiasco of the Jubilee celebrations.[7] Louisa obtained an old printing press and together with Walker, Black, Keep and her son Henry, she planned the first edition of the *Republican*. While the family dined and slept in the front rooms, the first edition of the *Republican* was produced in the back room of the Phillip Street cottage and issued from a small room which Keep had rented at 45 Stanley Street. The beginnings of the *Republican* were humble and comic as Henry Lawson related when he looked back many years later:

Nation and Republic 155

Louisa Lawson and Henry Lawson
Louisa Lawson, above, founder of the *Republican* and one of the most important figures in the struggle for women's rights in Australia's history. Below, the man himself, Louisa's son, Henry, photographed in his early twenties, his greatest republican writings already behind him.
(Image Library, State Library of New South Wales.)

The life of the *Republican* was a tragical farce now I come to look back at it. We got hold of a little old printing press that had been over the mountains in the early days—and Keep had been a draper in London. He was a weed then, but with the vitality, energy and blind self confidence of a dozen fat men . . . We had to turn the press by hand and it ran like a dray most of the time; we had to feed and fly by hand, too—when the press *was* going . . . there'd be a break-down or smash-up somewhere and Keep would go round briskly and cheerfully in front of the machine, behind it and under it, and squeeze between it and the wall, with a couple of spanners and a screw-wrench for odd nuts and screw up a nut here and loosen one there, and try her again, until at last, by some accident, or wonderful combination of accidents incomprehensible to me, he'd get her going all right . . . Then, towards the end, Keep would get excited, and, if it were a hot night, peel to his pants and shirt and rustle up every damaged or soiled sheet of paper from the floor and put it through. I believe if such a contingency had arisen to make it seem necessary, he would have put his shirt and pants through too, rather than disappoint two of our subscribers.

. . . The night after we'd fold, wrap (there wasn't much folding) and carry the papers to the post in the early hours in a clothes basket; and, before daylight we'd have a public breakfast at the old coffee stall outside the *Herald* office where Keep would argue politics and freethought and other things with cabmen and others.[8]

During its short lifespan, the *Republican* was kept afloat by Keep, swinging on a hammock over the printing press, dreaming of special editions. Although Walker, Black and the Lawsons all contributed at various levels it was Keep who did the bulk of the work. The first edition on 4 July carried a portrait of English republican, Charles Bradlaugh, on the front page, under the masthead 'Liberty, Fraternity, Equality'. The challenge, which the *Republican* acknowledged, was to organise the hitherto isolated and confused group of reformers who were sympathetic to the idea of an Australian republic. On the second page, under the title 'Australian Independence', the author (most probably Henry Lawson) pleaded for separation and independence instead of the 'abject grovelling to Royal ermine and jewelled heads' that occurred during the Queen's Jubilee. The events of June had been the primary factor behind the publication of the *Republican.* Articles focusing on 'Czar Parkes and his attempts to close public theatres' as well as frequent mention of the Jubilee made that much clear. But what of the *Republican*'s 'republicanism'? There was the predictable *Bulletin*-like nationalism—breast beating lines about the need for Australians to assert their 'manhood' and 'walk alone'. Otherwise, the journal was a grab-bag of familiar socialist and secularist philosophies. Articles on the wealth of the clergy—essays on labour and capital outlining the virtues of unionism and arbitration or articles of 'faith' from the old country, such as Annie Besant's 'Why I am a socialist'—together with portraits of Bradlaugh, Henry George, Herbert Spencer and the Italian republican hero, Garibaldi.[9]

Although the *Republican* was attempting to achieve unity among radicals by throwing a blanket of nationalist rhetoric on top of a splintered reform movement, the first two issues offered little hope that this aim would be achieved. As expected, there was no platform outlining principles, only various attacks on imperialism and established institutions. The editorial of the second issue in August spent most of its time arguing for a republic on the grounds that an Australian president would cost only £5000 a year. At the same time, the editors had little faith in the capacity of the people to take up the republican cause. According to the *Republican*, the voting population of New South Wales was 'apathetic' and in any case republicanism 'was a new ism' in the colonies; and there was no prospect of weekly issues until public opinion turned in favour of a republic.[10] While the *Republican* can hardly be criticised for relying on the same theorists that had excited the rest of the labour movement in England and America, the distinct lack of a coherent and detailed programme is a different matter. Although Keep had attended the Republican Union's first meeting there is no evidence to suggest that the two initiatives (the Union and the journal) were linked in any way. The Union was instigated largely at the behest of labour reformer J. D. Fitzgerald and included many of the men who had been involved in the June demonstrations, such as John Norton and Charles Jones. Led by Fitzgerald, twenty 'gentlemen' met at the Temperance Hall and decided to form an Australian Republican Union with the following objectives: 1 To encourage a national Australian sentiment; 2 The abolition of titular distinctions among Australians; 3 To ripen the desire of Australians to conduct their own business; 4 To build a Federated Australian Republic; 5 To encourage Australian talent.[11] None of the objectives would have been objectionable to the staff of the *Republican* but subtle differences between the two bodies soon began to emerge. The secretary of the Republican Union, W. M. Foote, publicly distanced the Union from the journal on two occasions.[12]

Foote dreamt of a grand republican union which would focus purely on the object of an Australian republic and eschew all other political issues or affiliations, but in the political climate of the late 1880s this position was unrealistic. Free trade and protection, labour reform, the role of the trade unions, foreign policy and defence were all issues tied closely to the debate on imperial relations. One only has to look at the report of the Republican Union's second meeting on 23 August to realise that the same fears which plagued the republican debate in the 1850s were also surfacing in the 1880s, in particular, the fear of invasion. Like J. D. Lang, members of the Republican Union believed Australian society would be best served by separation from Britain and avoiding the possibility of imperial war.[13]

The second meeting was, from all reports, a great success. The *Sydney Morning Herald* reported that over '200 people were present, including a few ladies'. Speakers alluded constantly to the inspiration provided by the American Republic and the Declaration of Independence. America, it seemed, was the 'model' of Australian 'destiny' for the Republican Union.[14] But perhaps the most interesting aspect of the meeting was the way in which it revealed the role of the Jubilee in crystallising 'national sentiment' in Sydney. The talk of 'national Australian sentiment', and Australian 'manhood' which dominated the meeting was in direct response to the sycophancy of the loyalist minority which had led the Jubilee celebrations. An excess of British loyalty had sparked the articulation of a brazen Australian nationalism. But part of the republican dilemma, both for the Union and the journal, was the lack of a nationalist mythology, with the possible exception of Lang and Eureka. There was no glorious past for republicans that would serve as an inspiration. In many respects the republicans of the 1880s felt that they were pushing out the nationalist boat for the first time.

Although the Republican Union and the *Republican* were not officially affiliated much of their rhetoric held common threads. True, many republicans had been led to the Union after the events of June for various and sometimes conflicting reasons, but underneath these differences both parties were contributing to the bonding of a particular Australian national sentiment with republicanism, a connection which would be far stronger by Federation than it had been at the granting of responsible government. In the October issue of the *Republican* Henry Lawson acknowledged these changes in his piece 'Sentimental Loyalty'. 'Sentimental loyalty has gone on whining blundering and bullying through this year of Jubilee until it brought to the surface an undercurrent of republicanism.' The Jubilee had forced the hand of the republicans. As far as the meeting of the Republican Union was concerned, the large crowd augured well. Foote, who had arrived from London in 1884, had managed to assist in the formation of a Union which he believed would soon set up rural and interstate branches and lead the nation to a republican Federation.[15] Unfortunately, the reaction of the press demonstrated a distinct lack of interest. The *Bulletin* took more than three weeks to mention the Union, while the conservative press ridiculed it as a fancy of youth. The *Sydney Morning Herald* reacted in a patronising tone:

> Can we not all of us look back to that pleasant period when we were 20; when the hair on our heads was in an inverse ratio to that on our faces to what our shaving-glass reveals to us now; when all legislation was so simple, all wrong so easily remediable; when we revered the horny hand of labour more than that of all the dukes of all the ages; when we dreamed some day of revolution

and heroism, and subsequent execution to slow music accompanied by the sobs of a people? Yes, the outlook is hopeful. We grow out of those things. We conclude later on that we can enjoy our cakes and ale, . . . We remember the dog and the bone; we prefer the substance of liberty to the shadow . . .[16]

To keep the anti-republican flag flying, the *Illustrated Sydney News* chimed in with an amusing, if not familiar refrain, which demonstrated just how little such rhetoric has changed since 1887:

> Why, in the immortal and historic name of the Three Tailors of Tooley Street, do those mercurial theorists, who magniloquently style themselves the 'Australian Republican Union,' continue to mildly menace our meek and placid public? In season and out of season, these gentlemen seek to impose upon us their alien and unnecessary 'fad'. Republicanism! What do we want with it? What would it do for us? . . . it would unsettle many stable interests; it would materially augment the cost of Government, and import amongst us a whirling element of discord . . . At the very least and lowest, we intend to remember the wise and politic maxim: 'Striving to better, often we mar what's well'.[17]

Apart from the response of the 'if it ain't broke don't fix it' school there was the predictable support of the *Bulletin* and a number of each-way bets from papers such as the *Daily Telegraph* and the *Age*, which both preferred to see the republic as something for future generations to consider. Despite the initial flurry of interest at the meeting in August, support for the Republican Union waned quickly. For Foote and the committee, maintaining the momentum in the Sydney branch proved difficult enough, let alone setting up new branches elsewhere. The problem was twofold. In the first place Foote's insistence that the Union cling to a vague non-political platform was causing dissent. Many members, especially George Black and Thomas Walker, wanted republicans to come out in support of land nationalisation, and generally adopt broader and more prescriptive policies. It was clear that republicanism could not be sustained on nationalist rhetoric alone. Only so much support could be gathered around the need to foster Australian talent and sentiment. In their criticisms of the Union members displayed a distinctly Australian preference for practical reforms. The 'Dictionary for Working Men' published in the *Republican* listed 'Socialism' as 'a word used to keep men from studying the labour question', and by the end of 1887 it was becoming clear that many members of the Republican Union felt the same way about Foote's brand of republicanism.[18]

The second problem faced by the Union was that the bulk of the people showed little interest in joining political movements. By January 1888 the *Republican* had become so frustrated with the lack of interest displayed by its fellow colonists that it was unable to hold back its anger:

Daily, nay-hourly, our prospects are darkening and the whole sky is covered over by the frowning menaces of dire despair. What is the cause of this? Apathy! Want of sound public spirit and native patriotism. We are too servile, too thoughtless, too indifferent to our best interests.[19]

Like the Republican Union, the *Republican* had struggled. Henry Lawson had left for Melbourne in November 1887 and would not return until January. In the meantime Keep and Louisa battled on with meagre resources and a small readership which showed little sign of improving. In political terms, republicanism was still nourished by the memory of the Jubilee, the coming Centenary celebrations and especially by public debate over the Naval Defence Force bill. Conditions were certainly ideal for an upsurge in republicanism, something which must have rankled with Black and Walker as they saw the Republican Union faltering in late 1887. Meetings of the Australian Republican Union continued on a monthly basis between September and December, but political differences only increased as numbers dwindled. The Queen's Jubilee had provided the catalyst for the emergence of a nationalist republicanism and yet, after only six months, it seemed that the cause was losing its way.[20]

1888—The Centenary Year

> Heavy feeding is almost inevitably an incentive to Conservatism . . . The flame of loyalty burns brightest in the soul of man who is gorged and somnolescent with turtle . . . Conservatism in fact, is a parochial sentiment of self congratulation propelled and kept in motion by food.[21]

This amusing reflection on loyalist sentiment from the *Bulletin* was typical of nationalist and republican opposition to the Centenary celebrations of 1888. Throughout the month of January the colonial calendar was littered with banquets, charity dinners, concerts, openings, dedications and unveilings which extolled the virtues of British civilisation and the Empire. If the *Bulletin*'s theory on conservatism was correct there was certainly a plentiful supply of food in early 1888 to stem the republican tide. On the other hand, the *Bulletin*'s remarks did contain a kernel of truth. As with the Jubilee celebrations of the previous year, the Centenary celebrations witnessed obsessive preoccupation with public declarations of loyalty on the part of politicians, community leaders and the conservative press. As the *Bulletin* pointed out, the fact that the bond between the colonies and the mother country was so often being 'cemented' was itself a sign that the bond was in need of repair. The Centenary celebrations did not turn out to be a unanimous festival of British imperialism.

Instead, 1888 was a year in which the tremendous diversity of colonial identity again came to the fore. Already, in late 1887 signs of confusion were evident in Henry Parkes' attempt to change the name of New South Wales to 'Australia'—a measure strongly resisted by the other colonies. The celebrations were naturally centred in New South Wales and Sydney in particular, something which only encouraged other colonies to remain unenthusiastic;[22] 26 January was not a date which inspired 'national' sentiment or a 'national' mood of celebration. If anything, it provoked feelings of bitterness and embarrassment and a determination to deny the past. There was no better example than the *Bulletin*'s editorial on 21 January 1888, 'The Day We Were Lagged': 'Australia ... celebrates a century which began and ends alike in nothing. A hundred years have left her as they found her—a name but not a nation—a huge continent content to be the hanger on of a little island ...'[23]

The *Bulletin* was not the only source of dissent. Even the *Sydney Morning Herald* saw the Centenary as a reminder that Australia began as a convenience to Britain—'a distant prison'. When the celebrations of January had passed the *Herald* could only express relief: 'We can all be thankful that the centennial is over'. Neither conservatives nor radicals could deal with the convict 'skeleton' in the context of celebration. Some newspaper editorials openly declared that they wished Australian history 'had been otherwise'. Others even denied that New South Wales had ever been a penal colony.[24] This constant guilt meant that for most colonists the celebrations presented a dilemma. Unable to find any pride in the idea of a society which had sprung from the overcrowded gaols of Britain, they were at a loss as to what they should celebrate. They could turn to the imperial propaganda so readily embraced by the likes of Henry Parkes, but there seemed to be an awareness, across all classes and political boundaries, that an 'Australian' celebration demanded more than fealty to Queen Victoria. The indulgence of the Centennial Banquet, with its predominantly 'imperialistic tone', was seen to be 'foreign' and 'un-Australian'—an opinion endorsed even by the normally ossified *Town and Country Journal*. Everyone seemed to agree that they wanted a 'national' celebration but no one seemed to know exactly what a 'national' celebration should entail. Weeks before the main celebrations on 26 January, the *Herald* admitted that the authorities were 'hunting' for 'methods of demonstration' and 'objects on which the national pride might waste itself'.[25]

The unveiling of the Queen's statue on 24 January was one of the major events of the Centenary, together with the official Banquet and the opening of Centennial Park two days later. It said much about the development of nationalist and republican sentiment in Australia that the focal points of celebration in 1888 were imperial. At least unveiling the

Queen's statue (which the *Bulletin* referred to wonderfully as 'a bilious effigy of tinted bronze') allowed the people of Sydney to forget about their convict past and solved the problem of what to celebrate. Perhaps one of the strongest reasons for the longevity of the imperial connection in Australia has been the inability of nationalists to deal with the sordid beginnings of settlement in 1788. The Queen was at least glorious and powerful, much easier to devote one's allegiance to than an unheroic nation of thieves and criminals—the 'festering vileness' of England. None the less, the essential dilemma remained. The *Herald* complained that people were being forced to rejoice when there was no such feeling within the community. The unveiling of the Queen's statue, said the *Herald*, was not an 'outstanding event toward which the national and international attention might be directed'.[26] One independent observer, the Englishman, Viscount Merionath, had this to say about the Centenary:

> There is the admitted prevalence of democratic and republican notions among the working classes here ... the hurraing crowds, the military display, the blazing bands, the official oratory, the jubilant newspaper rhetoric, everything loyal and monarchical on one side and on the other, the reluctant masses of the working trades brought here reluctantly and hating and scorning the whole thing.[27]

The consensus seemed to be that the celebrations were void of national feeling, 'signifying nothing' save the same old dreary imperialism of the previous year's Jubilee.[28] There seemed to be a yearning for a nation that did not yet exist—a future that time demanded remain far away, and underlying all this, the belief in the singularity of the Australian expressed so succinctly two years later by the *Australian Star*: 'The Australian is not a Briton by birth, nor is he a Briton in sentiment. He has aspirations and sentiments, habits and capacities of which a Briton knows nothing and cannot share ... He is of a new denomination and has new thoughts, beliefs and aspirings ...'.[29] The *Star* failed to mention that the Australian, just like his more British-centred compatriots, was ashamed of his past. Although the Australian was of a new denomination 'he' had not yet constructed a national mythology of 'his' own making.

So, when the royal statues were unveiled and the imperial speeches made, 'he' stood by unenthusiastically, unable to be fawning in his loyalty to the Queen but equally unable to follow the republicans who had only a convict past and a grab-bag of dreams of independence. Compliance was the only sensible option. It did not matter that republicans were few in number, what mattered was that on every occasion of celebration the question of a future Australian nation had to be addressed. Why else would Parkes have used many of his public speeches throughout January 1888 to stress that the colonies were already in fact 'republics' without the 'dangerous polity of a real republic'? Why else would countless public speakers in the same month go to extreme lengths to assert the continued loyalty of the Australian people to the British throne, and why else would newspaper editorials throughout the Centenary celebrations preoccupy themselves with those 'eccentric people' who advocated separation and a republic?[30] For the first time in almost half a century there was doubt about the value of the imperial connection. The actions of a few rowdy republicans had succeeded in shaping the framework of political debate. Far from being an inconsequential minority they had forced colonial elites to defend the connection and address the prospect of a future Australian republic. The *Daily Telegraph* came close to recognising the change that had come over colonial politics, only a few days after the Centenary celebrations were over. Referring to the tendency of Governors and politicians to defend the connection in their public speeches throughout January, the *Telegraph* realised that their constant carping also revealed a fundamental insecurity. The *Telegraph* saw that 'for the first time' in Australian history the merits of the connection were being seriously questioned:

> Hitherto we have been content to take the English connection as we take the English language—as an essential part of the general framework of things. We took it as the air we breathe as a thing not to be discussed or justified or defended or apologised for but simply as one of the general conditions of our existence.[31]

But now, especially since the Jubilee of June 1887, all this had changed. It was as if a door had been pushed ajar, a door that many of the colonial elite had assumed would never be opened. The Republican Union was only the small, formal and political manifestation of a much wider sentiment.

Although it was non-committal at times, throughout 1888 the *Daily Telegraph* stood for an independent Australia—free of 'the dangers and responsibilities of the Imperial policy'. The *Bulletin* adopted the slogan 'Australia for the Australians' and continued its republican campaign, vainly attempting to build the dream with the few heroic names it could muster.[32] Sydney nationalist, Robert Thomson, published his *Australian Nationalism*—an appeal for an independent federal republic written in a style similar to Lang's *Freedom and Independence*. Anonymous pamphlets were published pleading the case for separation. There was also enormous public disquiet, for example, over the issue of Chinese immigration, so much so that countless threats of separation were made in 1888, primarily due to the fear of the *Bulletin*'s Mongolian Octopus, the threatening tentacles of Asian domination. Conservatives worried that if the British government did not agree to the decision of an Intercolonial

Conference in June to put a complete halt to Chinese immigration that the clamour for separation would become louder still. Republicans used the supposed Chinese threat as a drum to beat up anti-British feeling, and everyone agreed that if the colonies had not acted for themselves by introducing harsh immigration restriction Acts a flood of Chinese immigrants would have been the result.[33] When the vessel SS *Afghan* arrived at Port Melbourne on 27 April 1888 with 268 Chinese passengers aboard, the ship was forced on to Sydney in a manner which evoked memories of the transportation crisis forty years earlier. In Sydney, an anti-Chinese demonstration attracted 40 000 people to the Domain, by far the largest public gathering ever seen in the colonies. Only three months earlier there had been little public enthusiasm for the Queen's statue and little for the Republican League. Now, republicans and loyalists joined with the mass of normally apathetic colonists to show the ugly face of Australian nationalism. The *Bulletin* led the charge—'Australia must choose between independence and infection, between the Australian republic and the Chinese leper'.[34]

If there was one issue which had the potential to force Australians to actively threaten independence it was the fear and hatred of the Chinese. It comes, then, as no surprise to say that the best chance for an Australian republic in the nineteenth century probably hinged on the British response to the colonies' stance on the Chinese question. But the British reluctantly allowed the passage of the restrictive laws and Australia progressed along a similar path under the imperial connection. It seemed Australians would always remain loyal so long as their nation was white.[35] Compared to the Chinese question, other issues which helped to keep the republican issue prominent—such as the British government's veto of New South Wales parliament's liberal divorce laws in 1887, and the dispute over the appointment of colonial Governors in late 1888—had a relatively minor impact although they did help to keep the debate about the merits of the connection alive. In Victoria, South Australia and Western Australia the spectre of a federal Australian republic permeated most of the public meetings of the Australian Natives Association during 1888. While it is true that there were far fewer republicans in Melbourne, debate on the merits of an Australian republic was still prominent in the Victorian press, thanks largely to the muddled policy of the ANA executive on the issue of separation.[36] One further means of explaining the lack of interest in republican nationalism in Victoria when compared to New South Wales is to acknowledge the more radical nature of Victorian liberalism. The success of reformers such as George Higinbotham had been founded on an ability to promote the ideal of citizenship and local autonomy under the Crown. Alfred Deakin explained the loyalty of the Victorian federalists by giving most of the credit to Higinbotham: 'None of the other colonies exhibited just the same firm alliance between radicalism and loyalty to the mother country because no other colony had a Higinbotham'. Unlike New South Wales, in Victoria the concept of Australian nationhood within the Empire was less of a contradiction.[37]

At the other end of the political spectrum, Joseph Symes' *Liberator* continued to publish a belligerent and provocative brand of republicanism. Sent to Victoria by Charles Bradlaugh in 1884 as the potential saviour of the Victorian secularists, Symes gave the *Liberator* its wonderful sense of humour of which the following example is typical: 'At present our government stinks like the Yarra . . . really, a breath of republican air would be refreshing'.[38]

Once we acknowledge the extent of debate on the question of a republic we can appreciate that 'Independence', as the Perth *Inquirer and Commercial News* observed, was a cry which could be heard 'through the length and breadth of Banana land' and 'echoed and re-echoed in Victoria and NSW'—especially in the first half of 1888.[39] In this light, the activities of republicans in Sydney in early 1888, including their attempts to revitalise the movement, do not appear as an isolated and marginal articulation of national sentiment but a determined (albeit rare) contribution to the organisation of a much wider phenomenon.

George Black
George Black, leading republican, journalist, Member of Parliament and founding member of the Australian Labor Party.
(*Sydney Morning Herald*, 20 July 1936, Image Library, State Library of New South Wales.).

The Coffee Palace Republic

> The *Bulletin* shook out the folds of the blood red banner of republicanism on which was emblazoned the five silver stars of the Southern Cross and some of us founded a republican union in Sydney ... When our union died from official anaemia I built from its vertebrae a Republican League and had the energy to form branches in Melbourne, Adelaide and elsewhere in 1886 while on my way to Broken Hill.[40]

This was the way George Black incorrectly remembered the beginnings of the Republican League when he commenced the revision of his history of the New South Wales Labor Party in 1926. Born in Edinburgh in 1854, Black had emigrated to Australia in his early twenties after graduating in arts at Edinburgh University. From the moment he arrived in Sydney, Black quickly gained notoriety as an orator and political activist.[41] Like the Lawsons, Walker and Keep, he had been led to republicanism by the events of June 1887. Later to become one of the founding members of the Australian Labor Party, Black had been frustrated by the Republican Union's failure to annunciate a clear and detailed political programme.

By early 1888 Black was winning acclaim with the Sunday crowds at the Domain, regularly attacking the 'milk and watery' policies of the Republican Union in his speeches. It was already clear that the Republican Union was faltering. Membership was barely more than a few hundred and attendance at meetings was poor. Black, Walker, Keep and William McNamara (also a founding member of the Socialist League) were determined to set the republican movement on a better footing before the Centenary celebrations got underway. At a special meeting of the Republican Union on 3 January 1888 in Tattersall's Chambers in Pitt Street, it was decided that the Republican Union should 'cease to exist' and that it should be replaced by a movement with a broader political platform. Down at the Domain, and in the pages of the Newcastle *Radical*, Black continued to hammer the Centenary celebrations by juxtaposing the city's poor with the 'flatulent' loyalty of public officialdom.[42] Finally, on Sunday 29 January, Black stood on a stump underneath the giant figs at the Domain before a crowd of between 1000 and 2000 people and announced the formation of the Australian Republican League. While Keep, McNamara and others walked among the crowd handing out copies of Black's open letter to Queen Victoria, Black outlined the objects of the League: 1 Abolition of the office of Governor; 2 Payment of members; 3 Abolition of the Upper House; 4 Abolition of all titular distinctions; 5 Revision of the penal code; 6 The championship of liberty at all times; 7 Nationalisation of the land; 8 Federation of the Australian colonies under republican rule.[43]

The inclusion of the republic as the last plank on the platform was an indication that for Black and the League the most important reforms were those which preceded number 8—at least these were more practical and more achievable. The platform was a pot-pourri of socialist and nationalist doctrines, many of which would later be adopted by the Labor Electoral League. As for the Republican League's chances of success, republicans were still 'wandering through a Sabbatarian wilderness of Sunday concerts and squash shops varied occasionally by the oasis afforded by Domain stumps'. Black had used these words himself to describe the situation of secularism in Sydney, yet they applied equally to the Republican League.[44] Throughout February and March the League held regular meetings on Sundays in the Domain—along with the Australian Socialist League, the secularists and anyone capable of mounting a stump and holding the attention of a large crowd for half an hour or so. In the weeks which followed the League's formation, members debated the League's platform. Each Sunday a different plank would be chosen, and occasionally Black would deliver his well-tuned lecture 'Why I am a Republican'.[45] Now that it was more clearly in agreement, the *Republican* provided enthusiastic support.

Henry Lawson had apparently found Keep and Louisa struggling with the *Republican* on his return from Melbourne. But Black's Republican League must have given Lawson cause for optimism, because by February 1888 Lawson was editing the *Republican*.[46] Under Lawson the *Republican* continued with its usual collection of articles—criticising the Centenary celebrations, despising the Chinese, warning against Imperial Federation, syndicating articles from English socialists, eulogising anarchists from Chicago—and all the while supported by the sponsorship of the celebrated Danish herbalist, Herr Rasmussen of 247 Crown Street, Surry Hills. The uniqueness of the *Republican* lay in its utopian nationalism. Readers were encouraged to compose a national anthem which would become the 'voice of Australia's swelling spirit' and prizes were awarded for the best republican poetry. The Lawsons were most responsible for the *Republican*'s nationalism. Louisa composed poems such as 'Australia', where she wrote of Australia as a 'beloved home giver' and 'bright haven of rest' for the immigrants who came to her 'bountiful shores' full of hope for a better life.[47] Henry, determined to assert an Australian identity, highlighted the neglect of Australian history in an essay which appeared in April 1888:

> . . . If this is Australia, and not a mere outlying suburb of England: if we really are the nucleus of a nation and not a mere handful of expatriated people dependent on an English Colonial Secretary for guidance and tuition, it behoves us to educate our children to a knowledge of the country they call their own.

> It is a matter of public shame that while we have now commemorated our hundredth anniversary, not one in every ten children attending Public schools throughout the colonies is acquainted with a single historical fact about Australia.[48]

The Lawsons were searching for a new mythology, a new dreaming which, ironically, was supposed to remain just as Anglo as the Empire which Henry despised. While much of the *Republican*'s rhetoric betrayed the influence of the *Bulletin*, the nationalism of Louisa and Henry was more positive and more romantic than that of Archibald. The *Republican* spent much time acknowledging the need for new symbols of national life, new anthems, flags, histories and art. Yet, like the *Bulletin*, it knew that these things would not appear overnight.

In early March 1888 George Black decided to travel to Adelaide and Melbourne in an effort to stimulate interest in the Republican League. Considering that interest in Sydney was not exactly overwhelming and that Melbourne and Adelaide were even less likely to embrace republicanism, Black's decision was more an exercise in wanderlust than political agitation. From what we can glean from Black's speeches in Adelaide, it seemed he must have known there was little hope for a strong Republican League in Australia.[49] His presence stirred little curiosity in a city where the Adelaide *Advertiser* was already convinced of the colony's republican status:

> South Australia is a republic in the best sense—that is, the state is the public concern of every citizen. Neither birth nor wealth—inherited or acquired, constitutes a qualification for office, nor the want of them a disqualification. We enjoy in the fullest sense government of the people, by the people, for the people.[50]

In Melbourne, Black did manage to set up a branch of the League, albeit briefly. It was there that he inspired the likes of poet Bernard O'Dowd to advocate republicanism and discovered the prejudice of the Melbourne press, which largely ignored the meeting. After his return to Sydney, Black wrote a letter to the Newcastle *Radical*, explaining the events surrounding his trip to Melbourne. The letter tells the story in a manner which captures the atmosphere of the late 1880s, especially that of the coffee palace debaters.

> On the day of my arrival, I happened, in looking for the amusement column, to drop across an advertisement which notified that Mr Montague Miller would open a debate on the 'Gullibility of the Australian Native,' at the Hall of Science on that evening; being somewhat interested in subjects of this character, and

recognising the wide field for debate presented, I attended. In his speech Mr Miller ... uttered some warmly republican sentiments, these revived my somewhat exhausted frame (I had been travelling 20 hours by train without sleep.)

... I jumped up and asked those who were interested in the matter to join with me in forming a National, or Separation League. About thirty persons did, so some money was raised and a meeting called in an upper room of the Bourke St. Coffee Palace ... I then invited those present to join the League, naming one shilling as the entrance fee, and sixpence as the monthly subscription, and declared the intention of my co-workers to hold a mass meeting at an early date ... There were three reporters from the *Argus*, *Age* and *Herald*, present. The latter two ignored the meeting altogether, while the *Argus* scribe deliberately lied in his reference to it.[51]

Black was right to expose the bias of the Melbourne papers, but this was hardly the reason for the failure of the League in Melbourne. The small group of twenty-five met again on only one occasion, before disbanding. Melbourne was a great place for coffee but not so good for republicans. When Black arrived back in Sydney more bad news awaited him. The Republican League had broken into warring factions and all but disintegrated. Even before Black's departure members of the Republican League had taken part in debates which began with the proposition that 'modern republicanism' was 'a failure'.[52]

Without Black's skill to galvanise the disparate political forces in the League, it quickly became just another stump 'ism' touted around on a Sunday afternoon at the Domain. Socialists and anarchists frequently attacked republicanism for its failure to deliver practical programmes and kindle popular support. Divisions arose over definitions of key terms such as 'democracy' and 'republic' as well as political strategy. Many republicans were Christians and disliked the arrogance of fellow republicans who thought it an absurdity 'to believe in republicanism on earth and autocracy in heaven'. The atheism of secularists, like Thomas Walker in Sydney and Joseph Symes in Melbourne, discouraged many from supporting the republican movement. The *Bulletin* often suggested that the cause of Australian democracy was disgraced by its association with atheism and it gave scant coverage to the activities of the Republican League—something which greatly angered George Black.[53] Black scorned the *Bulletin* for 'consistently ignoring the Australian Republican League' in a tersely worded letter which was published in the *Bulletin* just after his return to Sydney:

Have you forgotten, or if not, why do you so persistently ignore the Australian Republican League.—'Tis true its president is not a Q.C.; 'tis true that most of its meetings are held in the Domain, or at the Queen's Statue; 'tis true that none of its members are wealthy, or *respectable* 'tis true that its propagandistic work is done by working men among working men; but surely these are the very things that should above all others recommend it to a journal professing advanced democratic principles.[54]

By May 1888, less than one year since the Republican Union had held its first meeting in Sydney, any chance of an organised republican movement seemed lost. Although republicans like Norton, Keep and Black continued to attend debating club meetings at the School of Arts and stir up trouble at public meetings, both the Jubilee and the Centenary had now passed. Black, however, did not give up easily. He repeatedly argued that the people should refrain from joining socialist movements and concentrate their energies on republicanism.[55] But by May he had also lost the support of the *Republican*, which had published its last issue in April. Louisa Lawson had decided that the fight for women's suffrage should take precedence over republicanism. In May, Louisa, together with Henry, published the first issue of the *Dawn*, a journal of far greater longevity than the *Republican*. The germ of the *Dawn* was already present in Louisa's women's column in the *Republican*, and for the next decade the *Dawn* would continue to champion the same nationalist concerns of the *Republican*.[56]

The simultaneous demise of the Republican League and the *Republican* indicated just how tenuous a hold the organised arm of the movement had on its followers. The men and women who had been inspired by the events of June 1887 were unable to sustain their fervour for republicanism once the imperial festivals were over. The publication of George Black's *Why I am a Republican* in mid-1888 subsequently made little impact. Black's thirty-page pamphlet, which ended with a maudlin ode to 'dear Australia', was largely a regurgitation of Morrison Davidson's *Book of Kings* and Max Nordau's *Conventional Lies*, a fact which did not endear it to radicals. Basically, they had heard it all before, and the arguments, while convincing, did not really carry the capacity to effect change to a republic in an Australian context. Everyone agreed that the history of the English monarchy was a sordid tale of hoary lechers, bigots, butchers, fools and madmen. But that was beside the point and as Black himself asked: 'What did all that have to do with Australians?'.[57]

Although he tried to convince his readers that the monarchical connection meant greater taxes, Imperial Federation, the perpetuation of a colonial aristocracy and imminent war, Black's conspiratorial tone was not in concordance with the feelings of the wage earners of Australia to whom his pamphlet was dedicated, most of whom did not perceive the connection as an obstacle to political reform although they bore a dislike for monarchy in principle. Despite the League's failure Black soldiered on, attending debating club meetings while William Keep took greater interest in Louisa Lawson's *Dawn*.[58] As for Henry Lawson and the others who had joined the Republican League, there was still cause for optimism. A large percentage of the Sydney working classes were still unhappy with the Australian Natives Association's status as the sole voice of national sentiment. They were unhappy with the ANA's somewhat equivocal stance on the issue of Federation and independence, and even more displeased with the exclusive membership rules which excluded all those who had not been born in Australia.[59]

At the same time as the ANA made its push into New South Wales, Thomas McIlwraith's National Party scored a remarkable victory in the Queensland elections of May 1888 after standing on a platform which included the expressed goal of a federated independent government for the Australian colonies. While republicanism had not been an election issue McIlwraith's victory was hailed by the *Bulletin* and Sydney's weather-beaten republicans as the harbinger of a new move towards independence. Having been so unsuccessful with the 'r' word, they realised that many people were simply too timid or too apathetic to join a republican league, whereas McIlwraith's use of the word 'National' had not harmed his election prospects in the slightest.[60] McIlwraith's success also pleased the likes of the more liberal nationalists led by the *Daily Telegraph* and Robert Thomson. It seemed for a moment that McIlwraith's victory might provide the spark for a more unified nationalist movement with broader appeal.

On 12 July 1888 at the Royal Hyde Park Hotel in Sydney a 'few gentlemen' gathered to form 'The Australian National Association', a body which planned to affiliate immediately with McIlwraith's party in Queensland. Among those present were Robert Thomson, W. H. Traill from the *Bulletin*, and the republican nationalist J. H. Byrne.[61] The platform adopted was almost identical to McIlwraith's National Party: the cultivation of Australian national sentiment; an independent federal nation with full responsibility for its own defence; the exclusion of the Chinese and all convicts, together with some quasi-socialist ruminations about the dangers of monopolies and the privileged classes. But above all, there was no mention of the word 'republic', a tactic which seemed to be perfectly sensible to the Lawsons, who embraced the National Association and undertook to publish a monthly journal, the *Nationalist*, as the Association's official mouthpiece. The first and last issue, ostensibly a reincarnation of the *Republican*, appeared on 8 August 1888 with the sub-title 'A Monthly Journal for Men and Women'. Louisa's influence was not hard to discern.[62] Despite the talk of Australian nationality there was not much new about the *Nationalist*. Henry Lawson chipped in with a short harangue on the word 'colony', demanding that Australians rid themselves of the inferiority and subjugation associated with the word. But he was sounding more and more like the *Bulletin*, berating the Chinese and repeating the same old filial metaphor as proof of the need for an Australian independence. For Lawson and the nationalists, the nation's *raison d'être* was its racial composition.[63] The pages of the *Nationalist* carried letters from founding members of the Association, Louisa's women's column, a potted biography of John Dunmore Lang, reports of the Australian Socialist League meetings, not to mention the advertisements of the celebrated Danish herbalist, Herr Rasmussen—who also offered to do his bit for the emancipation of Australian women: 'Married ladies, having no children, should send for Herr Rasmussen's Free Medical Book which contains valuable advice. Sent, post free, anywhere, only a few left. 157 Liverpool Street, Hyde Park, Sydney. Consultation free'.[64]

Unfortunately, Herr Rasmussen had no tonic for political apathy. The Australian National Association and its journal were dead within two weeks of their inception. Once again, attempts to form an organised political wing of republican sentiment had failed miserably. Like the Republican Union and the Republican League, the Australian Nationalists were buried quickly in an unmarked grave. The energy and commitment of Keep, the Lawsons and Black had not been enough to carry the day. It would be a long time before the citizens of New South Wales would again join a republican movement.[65] The reasons for the collapse of the republican movement were many, but primary among them was the failure of the intelligentsia to stir the working classes into action. One of the most interesting facets of the Sydney republican movement was that it was led largely by men born in the United Kingdom—that is by 'new chums' and not the native-born, something which did not escape the notice of George Black:

> The man who in this and the other colonies, most strenuously preaches separation, is not as a rule the native, but the travelled European, not the rich globetrotter or imperialistic toady, but the man who has travelled in search of a livelihood, or for the sake of acquiring information.[66]

Although the republicanism of the late 1880s may have been presented as the ultimate destiny of the native-born, it was most certainly not the product of the native-born. There was little about the Sydney republicans (with the possible exception of the Lawsons) which was in anyway unique or different from the republicanism of Charles Bradlaugh or radical journals like the *Reynolds News* in England. Even Archibald's republican nationalism was influenced by the time he had spent in England in touch with radical political movements in the early 1880s. In fact, a quick glance at the birthplace of the leading republicans in 1888 says little for the influence of either Australia's 'native sons' or the 'Irish' on republicanism. David Buchanan, George Black and Thomas McIlwraith—like John Dunmore Lang—were born and educated in Scotland. Thomas Walker, William Foote, Joseph Symes, William Keep and William Lane were all born in England and informed largely by the political language and conflicts of English industrial society. In terms of political participation, the native-born made little contribution to formal republican movements in Sydney. George Black spent much of his time bemoaning the political apathy of a generation of Australians. On one occasion he even suggested that the native-born (especially in Adelaide and Melbourne) were actually more in favour of monarchy than a republic, claiming that it was only those who had experienced the evils of monarchy in the Old World who cried out for republicanism. To some extent Black was correct, but it may have been easier to gather the support of the native-born if the republicans themselves had not been so divided. By mid-1888 the conflict between republicans, socialists, anarchists, secularists and combinations thereof had descended into petty recriminations.[67] The 'bourgeois-public-sphere' was a messy and confused space. Yet while republican movements and their enlisted adherents may have been numerically insignificant, their effect was not. The Sunday stump republicans had disbanded by mid-1888, but the debate on the future prospect of an independent federal republic continued. In 1889 the American Consul in Sydney, G. W. Griffin, wrote in a letter to the Assistant Secretary of State in Washington: 'It is difficult always to gauge public sentiment but it is impossible for even the imperialist to overlook the growth of a strong republican sentiment in Australasia'.[68]

When Griffin talked about republican sentiment, he was not only referring to the formal republican movement in Sydney. This republican sentiment also included the new perspective on the British connection as articulated by the likes of Sydney's *Daily Telegraph*, a perspective which was not necessarily anti-British but a spirit of independence none the less.[69] Beyond the Domain, there was an undeniable awakening of national sentiment of which the Blacks and Lawsons represented only a minority; the belligerent, radical and publicly anti-British minority.

Debate on the merits of the British connection, largely in the context of imminent federation, continued unabated throughout 1888. In the press, in parliament, and at public meetings the merits of separation and a republic continued to be discussed.[70] Generally, this debate centred on the question of 'timing' and whether the republic would be forged by a rejection of Britain or an amicable and peaceful separation. For those men and women who joined the republican movements in Sydney, the demand for a republic was obviously driven by a repudiation of British monarchy and aristocracy but not of Britain itself, for much of their political rhetoric embraced the same class rivalry espoused by radical political movements in Britain. More importantly, it should be understood that even the leaders of the republican movements did not believe the republic was an immediate and realistic possibility. Instead, like many of their political opponents, they saw the republic as a future event. Lawson's *Republican* realised that its supporters were 'not at present in a position to enforce the dogma' of an Australian republic but hoped that the day would be 'not far distant'. When George Black finished his speech at Botanic Park in Adelaide in March 1888 three cheers were given 'for the coming of the Federated Australian Republic'. Black knew that the republicans had little chance of success in the immediate future. Other republicans, like J. A. Byrne, saw the republic as the 'great inheritance' in store for the native-born.[71] The republic, as always, was just as the *Telegraph* had described it: 'the road we were travelling on, the goal we were moving towards'. These were the same sentiments which echoed within the walls of New South Wales Parliament House. During the debate on David Buchanan's motion of separation in November 1888 several members insisted that the time was not yet ripe for republican government while offering tacit support for the idea in the future. It was as if all those in favour of an independent Australia sat patiently on the edge of a sandstone coast, gazing out to sea, searching the horizon for the 'inevitable arrival of the good ship republic'.[72]

The debate had been intense and widespread but the tide was definitely beginning to turn by mid-1888, except in Queensland, the one colony where strong republican sentiment would continue to emerge until the early 1890s.[73]

Queensland—The Banana Republic

For much of its post-European history Queensland has been the playhouse for speculators, tricksters and the would-be barons of colonial fiefdoms, and the 1890s were little different. Separated from New South Wales in 1856, Queensland was a colony in the midst of an economic boom by the mid-1880s. Buoyed by a massive influx of overseas capital, especially from Great Britain, Queensland's flourishing mining and pastoral industries attracted a predominantly literate and itinerant wave of immigrants in the 1880s. The flood of money and employers hungry for profits encouraged a marked increase in the growth and strength of trade unions. It was not surprising that Queensland trade unions provided the wellsprings of the Australian Labor Party.[74] Nowhere in Australia were the forces of labour and capital so opposed as they were in Queensland between 1888 and 1893. The fact that the bulk of incoming capital came from Britain laid a strong material basis for potential republican sentiment. When relations between workers and employers soured, as they did frequently during these years, the temptation to blame British capitalists, the monarchy or the 'connection' was great. At the same time as Federation was being debated throughout the colonies there was also an impression that Queenslanders harboured a different view on Federation, as the English republican Sir Charles Dilke observed in 1890: 'The prevailing sentiment in Queensland is certainly that Australian Federation is workable, but implies ultimate separation from the mother country. Both are looked upon as inevitable in a more or less distant future'.[75]

There was a common perception in the late 1880s that Queensland was a young community which bore a discernible spirit of independence, something that was lacking in the other colonies. On many occasions this 'spirit of independence' was thought to extend to a desire to sever the 'last constitutional link' with the mother country, thanks largely to the election of Thomas McIlwraith's National Party government in May 1888.[76]

McIlwraith's party preached 'alliance not dependence', and while this was hardly a call for a republic it did not stop conservatives and the representatives of big business, such as the Bankers' Institute of Australia, from referring to the National Party as 'anti-monarchical' and 'republican'. In part, this perception was fuelled by the willingness of certain sections of the New South Wales press, in particular the *Bulletin* and the *Daily Telegraph*, to champion McIlwraith's election as a portent of the inevitable republic. On the other hand, McIlwraith's stance on the appointment of colonial Governors in late 1888 struck fear in the hearts of many conservatives who interpreted his insistence on the right of colonial and national interest to override imperial concerns as a threat to the steady flow of British capital.[77] In the space of only three months McIlwraith had asserted the supremacy of ministerial responsibility by securing an acceptance from the Colonial Office that colonial Governors should abide by the convention to accept the advice of ministers. In addition, he had successfully forced the Colonial Office to accept the right of colonial governments to be consulted with regard to vice-regal appointments. While this stance was seen by many as the first step on the road to independence, it was actually one way of ensuring that formal separation from the Empire would not be necessary. Only five Acts emanating from the Australian colonies were disallowed between 1856 and 1900, a statistic which demonstrates that the opportunities for serious friction between the colonies and London were extremely limited.[78]

Even the *Australian Star* acknowledged that, except in one or two matters, Britain did not interfere in any way with colonial legislation, nor did it attempt to make the colonies feel as if they were dependencies. If it did so, said the *Star*, the halls in the city would not be large enough to hold the crowds that would assemble to demand independence. McIlwraith's National Party played a large part in this process. By forcing the Colonial Office to declare its policy on the powers and election of the Governor, McIlwraith—like Higinbotham in Victoria—asserted the supremacy of colonial self-interest within the bounds of the imperial connection. In Queensland, loyalty to Empire was learning to coexist with loyalty to Australia. One did not necessarily preclude the other. The National Party was not interested in immediate separatism but in the 'reciprocity of rights' between colony and mother country.[79]

Aside from McIlwraith's National Party, republicans in the separatist anti-British mould were still plentiful in Queensland. Leading the charge was William Lane, the man most responsible for the early direction and philosophy of the labour movement in Queensland. Born in Bristol in 1861, Lane arrived in Brisbane in 1885 at the age of twenty-four. Described as 'a frail little man, with gold rimmed spectacles and a club foot for which he needed a walking stick', Lane was able to forge a genuinely original blend of English and American radicalism into a campaign for republican independence.[80] Lane dreamt of an Australian republic as the isolated fortress 'left alone' in the South Pacific. A white

William Lane
William Lane, editor of the Brisbane-based *Boomerang* and one of Queensland's most idealistic republican intellectuals.
(Image Library, State Library of New South Wales.)

socialist utopia, free of the corrupt influences of capitalism—a nirvana which would eventually force him to sail to Paraguay like a prophet in search of the promised land.[81] For Lane, protection and Federation were the first steps towards complete nationality. During the two and a half years he edited the *Boomerang* from 1887 to 1890 Lane projected a sophisticated republican voice to the thousands of workers throughout Queensland who read the *Boomerang*.

In certain respects, Lane's vision of a republic was not dissimilar to that of the *Bulletin*. Monarchy was seen as a 'remnant of barbarism' and the British sovereign was 'a worthless and brainless individual' who did 'nothing but draw a big salary'. This was familiar rhetoric, but Lane thought far more critically than the *Bulletin* or the Sydney republicans. He frequently reminded his readers that a republic would not be a panacea and that Australians had to be just as careful of monopolists in a republic as under a monarchy. For Lane, a republic was nothing if it did not include the nationalisation of land, women's rights, electoral reform, free education and the expulsion of all alien races.[82] While he drew freely on the democratic rhetoric of the American Declaration of Independence for inspiration, he recognised that American society was characterised by extreme social inequality and this perception continued in the pages of the *Boomerang* long after Lane had left: 'To simply shift the name isn't good enough . . . the whole system must somehow or other be shifted . . . If republicanism is made a means to this end—it is good, otherwise it is no more worthy struggling for than a game of whist with ha'penny corners'.[83]

Unlike McIlwraith, who talked of Australia's independence in non-committal terms, Lane was not afraid to stand openly and proudly as a republican.[84] The *Boomerang* editorial of 30 November 1889 was proof enough, but it also showed that Lane was much more than a republican propagandist:

> The whole civilised world is republican . . . Republicanism is weakening nowhere, it is getting stronger everywhere. The deduction is self evident. A monarchy will soon be as scarce in the civilised world as a hairy man or a woolly horse. It will be, indeed, just such another monstrosity, whilst a king will be exhibited with a boneless boy and Siamese twins.[85]

Like Harpur and Lang, Lane saw republicanism as the symbol of a modern, enlightened and progressive society. But unlike the *Bulletin* and the Sydney republicans he knew that the possibility of an Australian republic depended very much on the existence of an 'irritating cause', and although he despised the hereditary principle of monarchy, the reasons for the eventual survival of the British monarchy in the Australian Constitution were already planted in his argument. The monarchy had learnt to reign instead of rule, and hairy men would continue to flourish in Queensland. Perhaps this was why Lane, like nearly every other vocal republican in the nineteenth century, spoke more of the republic as a 'coming' event than an urgent necessity.[86] But the *Boomerang* still had a profound influence on the workers of Queensland, and republican ideas were varied and widespread throughout the colony. By the time Lane had left the *Boomerang* to write for the Queensland *Worker*, a strong republican movement was about to emerge in Charters Towers in north Queensland.

The Republicans of Charters Towers

> What will the world think when they become acquainted with the fact that a municipal town of Queensland resolved to form a republican institution for the whole of Australasia.[87]

Geoffrey Bolton has described Charters Towers in the 1880s as 'one of the longest established North Queensland mining centres, the most prosperous [and] the most populous'.[88] Second only to Bendigo in the production of gold, the first sixteen years of Charters Towers' existence between 1872 and 1888 had been largely characterised by economic prosperity. By the late 1880s the Charters Towers mines employed almost 2000 miners with 550 carriers, timber getters and attendants on machines, as well as 1600 merchants and tradesmen who were dependent in some way on the industry. This image of a thriving mining centre was a far cry from the Northern Queensland towns visited by Queen Elizabeth II almost 100 years later. In the twentieth century the Queen was greeted by the floral frocks of the Country Women's Association and a flotilla of tea and scones. But if any member of the British royal family would have dared to appear in Charters Towers in 1888 the welcome might not have been so agreeable. At that time, Charters Towers was a community steeped in socialist and democratic ideas, a community of workers with little tolerance for hereditary institutions such as monarchy.

The Charters Towers press had been anti-royalist since 1887, with the Irish editor of the *Northern Miner*, Thadeus O'Kane, probably the most conspicuous of early republicans.[89] For miners who were familiar with the republican ideas of the *Bulletin*, the *Boomerang* and the *Worker* it was only a short step from blaming the greed of British entrepreneurs involved in the mining industry to the advocacy of separation and a republic—especially for the small band of intellectuals in Charters Towers who had been exposed to the same diet of radical British and American literature as their counterparts in Sydney. When John Dunsford, one of the founding members of the Australian Republican Association in

Charters Towers, was asked to explain the initial success of the republican movement in Charters Towers, he replied: 'They [British Capitalists] have in this locality bought up our best dividend producing mines and now our working classes feel the disadvantageous difference between the dividends being paid in London instead of in Charters Towers'.[90]

This may have explained why a republican organisation formed initially in Charters Towers, but Dunsford's words disguise the degree of confusion which existed among the vanguard of the working classes of Queensland in the 1890s. Primarily, this confusion emanated from the need for workers and unionists to decide on the most appropriate political platform and industrial relations strategy which would best represent their interests. We can more easily understand the formation and failure of the Australian Republican Association in Charters Towers if it is placed in the context of the ructions inside the union movement as a whole.

At the time of the Republican Association's formation in February 1890, Queensland unions were fighting hard to force employers to agree to a closed shop, something which they succeeded in obtaining, at least from pastoralists, in May 1890. Throughout the year this victory would encourage union members across Australia to struggle for similar concessions, the most notable example being the maritime strike of August to November 1890, which saw over 25 000 unionists in New South Wales, Victoria and South Australia go out on strike—a display of unity which would eventually be defeated by strike-breaking labour and internal divisions.[91] The failure of the maritime strike raised questions for the labour movement which had become steadily more urgent since the flurry of union activity began in the 1880s. In April 1890 William Lane published the first edition of the *Australian Worker*, the paper which would announce Lane's programme for a national labour federation—a plan which was partially realised in August 1890 when Queensland members of the Australian Labour Federation held their first general council in Brisbane. The formation of the ALF, the maritime strike, and the shearers' strike of 1891 were all signs of the enormous tensions in the labour movement. By 1890 economic depression had forced unionists to confront the political divisions which had plagued radical and working-class politics for the previous decade. It was clear that a broad, co-operative, and 'national' strategy was required to enable workers to mount an effective campaign for social and political reform. What was not clear, however, was how this aim should be achieved. When a small number of men gathered at the ANA hall in Charters Towers on 2 February 1890, they carried the same doubts and aspirations of unionists throughout Australia. How should the interests of workers best be promoted? Parliamentary representation? Repeated strike action? A national trade union movement? And how should the movement structure its political platform? What issues should be given priority and what name should be given to the workers' movement?[92]

When the newsagent and bookseller, John Dunsford, rose to address the meeting he reminded those present that radicals were scattered throughout Australia like chaff. In Dunsford's eyes, the hope for cohesion and stability lay in the consummation of an Australian republic. Even allowing for the fact that there was considerable anti-British sentiment in Charters Towers at the time, this was still a startling conclusion to make. As the meeting progressed, the confusion which characterised the wider labour movement soon became evident. There was much disagreement about the title the new radical association should adopt. When Dunsford put forward the name Australian Republican Association many thought it inappropriate, so much so that they walked out of the meeting when the republican title was passed.[93] Alternative names were proposed such as the Australian Radical Republican Association, the North Queensland Radical Association, and the Australasian Democratic Association. Regionalism, political differences, and the need for a national political strategy for the union movement which would carry broad appeal were the reasons for the Republican Association's eventual demise, and each of these factors was already causing tension at the first meeting in February 1890. Although the majority of those present supported the name 'Australian Republican Association' the word 'republic' was still too loaded, too ambiguous, too much of a gift to the opponents of labour to inspire a national political movement. This became clear when the editorial of the *Charters Towers Times* slammed the meeting's choice of the title only two days later. The *Times* thought it absurd that Charters Towers' radicals should have the audacity to attempt to lead a national republican movement when those in Sydney and Melbourne had failed. For the *Times*, radicalism and republicanism were not interchangeable synonyms, but distinct. 'Republicanism' said the *Times* 'had no show' in Charters Towers.[94]

Throughout the brief eighteen-month life of the ARA, the movement's leaders would spend much of their time explaining or defending the republican appellation.[95] The platform of the ARA was a synthesis of the *Bulletin/Boomerang* political programme. Universal suffrage and triennial parliaments, direct tax on land values, simplified procedure of law courts, abolition of capital punishment, Australia for the white man, free education, government control over monetary policy without the intervention of banks, no foreign labour, and finally, almost as an afterthought, came this *sequitur*:

> We call upon all who seek the emancipation of labor and who would make Australia a democratic commonwealth of free and independent people ... by

constitutional methods, to build up the republic of the Southern Seas, to establish justice, to preserve liberty, to extend the spirit of Australian nationality and to elevate humanity.[96]

Reading this platform, it isn't difficult to identify the authors. The town's reformers, Andrew Dawson, John Dunsford and Charles McDonald, were men who had read the works of Henry George, Bellamy, Paine, Carlyle and the interstate journals which thrived on a similar diet of radical literature. John Dunsford's newsagency and bookshop in Charters Towers was the focal point for ARA members, just as Henry Parkes' toyshop had been for the Sydney democrats in the 1850s.[97] Like Parkes, the leaders of the ARA would later soften their attitude to the colonies' connection with the motherland. Dunsford, McDonald and Dawson would all later be elected as Labor members of parliament in Queensland. In February 1890, however, they were convinced that republicanism was the most appropriate 'ism' for the labour movement to advance its cause.

Within two months the ARA, which had begun with a mere thirteen members, boasted more than 500 members. On 21 June 1890 the Association published the first volume of the *Australian Republican*, a fortnightly journal which would have a wider circulation and longer lifespan than Louisa Lawson's *Republican* in Sydney.[98] By the end of the year branches of the ARA had been set up in Bundaberg, Ipswich, Townsville, Cairns, Brisbane and several other rural towns in Queensland. While the membership never numbered more than several hundred in any one centre, there was clearly far more overt support for an explicitly republican platform in Queensland throughout 1890–91 than there had been at any previous time in Australia's history. Each branch held regular weekly or fortnightly debates on various aspects of the Association's platform in much the same manner as the Sydney republicans had done in 1887–88.[99] When the *Australian Republican* reached the desks of the rural press in Queensland the reaction was mixed. In Cairns the *Post* saw it as 'healthy and refreshing', 'another big brick in the bulwark that labour' was 'endeavouring to erect in defence of its rights'. The *Bowen Observer* agreed with almost everything the ARA stood for except the desire 'to cut' the colonies 'adrift from the old country'. The ARA's journal overflowed with letters from shearers and working men on the road who wished to send their messages of support.[100]

For a short while (during the maritime strike in 1890 and until the onset of the shearers' strike in February 1891) the *Australian Republican* filled a vacuum for many working men by providing an intelligent and widely circulated journal—published in Charters Towers, a fact which would have endeared it to many workers in outback Queensland.[101] The initial success of the ARA throughout the colony was sufficient evidence that Queenslanders were more sympathetic to republicanism. But exactly what kind of republicanism was articulated by the ARA? And why was it taken up so enthusiastically, at least in the early stages of the movement?

To begin with, perhaps the most interesting aspect of the ARA is that its manifesto, which listed the ten 'objects of the Association', did not include the specific object of a republic.[102] The word 'republic' only appeared in the paragraph underneath the objects, and even then it was more in the context of a rhetorical flourish. More than anything else this points to the fact that Dunsford, Dawson and the other leaders of the ARA wished to promote the Association as a broad labour movement in which a republic was an end goal. The choice of the title 'Republican' owed more to the founding members' distaste for other words such as 'Socialism'. On 23 August 1890 the opening page of the *Australian Republican* led with an editorial entitled 'Republicanism and Socialism' which was sympathetic to both 'isms' and tried hard to provide separate definitions. Republicanism was supposedly about 'ensuring the public good by identifying those governing with the governed', while socialism was securing the 'welfare of the individual'.[103]

But beyond the addition of a few Jeffersonian phrases about government for the people and the inclusion of a vaguely Benthamite notion of public welfare there seemed to be little to distinguish the ARA's republicanism. The very fact that the editorial seemed unsure about the difference between republicanism and socialism revealed just how much uncertainty there was over the choice of appropriate 'labels' among the working classes. Another thing that was lacking was one good reason why the ARA's democratic and constitutional republicanism could not be achieved under the auspices of the political connection with Great Britain. The motto of the ARA was 'Independence peacefully achieved if it may be but independence'. The manifesto emphasised that republicans strove to achieve the aims of the Association by 'constitutional means' only. While there was still the usual nonsense about the need for 'powerful manhood' in the ARA, there was never any intention to press the point beyond the institutionalised methods of political reform. The ARA were still British constitutionalists, the only difference was that they were now appealing as Australians instead of exiled Britons.[104] There was also an underlying pragmatism in the republicanism of the ARA. Even Albert Dawson's pamphlet, *The Case Stated*, preferred the euphemism 'independence' to 'republic'. Although Dawson, Dunsford and McDonald had succeeded in convincing about 5 to 10 per cent of the electorate in Queensland that republicanism would best advance the cause of the labour movement, by the end of 1890 the ARA was under siege from within its own ranks.

The *Australian Republican*'s support for the workers involved in the maritime strike was beginning to irk many of the small businessmen and shopkeepers who were dependent on imported foodstuffs for their livelihood. Support for the ARA in the town started to drop off, even spilling over into violence on some occasions. In November 1890 a gang broke into ARA offices and 'pied the type of a forthcoming issue'.[105] When the shearers' strike began early in the following year, the fault lines which had always been present in the ARA began to crack wide open. Miners, artisans, and other sections of the pro-labour press began to bicker over strategy. Increasingly, the immediate relevance of a republican movement was being questioned and, as the shearers' strike dragged on, the need for a body such as the Australian Labour Federation began to distract the leading members of the ARA. Republican meetings were cancelled on several occasions to allow members to attend mass meetings in support of the maritime strike.[106] The *Boomerang*'s criticism of the Brisbane branch of the ARA in September 1890 was typical of the mounting opposition facing the ARA. The *Boomerang* thought the Brisbane branch an example of 'shoddy republicanism', a group which lacked the gumption to stand up for radical change:

> Unless republicanism is thoroughly progressive and democratic practically as well as normally, we might as well remain exactly as we are. Because we are discontent with King Log we do not want to place ourselves in the hands of President Stork ... The republic we want is a land of free men whereon the government rests on the people, and is by them and with them and for them. No other form of republicanism will suit us not even though it does a few who follow the will-o'-the-wisp of a mere name.[107]

The secretary of the Brisbane branch of the ARA, Fred Passey, acknowledged in a letter to the *Australian Republican*, that republicans in Brisbane 'faced a lot of opposition from those who ought to push us on'. The labour leaders and the *Boomerang*, said Passey, were afraid that the republicans 'would split their party'.[108]

By the time of the shearers' strike the feeling that the labour movement could be split by republicans was widespread. When Frederick Charles Burleigh Vosper took over the editorship of the *Australian Republican* in October 1890 the journal entered a more radical phase. Straight away, Vosper turned the paper into a weekly and tacked the direction of the movement into more dangerous waters. Instead of 'independence peacefully achieved' it was now independence by 'such methods as may be necessary'. Vosper's rhetoric was evocative and forceful. His first editorial spoke of the need for a 'merciless attack on all kinds of political sham and abuse'. He called on all those who believed in 'Australia for the Australians' to stand up and be counted and declare that they were an 'upright down straight uncompromising democrat and republican'. One could be forgiven for thinking that Vosper was about to lay his life on the line for his beloved 'United States of Australia'. More than any other republican Vosper brandished a truly revolutionary sword. He was a republican in the tradition of 1789 and 1848, a man whose 'single aim' was the declaration of an Australian republic — a coming event which he dramatically described as the 'sole cause' of his existence.[109]

Born in Cornwall in 1867, Vosper had emigrated to Bolivia at the age of only fifteen where he participated in two 'sporadic revolutions'. After arriving in Queensland in 1883 he worked as a timber miller, drover, boundary rider, miner and journalist. Later, he became a member of the Australian Institute of Mining Engineers and was one of the founders of the Geological Society of Australia. At the age of twenty-four, Vosper had a thorough command of the craft of political journalism, and a knowledge

Frederick Charles Burleigh Vosper
Frederick Charles Burleigh Vosper was probably Queensland's most radical republican. Vosper is shown here in 1895, shortly before his death on the Western Australian goldfields.
(Albert Calbert, *My Fourth Tour in Western Australia*, 1897, Image Library, State Library of New South Wales.)

of political and social theory which would have made others envious. He was described as 'highly intellectual, a deep student, a magnetic personality and a wonderful platform speaker', standing about 'six foot high, stout and ruddy, with a big head' and with a fondness for whisky.[110] It seems 'inevitable' that Vosper will be the subject of a mini series at some future date, either that or his giant effigy will stand on the highway at Charters Towers—the big republican, Frederick Charles Burleigh Vosper.

When Queensland shearers decided in early 1891 to fight the graziers' attempts to destroy the principle of the closed shop, the beginnings of a bitter and protracted strike emerged. Before its conclusion and ultimate failure, shearers would mass in camps at Barcaldine and Clermont, violent clashes between union and non-union labour would ensue, and the Queensland government would react draconically by deploying troops and artillery against the strikers.[111] On 21 February 1891, as the shearers' strike reached its height, Vosper entered the fray by publishing a highly inflammatory editorial, an editorial calculated to elicit a response from the authorities and inspire the strikers to new heights:

> The men are placed in this position—they must either have BREAD OR BLOOD—WOOL OR HEADS—and if the government be not careful they will have BOTH ... The Government ought to know that in no country is revolution so easy as here; and once let the masses be roused, then good-bye to capitalistic domination and the sham royalty which is inflicted on us now, and hurrah for the Republic![112]

These words, plucky, taunting and swaggering as they were, were far in excess of anything John Dunmore Lang or Henry Lawson could ever have penned. The fact that the editorial was published at a time of extreme political crisis prompted a reactionary Queensland government to respond swiftly. Before copies of the *Australian Republican* could even be distributed throughout the colony, the authorities had all issues confiscated from postal offices in Charters Towers. Vosper, the man who saw himself as 'the leader of republicanism' in the region, was swiftly placed under arrest and put on trial for seditious libel. Detective Constable James McQuaker of Charters Towers, the person who initiated the charge against Vosper, typically described the editorial as 'wicked' and 'scandalous'.[113] Vosper had tested the waters and received an unambiguous reply. There would be nothing like 1848 tolerated in Queensland. But convicting Vosper was another matter. The bitter wrangling over jury selection which took place before and during Vosper's trial between May and August 1891 was an indication of the divisions which existed in the Charters Towers community over the 'bread or blood' editorial. When a jury panel acceptable to both parties was finally agreed, they were unable to reach a verdict. Then, at the retrial in August, Vosper was eventually acquitted. The specially selected jury found that Vosper's editorial was seditious but not published with the intention to incite the shearers to commit deeds of bloodshed, burning revolution and riot. Vosper, conducting his own defence, had successfully managed to evade prison but not the condemnation of many of his comrades, many of whom denounced his revolutionary tactics. Editorials from competing papers such as the *Charters Towers Times* claimed that talk of republican revolution would only play into the hands of the shearers' enemies.[114]

In many ways, Vosper's editorial and the eventual failure of the shearers' strike sealed the fate of the ARA. Vosper's call to arms was not one favoured by the majority of those pressing for the strengthening of the Australian Labour Federation. By August 1891 the *Australian Republican* was mourning the end of the great strike.[115] There was less correspondence from affiliate branches and the editors now highlighted individual requests for subscription instead of the formation of new republican associations. The political utility of the republican label for labour reformers in Queensland was now exhausted. After the shearers' strike, parliamentary representation and the achievement of practical reforms through collective bargaining were given priority. As one letter writer from Sydney explained to the *Australian Republican* in May:

> [Republicanism] can't be realised in our generation . . . We cannot hope for republican institutions till there is an upheaval or general insurrection throughout the colonies . . . [Republicanism] is not within the range of practical politics in the present time . . . and all your little paper might say does not advance the cause one iota.[116]

'Practical politics' was definitely the chief aim after the strikes of 1891 and separation from Britain was certainly not considered to be 'practical'. More often it was seen as an abstract fancy or 'premature'. Vosper's firebrand enthusiasm for an Australian republic was an exception. In August 1891 the *Australian Republican* published its last edition. It led with a frustrated editorial entitled 'Ballot or Bayonet', a question which was itself symptomatic of the movement's demise.[117] Vosper's transformation of the *Australian Republican* from constitutional republicanism to revolutionary republicanism had failed to stimulate the support the ARA needed to survive. Vosper was eventually ostracised by the ALF in Queensland. Radical, maverick and a political hero for many shearers, he later fled Queensland for the goldfields of Western Australia, vowing never again to cut his hair after prison authorities had given him the customary shave during his brief imprisonment for inciting leading strikers to riot in 1892. Vosper's last years in Queensland were representative of the difficulties which had beset the ARA from the beginning: plagued by internal division, distracted by regionalism, particularly the movement for north Queensland separation, and finally, faced with the repression of the Queensland government.[118] If this were not enough to kill off Vosper's republic there was the added burden of that old chestnut, the inevitable republic.

When Justice Chubb addressed the court in his three-hour summation during Vosper's first trial in May, he referred especially to republicanism:

> There is no moral harm in advocating a republic provided peaceful means are recommended. I believe and I think, in common with most intelligent men that the conversion of the Australian colonies into a republic is inevitable and I am of the opinion that a person who does not in some measure, agree with that idea is one who is incapable of comprehending the destiny of his country.[119]

As Albert Dawson, one of the founding members of the ARA well knew, Chubb's remarks were simply a means of satisfying 'the multitude and justifying inaction'.[120] The Australian republic remained the stuff of destiny rather than politics.

CHAPTER NINE

The Common Weal—
Republicanism and Federation

> Will we make Australia a grand whole commanding the respect and the admiration of the world, or will we split it up into a number of jarring, petty, squabbling states, at once ridiculous and contemptible?
>
> *Argus*, 3 April 1888

On 15 June 1889 New South Wales Premier Henry Parkes had a long conversation with the Governor of New South Wales, Lord Carrington, on the topic of Australian Federation. During the course of this conversation Parkes boasted that he could federate the Australian colonies in twelve months if he wanted to. Knowing Parkes well, Carrington pandered to his vanity and dared him to do it.[1] By the end of the year Parkes had visited Queensland and northern New South Wales, delivered his famous Tenterfield speech, and instigated the convening of a Federal Council which would be held in Melbourne.

Throughout the next decade, Federation was the 'inevitability' through which much political debate in the colonies was filtered. For most of this time, but especially in the early 1890s, there were many Australians who articulated a strong preference for an independent federal republic. Republican movements may have disintegrated, but a strong republican spirit had survived the 1880s and as always it was variable and not bound by class or ethnicity. Yet regardless of whether Federation was sought under the Crown or separate from it, almost every party agreed that the primary unifying force for Federation should be purity of race. For Parkes this race was 'British', as it was for many others who supported a republican Federation. Either way, the resulting Federation of the colonies was bound to be founded on the principle of exclusion rather than inclusion—a principle which might otherwise be described as racism. As far as Aboriginal Australians were concerned, or the thousands of Chinese Australians, it mattered little whether Australia became a republic or a constitutional monarchy in 1901. Both scenarios meant the continuation of discrimination, exclusion and persecution. If isolation in the South Pacific had caused many Australians to become more British than the British themselves it also contributed to the exacerbation of racism. Fear of invasion and the loss of a white man's fortress were central to much of the debate on Federation. Consequently, much of the argument about the merit of republican Federation focused on the issues of 'defence' and the

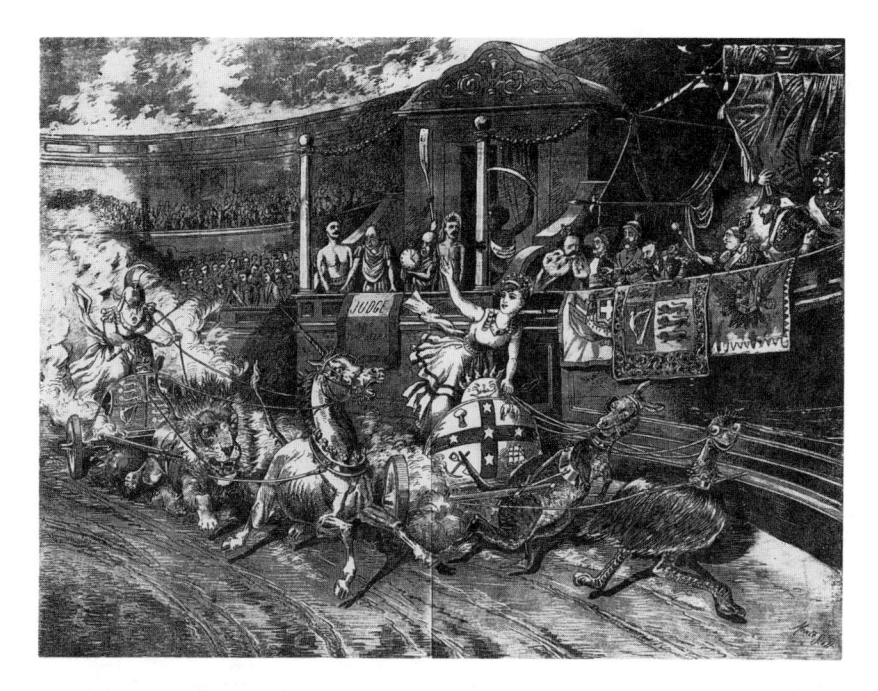

'Australia first'
The young, female Australia drawn by the spirit of Eureka and a delirious kangaroo and emu leaves the tired old English lion behind in the race to Federation.
(*Boomerang*, 1 February 1890, Image Library, State Library of New South Wales.)

flow of British capital.[2] The *Sydney Morning Herald*'s fears in 1891 were typical: 'As sure as we enjoyed the luxury of being cut adrift from the "effete" system of Great Britain, that moment would the fair fields of Australia become the cynosure of millions of hungering eyes in Europe, to say nothing of the yellow barbarians of the Flowery Land'.[3]

Although many republicans attempted to turn this argument on its head by supporting John Dunmore Lang's claim that the maintenance of the connection would simply embroil Australia in imperial war (a claim which was proved to be correct several times over) the fear of isolation was to prove far stronger. Australians preferred to sacrifice their citizens in a foreign war in the hope this would ensure British protection in their hour of need.[4] But the fear of geographical, economic and political isolation was still not strong enough to stop a significant number of republican voices being heard on the subject of Federation. While the early debates were often characterised by the polarisation of republican Federation and Imperial Federation, once the colonies had begun in earnest to address the prospect of Federation in the 1890s, the concept of Imperial Federation was never seriously entertained.[5] Republican Federation on the other hand was an idea proposed more frequently. In 1889 Sir Charles Lilley, the Chief Justice of Queensland, provoked a good deal of consternation when he publicly came out in support of a republic. Lilley's views were not aired from a park stump but from his desk at the Supreme Court in Brisbane:

> since 1856—and probably from before that time—there has been a strong democratic and republican element in these communities which is steadily growing, ... In truth, Australian independence is in the air and in the hearts of men, and although no man can foretell the hour of its birth its advent sooner or later is sure ...[6]

Lilley was a republican in the tradition of John Dunmore Lang: liberal, democratic, and fundamentally loyal to British institutions. Despite the support for a republic shown by Lilley and others, when colonial politicians finished their deliberations in Melbourne during a trying week of heat at a Federation Conference in February 1890, there was a clear signal that the issue of republican Federation was not open for discussion. The final motion of the Council stated: 'that in the opinion of this Conference, the best interests and the present and future prosperity of the Australian colonies will be best promoted by an early union *under the Crown*'. At the banquet which followed the first day of the Conference, Henry Parkes spoke not of an Australian nation, but the 'crimson thread of kinship that runs through us all'.[7] Parkes was as determined as ever that Federation should not mean severance from the mother country. During the twelve months that followed the meeting in Melbourne, there was a wide-ranging discussion on the task before the planned Federal Convention in early 1891. Predictably, republicans of the *Bulletin* mould saw the decision to federate under the Crown as a betrayal of Australian independence, a contradiction which simply swapped one form of provincialism for another.[8]

In New South Wales parliament there were four schools of thought on Federation under the Crown. First came those who wholeheartedly supported the resolution; the ones who recoiled in horror at any mention of 'red raw republicanism'. Next came those like Parkes, who simply tried to argue that the colonies were already republics in disguise.[9]

Close on the footsteps of the 'disguised republic' came republicans who saw independence as Australia's natural destiny but thought that the time was not yet right. Among them was W. H. Traill, a man whose radicalism had clearly been tempered by the trappings of political office. As Traill admitted, being a republican in New South Wales meant carrying the burden of significant social disabilities—to be a republican was to be a professional *persona non grata*.[10] Joined by Copeland, Melville, Greene, Wilkinson and others, Traill led the charge of the inevitabilists, otherwise described as 'philosophical republicans' or 'cold white' republicans rather than 'red hot' ones.[11] While this approach may have seemed politically astute at the time it certainly played into the hands of those who wished to exploit the inevitability argument to delay separation for as long as possible. Moreover, it left those republicans, such as Thomas Walker, who were brave enough to demand immediate republican Federation very much alone. William McMillan, member for East Sydney, explained the position of the 'theoretical republicans':

> I can quite understand a man being theoretically a republican and at the same time, a loyal citizen of Her Majesty the Queen ... I consider that a man may be a loyal Australian and yet may think that a change should take place in the Constitution of the country when the time is ripe.[12]

This detached, non-confrontational approach of the theoretical republicans in the 1890s virtually ensured that the Australian republic would be kept at bay.[13] Finally, there were the 'kamikaze' republicans led admirably by the member for Glen Innes, Alexander Hutchison:

> I maintain that to federate under the Crown is one of those conditions which is opposed to national spirit ... If we were to federate under the Crown and the present heir to the throne become our ruler, I should feel my human nature so degraded that I am not sure that I would not commit suicide.[14]

New South Wales parliament harboured more republicans than any other colony, but in every colony it was a minority of parliamentarians who denied the inevitable coming of an Australian republic. Although the reasons for being an inevitabilist varied the result was similar—Federation under the Crown.[15]

Commonwealth

For the majority of Australians in the late twentieth century, the name 'Commonwealth' is linked primarily to the British monarch and the commonwealth of nations. If asked to explain why their new Federation was given the title 'Commonwealth' in 1901 few Australians would link the word with the notion of government 'formed for the common good of its people' as Alfred Deakin did in 1891.[16]

When forty-five delegates from the six colonies and New Zealand met in Sydney in March 1891 at the Federal Convention they came to draft a bill for the Federal Constitution of Australia. One of the three select committees appointed by the Convention was first given the task of deciding on an appropriate name for the new Federation. On 31 March the chairman of the constitutional committee, Sir Samuel Griffith, presented to the full Convention a draft bill to constitute the 'Commonwealth' of Australia. The committee had voted by a majority of one to confer the title of Commonwealth on the proposed Federation. During the course of the Convention debates there was considerable discussion on the committee's choice of the term 'Commonwealth'. We know that 'Commonwealth' was a name put forward largely at Parkes' instigation.[17] Alfred Deakin relates the events surrounding the committee's choice in his book, *The Federal Story*:

> [Parkes'] literary tastes and habits led him to take a deep interest in the title of the new Union. He had been accustomed to lecture upon the heroes of the great political convulsion which culminated in the Great Civil War and it was but natural therefore that the name 'Commonwealth' should occur to him. It was received however with scanty favour by the Committee because of the flavour of Republicanism and the suggestion of Separation that it was considered to convey.[18]

Deakin was correct. The Convention debates saw much heated discussion, of which the following example is typical:

> Sir John Downer—The popular understanding of the word Commonwealth is certainly connected with republican times.
> Mr Deakin—No!
> Sir John Downer—It is, in my opinion connected with republican times, and it is certainly disconnected with that loyalty which we all . . . feel towards the Crown.
> Mr Deakin—The most glorious period of England's history!
> Mr Clark—Hear! Hear!
> Dr Cockburn—Was it under the Crown?
> Mr Deakin—There was then no Crown![19]

Much of the dispute which followed centred on whether or not the word 'Commonwealth' was connected with the 'glorious' phase of English history. Put another way, delegates could not agree whether the word 'Commonwealth' denoted a state which included monarchy or excluded monarchy, as it did under the protectorate of Oliver Cromwell. There were various means of proving the point. Those in favour reached for Shakespeare and Roget's *Thesaurus* in an attempt to prove that 'Commonwealth' was a term which simply described a government formed for the common good ('respublica') and a government which, for the majority of English history, had included monarchy as an essential component.[20] Those against, feared that if the new Federation adopted the title 'Commonwealth', it would send a signal that Australia was disloyal and republican or, as one delegate put it, a situation would be created where a future Oliver Cromwell would destroy the allegiance Australians had traditionally shown to the throne.[21] Although the motion to omit the word 'Commonwealth' from the draft bill and replace it with 'federated states' was lost by a 2:1 majority, it was clear that there was a substantial degree of confusion among delegates about the meaning of the word. Between 1891 and the year of the next major Convention in 1897, members of parliament in all colonies would continue to debate the meaning of 'Commonwealth', continually arguing over its republican connotations.[22] Essentially, they were doing to the word 'Commonwealth' what many have done to the word 'republic'—taking one set of associations (such as anti-monarchical or mixed government) and claiming these to be the true ones. Of course, there were always those who gave up. The Melbourne *Commonwealth and Worker's Advocate* remarked in 1891 that the word was of 'such deep meaning' that its 'full and complete import' could 'never be comprehended'.[23]

When Henry Parkes spoke at the beginning of the Convention, he made it clear that he had 'no time to talk' about 'republicanism':

> If a time should come when it would be necessary to sever the connection with the mother country, it will come, as it came in America, in spite of the loyalty, in spite of the good feeling of the chief men of the time. It will not come to meet the wild ravings of some person who may call out 'Republicanism', without the slightest knowledge of what he is talking about.[24]

For Parkes, 'true' republicanism had always been grounded in the English Civil War period of 1649–60. Parkes believed that the spirit of republicanism and the commonwealth was not anti-monarchical, but anti-tyrannical. This explains why he consistently argued that the United States could not strictly be called a republic because its system of government allowed for a president who was more powerful than the monarch in the English Constitution, the very Constitution which Parkes wished to embrace by suggesting the title of 'Commonwealth' for the new Australian Federation. When Parkes asked Edmund Barton's 'journalist–brother', G. B. Barton, to write an 'annotated version' of the Convention's draft bill, Barton's introduction explicitly set out to connect the title of 'Commonwealth' with pre-Cromwellian England.[25] Quoting Shakespeare, Harrington and Locke, Barton stressed that the word 'Commonwealth' simply described a state or community which in turn did not necessarily exclude monarchy. 'It corresponded', said Barton 'with the term respublica, as used by the political writers of ancient Rome . . . King James the First was even pleased to call himself "the Great Servant of the Commonwealth"'.[26] For both Parkes and Barton the choice of the word 'Commonwealth' was the achievement of one type of republic. It was not the republic of Lawson or Black but it was Parkes' 'true' republic none the less. In this sense, many Australians have yet to appreciate the submerged 'republican' legacy in their present Constitution. While this legacy is not the dominant and more active anti-monarchical strain with which we are familiar, it still deserves to be acknowledged.

After the French Revolution, and the separation of the United States from Great Britain, for Parkes and many others the word 'republic' had become 'sullied' by its connection with violence, separation and anti-monarchical sentiment. This was why he preferred the word 'Commonwealth' and why he distanced himself from the term 'republic'. Ever since 1850 he had preferred the 'substance' of republicanism without the 'shadow' of its name. Parkes' fear of tyranny was also shared by other delegates during the Convention debates. Sir Samuel Griffith rejected Sir George Grey's proposal to elect the Governor-General because he did not want to see Australia develop a similar situation to many states in America where governorships were kept as heirlooms by wealthy families. For Griffith, the Governor-General had to be 'above party politics'. Other delegates, such as Sir John Downer, feared the potential power of a popularly elected Governor-General. Alfred Deakin preferred a ceremonial Governor-General representing the sovereign of Great Britain to an elected office similar to the President of the United States.[27] The preservation of the link with the Crown was, for many delegates, one way of ensuring that the monarchical excesses of American presidential government were not enshrined in the draft bill for Australian Federation.[28] Even George Dibbs, the man at the Convention who confessed to 'possessing a slight tinge of republican notions', relied on that 'germ of liberty' planted by his English forefathers. Dibbs' vision of a republic was akin to William Wentworth's—'a New Britannia'—a republic which enshrined all of the virtues of the English Constitution and would simply fly 'a new flag'.[29] The Tasmanian-born delegate, Andrew Inglis Clark, was another delegate who brought a strong sense of republicanism to the debates. Clark's draft bill was an attempt to ensure limited legislative independence for both State and Federal governments in the new Federation. Clark strove to maintain the spirit of American republican government, working under the constraint of the retention of links with the Crown.[30] Like many theoretical republicans, he did not think Australia was quite ready for complete independence. Thus, Clark did not propose to alter the monarch's power to veto Commonwealth legislation.[31] Aside from Clark, there were others who were more openly 'republican', such as the South Australian, Sir Richard Baker. In his public speeches on Federation, and as a member of the South Australian Legislative Council, Baker declared that 'he was a republican, but was as loyal to the Queen and as strongly attached to Great Britain as anybody'. While his colleagues in the Legislative Council spoke of shooting the first rebel who professed republican principles, Baker, like Parkes in New South Wales, politely informed them that they did not know what they were talking about. The concept of republicanism, said Baker, was simply consistent with 'government by the people, for the people'. The proposed Federation 'under the Crown' was no obstacle to the essentially republican nature of the Australian Commonwealth. For Baker and Clark, republicanism did not mean choosing a president over a monarch, rather, it was the word which best expressed the democratic nature of the Australian Constitution.[32] Yet for all of this sympathy for the spirit of republicanism, the simple fact was that the label 'Australian republic' was unanimously rejected at the Convention because its active adoption symbolised separation from Britain.

By the time the Convention had completed its task in April, however, there was an extremely loud and discordant chorus of 'hot' republican opposition to the draft bill.

For the *Bulletin* and its bedfellows, the concept of a future Australian republic had nothing to do with the seventeenth-century Commonwealth men of England:

> The Englishman, more than any other individual on earth, reverences anything that is old, merely by reason of its age. The principle of hereditary monarchy is old—like mud and leprosy and premeditated homicide—and, therefore, its hideous grotesqueness never occurs to his intelligence. Most dynasties begin with one strong and vigorous sovereign, and after him come, as a rule, a long succession of dreary imbeciles.[33]

In the *Bulletin*'s eyes, the draft bill for Federation under the Crown was nothing more than 'an alienation of essential sovereignty'—a bill which set out to deny Australian nationhood and freedom.[34] This view was reflected throughout the Labour press. There was no shortage of opposition to the bill, as the Hobart *Mercury* acknowledged, there were persons actively working for separation, especially in New South Wales and Queensland.[35] Sir Charles Lilley rejected the draft bill, and claimed that it was a 'danger to the independence of Australia'. Other liberal opponents attacked the bill because it was the product of an undemocratic Convention.[36] In 1891 'hot' republicanism was still a priority for men like George Black and John Norton. Norton's colourful journal *Truth* kept the English radical criticism of monarchy alive, with a touch of healthy excess to add Australian flavour. The *Truth* saw Parkes' plans for Federation as a plot 'to rivet the links that bound Australia' to a land in which the 'whisky and Apolliniaris water drinking Victoria' was Queen.[37] Norton's approach was similar to the *Bulletin*'s: juxtapose the 'polished and cultured imperialists of Potts Point and Toorak' with that fount of all virtue, the Australian working male. Letter columns carried correspondence from 'The Grand Central Coffee Palace in Sydney' proclaiming the coming republic.[38] In South Australia, one of the few socialist organisations in the colony, the 'Allgemeiner Deutscher Verein', provided an interesting contrast to the republicanism of the eastern colonies. Whereas much of the explicitly republican sentiment in New South Wales was driven by the need to assert a manly sense of Australian independence, pockets of the German–Australian community in South Australia were sympathetic to a more philosophical and humanitarian vision of republicanism which had its roots in the radical traditions of European democracy. From the mid-1870s to the 1890s, through the publication of the *Süd-Australischer Zeitung*, the man who had participated in the 1848 revolutions in Germany, Dr Carl Mücke, together with the Hanover-born schoolteacher, Friederich Basedow, consistently proclaimed an Australian identity based on separation from Great Britain, Federation, and the civilising virtues of education and political participation. These beliefs were also present in the Allgemeiner Deutscher Verein, formed in 1886. In 1890 one of the organisation's more active members, A. A. Timmann, began the publication of a small journal, the *Pioneer*, from his Adelaide bedroom. Although the paper's existence was largely due to Timmann's desire to campaign for land nationalisation, its platform also included support for Federation on 'stringent democratic principles'—the 'true' republic:

> [We] desire the establishment of a true republic, not a sham one like that of America and France. Not a republic of Millionaires and Paupers, Masters and Slaves, but a Republic of free independent and interdependent citizens; a Republic based upon true democratic and equitable principles, securing equal opportunities to all, [and] favors to none. A Republic in which Liberty and Equality shall produce Fraternity, and shall be real active factors in the lives of all instead of being now mere ideals of which people speak much but feel little.

In Timmann's eyes, it was a sign of political immaturity to simply focus on the exchange of 'a King for a President' (as the republicans in the eastern colonies often did). The only remedy for social inequality was the introduction of reforms which sought to 'communalize national resources' thereby threatening the wealth of the landed classes. This was an ideal form of republicanism, one which was not preoccupied so much with names and titles like the Sydney *Bulletin*, and one which was far more thoughtful. Timmann placed little importance on the form of government, concentrating more on the practical democratic spirit and policies of government. This was the essence of his true republic.[39] Perhaps this was why the Allgemeiner Deutscher Verein immediately affiliated with the Labor Party in 1891.

Throughout the country, newspaper editorials had spoken of the opposition of the 'Labor Party' to Federation under the Crown. The 'Labor Party' was, of course, the Labor Electoral League of New South Wales, which had formed in April 1891 and emerged with such stunning success at the polls two months later. The LEL had won seventeen out of fifty-three seats contested at the June elections, a result which gave Labor a total of thirty-five seats in the new Legislative Assembly. The League's platform included the aim of Federation 'on a national as opposed to an Imperial basis'.[40] There were many republicans among the new Labor members, including George Black and Jack Fitzgerald, but it would be naive to believe that Labor's success at the polls was due to its position on Federation. After all, the LEL had purposefully left the word 'republican' out of its platform and substituted 'national' in its place. In addition, the League made no attempt to outline a timetable for this 'national' Federation, let alone provide details on the specific federal structure envisaged. The platform of the LEL was, in fact, a clear sign that the labour movement was turning away from republicanism to concentrate on securing political representation and practical labour reforms. Implicitly, this focus was bound to involve compromise with republican views. All Labor members swore an oath of allegiance to Her Majesty before entering parliament, and the more accustomed they became to the trappings of office, the more they realised that the links with the Crown were no obstacle to their reforms. Whenever 'hot' republicans in colonial parliaments did dare to speak up against the idea that Australians should continue to worship an 'old lady 16 000 miles away', they were forced to retract their words immediately. The parliamentary oath of loyalty ensured that open advocacy of republican views could always be censured.[41]

In the six-year period between the Federal Conventions of 1891 and 1897, there were occasions when Federation under the Crown itself seemed nothing but a pipe dream. Every colonial parliament rejected the draft bill of 1891, and if it were not for the determination of townspeople in southern New South Wales who brought together Federation leagues and branches of the ANA at Corowa in 1893, regional rivalry may well have triumphed. It was at Corowa that the idea of a Federal Convention elected by the people was first mooted. In turn, the Corowa Conference agreed that the draft bill of the elected Convention should then be sent to the people at a referendum, which was precisely what occurred in 1897–98. Finally, after amendments were made to the draft bill to satisfy doubts in New South Wales, the path to Federation under the Crown was clear.[42] But the chances of republican Federation were lost long before the people's representatives met in 1897.

Federation proved difficult enough to achieve without the added burden of forcing agreement on republican Federation. At Corowa, discussion of a republic was ruled to be out of order by the chairman.[43] E. W. O'Sullivan caused a stir at a public meeting in the Oddfellows' Hall on the evening of Monday 31 July, the first day of the two-day Conference. O'Sullivan moved that Federation would only be acceptable if it embodied the principle of 'one man one vote and the direct expression of the people'. The following morning when Conference delegates reconvened at Corowa Courthouse the formal motion that the Australian colonies move to an early union under the Crown provoked a republican outburst from William Maloney, the maverick socialist member of the Victorian Legislative Assembly. As Maloney declared in full voice that Australia was marching towards a republic, he (and his small band of Labor Party supporters) were shouted down with cries of 'No! No!'. Corowa may have been an important turning point on the road to Federation, but it was certainly no haven for men who rejected the restrictive definition of democracy championed by the majority of delegates.[44] Four weeks before Corowa, the Sydney republicans George Black and John Norton made one final gesture when a predominantly pro-Labor crowd dominated the meeting where the Australasian Federation League was established at Sydney Town Hall on Monday 3 July 1893. When an amendment was proposed by the president of the South Sydney Labor Electoral League that Australian Federation should be established on a democratic and republican basis it was carried by a majority of 2:1. Republicans had tried similar tactics in 1887 and 1888, stacking public meetings which the majority of citizens were too apathetic to attend. The authorities responded in much the same manner as they did six years earlier. Despite the vote, the chairman declared the original non-republican resolution carried and the meeting ended in uproar with police called in to clear republicans from the platform.[45]

In the same way that any Federation other than that 'under the Crown' was not open for discussion, 'hot' republicanism was never tolerated by colonial governments or the police under their control, especially if it moved beyond inevitabilism to immediate action. When the officers of the Australasian Federation League met in Sydney they made sure that the republican overtones that had marred the meeting earlier in July were not repeated. The so-called 'general meeting' was limited to just forty people. Republicans had been organised out of the debate on Federation, something which would occur again at the Bathurst Federal Convention in 1896 and the Federal Convention of 1897.[46] Republicans faced insurmountable odds and there were too many people in powerful positions who saw the very word 'republic' as anathema. One member of the Victorian Legislative Assembly, for example, had this to say about republicanism in 1891: 'For myself, . . . rather than see Australia a republic I would pray Almighty God to send it to nethermost hell. So little do I like the idea of a republic'.[47]

Although many 'hot' republicans in 1891 believed that a referendum on the question of Federation under the Crown would end in a victory for republicans, the more likely scenario would have been a convincing victory for those who favoured maintaining the links with Great Britain.[48] By this time republicanism was less of a priority for the labour movement. There was still the dogged persistence of journals like the *Hummer* in Wagga, which described itself as the official organ of the Associated Riverina Workers. Unlike the Labor Electoral League, the *Hummer* unashamedly declared in its platform that it favoured 'the complete political independence of the United Australia Commonwealth on a basis of pure democratic republicanism'. The *Hummer*'s claims made in support of republicanism were certainly more extravagant. 'Everyone knows', said the *Hummer*, 'that nine out of ten Australian workers are republicans'. Yet even if it were possible to substantiate this claim, an inclination to republicanism did not necessarily mean a 'willingness' to campaign actively or vote for the immediate introduction of a republic. The editors of the *Hummer* were 'philosophical' republicans.[49]

By 1894 even the *Bulletin* had decided that it was willing to accept Federation according to the plan of the Convention.[50] Although it did not completely 'haul down the Republican flag' in 1894, as Sylvia Lawson has claimed, the 'hot' republican spirit which it had displayed since the late 1880s had all but evaporated. The only signs of republicanism in the *Bulletin* after 1894 were the occasional call for separation accompanied by an awareness that this would be a future event.[51] It was far more common to encounter cynicism in the *Bulletin*. In October 1896 it admitted that there were far fewer people who objected to the British connection than there had been ten years earlier. One month later, its remarks on Federation applied equally if not more to republicanism: 'The average Australian has no definite opinion about the matter . . . He is all tarred with the same apathetic brush. "Federation—What is Federation?" "Oh! Something they talk about in Parliament." "Have anything on Newhaven for the Cup?"'.[52]

Scarred by economic depression and the failure of the strikes of the early 1890s, the republican radicalism of the labour movement subsided soon after the entry of Labor members to New South Wales parliament in 1891. John Norton recognised this trend when he berated the Labor Party for failing to vote against Parkes' Federation bill: 'The great majority of them were avowed republicans. Yet these are the very men who now turn round and bolster up Parkes, the chief of the Convention conspirators, and the greatest enemy of Labor in Australia'.[53]

Norton was one of the few Labor campaigners who consistently managed to maintain the rage, but by the time of the next Federation Convention in 1897 his republicanism had been submerged beneath the new pragmatism of a Labor Party accustomed to the compromise that accompanied political power. Thus, in 1896 we find the *Australian Workman*, the official organ of the Trades and Labour Council of New South Wales, specifically insisting that the contentious issue of 'separation' be kept out of all discussions on Federation. Although the *Workman* still refused to 'grovel to effete conceptions of loyalty', it had realised that supporting the connection with the Crown would actually aid the prospects of reform.[54] In every sense, the Labor Party and the trade unions had gathered the previously splintered landscape of labour reformers under the umbrella of parliamentary representation and collective bargaining, something which Henry Lawson foresaw as early as 1890:

> Trade Unionism is a new and grand religion, it recognises no creed, sect, language or nationality. It is a universal religion . . . open to all and will include all—the Atheist, the Christian, the Agnostic, . . . the Royalist, the Republican, the black, and the white, and a time will come when all the 'ists', 'isms' etc., will be merged and lost in one great 'ism'—the unionism of Labor.[55]

Concentrating on achievable and practical reforms through parliamentary representation was also one way for Labor to avoid the philosophical divisions of the 1880s. 'Cold white' philosophical republicanism was therefore much more attractive. By the time of the proceedings of the 1897 Convention there was a new consensus on 'Federation under the Crown'. Delegates agreed that the question of republicanism was not open for discussion, and instead spent most of their time arguing about tariffs and the powers of the Senate.[56] It seemed that the *Sydney Morning Herald*'s remarks back in 1891 on Federation had proved to be correct. The 'braggadocio' of republicans and the 'sentimental loyalty' of imperial federationists had been rejected for the 'utilitarian argument' in favour of retaining the connection. The colonies needed British power to protect themselves against potential attackers. But there were many other reasons besides the fear of invasion to explain the failure of Bulletinesque republicanism in the 1890s.[57] John Norton blamed 'the great lack of national spirit and ambition' which he thought noticeable in the rising generation of Australians. This was due, he said, to the 'sporting mania' and the moderating influence of liberalism. For Norton, the Labor victory at the polls in 1891 soon lost its lustre when it became clear that after entering parliament—or the 'Macquarie Street den' as he referred to it—Labor men suddenly transformed into 'namby pamby and respectable republicans'.[58] Norton's remarks point to the fact that republicanism did not 'disappear' or suddenly self-destruct. Rather, a consensus emerged that republicanism be 'postponed'. Even in 1897, after already having reluctantly acquiesced to Federation under the Crown, the *Bulletin* could still find some of its old fire to reply to the *Brisbane Courier*'s assertion that the Australian people identified thoroughly with the mother country:

> The average Australian doesn't yearn to identify himself with the foreign scoopful of dirt that the pious editor calls 'the mother country'. The average Australian's mother country is Australia. The average Australian doesn't care a rap about identification with England, a place he has never seen. He'll hooray for the Queen, if there is beer about; but he'd hooray for a man who rode a bicycle over a bar counter and set up the drinks for the township.[59]

Republican sentiment had not disappeared but republicans had decided, as Robert Thomson observed in 1891, that 'the proclamation of an Australian republic was a practicable impossibility'.[60] In New South Wales parliament the new Labor members who so annoyed Norton did not lose their republican beliefs, they simply became inevitabilists. We find a chorus of inevitability in parliamentary debates between 1891 and 1897. George Black MLA, now removed from his stump at the Domain to the more comfortable chairs in Macquarie Street, was typically relaxed. 'I am in no hurry. I would not precipitate federation.'[61]

E. W. O'Sullivan, another one-time republican, was more eloquent than Black:

> We ... who desire a republican form of government can afford to wait. Time fights on our side, and just as surely as the sun will shine tomorrow before all of us who are here tonight are in our graves there will be a republican form of government in Australia.[62]

It was precisely this view of an Australian republic which was to keep the grave-diggers so busy. The graveyard of the inevitabilist, cold white, philosophical, namby-pamby republicans would grow steadily over the next century. Lawson, O'Sullivan, Black, Traill—and so the list goes on. All that remains to be seen is whether Turnbull and partners are to join them. The fact that so many republicans in the 1890s turned to

A new leaf
The inevitable Australian republic—always close at hand.
(*Bulletin*, 4 January 1890, Image Library, State Library of New South Wales.)

inevitabilism when faced with the reality of Federation under the Crown simply made them even more indistinguishable from their opponents. It also played into the hands of those who argued that Britain and her colonies already lived under a republican Constitution.[63] The longer the republic could be delayed, the more difficult it would be to substantiate arguments for change. The conceptual greyness of republicanism would always make sure of that. After 1890 Australian republicans would constantly be faced with the alleged republicanism of their own Constitution, a perception which the self-described republicans of the 1890s certainly helped to encourage and cement. To be fair, however, they could hardly be blamed for this. From their perspective, they probably saw the limited degree of independence in the Australian Federal Constitution as republicanism enough at the time.[64] In addition, racial purity was as prominent a theme in the new Federation as it had been in the platforms of republicans in the 1880s and 1890s. Federation under the Crown posed no threat to Anglo-Saxon supremacy and White Australia.

Another factor which contributed to the undercutting of republicanism in the 1890s was the lack of positive republican role models. This may come as a surprise, as for much of the nineteenth century the United States of America had been the beacon for Australian republicans. But by the 1890s the majority of republicans saw America in a different light. The American Civil War of 1861–65 and the increasing knowledge of patronage, inequality of wealth, and widespread poverty in the United States, made it easier for those in favour of maintaining the links with the Crown to portray the British Constitution as the guarantor of greater freedom. The stability of Canadian government under 'nominal royalty' was seen as preferable to the 'oppressive' republican governments in the United States and South America. Republicans found themselves in agreement with the likes of Parkes when they described the American republic as 'despotic', or exhibiting a 'lack of liberty'.[65] The waning impact of the United States as a positive role model encouraged many in the labour movement to be sceptical of future republican government in Australia. In the eyes of many reformers, the 'money kings' of the American republic were just as repulsive as the crowned kings of England. Perhaps this was why the *Bulletin* admitted as early as 1888 that it held 'no profound faith' in the honesty of republican government. Like the letter writer to the *Hummer* in 1892, the *Bulletin* agreed that 'America was anything but a paradise for the worker with long hours, wretched pay and corrupt judges'.[66] The Australian republican who detested British capitalism with such passion had also retained much of the traditional suspicion of tyranny inherent in British constitutionalism.

When the Australian colonies federated in 1901, the majority of Australians were content to remain under the protection of the Crown.

Henry Parkes' preference for substance over shadow had again won the day. But the Constitution of the new Commonwealth still bore the stamp of dependence. Ten years before Federation, George Black had scribbled some ominous words on his copy of the draft bill of the Federal Constitution. Black thought that the powers prescribed for the Governor-General were 'dangerous'. Carefully, he wrote in the section headed 'executive government' on page 44 of his copy of the bill: 'The Bill has no provision for the dismissal of ministers. In no line does it imply their responsibility to Parliament. The Governor-General . . . might defy parliament'.[67]

Unwittingly, Black had come close to identifying the catalyst for the emergence of the next extensive period of republican debate, more than three-quarters of a century later.

CHAPTER TEN

The Imperial Mardi Gras 1901–1963

> The British monarchy in its purely business aspect is practically unobjectionable . . . So long as it is understood that the British monarch holds his or her position by the will of the nation and for the convenience of the nation, there is no reason for complaint against the monarchical system.
>
> *Bulletin*, 2 February 1901

In 1911, the pathetic figure of Henry Lawson, the great republican of the 1880s, could be seen wandering the streets of Sydney begging for alcohol. Only one year earlier, Lawson had written two poems in honour of the Coronation of George V. In the last years of his life, Lawson was an apologist for monarchy and the British connection. Like most of those who were associated with the early labour movement, Lawson could find no reason to maintain his republican rage in the twentieth century. By the time the Australian colonies federated, the republican fire of the *Bulletin* and the majority of the radical press had been extinguished. All that remained was occasional grumbling about the pomposity of imperial culture. The *Bulletin*, like the Labor Party, had come to see that the imperial connection was appropriate for the new nation, at least for the time being.[1]

On Tuesday 1 January 1901 the people of Sydney gathered in Centennial Park to witness the inauguration of the Commonwealth of Australia. Before them, on a platform draped in imperial regalia, an assortment of public officials sported the latest designs in imperial fashion. Cocked hats, swords, wigs and military uniforms abounded. For colour, costume and florid language, the platform and speakers rivalled the best Mardi Gras floats of the 1990s.

Earlier that day, crowds had lined the city streets to watch the imperial mardi gras parade pass underneath a succession of triumphal arches on its way to Centennial Park. Australia celebrated its nationhood by stressing its Britishness, something which was reflected in the text of the new Constitution, a document which was always intended to emphasise the subordination of the Commonwealth rather than its independence. The Constitution, an Act of British parliament, stated in the preamble that the people had agreed to unite in one 'indissoluble Federal Commonwealth under the Crown of the United Kingdom of Great Britain and Ireland'. The language of the Constitution was dry, legalistic and imperial.

Superficially, it seemed that the document paid greater attention to 'the Queen's pleasure' than the needs of the Australian people. This was the first time that the 'boundaries of a nation–state had coincided with those of a whole continent', but this was a nation without independence; a nation without its own flag, a national anthem, a currency, an honours system, a navy and the power to conduct its own foreign policy.[2] Even as the gun salutes heralded the birth of the nation on 1 January, Australian soldiers were dying for the Empire in South Africa. Further indication of the dependence of the new Commonwealth could be seen in the office of Governor-General. For the first thirty years of the Commonwealth's existence the Governor-General was the 'visible link' with London, appointed by the reigning monarch, never Australian, and primarily presiding to protect imperial interests. Some historians have bemoaned the lack of independence in the Constitution and the absence of any Australian flavour in the celebrations that accompanied it.[3] Yet both the Constitution and the celebrations of 1 January were an accurate reflection of the priorities of the Australian people in 1901.

The road to Federation had been difficult, but the truth was that it was only through devotion to monarch and Empire that Federation was able to take place. Loyalty to Britain was the common bond which united a group of suspicious and distrustful colonies. Imperialism, for all its gaudy symbolism, provided the vision, the grandeur and the glorious past that Australians were not able to find in their own beginnings. The comments of the *Sydney Morning Herald* after the opening of the Harbour Bridge in 1932 were typical of the need Australians felt for the British connection: 'The King's message and the presence of the Governor General brought the empire into prominence as the Union Jack, floating aloft in its place with our own Australian flag marked the unity without which our strength as a Commonwealth must be but pitiable weakness'.[4]

In 1938 the Sesquicentenary celebrations continued the theme of Australia's 'march to nationhood' and material progress as a member of the British Empire. Attachment to Britain solved the quandary posed by Australia's geographical position. Under the imperial umbrella Australia and her 'British race' would be safe from harm. The crisis of belonging, whether to Britain, America or Asia, was easily solved in the first decades after Federation.

The Australian colonies had federated at a time when the British monarchy played a vastly different role to the one it had occupied at the time of American Independence. By the time of Queen Victoria's death— three weeks after Australian Federation—the Crown had become the emblem of the 'British race', and the monarchy had transformed itself into something 'splendid public and popular'. Viewed from the perspective of the increased closeness brought by communication media such as the telegraph and radio, Australia had little choice about its allegiance. At the very time nationhood beckoned, the nation's communication networks were flooded with imperial propaganda. Initially, this helped to ensure that the vigorous criticism of monarchy, which had been a feature of nineteenth-century political culture in both Britain and Australia, would not be as strong in the twentieth century. The monarch was now the bedrock of political and social stability, the source of all institutional authority, the legitimiser of war and the prop of class prejudice and cultural snobbery, factors which were only exacerbated in an isolated community like Australia.[5] Against this background it is not surprising that for the first fifty years of the Commonwealth's existence, Australian media, churches, schools, business and parliaments indulged in an annual imperial orgy known as Empire Day. Empire Day was the best example of the way in which British paradigms dominated Australian culture, paradigms which were continually bolstered by the public affection for the royal family. A succession of royal 'visitations' helped to bury internal political differences and boost the role of the monarch as a unifying national symbol.[6] The excessive displays of loyalty to the throne, which had always been a feature of Australian public life, were now amplified by electronic media. As we have so often heard, it was the Lord Warden of the Cinque Ports, Robert Menzies, who took over from where Parkes left off half a century earlier. Between 1952 and his retirement in 1966 Menzies played the role of bell boy to the Queen Goddess Elizabeth. His embarrassing protestations of love and affection for the Queen and her 'little' country were symptomatic of the desire to kneel felt by many Australians when in the presence of British visitors.[7] In 1954 the Federal government went to the trouble of publishing a small pamphlet entitled *The Royal Visit and You*. This booklet was an attempt to inform uncultivated Australian officialdom of the appropriate etiquette for social functions during the royal tour.[8] Retrospectively, it all seems very amusing. One can just imagine Australian officials checking their copies of *The Royal Visit and You* at royal functions. Have I gone to unnecessary expense? Should I be dancing on the right or left of Her Majesty? Should I be dancing at all? Perhaps the Menzies government published their 'little book' because they feared the young Queen would be greeted by a bevy of Sir Les Pattersons.

Although the 1954 royal tour was the climax of half a century of Empire worship in Australia, the absence of 'hot' republicanism during these years is not explained simply by the dominance of imperialism. Between 1901 and 1964 there were still substantial pockets of opposition to imperialism but they were now filtered through a political framework which was completely consumed by the prospect of external threats. For many Australians, it seemed that if the Germans or Japanese didn't take

WHEN YOU MEET THE QUEEN AND THE DUKE

If you are presented to Her Majesty the Queen,

the correct procedure is to address Her Majesty in the first instance as "Your Majesty," and thereafter as "Ma'am."

If you are presented to His Royal Highness

it is correct to say in the first instance, "Your Royal Highness," and thereafter, "Sir."

Procedure in presenting guests.

Her Majesty normally stands on the right of The Duke of Edinburgh. The host, or whoever has the honour of presenting the guests, stands on the right of Her Majesty. Guests approach from the right, husbands in front of wives, and the host introduces each by name in a voice clear enough for both The Queen and The Duke to hear. Each male guest bows, and the women curtsey, before The Queen and shake hands prior to passing on to The Duke, before whom they bow or curtsey. They then shake hands and pass on.

At a State Ball

Mostly no prior arrangements are made about partners for The Queen and The Duke of Edinburgh at an official Ball. Her Majesty and His Royal Highness might dance together for a time or they might dance with one or two partners. Most of the time they prefer to watch. Guests may begin dancing as soon as the orchestra plays after the arrival of Her Majesty and should not wait till Her Majesty moves on to the dance floor.

At public luncheons and dinners.

At public luncheons and dinners the host has The Queen at his right and The Duke of Edinburgh at his left. The hostess sits at the left of The Duke of Edinburgh. The next most important guest sits at The Queen's right. At more informal meals, The Queen and The Duke usually sit opposite one another across the table. When this happens, The Queen has the host at her right and The Duke the hostess at his right.

Royal Performance

When Her Majesty and His Royal Highness attend a theatre or similar function during the Australian Tour, it will be designated a "Royal," "Special," or "Gala" Performance. Guests always stand when Her Majesty enters a theatre or any other place.

WHAT DRESS SHOULD YOU WEAR AT PUBLIC FUNCTIONS?

WOMEN

Her Majesty has expressed the wish that no one should be put to unnecessary expense in buying clothes and accessories.

Long dresses need not be worn at Garden Parties or other daytime functions. Short afternoon frocks are correct.

Hats should always be worn at daytime functions.

Gloves should always be worn at daytime functions. They **need not** be white and **should not** be taken off before the wearer is presented to The Queen or The Duke.

If ladies possess long gloves, they should wear them at formal evening functions.

When opening a Parliament Her Majesty wears full evening dress, although it may be in the daytime.

Women guests at the opening of Parliament should not wear evening dress.

MEN

Her Majesty does not wish anyone to stay away from a function to which he has been invited because he feels he has not the correct clothes to wear.

At Garden Parties The Duke of Edinburgh and members of the Royal Household will wear top hat and morning frock coat, or alternatively, soft felt hat and lounge suit, according to the local custom.

The basic principle to be observed for Garden Parties is that men shall wear the best they have, whatever it may be.

Officers in the Services may have the option of wearing uniform.

On any occasion it will be correct for anyone not possessing a uniform or morning dress to wear a lounge suit.

In the evening a dinner jacket may be worn at a ball or other function by anyone not possessing a white tie and tails. A lounge suit may be worn by anyone not having a dinner jacket.

When you meet the Queen and What dress

One way of understanding the loyalty and affection Australians have always held for the British monarch is to read *The Royal Visit and You*, a small publication produced by the Menzies government in 1954 for the visit of the newly crowned Queen Elizabeth II. If Australians were unsure of what to wear, what to say or how to dance when in the Queen's presence, they could refer to the relevant pages.

(*The Royal Visit and You*, 1954, Government of the Commonwealth of Australia, Commonwealth of Australia copyright reproduced by permission.)

Australia then the Communists or the Catholics probably would. The fact that so much of Australian politics between 1901 and 1963 was dominated by the ideological battle between capitalism and communism and the bitter divisions of religious sectarianism meant that republicanism was not seen as the primary threat to Australia's 'British' way of life as it had been in the nineteenth century. Communism became the new bogey, while republicanism became something which was primarily associated with Irish separatism. When one member of the Communist Party dared to write an article critical of the coronation of Queen Elizabeth in 1953, the Menzies government went so far as to order the Federal Police to raid the offices of the Communist Party of Australia and charge the author, Rex Chiplin, with 'seditious intention' under section 24A(1) of the Crimes Act (1914). Even though the charge was dismissed, by attempting to prosecute Chiplin under the Crimes Act, Menzies 'had tried to insist that public loyalty to the Crown was an essential component of political stability in Australia'.[9] The Act effectively interpreted open declarations of republicanism as seditious, although it is unlikely that advocating a minimalist republic without the Communist overtones would have attracted such a reaction from the Federal Police.

As far as the Irish are concerned, the popular assumption that Australian republicanism has traditionally been the domain of Irish–Australians stems largely from the misconception that the Irish who campaigned for a republic at home also wanted to see a republic in their adopted land. On a more basic level, when the word 'republic' was heard or read in Australia after the Easter Rebellion of 1916, the words 'Ireland' or 'Irish' were usually close by. In 1921 one Protestant minister in Sydney warned that Rome's agents in Australia were just as Sinn Fein as Rome's agents in Ireland and if they had their way there would be a republic in Australia dominated by the Vatican.[10] There is no doubt that Irish–Australians harboured a deep mistrust of British rule and that they were healthily sceptical of both the British class system and the monarchy. Yet it is partly because of this image of Irish–Australians as anti-British revellers that historians have arrived at dichotomies such as the one below from Gavin Souter. Souter writes of Australia at the end of the First World War:

> There were clearly two types of Australians now, probably about equal in number, and not easy to define. There were the British–Australians, unchanged in their imperial loyalty, predominantly middle class, Protestant, and politically conservative, and there were those who had rejected, outgrown, forgotten or simply never known the British inheritance. To this second group which might be called the Indigenous Australians, belonged a large part of the working class, most Irish Catholics, the children of European immigrants the industrially militant and the politically radical.[11]

While there are elements of truth in this dichotomy, there are also many problems. To begin with, it encourages the misconception that WASP (White Anglo-Saxon Protestant) Australians were somehow 'British' and not Australian—or more generally that loyalty to Britain was antithetical to Australian nationalism. Secondly, it stereotypes Irish and European immigrants and native-born Australians as politically 'radical' and anti-British. From this it follows that republicanism in Australian history can then be stereotyped as an Irish plot, ethnic troublemaking, or a predominantly working-class movement. If this is the case, then how do we explain the fact that many of the Australians who waved enthusiastically as Queen Elizabeth passed by in 1954 were of Irish extraction? The statement of ALP Senator James Ormonde in the Senate in 1964 might provide a useful starting point: 'The principal buttress of the Royal Family is . . . I was about to use the expression "the working class"—the little people of the British Commonwealth'.[12]

It is precisely these 'little people' that Stephen Alomes refers to less condescendingly when he writes of imperial ritual in early twentieth-century Australia:

> The ideological impact of the popular rituals and the socialisation involved in these processes [of Imperial propaganda] was fundamental. The co-option of the larger population, especially the working class, into Imperial patriotism, monarchism and militarism successfully weakened class identifications and radical sentiments.[13]

The belief that republicanism in Australia has largely been the work of Irish–Australians conflicts with the fact that the Irish working class have always been very much a part of the political conservatism of Australia, especially during the Menzies years. In addition, the majority of Australian republicans we have met so far were English- or Scottish-born. In an Australian context the Irish have supported the maintenance of the connection with Britain.

When the Catholic Archbishop of Sydney, Cardinal Patrick Moran, was dissatisfied with his allotted position in the Federation procession to Centennial Park in 1901 the Irish Catholic community did not take up arms, instead, led by Moran, they organised their own ceremony outside St Mary's Cathedral and loyally sang 'God Save the Queen' at its conclusion.[14] Thirteen years later, at the outbreak of the First World War, the Irish–Australian community supported Britain. Speaking at the Melbourne Town Hall in 1914 John Gavan Duffy, the self-described 'Irish Catholic nationalist', claimed that Irishmen were willing to forget 'all the injustices of the past' in Britain's 'hour of need'. While the Irish were never willing to be part of nonsense such as Empire Day, they were rarely agitators for an Australian republic (Daniel Mannix included), simply because this was the most obvious way for the Irish to be accepted as Australians. The republicanism of Irish–Australians between the wars was connected foremost with Ireland and if we must make them Australian republicans, we can only do so by implication.[15] On the occasions that they did allow their republicanism to spill over to Australia, it was often as an aside or afterthought.

The case of Hugh Mahon, president of the Irish Land League and member of federal parliament, is one example. Speaking in 1920 in front of a crowd of 10 000 supporters of the League in Melbourne, Mahon called for an end to the 'foreign occupation of Ireland' and pledged the League's support 'for any movement for the establishment of an Australian Republic'.[16] Typically, Mahon invited someone else to start the movement but was unwilling to initiate it himself. Even if Mahon were serious, the reaction of Hughes and the House of Representatives was an indication of just how much things had changed since the nineteenth century. Then, it was at least possible for members of parliament to declare their support for a republic, however immediate or inevitable. In the 1920s, however, open advocacy of republicanism was completely taboo. In Federal parliament Hughes accused Mahon of treason and successfully demanded his expulsion. For a short time, parliament resembled a kangaroo court, with Mahon being painted as a 'traitor to his country'.[17]

When the Victorian parliament sought to expel Edward Findley, the editor of the radical weekly *Tocsin*, for his syndication of a republican article from the *Irish People* in 1901, another farce ensued. When the article was read to the House, Premier Peacock ordered Hansard reporters and members of the public outside because he thought the article too scandalous. One member taunted the Speaker, 'Supposing you do order Hansard out—you cannot prevent me from [later] . . . quoting what has been said'. 'Yes I can' said the Speaker. 'If you like by force to silence me you can do it' came the reply. This was the kind of madness that as one member remarked 'the King of England himself would not adopt'.[18] There was little chance of republicanism being able to surface when the mere hint of disloyalty meant instant public humiliation. After 1901 Australians were certain about their loyalty to Empire, not so much because they identified with imperialism but because they would have felt vulnerable and insecure without it. There was still evidence of republicanism in the labour movement, at least until the 1920s, but it was sporadic, non-committal and mostly confined to the far left wing. For a short while, *Tocsin* in Melbourne under Bernard O'Dowd's editorship maintained occasional republican opposition to Federation, as did the Broken Hill *Flame* and the Hobart *Clipper*.[19] Sections of the Labor Party were still uncertain about their attitude to the monarchy before the tour of the Prince of Wales in 1920 while the left wing seemed to mention a republic mainly in the context of eradicating capitalist class ownership.[20] After Federation the bulk of the parliamentary Labor Party were loyal socialists. As the Sydney *Worker* observed in 1911, Labor worked towards 'practical' goals and the British tie should be allowed to remain.[21] What preoccupied the labour movement now was not the need for a republic—which could in any case be had simply by asking for it—but deciding on the most appropriate political strategies to achieve class equality. The Great Depression, two world wars and the Cold War only encouraged the left wing to concentrate on international class solidarity rather than Australian nationalism.

When New South Wales Premier Jack Lang refused to pay back British loans during the Great Depression, he was not branded a republican but a Communist, even by ultra-loyalists such as the New Guard. Equally, by the 1930s the radical wing of the labour movement did not prioritise republicanism as it did in 1890s, but Communism.[22] The Communist Party of Australia sought to establish a 'workers and farmers republic' with a Soviet form of government led by the workers—the dictatorship of the proletariat.[23] While it is true that the most frequent calls for a republic between 1930 and 1963 came from the CPA, theirs was a republicanism of ideological imperatives and when the CPA used the word 'republic' it carried little of its previous cultural or political baggage.[24] Jack Lang's staunch independence and his determination to assert Australia's interests, actually had more in common with the separatist republicans of the nineteenth century than that of the CPA, as did P. R. Stephensen's *Foundations of Culture in Australia*, published in 1936. Lang and Stephensen both tried to distinguish Australian nationality and Australian self-interest from that of Britain or the Empire. Although they never referred to themselves as 'republicans' they were part of one strain of Australian nationalism which would not accept the notion of 'divided' loyalty. For Stephensen especially, there was only one loyalty and that was to Australia. *Foundations of Culture in Australia* was a brilliant and influential polemic on the cultural cringe, and despite the Australia First movement's Fascist overtones, what strikes home very clearly when reading it today is the manner in which many of Stephensen's arguments prefigure those of the republicans of the 1960s and 1970s. Stephensen wrote in 1936:

> It seems to me that while Australia remains in the British Empire, and while the British Empire is controlled from London and while Australia accepts mentally or politically a *subordinate or subsidiary status* within that empire, it will be quite impossible for Australians to develop a culture here with distinct national features.[25]

Stephensen had refined the *Bulletin*'s nationalist rhetoric which he regarded as 'larrikin, rude, slangy and naughty',[26] but his emphasis on the 'subordinate' status of Australia under the Empire would be picked up later by Donald Horne and Geoffrey Dutton. In the nineteenth century, republicanism had revolved very much around the debate concerning the extension of political and constitutional rights. Stephensen's book was actually one of the first signs that this focus was beginning to shift or at least broaden. As soon as Australia federated in 1901 the gradual process of granting the new Commonwealth greater political and legal autonomy began almost immediately. The Australian Commonwealth may not have been an independent or sovereign nation in 1901, but by the time of the Statute of Westminster in 1931 Australia 'had federal parliaments free of United Kingdom control' and a head of state who could act only on the advice of Australian ministers.[27] This was evidenced by Prime Minister Scullin's appointment of Isaac Isaacs as the first Australian Governor-General in 1931. Although King George was extremely dissatisfied with the appointment, his conversation with Scullin at Buckingham Palace revealed that the independence of the elected Australian minister was not in doubt. After forty-five minutes of quite heated debate between the two men the King said: 'I have been for 20 years a monarch and I hope I have always been a constitutional one, and being a constitutional monarch I must, Mr Scullin, accept your advice which, I take it, you will tender me formally by letter'.[28]

The role of the Governor-General had already been altered by the resolutions of the Imperial Conference of 1926. After 1926 the Governor-General was no longer the diplomatic representative of the British government. The Balfour Declaration of 1926 paved the way for a Federal Department of External Affairs in 1935.[29] This is not to say that Australia exercised full independence in its foreign relations, but the trend was clearly one of moving away from dependence to independence—a trend which had begun back in 1856 with the granting of responsible government. It is important to acknowledge that Australia's independence from Great Britain evolved gradually and peacefully in the four decades between Federation and the end of the Second World War, but it would be wrong to imagine that this evolution was given much prominence within Australia at the time.

At the Paris Peace Conference in 1919 Australia possessed separate dominion status, thanks largely to the persistence of Prime Minister Billy Hughes. Hughes was determined to carve out an independent Australian voice within the Empire. In the tradition of Australian political leaders in the nineteenth century he was not afraid to threaten the withdrawal of Australian loyalty if he thought this voice was being ignored. On one occasion, Hughes' staunch defence of Australian interests at Paris resulted in his cabinet sending an urgent telegram to remind him not to endanger the British connection.[30] Hughes was always aware that he could never risk being seen as anti-British on a domestic front in which 'rational discussion of Empire or the United Kingdom connection had become difficult'. Australian fear of losing British military and naval protection was too great after the First World War to contemplate complete severance from Britain.[31] If we accept the argument of Hudson and Sharp, Australia obtained its diplomatic independence in 1923 when the dominion governments were effectively given full and free access to the sovereign, free of interference from the British government. This was closely followed by executive independence in 1926, with the Australian Governor-General now able to act only on the advice of his dominion ministry. Finally, in 1931 Australia attained its legislative independence when the Statute of Westminster ensured that no British Act of parliament could apply to an Australian federal parliament without Australian consent. Our federal parliament was now free to enact laws repugnant to English law and to repeal or amend Westminster Acts applying to them.[32]

Yet this reading of 'independence' may be too legalistic and narrowly defined, as Hudson and Sharp admit. The States were not affected by the Statute of Westminster. State governments continued in a legal status of dependent colonialism until the passing of the Australia Act in 1986. In addition, Australians were still 'British subjects', appeals to the Privy Council remained and the British dominance of Australia's intellectual and artistic life was barely challenged. The Statute of Westminster was not even ratified until 1942. As George Winterton has remarked, 'the outstanding political feature' of Australia's march to legislative independence is 'how little part Australia played in it'. Between the wars, it did seem that Australia was determined to cling to dependence.[33] Australia's federal parliament may have been freed in 1931 but the public heart of its culture remained in imperial chains. State and federal governments continued to accept British imports as Governors and Governors-General.[34] Throughout the 1930s and beyond, in public ceremonies, in schools and community organisations, universities, business associations and hotel foyers, affection for Britain and the comforting cloak of the connection remained strong. But the evolution of independence was still central to undercutting appeals to anti-British or radical labour-inspired republicanism. Essentially, this meant that the old arguments against the need for a republic carried more weight, at least as far as political independence was concerned. Loyalists could continue to reply that like Britain, Australia was already a republic in disguise. More importantly, many of the arguments which loyalists used to support the continuation of Australia's links with the Crown incorporated many of the arguments used by liberal reformers such as Parkes in the nineteenth century. Then, 'loyalists' spoke of the virtues of the English Constitution. In the twentieth century, after the formation of the Commonwealth and the writing of the Australian Constitution, much of the old rhetoric concerning the 'Constitution' was simply transferred to the 'Crown', the last visible link with Britain. Thus it was common to find the monarch being portrayed as the protector of democracy and national security, the symbol of civic virtue and 'service', and the bulwark against tyranny, corruption and the 'despotic whims' of oppressive government.[35]

When Keith Hancock eulogised the monarchy in 1943 he may have hoped that anti-republicans would be saying much the same thing half a century later:

> Australia has achieved sovereignty without the pain and loss of separation. Australia belongs to a family, a Commonwealth of democratic nations. Each member of this family declares its independence; each, proclaims its interdependence. Here, in this sundered world of snarling nationalisms, is a true political miracle. All the cleverest professors of the nineteenth century argued that it could never happen. They proved to their own satisfaction that national freedom must inevitably mean imperial disruption. But something quite different has happened, and is still happening. Monarchy grows into democracy, empire grows into commonwealth, the tradition of a splendid past is carried forward into an adventurous future.[36]

Between 1945 and 1975 this kind of reasoning, so succinctly articulated by Hancock, claimed almost complete ascendance. If Hancock's argument was accepted then there was no need for 'hot' republicanism in Australia. This probably explains why republicans in the 1960s and 1970s based their case on cultural independence and nationality rather than points of constitutional independence, at least until Sir John Kerr helped them out in 1975. Ever since the catharsis of Gallipoli and the First World War there had been growing signs that Australia's loyalty to Empire was being 'tempered' by an awareness of the uniqueness of Australian society, its different needs and interests and its different nationality.[37] The fact that Empire Day finally ended up as 'cracker night' in the 1950s showed that the thrill of putting a thunder-bunger in someone's mail box mattered more to many Australians than the virtues of the English Commonwealth and the Queen.

The reaction to the bodyline bowling of Jardine's touring English cricket team in the 1930s was another example of the way in which the mystique of the Crown was beginning to be balanced by the not-so-mysterious cry of 'Pommy bastard'.[38] When Jardine entered the Australian team's dressing-room to complain that an Australian player had referred to one of his players as a bastard, Captain Bill Woodfull is alleged to have replied: 'Which one of you bastards called this bastard's bowler a bastard?'.[39]

While Pommy bastards could be found with increasing regularity, the growing awareness of Australian nationality was accompanied by an acceptance that Pommy bastards were good 'blokes' when all was said and done. Part of the male Australian larrikin identity was not only crudeness and vulgarity but jocularity, a fact which ensured that the insults were not really that heartfelt after all. There were good bastards and bad bastards and the Pommies were usually accepted as good ones.

When Australians were asked to declare their preference for British or Australian nationality in 1947 in a nationwide Gallup poll, 65 per cent of the sample stated their preference for British nationality.[40] Although Australians became Australian citizens with the passing of the Chifley government's Nationality and Citizenship Act in 1949, Menzies later revoked the Act's provision for Australian passports and Australians travelled on British passports until 1963.[41] This only demonstrated just how entangled notions of Australian and British nationality really were.

Looking back over the period 1901 to 1963, the obvious question arises: why did republican sentiment in Australia all but disappear during these years? Apart from the reasons already mentioned, there appear to be two crucial factors. First, the formation of the new Australian nation in 1901 had occurred at the very time that Great Britain was once again turning to its colonies to support a new programme of imperialism. As always, loyalty to Empire and loyalty to Australia were not antithetical but intertwined. As far back as 1912 the *Sydney Morning Herald* perceptively observed: 'Imperialism and Nationalism are not mutually exclusive but complementary, the one helps the other'.[42]

For most Australians in the years 1901 to 1963, the notion of Australian independence was rarely viewed in absolute terms. Instead, independence was a concept which was naturally limited and shaped to coexist with overall loyalty to the British Empire. It was for this reason that phrases such as 'the independent colonist' or 'independent Australian Britons' did not appear as oxymorons but as perfectly natural expressions of Australian nationality.[43] Related to this concept of limited independence was the second major reason for the decline of republicanism. The new nation had been forged not just through its loyalty to Empire but through its loyalty to White Australia. In 1919 the first plank of the federal Labor Party's platform stated the Party's desire to cultivate Australian sentiment and maintain White Australia.[44] Herein lay the essential paradox of Australian nationalism in the twentieth century. If being Australian meant being of white British stock, then the best way to nurture Australian sentiment was to maintain the connection with the protective fountain of that racial stock. This is why the Labor Party became such staunch defenders of the British connection. A republic could never have guaranteed the security of White Australia in the same way that the British connection did, as Richard Jebb observed in 1905: 'Australian patriots are predisposed to imperialism so long as it connotes the defensive co-operation of white nations rather than the exploitation of Australia by the coloured races . . .'.[45]

It was no coincidence that republican sentiment in Australia would not surface again until the 1960s, the very decade when the White Australia policy was finally put to rest. Australians would only be able to cast off from Britain when they had relinquished the racist dream of fortress White Australia.

CHAPTER ELEVEN

The End of the Affair   1963–1995

When Sir Robert Menzies farewelled Queen Elizabeth II and her husband Prince Philip at Mascot in 1963, it represented not only the end of another royal tour, but the end of an affair between Australia and Britain which had lasted for almost two centuries. Within three years of the Queen's departure, Menzies would retire and the enormous shifts in social and political attitudes that characterised the 1960s would ensure that visiting royals would never again encounter the adulation that Queen Elizabeth had received in the 1950s. Australia and Britain had finally reached the end of their 'colonial' relationship.

In 1967 the British government decided to begin the gradual withdrawal of its forces from Malaysia and Singapore, an act which simply completed the process which had begun in 1942 with the fall of Singapore. The long history of joint military participation between the two countries which began with the Sudan expedition in 1885 had come to an end. Britain retreated to Europe while Australia 'looked to America' to assist her in defining a new role in Asia and the South Pacific. Britain's entry into the European Economic Community, which had first been mooted in the early 1960s and caused Menzies such concern, finally occurred in 1973. Australia's trade links with Britain had already shown signs of a shift by the mid-1960s but the symbolic import of Britain's official entry into the EEC would never be lost on late twentieth-century republicans. In the 1960s the United States and Japan both overtook Britain as Australia's major trading partner.[1] Australian exports to Britain and British exports to Australia declined sharply and the largest proportion of incoming foreign capital to Australia now came not from Britain, but the United States. By the late 1970s economic ties between Britain and Australia would dwindle to 'relatively low levels'. From now on, if the two countries could be claimed to have a special relationship, it was primarily one based on memories of the past. The only claims left for loyalists were 'political stability', 'heritage' and 'cultural ties', but even these were showing signs of giving way by the mid-1960s.[2]

On 2 August 1965 the federal Labor Party formally dropped the White Australia plank from its party platform. Don Dunstan presented the

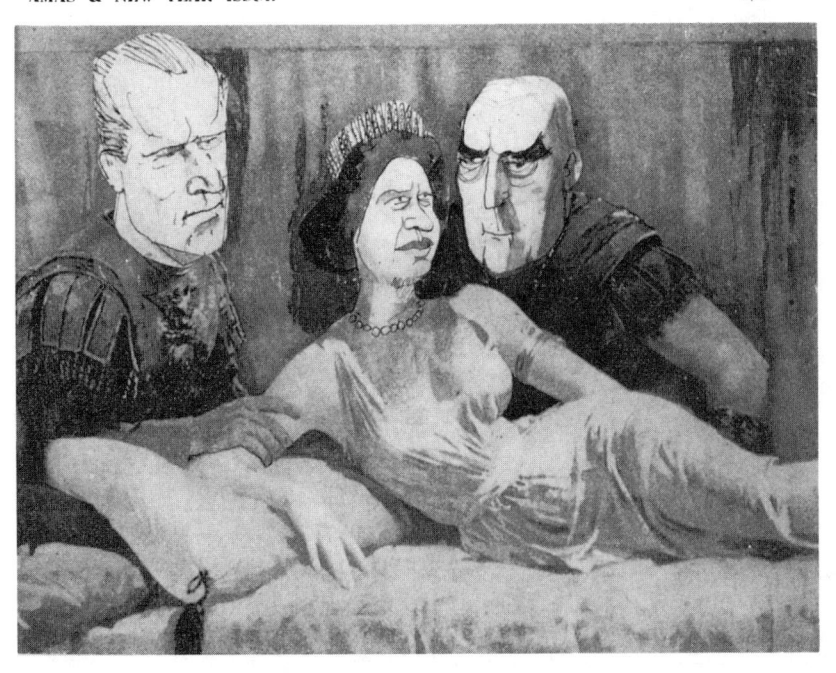

OZ

XMAS & NEW YEAR ISSUE 1/3

Oz
Twelve years later, *Oz* magazine produced a cover which would have brought in the Federal Police in 1954. Martin Sharp's ménage à trois of Prince Philip, Robert Menzies and Queen Elizabeth II was one indication that the period of gushing loyalty to the throne was at an end in the mid-sixties.
(Martin Sharp, *Oz*, Christmas and New Year issue, 1966.)

findings of the Party's immigration review committee at the twenty-sixth Party Conference. The committee recommended that the ALP support an 'expanding immigration programme' based 'on sympathy, understanding and tolerance'. The 'Great White Walls' of fortress Australia were 'crumbling' as was the steady flow of predominantly British immigrants which had helped to build them.[3]

Under a succession of Liberal governments the face of Australian immigration had already become more diverse, so that by the time of the election of the Whitlam government in 1972 the percentage of Asian immigrants arriving in Australia had increased from 1.6 per cent of total intake in 1947–51 to 11.2 per cent by 1966–71. It was during the 1950s and 1960s, under Menzies, that large numbers of immigrants from eastern and southern Europe first began to outnumber those from Britain. So far as immigration was concerned, Labor was certainly not the enlightened Party. While the ALP clung to the White Australia policy until 1965, it was a Liberal government that presided over the increase of non-white immigration to Australia which, by 1971, had reached 10 000 persons per annum.[4] This should remind us not to stereotype pre-Whitlam Australia as some kind of dark age from which Labor somehow saved Australia in 1972. Even when Menzies expressed grave fears about Britain's application to join the EEC in 1961 he emphasised that his government's first duty was to protect the interests of Australia.[5] However, by the time Menzies retired in 1966 the public values, beliefs and ceremony which had held Australia together for most of the twentieth century were no longer dominant. The belief in Australia's 'Britishness', the racial purity of White Australia and blood sacrifice to Empire, the very principles which had bound the nation together in 1901, were now being challenged. 'American' imperialism and not British imperialism was the concern of the left wing while the Australian soldiers who were dying in Vietnam were a symbol not only of Australia's inability to free itself from the need of a powerful protector, but that Asia was the most important sphere of foreign relations for Australia, not the Dardanelles or Sudan. So when Geoffrey Dutton and Donald Horne raised the question of a republic in 1963–64, the parameters of the modern republican debate were already evident. What Dutton and Horne said in the early 1960s did not differ greatly from what republicans would say in the 1990s.

Modern Australia republicanism would rest its case on almost predictable arguments:
- Australian 'nationality' was not British but uniquely Australian. The Queen was not an Australian head of state;
- The retention of ties with the British monarchy was an obstacle to the realisation of Australian nationality and independence and perpetuated a culture of political, economic and cultural 'dependence';

- The divergence of Australian and British national interest, as symbolised by Britain's entry into the EEC and her retreat from the Far East, demanded a commensurate adjustment of Australia's constitutional arrangements to more accurately reflect the new reality in Anglo–Australian relations;
- There was a need for an 'Australian' head of state to enable Australia to project a clear national identity in the Asian region;
- The Australian republic was inevitable.

After the 1960s arguments for a republic would be articulated largely by the bourgeois intelligentsia and the asinine political fringe. Essentially this meant that republican plots would be hatched over lunch or in suburban garages.

The most prominent 'hot' republicans were the South Australian academic, writer and author, Geoffrey Dutton, and the New South Wales journalist and public intellectual, Donald Horne. Dutton made the initial republican noises in 1963 in an article which was published in *Nation* magazine.[6] At the time, Dutton was serving a semester as a visiting professor at Kansas State University in the USA. After representing the University of Adelaide at a Founders Day Convocation at Kansas, Dutton woke the next morning to find his photograph on the front page of one of the local dailies, accompanied by a caption which read 'Professor Geoffrey Dutton sends his congratulations from England'. In his article, Dutton used this experience as the launchpad for a republican outburst. Although he acknowledged that the mention of republicanism was taboo in Australia, his solution to the dilemma of being British subject or Australian citizen was simple: 'Declare Australia a republic. Elect our own Governors. Abolish the use of the word British and substitute Australian'.[7]

Three years later, Dutton edited the first republican paperback published by Sun Books in Melbourne, *Australia and the Monarchy*, a book which collected essays from republicans such as Donald Horne, Max Harris and Richard Walsh.[8] There were no female or non-'Anglo' contributors. In his essay on 'Labor and the monarchy', Stephen Murray-Smith remarked that it was a 'staggering impeachment of the failure of Australian intellectuals to express in politically meaningful terms their sense of despair at our national habit of clinging to the maternal tit'. This was not that far removed from the *Bulletin*'s ravings about 'manhood' in the nineteenth century—boys wanting to leave mother and be real 'men'.[9] In his introduction, Dutton dated his conversion to republicanism at 1958 when, while 'having dinner with Rohan Rivett, then editor of the Adelaide *News*, Rupert Murdoch and Malcolm Muggeridge, he was surprised by Muggeridge's denunciation of the Australian attitude to the British monarchy:

I remember being puzzled at his vehemence, his genuine concern over the fact that Australians should, in his words, worship an image of power that has no power. Once again, typically Australian in my mental indolence, it took me a while to realise that I was completely in sympathy with Muggeridge's views and could not be anything else but a republican.[10]

Dutton's quip about mental indolence did not alter the fact that a British intellectual had 'awakened' a 'colonial' to his republicanism. After publicly declaring his views Dutton was expelled from the Adelaide Club, a crusty and conservative institution which would have at least agreed with him on the 'mental indolence of Australians'. He was then branded a traitor by the RSL president who demanded that he be 'sent back to Russia' where he belonged.[11]

While Geoffrey Dutton's contribution to the emergence of a modern republican debate in Australia was considerable, it was far outweighed by that of Donald Horne. One of the few intellectuals who had the capacity to think as a true 'generalist', Horne's most obvious talent was the ability to write intelligently and accessibly in a style of which *The Lucky Country*, published in 1964, is probably the best example. In *The Lucky Country*, a bestseller which was a 'set text in many schools', Horne identified the framework of the political and social debates which would face Australians over the next three decades. Subheadings like Women, Migrants, Racism in Australia, What is Asia? and A Republic? were signposts of the new priorities in Australian political culture. *The Lucky Country* was different, essentially because it was a book about Australia written in a language which spoke directly to the concerns of everyday Australians at a time when traditional belief systems were being challenged. As Horne himself has remarked, *The Lucky Country* put republicanism on the public agenda but it did so in a manner which linked a future republic with far more than the rejection of English monarchy. In little more than three pages Horne managed to map the priorities of late twentieth-century republicanism in Australia: national identity; the waning of traditional links with Britain; Asia and Australia's place in the region; minimalism.[12]

Through the popularity of *The Lucky Country* and Horne's republican articles in the *Bulletin*, which he edited from 1967, he influenced a large number of politicians, educators, journalists and a considerable section of the general republic who would no longer be so shocked by the mention of the words 'Australian republic'. For both Dutton and Horne, the coming republic and the patriotism which would accompany it would result in a new vision of Australian nationalism in which 'nationalism' would serve as the wellspring of creative endeavour.[13] This cultural nationalism was not prescriptive or chauvinistic, if anything it was simply a rejection of a perceived cultural cringe.

However, there were republicans who projected a more chauvinistic nationalism. The Melbourne-based Australian Republican Party, which had formed in 1956 in response to the playing of 'God Save the Queen' as Australia's national anthem during the Melbourne Olympic Games, had branches in New South Wales and Queensland by 1970. The Party suffered from low membership, internal division and a range of policies which were, to say the least, odd. In 1964, the Melbourne branch of the Party revealed some of its 'practical politics' in its platform and policy statement: pro-Vietnam war, US bases, conscription, selective quotas for Asian immigrants, and an expanded social welfare system. To pay for it all, the Party hierarchy had an ingenious idea—legalise SP betting. The revenue from this source could then be used to liberate Australian women by allowing them to perform their duty for the coming republic:

> [Half] of this new source of revenue would be spent on the now vital needs of a national maternity scheme, to allow every mother and mother to be, in all Australia, to carry out her highest sacrifice and noblest duty in presenting to her family and country our most precious asset, the newly born Australian completely free of cost to her of hospitalisation, doctor, medicine and transport charges.[14]

This was a vision of a racetrack republic with men at the Totalizator Agency Board performing their civic duty while women stayed at home with their little Australians. The prospects for success for the Australian Republican Party were never high, but there were still other republicans who were 'visible' and played a large part in demystifying monarchy for the youth of the 1960s, as Geoffrey Dutton explained in 1965:

> ... OZ has tried to stir up controversy about the monarchy by deliberately tasteless cartoons and skits, though these are mild compared with those published in satirical magazines in England, but the monarchy has so little relevance as a social symbol for Australian youth that no one cares.[15]

The contribution of OZ has often been overlooked, but during the mid-1960s it was the only journal to consistently lampoon the monarchy. For a satirical magazine like OZ, the monarchy provided an easy target. Front page illustrations depicting Robert Menzies as a latter day Marc Antony lusting after a reclining Queen Elizabeth, or of Prince Philip proclaiming 'My wife doesn't go to the lavatory, it bloody well comes to her' were typical of the OZ style.[16] OZ was, in fact, one of the first signs that the naivete of the 1950s had passed. Australians were once again free to poke fun at British royalty. Writing on behalf of Australia's 'youth' in *Australia and the Monarchy*, Richard Walsh, the co-editor of OZ and then medical student at

Dutton and Horne
Geoffrey Dutton, above, leading republican of the 1960s and one-time member of the Adelaide Club. Dutton's writings were instrumental in promoting republicanism within Australia's intellectual and artistic communities. Below, Donald Horne, the man who gave up cigarettes—and the monarchy. Horne was by far the most prominent republican in late twentieth-century Australia. (Image Library, State Library of New South Wales.)

the University of Sydney, concluded: 'So far as we are concerned, the soap opera is over, the players must find useful employment. The people, still clinging to their bread, demand a more inspiring circus'.[17]

That Australians weren't necessarily 'inspired' by monarchy was perhaps true, but whether they wanted to be inspired at all was another matter. Horne, Dutton, the *OZ* circus, the *Bulletin* (once again) and even the fringe republican groups had all contributed to forcing the issue of an independent republic into the public domain. Although 'hot' republicans were still a minority according to the polls, the time of undivided loyalty to the throne was over. What would prove difficult, however, would be to convince a majority of Australians that the issue mattered enough to want to change Australia's Constitution. Peter Coleman's chapter in Geoffrey Dutton's *Australia and the Monarchy* made the point bluntly by repeating an old theme:

> There is no royal oppression against which the republicans can appeal, there is no red republicanism against which royalists can appeal to God and King. This is another way of saying that there are really no republicans or royalists in the historically sanctioned sense in Australia. Almost everyone is a sort of republican—monarchist or monarchist republican and has more important issues to concern himself with.[18]

The mythology of Australian society was egalitarian, but to persuade Australians to countenance constitutional change in a republican referendum was more difficult. In the early 1970s the republic, as always, was seen as a matter for the future. Opinion polls showed dramatic shifts in public support. One poll in 1968 had support for a republic at 40 per cent, while two years later in 1970 it had dropped to 24 per cent.[19] These variations were an indication of just how unpredictable support for a republic would be in the years ahead. In *The Lucky Country* Donald Horne had spoken of the need for a dramatic event to usher in a popular push for a republic. On 11 November 1975 he would have his wish granted.

The Legacy of Kerr 1972–1988

> What is sometimes called a new nationalism, for which the election of this government is seen as a catalyst, is, I hope, really the beginning of self confidence ... My great hope for my government ... is that it will see the end of the old inhibitions, the self defeating fears about Australia's place in the world, and the beginning of a creative maturity.[20]

Gough Whitlam's election on 2 December 1972 brought the federal Labor Party to power after twenty-three years of conservative rule. Whitlam had become Prime Minister at a time of social upheaval. The same forces of social dislocation at work in western Europe and the United States—the protest movement, rock and roll, the women's movement and the power of television—were also at work in Australia in one form or another.

Even before Whitlam was elected Australians had already displayed a 'surface fidgeting about national symbols' and a willingness to engage in 'critical self-appraisal' about matters of national identity.[21] It was as if the tension created by the more detached relationship with the United Kingdom, and the influx of American television, cinema and popular music, had jolted Australian intellectuals and artists into an attempt at self-definition—or at least into appraising which particular political, economic and cultural directions might best serve Australia's self-interest. After the 1960s most Australians would receive their ideas about the Australian 'nation' from television advertising. Television images and jingles which distilled the essence of 'Australia' as a mechanism to boost consumption of petrol, cigarettes, beer or cornflakes played just as much a part in the so-called new nationalism as did Gough Whitlam's government. The surge of nationalism that coincided with the election of the Whitlam government had a dramatic effect on public sympathy for an Australian republic. Whitlam has since made it clear that his government 'was not republican' but this did not stop a large part of the electorate from perceiving his government as at least potentially republican.[22] Writing in the *Australian* in 1973 Robert Drewe quoted Manning Clark on the new spirit of nationalism that seemed to trail Whitlam:

> At the moment, according to Professor Clark, the larrikin nationalist is in the ascendancy after a twenty year rule by the Anglophiles led by Sir Robert Menzies. Now we've got the situation of the 1890s once more where people are cheeky or indifferent about the royals and reacting against the snob or English values.[23]

The perception that Whitlam was driving Australia towards an identity detached from Britain was understandable. Between 1972 and 1975 Whitlam gave Australia a new national anthem, a new honours system, abolished appeals from the High Court to the Privy Council, unsuccessfully tried to legislate for a new oath of citizenship which removed any reference to the Queen, and decided to appoint Australian Ambassadors without seeking the formal approval of the Queen.[24]

Superficially, this may have seemed like the first step down the road to a republic after the policies of Menzies. Many conservatives were horrified by Whitlam's attempt to destroy Australia's links with 'civilisation'. Liberal and Country Party State governments refused to relinquish their imperial honours system and the right of appeal to the Privy Council. Sir

Joh Bjelke-Petersen delighted in portraying the Whitlam government as the harbinger of a godless socialist dictatorship. In federal parliament some members expressed concern that a large percentage of Labor Party ministers did not acknowledge the existence of God alleging that they planned to cut Australia's ties with England so quickly that the Queen would not even know what had happened.[25]

Whether the Whitlam government was republican or not, it was in the interests of opposition parties to portray it as republican. There was still sufficient political capital to be gained from 'scaring' the electorate with the old republican bogey. Thus, the Liberals were only too happy to read out letters in parliament from extreme right-wing organisations such as the Australian Heritage Society, letters which warned that the Whitlam government was about to abolish the Crown in Australia.[26] The truth was the opposite. The Whitlam government did more to hamper republicanism than aid it. Under Whitlam, the process of naturalising the Queen and the British monarchy in Australian political life was accelerated. Far from severing ties with the monarchy the actions of the Whitlam government succeeded in cementing them even further. Aside from the fact that Whitlam stated several times in parliament that his government had no intention of moving Australia towards a republic, the changes which Whitlam introduced, especially the Royal Style and Titles Act of 1973, were simply designed to give the monarch an Australian 'flavour'; to 'modernise' the monarchical connection in a manner which more accurately reflected Australia's independent status. In 1973 Whitlam explained his position to the House of Representatives:

> The changes we have made or propose to make on such matters as the powers of the Governor-General, appeals to the Privy Council, a new national anthem, the Queen's Style and Titles and the amendment of the oath of allegiance are in no way directed against Britain. They are solely intended to put our relationship on a more mature and contemporary basis and to reflect the development of a more independent Australian identity in the world.[27]

This was not independence 'under' the Crown but 'with' the Crown. While there were several republican ministers in the Whitlam government, their republicanism rarely amounted to more than colourful posturing. The Royal Style and Titles Act of 1973 simply made the formal title of the Queen as Australia's head of state more explicitly 'Queen of Australia'.[28] Whitlam was merely attempting to assert the identity of the Queen as Australia's head of state over and above her role as British head of state. There was one member of the opposition, however, who was intuitive enough to realise the ramifications of this for republicans. After listening to a turgid and mournful speech from Jim Killen, Ian Sinclair rose to tell the House why he agreed with Whitlam's bill: 'I believe that this Bill presents for Australia a modern idiom and a modern expression of the monarchy as we in Australia understand it . . . Indeed, instead of promoting the substance of change towards a republic . . . I believe that this Bill will preserve the monarchy . . .'.[29]

With every further clarification of Australian independence under the symbolic function of the Crown, the harder it became for republicans to distinguish the future republic from the republic in disguise. Two months after Whitlam's election in 1973, when a euphoric sense of national awakening was still in the air, support for Australia becoming a republic with an elected president stood at 40 per cent in a Morgan Gallup poll. This was a higher level of support for a republic than in any similar Morgan poll between 1953 and 1991.[30] Remarkably, there were more Australians in favour of a republic in 1973 than in December 1975 after Whitlam had been dismissed by Sir John Kerr. This irony revealed something crucial about republicanism in the post-Menzies era. Australians were most likely to be sympathetic to republicanism at times of national self-confidence, primarily because in the early 1970s republicanism was still more about 'sentiment' than policy. In times of political or economic crisis this sentiment was quickly forgotten and the events of November 1975 were no exception.

The Queen's Australian

Six days after Governor-General Sir John Kerr dismissed Prime Minister Gough Whitlam on 11 November 1975, the (London) *Economist* made an interesting observation:

> When they [the residual powers] are invoked in a crisis, people are bound to ask whether they are compatible with a modern democracy and to question the institution of the monarchy itself. There will be more republicans in Australia after Tuesday, than there were before.[31]

In one respect, the *Economist* was right. John Kerr's dismissal of Gough Whitlam certainly caused Australians to think about their Constitution. But the dismissal did not cause an increase in public support for republicanism. Instead, it was the catalyst for a protest movement which, even at its height, could not manage to attract the same level of enthusiasm Whitlam had achieved for the republic in December 1972. In 1976 Gareth Evans, then senior lecturer in constitutional law at Melbourne University, wisely remarked that 'given the extreme caution with which British monarchs have exercised their prerogatives in recent centuries it

CITIZENS FOR DEMOCRACY
presents

REPUBLIC DAY

TOWARDS A NEW CONSTITUTION

11th November, 1979

μερα Δημοκρατίας

SYDNEY TOWN HALL
SUNDAY 2.15 — 6pm
$3.00
$1.50 concession

SPEAKERS (3.00pm)

Gough Whitlam
Manning Clarke
Lionel Bowen
Patricia O'Shane
Donald Horne
CHAIR: Carolyn Simpson

ENTERTAINMENT
Topical songs, poems and danc

Cümhüriyet Günü

REPABLICKI DAN

GIORNO REPUBLICA

DIA DE REPUBLICO   **JOUR REPUBLIQUE**

TAG REPUBLIK

Citizens for Democracy
In the nineteenth century, the need to keep Australia safe for the 'white man' was one of the primary motivators for Australian republicans. In the late twentieth century, the situation was reversed—republicans now relied on multicultural Australia to legitimise their cause.
(Citizens for Democracy, Donald Horne Papers, Image Library, State Library of New South Wales.)

may be said indeed that the trouble with Sir John Kerr was not that he was too much the Queen's man, but that he was not enough'.[32] In other words, if Australia was a monarchy, it was a monarchy under the Governor-General. The fact that Kerr had acted independently of the monarch and that the Queen had refused to become involved in the crisis meant that it was not so much the monarch but the role and powers of the Governor-General which would be the focus of 'republican' anger. Before November 1975 the majority of Australians were blissfully ignorant of their Constitution. What Kerr did was to remind them that they had one. As Governor-General, Kerr was the Queen's representative in Australia, and his dismissal of Whitlam immediately raised questions about the broader symbolic role of the 'Crown' in the Australian Constitution.[33] Kerr may have acted as an Australian, but the public theatre which accompanied his office was British and imperial. With his top hat, tails, imperial honours, and warnings about republicanism, Kerr's appearance was a constant reminder to Australians that their 'republic' was disguised by a portly, champagne-soaked Governor-General who seemed to represent the British aristocracy more than the Australian people. For the Labor left, the republicans of the 1960s and many of those in the arts and academia, Kerr's action provided the motivation for the formation of a broadly-based movement for constitutional reform which incorporated republicanism as part of its platform.

Citizens for Democracy (CFD) formed in November 1975 as a non-party group primarily to contribute money to pay for newspaper advertisements. Its role in the first twelve months after the dismissal was one of placing advertisements, circulating petitions and general rage maintenance.[34] It was only after September 1976 that CFD took on the role of a structured political movement. After a successful meeting at Sydney Town Hall a small group of authors, academics, artists and politicians decided to adopt the title Citizens for Democracy to wage an ongoing campaign for a democratic Constitution. The decision to hold the September meeting, as Donald Horne recalled in 1977, was made over lunch:

> Somewhere in the middle of the second bottle we decided that as two individual citizens we would hire the Sydney Town Hall and call a public meeting. My wife [Myfanwy Gollan] suggested we call the meeting 'Kerr and the Consequences' so that we could test the political temperature.[35]

Death of a Lucky Country was written in three weeks while Horne convalesced in Sydney Eye Hospital. In the book, Horne described Australia as a 'Governor-Generalate' struggling to recover from 'Menzies' banana monarchy', and a derivativeness sustained by 'the British whimsy of its monarchic constitution'.[36] When 2500 people gathered at the Sydney

Town Hall on 20 September 1976 for the 'Kerr and the Consequences' meeting they heard much about Australia's 'monarchic Constitution'. This was the first time that 'potential' republicans had gathered at the Town Hall since the Queen's Jubilee in 1887, although on this occasion the ambience was somewhat different:

> As the audience arrived inside the Town Hall works by Albinoni, Bach and Vivaldi were played softly over the amplifying system. At starting time John De Luca played his arrangement of *Advance Australia Fair*, and the audience sang clearly because the words had been printed in the program.[37]

On the platform, a large banner which incorporated a golden orange Southern Cross on a blue background was bordered with the words: 'It's time for a new Constitution'. Seated in front of the banner were the speakers: Chairman Donald Horne, Pat O'Shane, Manning Clark, John Gaden, Joan Evatt, James McLelland, Bob Carr, Sarah Sheehan, Bruce Petty, Jack Mundey, Franca Arena and one of the most important of the 'unheard' contributors, Myfanwy Gollan. The resolutions called on Australians to engage in 'extra parliamentary activity', and to demand a democratic Constitution in which the powers of the Senate and the head of state would be curtailed. As far as the republic was concerned, there seemed to be a cautious acknowledgment that republicanism was to be included but not over-emphasised. The very fact that the words 'democracy' and 'democratic' were favoured over 'republic' and 'republican' both in the movement's name and in the majority of the resolutions was an indication that republicanism was not to be the main focus of CFD. The resolution which referred to a republic stated: 'To symbolise its maturity as a nation, Australia should become a republic'. This was a clear attempt to connect republicanism with national identity rather than the dismissal—a strategy which would continue in the 1990s. Only two speakers, Donald Horne and Jack Mundey, specifically called for a republic.[38] It was left to Jim McLelland to read the resolution for the republic and his trepidation was probably indicative of just how much uncertainty there was about republicanism within CFD.

McLelland was astonished to see the resolution carried, most probably because he was aware that some of his colleagues on the platform were ambivalent about a republic. Patrick White, for example, who spoke several weeks later at the 11 November rally at Town Hall Square, saw the question of a republic as one of 'secondary importance' when compared to the need for a 'trustworthy constitution'.[39] None the less, the republican motion was passed, more as an accessory of democratic reform than as the centrepiece.

In the aftermath of 'Kerr and the Consequences', CFD set up branches in the Sydney suburbs, Newcastle, Perth, Adelaide, Melbourne and Brisbane. There was a formidable minority of citizens now willing to call for a democratic Constitution and 11 November became the rallying point for republicans and all those who wished to see Kerr removed from office.[40] Within a few weeks of the first anniversary of the dismissal, meetings had been held in almost every capital city. Polls were conducted on the republican issue, John Kerr was forced to speak out publicly against any move to a republic, and Gough Whitlam, still restrained by his role as leader of the Opposition, declared a republic would come but not in his lifetime. Although the polls showed varying levels of support for a republic in 1976—anywhere between 25 and 39 per cent—some sections of the press saw republicanism as being on the rise.[41]

In Queensland, where all roads led to Kingaroy (home of the Bjelke-Petersens), the mere mention of republicanism was enough to unsettle law-abiding citizens. In December, Premier Bjelke-Petersen successfully passed legislation which entrenched the British monarchy as part of the Queensland parliament. Appropriately endorsed by so-called constitutional experts in Britain, Bjelke-Petersen's bill was basically a silly attempt to thwart any plan by Canberra to force Queensland into a federal republic. There was no need for the Orangemen when Joh and Flo held the fort.[42]

Although the anniversary of the dismissal had sparked a vigorous movement for constitutional change, the event which kept republicanism alive was the Queen's visit to Australia in March 1977. Given the extent of public animosity displayed towards Governor-General Kerr after 11 November there were many who feared for the Queen's safety should she set foot on Australian soil. Prime Minister Malcolm Fraser personally assured the Queen that it would be safe for her to visit Australia.[43] When the Queen finally arrived the reaction of protest groups such as CFD demonstrated just how reluctant Australians were to involve the monarch in domestic politics. Republicans were not critical of Queen Elizabeth, they simply wanted the friendly severance of monarchical ties. But 1977 was the peak of republican sentiment in the years following the dismissal. After November 1975, every royal visit would be greeted by a public discussion on the prospect of Australia becoming a republic. Predictably, this pattern began with a surge in 1977, and tapered off in intensity until the Fleet Street tabloids and the royal family went to war in the early 1990s.

In March 1977 CFD organised a public meeting at the Sydney Town Hall under the title 'Towards an Australian Republic'. Donald Horne, the person most responsible for the decision to lead with the 'r' word, addressed the National Press Club on the eve of the meeting and told journalists that the Queen was a symbol of division for Australians.[44] 'Peaceful protests' were organised to coincide with the Queen's visit, protests which usually involved citizens holding up placards after a picnic lunch while the Queen's Rolls-Royce passed by on its way to another official function. In the same way that nineteenth-century reformers petitioned the Queen, twentieth-century protesters stood quietly and held their placards—constitutionalists above all else. The year 1977 was the first occasion Australia had witnessed substantial opposition to a royal tour. The decision of CFD to focus on the republic during the Queen's visit was sufficient to provoke a torrent of anti-republican vitriol. Peaceful protests, carefully considered arguments, and a distinctly non-confrontationist approach were not enough to earn republicans credibility. In the weeks after the Town Hall meetings and Donald Horne's Press Club address, the reaction of parliamentarians, newspaper editors and leading public figures demonstrated that Australians were still not ready for a mature debate on the republic. We need only look at some of the colourful euphemisms used to describe republicans in 1977: radicals; ratbags; political stirrers; professional protesters; larrikins; louts; anarchists; tasteless demonstrators; notoriety seekers; Marxists; socialists; 'two-bob republicans'; rootless intellectuals; a 'scruffy looking mob'; mental midgets; pseudo-academics; a vocal minority who should be sprayed with DDT.[45]

Donald Horne was variously described as a little old man, 'a little known author', 'leader of the republican stormtroopers', 'undistinguished', 'pathetic', 'a self-appointed prophet' and the 'high priest' of republicanism. Finally, the future republic was characterised by one federal Senator as 'a system where we would all be united under the machine gun', a vision which probably explained why the Australian Heritage Society believed the Queen to be commander-in-chief of the Australian Defence Forces.[46]

With abuse like this being directed at republicans through the press and in federal parliament, it is possible to appreciate just how difficult it was in 1977 for republicans to gain a fair hearing. Despite the gutter quality of much of the so-called loyalist opposition, CFD pressed ahead with the campaign for a republic as the end goal of its more important proposals for constitutional reform. Rallies and meetings were held in most capitals during March, a National Conference for a Democratic Constitution was held in Melbourne in September, and a historical exhibition, 'Struggle for Democracy in Australia 1788–1977', was launched by Manning Clark at Sydney Town Hall to coincide with the anniversary of the dismissal.[47] Organised by Myfanwy Gollan, 'Struggle for Democracy' was probably the first example of 'republican realism' in Australia. Australian history was presented in the exhibition as a succession of people's struggles for rights: 'Aboriginal rights, Women's rights', the rights to a free press, freedom of religion, the franchise and so on. The republic was portrayed as the end point of the people's fight for independence, with Eureka and Ned Kelly being appropriated to serve as its heroic antecedents.[48]

The year of 1977 also saw the publication of Geoffrey Dutton's second republican symposium, *Republican Australia*.[49] *Republican Australia* and *Change the Rules: Towards a Democratic Constitution*, edited by Sol Encel, Donald Horne and Elaine Thompson, were published in the same year. The books were an indication that republicanism was only one part of the debate about constitutional reform sparked by the dismissal. This is probably one of the strongest differences between the republicanism of the late 1970s and that of the early 1990s. In the 1970s CFD argued for a complete overhaul of the Constitution, arguments which happened to include the need to make provision for a republic, while republicans of the 1990s argued for a republic with minimal constitutional change. In one respect, however, the republican debate had changed little since the nineteenth century. It was still a minority of intellectuals fighting a minority of rabid loyalists—with the great majority of Australians showing little interest in the debate.[50]

John Kerr's dismissal of Gough Whitlam had certainly sparked debate on the republic, but it had other, more significant effects which have yet to be acknowledged. First, after November 1975 any future Australian republic would have to include the possibility of an elected president with codified constitutional powers. It may well be that the most important effect of Kerr's act on the Australian electorate was to convince the people that the head of state should be elected and directly accountable to the people. This seems to be one consistent factor to come out of the republican polls of the early 1990s.[51] Secondly, Gough Whitlam's election in 1972 and his dismissal three years later demonstrated that republicanism was politically driven. Although republicans kept chanting their demographic arguments for the inevitable republic like the rosary, it was not 'youth' or non-Anglo immigrants who brought republicanism to the fore but political catharsis.[52] After Kerr, debate on the republic would remain politically polarised. The intense bitterness that surrounded the dismissal only entrenched the lack of bipartisanship which was already evident on matters such as the national anthem, the flag, and the oath of allegiance. Since 1975 the achievement of bipartisan support has remained the greatest obstacle to substantial constitutional reform, but even more so to the declaration of an Australian republic.

The response of Donald Horne to Whitlam's dismissal also had important ramifications for the direction of republicanism in late twentieth-century Australia. Horne was the leading advocate of a republic and it was he more than anyone else who insisted that the republic was a separate issue. The minimalist republicanism of the 1990s has its roots in Horne's response to the dismissal. Speaking at the National Press Club in 1977, Horne told the audience that the significance of the Queen as Australia's head of state could only evoke two responses:

> One is the democratic statement about the political role of Australia's monarchic constitution and in particular the monarchic role of the Governor-General in our present democratic crisis; the other is a republican statement, or as I would put it, the Australian statement in our present crisis in National identity.[53]

This attempt to confine republicanism to the arena of 'national identity' can also be found in the platform of the Australian Republican Movement in the 1990s.[54] In one respect there were sound political arguments for this division. Considering the reticence of Australians to vote for constitutional change there was a danger that Horne's republic would sink quickly if it was too closely linked with substantive changes to the Constitution. But the link with the minefield of national identity also opened the door to a labyrinth of emotional arguments about which particular 'national identity' republicans espoused. The result was a procession of superficial television dinner debates about republicanism and Australian identity.[55] For many people this only seemed to bear out the fact that the Queen was worthwhile retaining so long as Australians could not easily define their own identity. Keeping the Queen as head of state allowed Australians to avoid talking about 'divisive' issues like allegiance and national identity. But in the 1970s a perceived crisis in 'national identity' was certainly one of the most important reasons for the emergence of republicanism. When we look at the speeches and writings of republicans like Geoffrey Dutton and Les Murray, it is possible to appreciate the manner in which Kerr provoked them into protest. Speaking at the 1977 meeting 'Towards a Republic' in Sydney, Les Murray told the audience:

> The prospect of living one's whole life in a timid late colonial society is a mediocre and galling one and Australians don't have to endure such a prospect. If the republic is about anything, it is about the dignity and potential of human beings in this country. It is about rejecting slurs. It is about casting off the psychological impediments to action. It is about confirming and strengthening the confidence of every Australian.[56]

For Murray, republicanism was a means of rejecting the cringe. For Dutton and Horne, who had both spent time in England in the 1960s, the republic was a means of asserting Australian identity over British identity, a response to the undoubted feeling of inferiority which they had all personally felt at some time in their lives. There must have been a time when Geoffrey Dutton and Donald Horne would have agreed with Patrick White when he told a republican rally in Brisbane in 1977 that 'London was still the great cultural centre of the world'. The dismissal of Whitlam by the

Queen's representative played into the hands of a generation of Australian intellectuals and artists who believed in the existence of the cultural cringe. The monarchic overtones of Kerr's act reminded Geoffrey Dutton that it was 'too much to stomach any longer that our head of state should be an English lady living in London or Windsor or Balmoral'.[57]

At a time when Australia had already shifted away from Britain to embrace the cultural models of the United States, the dismissal focused the issue of Australian independence through the traditional axis of Anglo–Australian relations. The heated debate over Australia–America relations which had formed such an integral part of Australian politics during the 1960s, especially at the time of the Vietnam War, was partially submerged by the dismissal. The mainstream republican movement in post-Menzies Australia was thus led by intellectuals who had belatedly decided that they no longer needed to feel inferior to Britain, although by the 1970s the bulk of the Australian population probably did not share the same intensity of feeling about the British connection as the men and women who were leading the republican crusade. One of the illusions created by the dismissal, and fostered by the vanguard of the republican intelligentsia, was that Australian independence would be attained by freeing the country from the last shackles of the British connection. It was only the smaller political movements on the far left which managed to maintain the independence debate in the wider context of Australia's relationship with the United States.[58]

When leading republicans could perhaps have been devoting more time to the lack of parity in Australia's relationship with the United States, they spent much of their energy writing about the lady in Windsor Castle. Consequently, one of the things which has been sadly lacking from the republican debate since 1975 has been the ability of prominent republicans to incorporate the question of Australia's relationship with the United States into the discussion concerning Australian independence. Admittedly, there were valid reasons in the 1970s for focusing the republican debate through the filter of Australia's relationship with Britain. The Crown was still the visible symbol of institutional authority, as well as being the centrepiece of many symbols of national value. It was only appropriate, especially after the dismissal, that republicans should point out the irrelevance of Australia's monarchical Constitution. The pity was that this focus consumed the independence debate and continued to do so until the early 1990s.

After the republican rallies of 1977 and the reasonably broad media coverage given to the issue in the same year, CFD splintered and republicanism gradually waned in influence throughout the late 1970s.[59] Lionel Bowen and Gough Whitlam continued to articulate their belief in a republic, especially on the anniversary of the dismissal, but as time passed the rage died or simply became divided or confused.[60] CFD tried to revive the republican spirit of 1976 by declaring the anniversary of the dismissal in 1979 'Republic Day', but even the presence of Whitlam at the rostrum could not stop the tide of indifference. Whitlam's commitment to the republic was sincere, but unlike Horne and Dutton it was based more on democratic and constitutional grounds rather than those of national identity.[61] In 1977 Whitlam took on the role of prophet and tried to imagine how future historians might view the republicanism which emerged after the dismissal:

> I believe historians of the future will agree that quite the most momentous event in Australia in 1976—all the more striking because it was unexpected—was the rising tide of republican sentiment and the growth of a new national spirit. This movement, amorphous, uncertain, unorganised, as yet largely undirected and unchannelled, was nevertheless real and spontaneous; and for those of us who shared its intellectual concerns and emotional springs, its appearance in Australia was as stirring as anything in our history. The movement will grow; it is the wave of the future. Its existence is the best guarantee that change is on the way, and the best evidence that Labor's present policies, no less than our past traumas, are helping to bring it about.[62]

To steal a phrase from Samuel Johnson, Whitlam's rhetoric was yet another example of the triumph of hope over experience. The most pronounced growth in national spirit occurred not in 1976 but in 1973 after Whitlam's election victory. By late 1976 the dismissal and economic recession had actually dampened the nationalist fervour of the early 1970s. Historians may well see the republicanism of 1976 as important, but it was by no means momentous nor was it unexpected. Given the circumstances, it seems more remarkable that republicanism made so little impact in the years after the dismissal. The truth was that the majority of those who had voted for Whitlam in 1972 were not the slightest bit interested in republicanism after 1975.[63] This is borne out by the fact that Whitlam fought the 1975 election on constitutional grounds and was soundly defeated at the polls. The public apathy which had so irritated John Dunmore Lang, Henry Lawson, Archibald's *Bulletin* and George Black was very much in evidence after the dismissal. If Australians were going to vote for a republic or for constitutional change, it seemed unlikely that they would do so at a time of political crisis.

When he addressed the National Press Club in 1977 Donald Horne brashly predicted that the republican debate would be a political reality by 1980, instead republicanism was a minor issue—only a shadow of what it had been in 1976 and 1977, and by 1979 Donald Horne and Myfanwy Gollan had parted with CFD. One thing Horne and many other republicans had learnt by 1980 was that the road to an Australian republic would be long and difficult. Although CFD had chosen to fight its campaign on 'constitutional' issues rather than republican ones, Horne had failed to convince the press and the general public that the two issues were separate. The period between 1975 and 1979 had shown that the media had a natural preference for 'republican' stories over those which related strictly to constitutional reform.

The republic was emotional and sexy—constitutional reform was dry and boring. But in the eyes of the public the two were still vaguely connected. Almost everyone had learnt that an Australian republic involved constitutional change. And as Australians headed towards the Bicentenary of Settlement in 1988, there was little sign of the bipartisan support needed to secure such change. The dismissal had entrenched one political party as constitutional fundamentalists and converted the other into cautious constitutional reformers. As far as the republic was concerned, there was still no one in the 1970s who seriously believed it to be a practical possibility. As the Brisbane *Courier-Mail* observed in 1979, there were few 'hot' republicans to be found: 'There seems to be no great enthusiasm for a republic even among many of those who support the principle'.[64]

Celebration of a Nation

> We Australians have trouble in identifying ourselves, in saying what we are and what we are coming to be.[65]

In 1988 historian Manning Clark became one of the heroes of the Bicentenary. Clark's prominence in 1988 said much about the character of Australian nationalism in the decade after the dismissal of the Whitlam government.[66] The elevation of Manning Clark's six-volume *History of Australia* to the status of secular bible, combined with his public persona—the oracle with the broad-brimmed hat—fitted comfortably with many of the official celebrations of the Bicentenary.[67] Like the Bicentenary celebrations, Clark and his history had not quite given up on a vision of Australia which attempted to assert one traditional and broadly homogeneous Australian identity.

Clark emerged as a leading public intellectual after Whitlam's election in 1972 and even more so after Whitlam's dismissal three years later. The cultural nationalism of the Whitlam government appealed to Clark and he was heartened by what he saw as Whitlam's 'missionary' zeal in teaching Australians that 'they could pursue an independent foreign policy and reach standards in the world of arts and letters which would once and for all rid them of the vestiges of their one-time colonial status'. In the same way that Clark saw Whitlam as the saviour of Australian nationalism, he explained the writing of the third volume of his history published in 1973 as an 'attempt to tell the story of how we began to acquire an identity and a conscience'.[68] The duties of government and the historian were not dissimilar—to reveal the nation to itself.

Clark's understanding of Australian nationalism was constructed on a traditional Anglo–Australian axis. The simplistic juxtaposition of the old dead tree of English philistinism and the 'young tree green' of Australian nationalism ran throughout his *History of Australia*.[69] For Clark, the wellspring of Australian identity was not so much the new multicultural Australia but the old Anglo–Australian legends. When the crowd gathered at the foot of the steps at old Parliament House on 11 November 1975 to protest the dismissal, Manning Clark was among them. Whitlam's dismissal angered and depressed Clark, he joined CFD, frequently spoke out against the 'treachery' of Kerr's behaviour and even wrote under the banner of a republican in 1977. It is here that Clark's role becomes most interesting. As one of the leading spokespersons for the cultural nationalist opposition to the dismissal, Clark was instrumental in interpreting Kerr's act as not only anti-democratic but anti-Australian. In Clark's eyes, the dismissal demonstrated that the greatest obstacle to Australian independence was the British connection, because it was this connection which represented 'the dead hand of the past' and only served to encourage a sense of inferiority and the tendency to 'grovel' and 'cringe'. So far as Clark was concerned, the nation could only become a nation by planting Henry Lawson's 'young tree green' on the grave of English philistinism.[70]

By the time of the Bicentenary Clark would be playing out the last vestiges of this essentially nineteenth-century version of Australian national identity. With the possible exception of Prime Minister Paul Keating (unleashed and unscripted), much republican rhetoric in the 1990s would leave Clark's traditional nationalism behind. There would be less talk about crucifying the cultural cringe and more discussion concerning multiculturalism and Australia's place in the Asian region.[71]

The demise of Clark's Lawsonesque nationalism was mirrored in the passing of the unitary vision of the nation at the end of the Bicentenary celebrations in 1988. In the words of Graeme Turner, the Bicentenary 'leaked alternative possibilities' and witnessed a 'decline in traditional nationalisms'. In its failure as a national festival it showed signs that a 'redefinition of Australian identity' was on its way. Peter Cochrane and David Goodman have also pointed to the travelling Bicentennial exhibition, which, with its Aboriginal and multicultural themes, represented a 'post-modern affirmation of diversity'.[72]

Although republicanism was conspicuously absent from the Bicentenary, the events of 1988 and the changes evident in the wider community were to have a profound effect on the republican debate of the 1990s. By the end of the Bicentenary it was clear that in the media, universities, and secondary schools traditional notions of Australian identity were being challenged. The influence of French structuralist theory within universities assisted in dethroning any 'real' or 'essential' notion of Australian identity. Proponents of multiculturalism were now beginning to speak of a 'nation without nationalism', while feminist and Aboriginal reconstructions of Australian history threw down the gauntlet to the Clark model of the past.[73]

The conflation of republicanism and national identity which had begun in earnest in the 1880s was about to undergo another significant change. The republic was now to become not so much about rejecting Britain but about remodelling Australian identity. Shortly before his death in 1991 Manning Clark spoke on the theme of multiculturalism and its relation to Australian identity:

> I think it is possible to identify an Australian . . . I think you identify him by the way he talks, even by the way he walks and his face. I would expect that despite the huge numbers of people coming here, there will always be a dominant culture, the Australian culture.[74]

The longing for a 'dominant' culture which Clark expressed may have been the hope of some Australians but the fact that it could not be identified, invented or distilled without considerable room for disagreement was an indication that the old European notion of a nation based on homogeneity was dying. The vacuum left by the transition from old monocultural nation to postmodern and multicultural nation would be one which would be partly filled by the republic. The republic would become one vehicle for redefining the nation. This did not mean that old concepts of the nation would disappear, but it did mean that they would have to be refashioned in the image of a more diverse society, something which the Bicentenary celebrations would certainly demonstrate.

The Dead Duck

> You realise don't you—this republican thing is a dead duck.[75]

One of the greatest myths about the republican debate in the post-Whitlam period has been the belief that there has been a republican movement in Australia since 1975. In part, this myth stems from the way in which we think about political participation in the late twentieth century. At a time when the membership of all political parties is in decline

***Time* and *Independent Monthly* covers**
By the early 1990s, after only two years of intense debate, sections of the Australian press began to represent the republic as an inevitable event.
(*Time Australia*, 12 April 1993; Reg Lynch, *Independent Monthly*, March 1992.)

and the mass media has become a more important political forum than parliament, political participation for the majority of citizens rarely extends beyond the ballot box.

The way in which the electorate's 'temperature' is gauged on any issue is through the interpretation of public opinion polls and this has certainly been the case with the republic. Since 1975 the pattern of republican debate has been predictable and largely repetitive. A small group of 'familiar' republicans—largely Sydney-based, and often associated with the Labor Party—have made public statements concerning the desirability or inevitability of a republic at times of convenient political occasion, such as a royal visit, the Bicentenary or an *annus horribilis*. This has usually resulted in a recycled media debate on the issue, followed by a considerable degree of frantic 'polling'. If the polls are favourable, then we have what is often referred to as a 'groundswell' of support for a republic or the 'growing movement' for a republic. Yet aside from a small and elite group of republicans, there is, in fact, no movement as such, only statements followed by the polling of a detached electorate largely sceptical of change. For some, this observation may seem cynical, pessimistic or even simplistic but it is probably the most truthful assessment of republicanism in the period after 1975. In the 1980s the republican debate followed this pattern but failed to recapture any of the 'poll movements' of the 1970s. The issue arose after the election of the Hawke Labor government in 1983, during royal visits, after the appointment of Bill Hayden as Governor-General in 1989 and within the Labor Party, but was conspicuously absent during the Bicentennial celebrations of 1988.

Bob Hawke's election in 1983 offered hope to all those within the labour movement who had been demoralised by the dismissal and the election of the Fraser government. Labor had moved to affirm its specific commitment to an Australian republic at its Federal Conference in 1981.[76] Consequently, when Hawke went to the polls he did so with a Party platform which included the goal of an Australian republic. As Prime Minister, however, Hawke was busier trying to legitimise Labor as a non-radical government on the consensus model. Advocating a republic was not seen as part of this process. Instead, Hawke spoke about the inevitability of a republic and revelled in the public theatre of royal tours. During his eight years as Prime Minister he avoided any open declaration of immediate support for a republic. Where he attracted criticism from loyalists was in his government's attitude to the oath of allegiance, the flag and the national anthem. The Hawke government tried unsuccessfully to delete references to the Queen from the oath of citizenship and alter the national flag before 1988, but it did manage to pass legislation which allowed Governor-General Sir Ninian Stephen to proclaim 'Advance Australia Fair' as Australia's national anthem in 1984.[77] This was more than enough to earn the label 'republican' from the Opposition.

244   *The Captive Republic*

The folksy right, led by Joh Bjelke-Petersen and Liberal member of parliament Michael Hodgman, flattered Hawke by describing his government as socialist and republican. Sir Joh placed advertisements in the 'deep south' warning Australia that atheists and drug addicts were about to republicanise Australia. Billy Snedden decided that the best way for the monarchy to survive in Australia was for Australia to have its own monarchy, primarily by transplanting one of Prince Charles' younger brothers to Australia and declaring him 'King of Australia'.[78] More intelligent ideas came from Michael Hodgman during the House debate on the Australia bill in 1986:

> Those republicans in the Hawke Socialist Republican Government . . . are in for a very big shock. We see the republicans coming out of the closet. Day by day I have to remind myself this is Canberra and not Moscow. It is only a matter of time before the coat of arms is changed. If those in the Moscow corner get their way, the kangaroo and the emu will be removed from the coat of arms and replaced with the hammer and sickle. If others get their way they will be replaced with a bandicoot and a ferret.[79]

Like Hodgman, the Australian Heritage Society was so depressed by the Hawke government's 'republicanism' that it placed advertisements in its quarterly journal *Heritage*: 'WANTED! AUSTRALIAN HUMOUR!'.[80]

Naturally, loyalists did not have a monopoly on original contributions to the republican debate. The platform of one republican Party set up in 1982 outlined its vision for a new social order: no alcohol at restaurants or clubs, one international airport at Alice Springs, no computers in the workplace, no nude scenes on television and no more Grassbyism. Groups such as Peter Consandine's Republican Party of Australia, formed in Sydney in 1982, continued the tradition of eccentric policy often associated with fringe republican groups. Consandine's Party platform included proposals for the reintroduction of 1-cent and 2-cent coins, and the abolition of the existing court system, policies which rarely attracted more than 500 members nationwide.[81]

In the land of real-politik, although political opportunists within the non-Labor ranks had tried to accuse the Hawke government of 'republicanism by stealth', there was no sign that the public perceived the government's initiatives as republican. In the 1980s the majority of debate on the republic tended to appear in the context of emotive disputes over national symbols or national celebrations rather than arguments over the specific constitutional role of the Governor-General. The constitutional debate did continue but mostly within the confines of academia or behind the closed doors of constitutional commissions. George Winterton, Professor of Law at the University of New South Wales, published *Monarchy to Republic* in 1986, the first book to address seriously the specific constitutional issues involved in establishing an Australian republic, and Gareth Evans worked hard throughout the 1980s to articulate the reasons for rewriting the Constitution and establishing a republic.[82] Others within the Labor Party, such as Neville Wran, Franca Arena and Gough Whitlam, contributed to keeping the question of a republic alive, while Donald Horne and Geoffrey Dutton never lost their commitment to the coming event. In the early 1980s Dutton had suggested 1988 as an appropriate time to declare a republic, yet if there was any event which revealed the fundamental conservatism of the Australian people and the crisis of belonging which faced them, it was the Bicentenary of 1988.[83]

The indecisiveness that reigned in the decade prior to 1988 over the appropriate theme for the celebrations demonstrated the inability of government to articulate Australian identity. In 1981 the Fraser government first decided on the theme of 'Living together' then suddenly reverted to the phrase 'The Australian achievement'. In 1984 the Hawke government returned again to 'Living together' before finally resting with 'Celebration of a nation'.[84] Here we can observe the tension between the old homogeneous concept of the nation and the new multicultural Australian nation. As early as 1985 the *Sydney Morning Herald* remarked that there was an 'ideological vacuum' at the heart of the planned celebrations.[85] As in 1888, the anniversary of the founding of a British penal colony raised a plethora of unpleasant dilemmas. In 1888 there was patent embarrassment over the convict stain. In 1988 the embarrassment was caused by what 26 January symbolised for Aboriginal Australians: decimation of a people and culture, invasion and immeasurable suffering. In addition, 1788 was hardly a date which carried significance for those Australians whose families had not emigrated from the British Isles. All in all, 26 January was an anniversary which reminded Australians that they had no founding myth of nationhood which could act as a unifying and defining force. The obvious lack of philosophical direction in the celebrations was therefore consistent with Australia's historical position— a multicultural society on the Asia–Pacific rim which had not yet managed to complete the transmission from colony to independent nation. The result was a Bicentenary which was big on spectacle but light on substance.[86] A harbour regatta, a barbecue festival, one nation in television (represented, appropriately, by the banal advertising jingle 'it's going to be great in '88, lend a hand mate'). The 'celebratory' nationalism of the Australian Bicentennial Authority was probably best described by John Murphy (with a little help from Milan Kundera) as the policy of 'laughter and forgetting'. It came as little surprise, therefore, that the *Sydney Morning Herald* should admit in December 1988 that 'it was never very clear what the Bicentenary was intended to celebrate, much less achieve'.[87] The suggestion of a republic was seen by the ABA and many people in public life as divisive. In fact, any discussion of republicanism was censored from the official channels of the ABA. In 1987 ABA chairman, Jim Kirk, ordered a republican article by Franca Arena MLC, commissioned for the ABA's quarterly magazine, to be withdrawn from publication, together with an article by Justice Michael Kirby of the New South Wales Court of Appeal which drew attention to the legal system's historical neglect of Aboriginal Australians.[88]

For republicans, there was much ground for pessimism by the end of the 1980s. The major speech on Australia Day had been delivered by Prince Charles and there had been no serious attempt to raise the issue of a republic in 1988.[89] The 1988 Constitutional Commission had recommended, in a somewhat despondent tone, that a referendum for a republic should not be held because 'on the evidence available to it, and regardless of the merits of the arguments, there was no prospect . . . of a change in public opinion in the near future which would result in there being majority support for a republic'. The Commission added that because of 'the fact that for many people the issue is an emotionally charged one, we believe that a recommendation to hold a referendum on this question at the present time would detract from other aspects of the report'.[90]

To rub salt into the wounds, the culmination of a decade of assiduous and detailed consideration of the Constitution within the labour movement was soundly defeated in the referendum of 1988. Lionel Bowen's four seemingly innocuous referendum questions, providing for four-year terms, one vote one value, the recognition of local government and the acknowledgment of basic rights and freedoms, were soundly rejected thanks largely to a brilliant spoiling campaign from the Liberal Party's Peter Reith. This only emphasised just how important it would be for any future referendum on the republic to have bipartisan support if it were to be a truly unifying national force. Meanwhile, the Australia Act of 1986 had completed the process of gradual evolution to independence under the Crown by formally terminating the power of the British parliament to legislate for State governments, abolishing all appeals to the Privy Council, and giving States the power to make laws repugnant to imperial legislation. Opposition members supported the Australia Act, conscious of the fact, as one member observed, that the legislation would take away ammunition from republicans and 'further enhance the position of Her Majesty and her heirs as monarchs of Australia'.[91] The Australia Act continued the drift away from England, but it also continued the process of making the monarchical connection less of a practical impediment to Australian independence. Equally, the appointment of ex-Labor leader Bill Hayden to the office of Governor-General in 1989 could either be seen as republicanism by stealth or the detoxification of a potential

Citizen Queen and ARM
Above, Queen Elizabeth II lives it up at the people's expense. Not unlike the images of Queen Victoria in the republican press of the 1880s, but a far cry from the 1950s. Yet another indication that the tide was turning. Below, the launch of the Australian Republican Movement in July 1991. The brainchild of New South Wales Labor MP Franca Arena, the ARM was run out of the offices of Malcolm Turnbull and Neville Wran in Sydney. The 'mixed media' of the ARM was a clever marriage of celebrity and respectability.
(John Shakespeare, *Sydney Morning Herald*, 15 February 1992;
Tasso Taraboulsi, *Daily Telegraph Mirror*, 8 July 1991.)

republican by the trappings of monarchical office. After taking up his appointment in 1989, Hayden earned the respect of all political parties while occasionally entering debate on the republican issue, usually with comments that tended to help the monarchist cause.[92]

In 1990, fifteen years after the dismissal of the Whitlam government, there was little sign that the republican debate was about to renew itself. The republic was still very much about emotional issues of national identity and still led by the same individuals. In political terms, however, any republic would have to be asserted through constitutional change. The two issues, republic and constitutional change, were interdependent—at least minimally.

The Dead Duck Flies 1990–1995

> I am delighted to announce that the British government has agreed to make a gift to Australia of an original document containing our Australian Constitution. The document is an original copy of the Commonwealth of Australia Constitution Act—the British Act of Parliament which was passed in 1900 and which brought our nation into existence on 1 January 1901. . . . In a very real sense, our birth certificate as a nation will be returning home.[93]

Almost one hundred years after the Federation of the Australian colonies in 1901 Australia received the original copy of the British Act which contained the Commonwealth Constitution. The irony was that Australians had never realised it was missing in the first place. The gesture of the British government in 1990 was a reminder to Australians of their colonial origins and an omen for the direction of political debate in the decade ahead. Metaphorically at least, it seemed that Australians now had the opportunity to recast the Constitution in their own image.

In June 1990 Prime Minister Bob Hawke opened discussion on the prospect of constitutional change by suggesting that the 1990s should be a decade of constitutional re-evaluation, especially in the sphere of federal–State relations. Hawke was aware that the centenaries of the Constitutional Conventions of the 1890s would offer the opportunity for what he called 'sensible and practical' proposals for constitutional reform.[94]

In April of the following year Hawke attended a Constitutional Convention at New South Wales Parliament House in Sydney convened to commemorate the National Australasian Convention of 1891. The 1991 Convention proved significant for several reasons. Aside from setting the process of constitutional re-evaluation in train, it was the first Constitutional Convention in Australia to conclude with majority support for an Australian republic. By early 1991 there were signs that the 'duck' was only sleeping after all. John Kerr's death in March brought home the fact that the bitterness surrounding the dismissal had passed, while the Hawke-led debate about constitutional reform ensured that the republican question would arise at some time throughout the 1990s. More generally, an obsession with the next millennium was beginning to emerge in the media. In 1991 cartoonists were already depicting republicans as astronauts leading Australia on some kind of Stanley Kubrick spacewalk into the future.[95] 2001 was also the anniversary of Federation, a coincidence which encouraged republicans to exploit the belief that constitutional change should take place in the 1990s to prepare Australia for the twenty-first century. If Homebush Bay could be detoxified in time for the Olympics, perhaps the Constitution could be reconditioned as well. The republic could become part of an Olympics marketing strategy just as the Olympics could justify the need for a republic.

In June 1991 the Labor Party held its Federal Conference in Hobart. It was here that the centre left faction, led largely by John Dawkins, succeeded in passing a resolution which committed the federal Australian Labor Party to encouraging a process of debate to facilitate the declaration of an Australian republic by 2001. On passing the resolution, national president John Bannon observed that it had been carried 'not very vigorously', an impression which proved accurate in the weeks ahead as both Bannon and Queensland Premier Wayne Goss described the republic as a distraction from the more important economic problems.[96] Leader of the Opposition, Dr John Hewson, agreed, claiming that the republican resolution was an example of the influence of the 'loony left' in the Labor Party. Meanwhile, those at the opposite end of the spectrum, such as Bruce Ruxton, president of the Victorian branch of the RSL and deputy national president, tried to draw on the speeches of Leon Trotsky but could not quite get the words right. Ruxton said the ALP would end up on the 'dungheap of history' because of its republicanism. The dustbin Ruxton was looking for was elusive but he eventually found it. After the initial period of republican debate had passed, Ruxton was no longer sought by the media as a credible anti-republican voice.[97]

As it was, what lifted republicanism into mainstream political debate was not the Labor Party's resolution but the launch of the Australian Republican Movement in July 1991 at The Rocks in Sydney.[98] The genesis of the ARM lay with ex-New South Wales Premier Neville Wran and especially with New South Wales Labor member of parliament, Franca Arena, who had long argued for a non-partisan national committee of prominent Australians to lead the republican debate. In 1989 Arena secured the support of Neville Wran and Wran, in turn, was able to convince author Thomas Keneally to stand as chairperson.[99] The contribution of Franca Arena was probably (unintentionally) under-emphasised by

Thomas Keneally in his book *Our Republic*. The genesis of the ARM was colourfully described by Keneally:

> The lunch at Jill Hickson's and Neville Wran's table had now reached the point where nearly all the fish they bought the day before at the Sydney Fish Markets had been eaten. In a manner all too typical of generous Sunday lunches in Sydney, a number of bottles of Hunter Valley Chardonnay had also been drained. Neville Wran leaned over the table and said, 'The other thing I want to see happen before I bloody well die is an Australian Republic'.[100]

If oppression was the catalyst of the French and American republics, wine will surely be the wellspring of the Australian republic. Despite its honesty, Keneally's image of a boozy lunch was not politically astute. The concept of a group of citizens to lead the republican debate proved to be effective but it would also lend itself to allegations of elitism. From its inception, at least until 1994 when it began to broaden its base, the ARM was not so much a people's movement as a media-offensive by a minority of influential individuals who claimed to have the people's interest at heart. The aim of the ARM was straightforward: legitimise the republican debate through celebrity identification and ensure that the 'ratbag stereotypes' that had bedevilled republicans since the 1960s would not be heard again in the 1990s.

In terms of media exposure, this strategy was certainly a sound one. The belief that the Australian republic would be more palatable if removed from the arena of Party politics was well-founded. Australians would see respected national figures from all walks of life, journalism, the arts, sport, academia, medicine, the legal profession and politics, coming together to declare their support for a republic. In the weeks that followed, the reaction to the launch of the ARM was overwhelmingly positive. Newspaper editorials came out in favour of a republic by 2001 and the electronic media picked up the debate and for a short time the republican issue dominated the political agenda.[101]

The ARM was run from the Sydney offices of merchant banker and lawyer, Malcolm Turnbull. Without Turnbull and Partners' financial support the Movement could not have managed the level of success that it achieved in 1991–92. Turnbull paid for the services of a full-time media relations expert, Tony Pooley, provided office support and gave generously of his resources to ensure that the Movement had every chance of success. As far as the media was concerned, the ARM possessed the right contacts. Several prominent journalists were among its founding members and there was no doubting the ability of leading members to articulate the Movement's cause. Turnbull, Keneally and Horne led the debate for the ARM and their impact was evidenced by Turnbull's appointment to chair the Republic Advisory

Committee in April 1993. But only eight months after the launch of the ARM its role was superseded by the new Labor Prime Minister, Paul Keating.

Keating had come to power after a bitter struggle with Bob Hawke, and while his first months as Prime Minister were characterised by an identifiable reticence to embroil himself in controversy, by early 1992 he was willing to campaign openly for the declaration of a republic. Between February 1992 and 1995 Keating was the driving force behind republican debate in Australia. In the tradition of Whitlam and Fraser and far more than Hawke, Keating saw the federal government as the primary agent of national renewal. From the outset the legitimacy of Keating's prime ministership was based on his 'big picture' image as a leader seeking national reinvigoration and new definitions of Australian identity. Thus, the Keating government cast nearly all its policies in nationalist slogans—'One nation', 'creative nation', 'working nation', 'one of us'—and when it came to remembering the old Australia, Keating was blessed with the convenient historical occasion of the fiftieth anniversary of the Second World War. A procession of television images followed of Keating kissing the ground on which the diggers had fought and died. Keating was never without an opportunity to speak on the issue of Australian identity. Even when announcing the Australian of the Year in 1995, he managed to reduce Arthur Boyd's entire artistic oeuvre to an attempt to distil the essence of Australia on canvas. Wherever Keating went the 'nation' tagged along, waiting to be redefined. Politics, art, sport, the information superhighway, any cultural or political pursuit except the Liberal Party was conscripted to serve the cause of national identity.[102]

Beginning with his short speech in the presence of the Queen in February 1992 when he declared Australia's outlook to be necessarily independent, Keating, with a little help from the Fleet Street tabloids and speechwriter Don Watson, became the first Australian Prime Minister to make an Australian republic an integral and active part of a Party political platform.[103] For a government that had been almost a decade in power and was about to go to the polls at a time of high unemployment and economic recession, the republic provided Keating with a means of reinvigorating the government and distinguishing his prime ministership from that of his predecessor, Bob Hawke. Obfuscation aside, the republic was at least a welcome change from the 'economy'—a word which seemed to have become a euphemism for the nation by the end of the 1980s.

Keating's drive for a republic was assisted by Paul Kelly, editor-in-chief of Rupert Murdoch's *Australian*. Kelly was appointed editor in August 1991 only one month after the formation of the ARM and the republican resolution at the Labor Party's Federal Conference. From the time of Keating's appointment as Prime Minister, the *Australian* maintained a consistently pro-republican line, regularly leading editorials with

Keating
Paul Keating, Prime Minister of Australia, December 1991 to March 1996. Keating was the first Australian Prime Minister to campaign for an Australian republic.
(Peter West, AUSPIC.)

sympathetic headlines such as 'Our republic a historical opportunity'. Linked with the idea of a republic for both Keating and the *Australian* was the concept of Australia's 'push' into Asia. During Kelly's editorship the *Australian* placed a high priority on the integration of the Australian economy into the Asia–Pacific region. Asia was frequently projected in the pages of the *Australian* as a treasure house of economic opportunity awaiting Australian exploitation. The republic was connected to this future, being seen as both the logical 'result' of Asian integration and the potential catalyst of greater links with the region. At times, one could be forgiven for thinking that the *Australian*'s primary motivation for supporting a republic lay in the mistaken belief that the declaration of an Australian republic would transform Australia into the *wirtschaft wunder* of Asia. Just as Paul Keating linked Australia's independence to Australia's economic future in Asia, Kelly's *Australian* emphasised the links between national identity and economic prosperity:

> Mr Keating's latest speeches . . . are closely related. They set the scene for a broader, competitive opening of the economy in the Asia–Pacific region with

a 'progressive, pluralist, democratic—unmistakably Australian' society at home. Mr Keating also relates a projection of a dynamic economic presence in the region to a clearer sense of Australian national identity. This is not a quantifiable relationship but surely it is crucial to our fortunes. Any trading nation worth its salt—Japan and Germany are modern examples—has had a robust sense of self-identity.[104]

For the ARM, Keating and the *Australian*, there was a shared belief in the need for a dominant concept of Australian identity, a concept which was simply Australian (whatever this might mean) rather than being both Australian and British. Hence the need for a new oath of citizenship, a new flag, and a republic. The republic was thus the means of wiping away the old 'duality' of allegiance and nationality which had characterised Australia for most of its history, a kind of psychological battering ram which, in the mystic words of Thomas Keneally, would finally allow Australians to 'cease' dividing their 'soul'.[105] But the event which provided the biggest boost for the government-led republican campaign was undoubtedly the re-election of the Labor Party in March 1993.

Within six weeks of his return to power Keating had announced the formation of the Republic Advisory Committee at an Evatt Foundation dinner in Sydney. Only two days earlier, *Time Australia* published the results of a Morgan poll which showed that 52 per cent of those polled supported a republic with only 38 per cent of the sample supporting the monarchy. The Morgan poll was the first national poll to reveal majority support for a republic. The election victory was widely interpreted as 'proof' that the republic was inevitable—especially by some members of the Liberal Party in New South Wales. New South Wales Premier John Fahey described the republican push as a 'train' which would leave the Liberals stranded at the station if they failed to enter the debate.[106] This sudden rush of republicanism was remarkable, given that only three years earlier the suggestion that republicanism would play such a central role in Australian politics would have been thought absurd. The fortuitous convergence of several historical factors had played a role: the rise to power of a Labor Prime Minister wearing a streak of republican nationalism like a badge of honour, the public farce of the 'private' lives of the English royal family, the formation of the high-profile ARM, an increased public receptivity to republicanism born of *fin de siècle* sensitivity and finally, the undeniable fact that the British monarchy was not perceived as an appropriate symbol for Australian society in the 1990s. The wheel of inevitability appeared to be grinding to a halt.

Within only three years of the ARM's launch and Keating's investiture as Prime Minister, an independent committee had outlined the options available to achieve a viable federal republic of Australia; an Australian

Prime Minister had discussed the proposed move to a republic with the reigning monarch, and the heir to the throne had endorsed the republican debate as 'a sign of a mature and self-confident nation'.[107] By any standard this was an astonishing degree of success in such a short period of time. Until the 1990s republicanism in Australia was often perceived by intellectuals as something akin to a fly at an imperial tea party, occasionally annoying but never able to make a significant impact on the afternoon's proceedings. Between 1990 and 1995 both the media and academia reappraised the role of republicanism. Historians and political scientists began to explore the broader traditions associated with republican citizenship, although this exploration was not necessarily prominent beyond academia and the opinion pages of the broadsheet press.[108] Rhetorically, the republic was seen as a vehicle of 'inclusion', but in 1995 there were few signs that Australian women or Australian Aborigines were about to lead the republican debate. This is not to say that women and Aborigines were not involved—the Australian Republican Movement, for example, held a women's forum in August 1994—but perhaps it does reveal that dry minimalist arguments about the minutiae of the Constitution did not excite much passion, nor did they speak about social justice or equality. Another difficulty with the debate was that it also showed signs of becoming too closely attached to the fortunes of one political party.

Between 1990 and 1994 the Federal Liberal Party maintained a stubbornly anti-republican line, not so much because of any heartfelt allegiance to the monarch but because of perceived political advantage from opposing 'Keating's republic'. But the debate was poorer for the Liberals' absence. The more that issues such as Australia's identity in the Asian region, multiculturalism and citizenship, became tied to the question of a republic, the harder it was for the Liberal Party to connect itself with those issues. The risk for the Liberal Party was that it would be painted into Keating's corner as creatures of the past—along with the 'Morphy Richards toaster, the Qualcast mower and the Astor TV'.[109] Keating's barbs aside, it did seem odd that a Party which championed individualism and meritocracy should forget these principles when it came to the head of state. In 1995 under John Howard's leadership, the Liberal Party became more equivocal in its stance. Keating's response to the Republic Advisory Committee's report, delivered in the form of a nationally televised speech in federal parliament and entitled 'An Australian Republic—the Way Forward', did force the Opposition parties to formulate a formal response. After some indecision John Howard committed his party to a Constitutional Convention. This was a clever ploy which had the benefit of allowing Howard to pay lip service to 'the people', maintain his long-standing support for the present Constitution

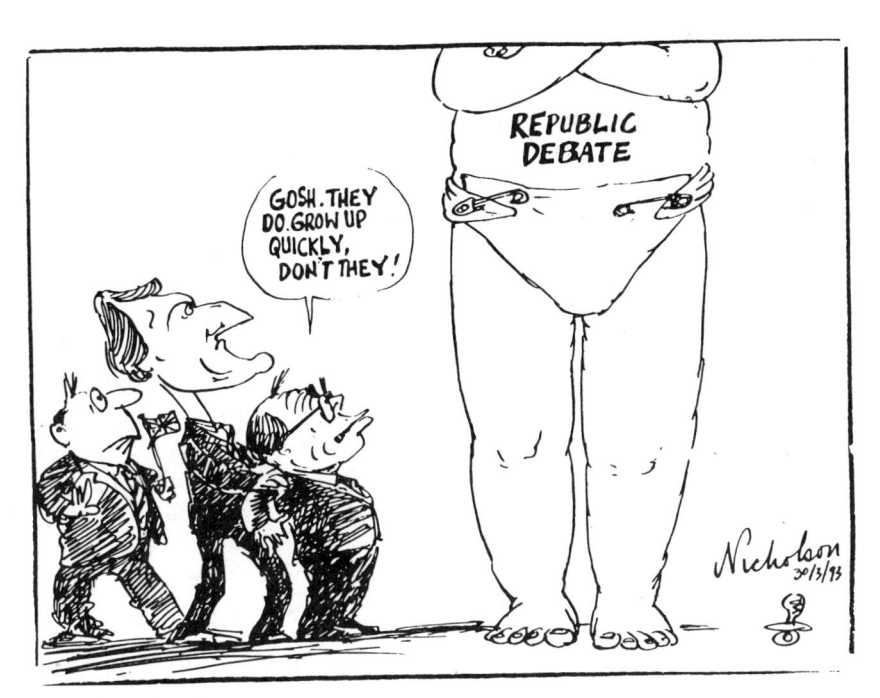

Nicholson cartoon and Moir cartoon
Cartoonists quickly pointed out the manner in which the republic became the property of partisan political debate. In these examples from Nicholson and Moir, the federal Liberal Party is left ossified at the station by the Keating government's advocacy of a republic.
(Peter Nicholson, *Age*, 30 March 1993; Alan Moir, *Sydney Morning Herald*, 1 May 1993)

and still oppose 'Keating's republic'.[110] The wall of conservative opposition to the minimalist republic was beginning to crumble in 1995 and Howard was aware that he could no longer afford to identify the Liberal Party with 'God, Queen and Country'. There was no surer sign that the Liberal Party's loyalty to the monarchy was waning than in August 1995 when ex-Liberal Prime Minister Malcolm Fraser admitted that the republic was both 'inevitable and right'.[111]

In other ways, however, the content of the republican debate in the 1990s has differed little from the debate of the previous two centuries. By 1990 the majority of arguments both for and against a republic had already been articulated, some as much as 150 years earlier. Aside from the fact that the recent debate has paid more attention to the legal and constitutional minutiae of republican government, the 1990s' debate on the republic is not new. In some respects Australians are still grappling with the questions of the late eighteenth century: colony or nation, Crown or country, child or adult. These questions have run like a river throughout our history since 1788. When we hear Thomas Keneally in the 1990s speak of Australia as a child longing to leave home we hear the echo of John Dunmore Lang in the 1850s. When we listen to Donald Horne stress the need for Australians to rid themselves of the colonial mind set that the monarchical connection engenders we hear a more sophisticated version of Henry Lawson's republicanism of the 1880s. Equally, when we hear Malcolm Turnbull use the phrase 'Australia comes first' in 1992 we hear the message of Lang, Lawson, Deniehy and many others.[112]

On the anti-republican side, we hear similar echoes: 'We are already a republic . . . Now is not the time . . . If it ain't broke don't fix it'.[113] While these fundamental dilemmas are 'old' we have not yet understood the links between the Australian republic of the late twentieth century and the republican debate of our past.

Aldous Huxley once observed that the most important lesson to be learnt from history is that human beings fail to learn from history. The history of republicanism in Australia has revolved around two focal points—constitutional reform and national identity, both of them underpinned by the notion of inevitability. When John Dunmore Lang first began to campaign for a federal Australian republic in 1850 there was a stark choice between the constitutional arrangements necessary to maintain colonial dependencies and those required to establish a republic. The same situation applied at the time of Federation in 1901. The choice between independent republic and dependent Federation was clear. Yet as Australia gained more and more independence under the Crown throughout the twentieth century the gap between 'republic' and 'constitutional monarchy' narrowed until, by the time the Australia Act was passed in 1986, the 'old' argument of Henry Parkes that Australia was already a republic effectively held true. In 1993 the report of the Keating government's Republic Advisory Committee agreed:

> Australia is . . . a state in which sovereignty resides in its people, and in which all public offices, except that at the very apex of the system are filled by persons deriving authority directly or indirectly from the people. It may be appropriate to regard Australia as a crowned republic . . .[114]

The Committee noted that this view was also one commonly expounded by constitutional monarchists. The ARM, the Keating government, and their opponents, are in broad agreement that the nature of Australia's political institutions is essentially 'republican'. The only point on which they differ is in regard to the role of the monarch as the head of state.

So far as 'constitutional' issues are concerned there is little difference between republicans and monarchists. The odd thing is that neither side is willing to admit that they are bedfellows. Both the so-called 'minimalist republicans' and the 'monarchists' are inheritors of the same political tradition—English constitutionalism. Each side's first obligation is to the Constitution and the rule of law. Both sides strive to protect the same 'republican' form of government: a government which enshrines the constitutional and political supremacy of an executive-dominated system of government. As Patrick O'Brien has remarked, both 'republicans' and 'monarchists' demand government 'for' the people not government 'by' the people.[115] Australian republicans are just as intent on preserving 'British' institutions as Australian monarchists. One need only look at the reticence of leading republicans to embrace a popularly elected president to realise their preference for 'British' models. John Hirst, historian, prominent republican and member of the Republic Advisory Committee, made this point in 1992:

> The Republican movement has declared that it wants our present system of parliamentary government to continue and that our President should not be directly elected like the American one. He would be elected by the parliament and perform the functions of the present Governor General . . . For the Republic to work well we should keep our well tried British political institutions. A republic which disowned our political and cultural heritage would be an apathetic and impoverished body.[116]

In 1991, George Winterton, another member of the Republic Advisory Committee and author of the first minimalist republican Constitution, commented on the monarchist argument that 'the system works well'. 'In general it is a sensible viewpoint, but the appropriate response is that a republic need not affect anything essential.' While it is true that the word 'minimalism' is a blanket term which actually disguises a range of options, as Cheryl Saunders has observed, the unmistakable emphasis of the ARM and the Keating government's republicanism was one of preservation rather than experimentation.[117] The Labor government's 1995 minimalist blueprint simply sought to insert 'one of us' as president. Appointed by parliament, with much the same reserve powers as the present Governor-General, the president's role would be to 'embody and represent Australia's values and traditions'. But the republic, in Keating's words, 'asserts nothing more than our unique identity . . . expresses nothing more than our desire to have a head of state who is truly one of us'.[118] In terms of substantial constitutional change Keating's republic was an empty vessel. This is why the republic was greeted with such eagerness by the mainstream press. As the *Sydney Morning Herald* enthused in 1994, the change to a republic will be 'smooth' and 'unobtrusive' nor will it 'conjure up idealism with political and social experimentation'.[119] Edmund Burke could not have said it better. Old boots with new soles and a spit of nationalist polish, but the same boots none the less.

In the 1990s we have arrived at a point where, in constitutional terms, there is little difference between our republicans and our monarchists. Constitutionally speaking, all they have left to distinguish between them is the person of the monarch. One wants to keep her; the other wants to remove her. The argument is not about altering the Constitution, but who should be the most appropriate symbol of its defence—an Australian president or a British monarch. In 1994 Malcolm Turnbull, speaking in his capacity as chairperson of the ARM, claimed that the Movement was not 'anti-British' nor was it 'anti-monarchy'. 'Thomas Paine' said Turnbull 'had observed that an hereditary ruler was as illogical as an hereditary author. But we have no need to make such a case in Australia. Our current head of state is inappropriate simply because she is not Australian'.[120] To be fair, Turnbull and the ARM have frequently pointed out the democratic arguments for a republic, but Henry Parkes would have been proud of the above remark. The republic of Turnbull and the ARM rejects any hint of radicalism, preserves the Constitution, and seeks only to replace the crimson thread with a ribbon of more native hue. Opposition to the monarch is motivated more by the monarch's nationality than the hereditary nature of her position.

Turnbull and the ARM are simply trying to complete the process of 'naturalising' Australia's political institutions which began with the Statute of Westminster in 1931, and continued with the Australia Act in 1986. The Republic Advisory Committee and the Keating government have already expressed their preference for the maintenance of the title 'Commonwealth of Australia' if Australia becomes a republic in 2001. Aside from minor alterations to the Governor-General's powers—changes which would only improve his ability to 'defend' the Constitution—the current minimalist model is the last step in the process Henry Parkes began in the 1850s. The substance of the republic will be finally complete, without the shadow of the name.

There are, of course, many republicans who wish to go well beyond minimalism, but political imperatives dictate that achieving even the minimalist model will be difficult enough.[121] In 1995, after four years of debate on the republic, republicans had won the nationalist argument for a republic, but they had not won the constitutional argument. Whether an Australian president would be popularly elected or appointed by parliament, as well as the question of the president's powers, were issues that still threatened to derail a republican referendum.

For most of our history, the republican debate has surfaced within a British-centred culture. Horatio Wills, John Dunmore Lang, Daniel Deniehy, J. F. Archibald, Henry Lawson, Frederick Charles Burleigh Vosper, and Geoffrey Dutton and Donald Horne in the 1960s and 1970s, all struggled to assert the priority of Australian interests over and above those of Britain and the Empire, whether it be in regard to foreign policy, the economy, constitutional autonomy or cultural identity. Historically speaking, Australia has only recently begun to move away from a belief which has dominated its history since 1788. This is the belief that Australian identity was somehow tied to, shared with or dominated by British identity. In the 1990s this concept of Australian identity has long departed. The date at which the departure began is contentious. Post-Menzies, post-Whitlam, post-Keating—there are valid arguments to support each of these periods. But the most notable difference about the republican debate of the 1990s is that it is occurring within the context of a perceived crisis of identity, a crisis which has been detectable ever since Australia began to move away from Britain in the 1960s. The republican debate is therefore no longer about whether we are British or Australian—it is about how we wish to be Australian. Although the issue of 'identity' has always been attached to the republican debate, it has never manifested itself with the degree of angst, emotion and urgency that has characterised the debate of the early 1990s. The important 'differences' between 'monarchists' and 'republicans' are not constitutional, they are differences concerning the ideas, beliefs and values which relate to Australia's national, social and cultural identity. The republican debate in the 1990s is as much about the way Australians wish to perceive themselves as it is about the role of the head of state. A debate about the past and the future, a debate about Australia's geographical position and the multicultural composition of its society. For some, like Donald Horne, the republic has become a way of turning away from notions of national identity and seeking to define Australian identity through concepts of civic identity. For others, like Don Watson, it is simply a way of 'exalting the nation less than the way of life'.[122] But underlying this 'republicanism' there is an emerging consensus that Australia must seek to reconcile the diversity of its society with the symbols of the political and institutional structures which give that society meaning. In 1994 Tony Abbott, leader of the anti-republican Australians for Constitutional Monarchy, accused republicans of promoting the 'black armband view' of Australian history:

> If Australia needs to become a republic to be complete all the achievements of non-republican Australia are devalued . . . The majority [of republican spokesmen] regard our pre-Whitlam history as a long dark age, blighted by genocide, patriarchy and capitalism—hence Paul Keating's desire to put a stake through the heart of the Menzies legacy . . . Republicans cite our ethnic diversity and multi-cultural achievements as the high points of Australian life without mentioning the Anglo–Celtic heritage.[123]

Abbott's attack on republicanism says nothing about the Constitution, but it says much about the true focus of republican debate in the 1990s and the essential differences between 'republicans' and 'monarchists'. Much of the Keating government agenda—such as a sympathy for political correctness, Aboriginal reconciliation, multiculturalism and Asian integration—is frequently linked to the republic by conservative opponents who fear the loss of British 'heritage'. Thus, we find John Howard accusing Paul Keating of forgetting that Australia 'is a predominantly Anglo–Saxon society', or we witness senior judges publicly deriding the Mabo decision as a cave-in to political correctness while launching an anti-republican book. When Prince Charles spoke at Darling Harbour on Australia Day 1994 he referred to the fact that Australia, like many other nations, was going through a period of, in his words, 'not quite knowing where we are'.[124] Charles' simple image identified the source of Abbott's angst and the point around which the question of an Australian republic now turns. No longer able to rely on monocultural definitions of identity through 'Britishness', 'whiteness' or traditional stereotypes of Australian identity, Australia now confronts the dilemma that its traditional British ties have always helped it to avoid. How does a multicultural society with predominantly European roots situated close to Asia manage to define itself?

Lurking underneath much of the republican debate are many of the traditional rivalries which have divided European Australia. Keating's republicanism, in particular, helps to stoke the fires of 'old' divisions, primarily because it is expressed in a political language which is itself 'old'. Much of Keating's nationalist rhetoric calls on an Irish–Australian working-class vernacular which is more representative of the 1930s than the 1990s. Phrases like 'tugging the forelock' and 'licking the British bootstraps' evoke the nationalism of the underdog, the working class and reek of traditional Irish resentment to British rule. Because Keating's language is steeped in 'old' working-class images we find equally 'old' reactions to his statements. One member of the National Party brought back memories of Anglo–Irish sectarianism when he labelled Keating 'bog Irish' in early 1992. Prominent right-wing historian Geoffrey Blainey then added to the nostalgia by referring to Paul Keating as 'pro-Irish'.[125]

Old class rivalries also stirred when Annita Keating failed to 'curtsy' when greeting the Queen in February 1992. While the Dutch do not curtsy to their own monarch, the Keatings had obviously not read their copy of *The Royal Visit and You*. When added to Keating's public distaste for the 'British establishment' and his forthright views on Britain's disregard for Australia's interests in the Second World War, there was a plentiful source of emotional material. Keating's rhetoric tapped into a language of traditional Anglo–Australian rivalry, evoking crude convict stereotypes from the British press and childish comments from the leader of the Opposition, Dr John Hewson, who remarked that Keating had never learnt a sense of respect at school.[126]

But the most startling fact about Keating's term as Prime Minister is that his statements concerning Australian independence created such a furore. When Keating 'dared' to mention that Australia's outlook was necessarily independent in his short speech during the Queen's visit in 1992, he was lambasted by sections of the press and, remarkably, accused of being 'republican'. The *Sydney Morning Herald* referred to his speech as an 'unfortunate lapse'. Other politicians used words such as 'embarrassing', 'impolite', 'shocking' and 'inappropriate'.[127] Similar outbursts ensued when Keating went one step further a few days later and criticised British policy in South-east Asia during the Second World War:

> I was told [by Dr Hewson] I did not learn respect at school. I learned one thing: I learned about self-respect and self-regard for Australia . . . Not about some cultural cringe to a country which decided not to defend the Malaysian peninsula, not to worry about Singapore and not to give us our troops back to keep ourselves free from Japanese domination.[128]

This was not the republican image which the ARM desired. But Keating's comments were not explicitly republican, and regardless of their historical accuracy the response of the British and Australian press proved two things. One, the British were not accustomed to criticism from Australia and two, Australia had not yet learnt to criticise Britain without fearing that the Queen would die of fright. The over-reaction to Keating's remarks demonstrated that remnants of the colonial mentality remained. Certain Australians had difficulty in accepting criticism of Britain or any mention of Australian independence in the presence of the monarch. As was so often the case in Australia's past, the crisis of loyalty was felt not in Britain but in Australia. Buckingham Palace even issued a statement after Keating's speech to the Queen in February which reassured Australians that the Queen had found the Prime Minister's remarks to be 'very warm'.[129] After two centuries it seemed Australians were still not free to think critically of Britain. So deep was the culture of fealty to Britain that the monarch and her 'little island' were still 'untouchable'. In some respects, support for the monarch was a cry for a time when 'identity' was one-dimensional, a form of nostalgia, a way of clinging to a time when the centre still held, when history was a pioneer march through the wilderness and the nation was one with Empire. If it is not this, then it is merely a refusal to accept that Australian identity—as Paul Keating and speechwriter Don Watson claimed—needs to be 'recast'; not so much an allegiance to the monarch but an unwillingness to seek parity between national symbols and the multicultural reality of Australian society in the late twentieth century.

Speaking at the Centenary dinner to commemorate the Corowa Federation Convention of 1893, Paul Keating revealed that it was the desire for this parity which drove his government's campaign for a republic:

> The monarchy has had family problems at other times in the past, but Australians did not draw the conclusion that the monarchy had lost its relevance.
>
> Today they draw that conclusion because the monarchy is remote from their lives and perceived as inappropriate to the sort of nation we must become.
>
> ... I am for the republic not for what I am against, but what I am for: not for what a republic will throw away, but for what a republic can deliver:
>
> It can deliver a new sense of unity and national pride in which Australians of this and future generations can share.
>
> It can deliver a re-cast Australian identity defined by the commitment of Australians to this land above all others, which will say unequivocally to the world who we are and what we stand for.[130]

In many ways, this history of republicanism has been an account of the pre-history of republican Australia. The history of Australian republicanism in the twenty-first century will be one which is fundamentally different from the republican history which has preceded it. It will be the story of Australia's success or failure in grappling with the dilemma which it was 'inevitably' bound to confront from the moment Governor Arthur Phillip took possession of the colony of New South Wales in 1788 in the name of the Crown.

How do we take possession of Australia, not for the Crown, not for white Australia, but for all Australians?—for her Aboriginal peoples, her ethnic majorities and minorities, her men and her women. How do we define the nation when the Crown which originally claimed this land is no longer an appropriate symbol of the people's aspirations?

Despite the continuity of specific arguments surrounding the idea of a republic—essentially a rehash of what the present generation has forgotten or half-remembered, the context of the debate has changed. The sighting of a 'republican' pig in Surry Hills in the 1990s takes on a significance far removed from its presence in eighteenth-century Sydney. Today, our pig walks free, no longer revolutionary, no longer a threat to civil society. It is difficult now to imagine any Australian wanting to shoot the republican pig, but equally, few would notice it as it passed them by.

Epilogue

If the role of the historian is not to be the advocate of one truth but to discover what men and women have believed to be true, then this book has been an attempt to reveal that there have been many 'true' republics in Australia's past.

The Australian republic has been attached to dreams of imperialist grandeur and to classical concepts of balanced government which have insisted upon the inclusion of the monarchical element. It has appeared as the spectre of revolution, the anti-democratic threat of squatters, the last resort of disappointed loyalists demanding responsible government and an end to transportation, the utopian dream of radical nationalists and the pragmatic platform of minimal constitutional change.

From a contemporary perspective, there are two broadly identifiable republican traditions in Australia, one conservative and the other Labor-inspired. For Australian conservatives, there is a republican tradition that is yet to be fully acknowledged. This is the tradition of David Blair, Henry Parkes, Alfred Deakin and George Higinbotham. The tradition of Australian liberalism which held that the essence of republican government was already built into Australia's State and federal Constitutions—the tradition of the disguised republic.[1] The conservative tradition was not anti-monarchical or anti-British and it insisted that the 'true' republic was one which embraced balanced government, the suspicion of executive power, the dispersal of power within a federal framework and an active yet moderate approach to constitutional reform. Finally, it acknowledged Australian aspirations to national independence, but did so emphasising the importance of British heritage and kinship qualities which, like Australian identity, were often projected as fixed and one-dimensional entities.

In contrast, the Labor tradition of Australian republicanism has always sought to frame the issue of national identity as a choice between Australian independence and loyalty to the mother country. For John Dunmore Lang, Daniel Deniehy, Louisa and Henry Lawson, and twentieth-century republicans such as Thomas Keneally and Paul Keating, the republic was the final assertion of national maturity, the catalyst for complete economic, cultural and political independence. While the initiators of the Labor tradition linked the introduction of republican government with various notions of social equality and democratic government, by the time of Federation in 1901 this connection was already severed. The conflation of Labor republicanism with one form of nationalism—the dominant strain of the romantic Labor left—was cemented with the rise of the Australian Labor Party in the 1890s. The Labor Party quickly decided that the republic was primarily an issue associated with national identity and largely detached from the party's program of parliamentary reform.[2] For most of the twentieth century the Labor Party shelved the dream of a republic in favour of imperial loyalty and White Australia. When the Keating government rekindled the flame in 1991–96 the form of republicanism espoused by Labor was perfectly consistent with the shift which had occurred in the labour movement in the late nineteenth century. Keating's republic was not driven so much by democratic resistance to inherited privilege but by the need to assert Australian identity through an Australian head of state—'one of us'.[3] Democracy was that which could be achieved through the vehicle of parliamentary legislation, the republic was merely the nationalist rump of that agenda.

Since the fall of the Keating government in March 1996 both the content and course of the republican debate in Australia are set to undergo a profound change. With a conservative government in power that is committed to a constitutional convention, 50 per cent of whose members are to be elected, the republican debate will be less dominated by nationalist rhetoric—at least of the Keating variety. On the one hand, the debate will be free of the 'Keating republic' barb, yet on the other hand it will be without Keating's passion and drive, not to mention federal government support. While certain members of the press gallery have been eager to dismiss Keating's republican campaign as a failure, it is unlikely that historians will perceive his role in the same light.[4] Keating's tenure as Prime Minister witnessed the most sustained and vigorous debate on the republican issue in post-Federation Australia. For just under four and a half years he dominated the debate, forcing the republic from the periphery of Labor's platform to the centre of government policy. Keating was responsible for making the republic a mainstream political issue, something it had never been beforehand. Without his commitment to the republic, expressed most succinctly in his speech to the federal parliament on 7 June 1995, the coalition parties would never have been forced into formulating an alternative policy—the constitutional convention. Keating's absence will place greater responsibility on pressure groups and individual citizens to sustain the momentum of the debate, as well as ushering in the decline of minimalism as the ascendant republican philosophy. In 1996 there are already signs that the debate is broadening. The parameters of the Howard convention are not confined to discussion relating to the head of state, but will include the gamut of proposals for constitutional reform. Influential lobby groups, such as the Constitutional Centenary Foundation, have called for the constitutional debate to be taken 'beyond the republic', while prominent republicans have demanded that the republic act as a 'trigger' for a more general dialogue on citizenship, the constitutional recognition of indigenous peoples, a bill of rights and the greater involvement of women.[5] With the departure of the Keating government the republican debate is likely to be more disparate and more disobedient. Controlled less by the political elite, it will also carry the attendant risk of fracturing, perhaps finding it difficult to attain the consensus and clarity of purpose which might have been possible under a leader insistent on confining the debate, such as Keating. In fact, given the longevity of the 'inevitable' republic, writing this epilogue may become a life-long occupation.

Yet in the broad historical sense the debate's importance is no longer contingent on the successful declaration of the republic on 1 January 2001. It is now a diverse and continuing national discussion on constitutional reform, citizenship and identity. In this light, it is useful to identify the relevance of Australia's republican history to the future direction of the debate.

Considering the important role played by Australian conservatives in demanding responsible government and the Federation of the Australian colonies, it is clear that latter-day conservatives have invested too much of their democratic heritage in the person of the British monarch, to the detriment of the contribution of their political antecedents. At the very least, this is how they have allowed themselves to be represented since the time of Menzies. Furthermore, the conservatives' most powerful argument in defence of the constitutional monarchy—that the monarch is above or 'beyond' politics—is one which panders to the populist disdain for the political, therefore implying that the system is at least morally 'broke' and in need of repair.[6]

In the nineteenth century, and even the first half of the twentieth century, allegiance to the British Crown made practical sense for Australian conservatives. Yet it would be unlikely that men of the calibre of Parkes and Deakin would agree that the British monarch should continue to act as Australia's head of state into the twenty-first century. Rather, they would see an Australian head of state as a natural evolutionary step for the Commonwealth—in keeping with the spirit of the Balfour Declaration of 1926, the Statute of Westminster of 1931 and the Australia Act of 1986.

In 1996 the more practical focus of a conservative defence of the

Australian Constitution does not lie in protecting the monarch but in ensuring that Australia's parliamentary traditions remain intact; in developing party positions on a wide range of constitutional reforms, especially on associated issues such as federalism and representative democracy. This would only be in keeping with their own 'republican' tradition—concentrating on the substance of the Constitution rather than the shadow of a name.

The Labor tradition of Australian republicanism is one which also has something to gain by reappraising its past. Since Federation in 1901, and particularly since the dismissal of the Whitlam government by Governor-General Sir John Kerr in 1975, the notion of a republic has been boxed into a nationalist corner. For reasons of perceived political expedience the republic and democracy have become mutually exclusive.

The first Labor visions of an Australian republic were not only attached to Australian identity but also to the ideals of social justice, one vote, one value, citizens' rights, and equal access to resources such as land and capital.

The original Labor vision may not have been inclusive but nor was it politically confined. In the 1990s both conservatives and Labor have focused the issue of an Australian republic through the filter of identity and heritage. As the centenary of Federation approaches, the greatest tension to be resolved in the republican debate will be between the desire to found the Australian republic on the basis of a shared identity and heritage, and the demand for a republic established on a shared and newly imagined democratic heritage. Perhaps the more substantial and potentially more invigorating republicanism is that which seeks to move the republican debate beyond the familiar framework of monarch or president to encompass the essence of 'respublica' and the commonwealth—government for the common good.

Notes

INTRODUCTION

1. McKenna, M., 'A history of the inevitable republic' in M. Stephenson and C. Turner (eds), *Australia—Republic or Monarchy*, pp. 50–71.
2. Ibid., pp. 64–7.
3. Burgmann, V., *'In Our Time': Socialism and the Rise of Labor 1885–1905*, pp. 137, 147–8, 163.
4. Turnbull, M., *The Reluctant Republic*, p. 255.
5. Gray, J., 'On liberty, liberalism and essential contestability', *British Journal of Political Science*, vol. 8, pt. 4, October 1978, pp. 385–402, at p. 392.
6. Appleby, J., 'Republicanism in old and new contexts', *William and Mary Quarterly*, vol. 43, January 1986, pp. 20–34, at p. 21.
7. Hamilton, A., Madison, J. and Jay, J. in Kramnick, I. (ed.), *The Federalist Papers*, Ringwood, Penguin, 1987, pp. 254–5.
8. Ibid., p. 41 (Introduction by I. Kramnick). Also Peterson, P., 'The meaning of republicanism in the Federalist', *Publius*, vol. 43, no. 2, Spring 1979, p. 44; Kerber, L. K., 'The republican ideology of the revolutionary generation', *AQ*, vol. 37, 1985, pp. 474–95, at p. 475; Shalhope, R. E., 'Toward a republican synthesis. The emergence of an understanding of republicanism in American historiography', *WMQ*, vol. 29, 1972, pp. 49–80, at p. 72. The same degree of uncertainty concerning the meaning of the republic existed in seventeenth-century England. See Robbins, C. (ed.), *Two English Republican Tracts*, p. 42; also Condren, C., *The Language of Politics in Seventeenth-Century England*, London, Macmillan, 1994, especially pp. 43–6, pp. 53–4 and p. 57.
9. *LS*, vol. 6, no. 2, Summer 1992, special issue on republicanism, pp. 21–43.
10. This contradiction is best explained in Galligan, B., *A Federal Republic*, pp. 12–37.
11. Winterton, G., 'Modern republicanism', pp. 24–6, and Evans, H., 'A note on the meaning of republic', pp. 21–3.
12. Appleby, J., p. 21.
13. 'Flicker'—see Ward, J. M., *Earl Grey and the Australian Colonies*, p. 146. The perception of republicanism as a minority movement can be evidenced by the scant attention given to republicanism in major histories such as Manning Clark's *History of Australia*, vols I–VI, and the *Oxford History of Australia*, vols I–V. For more specific evidence of republicanism as the work of a minority: Molony, J., *Penguin Bi-Centennial History of Australia*, Ringwood,

Viking, Penguin, 1987, pp. 171 and 175; Farrell, F., *Themes in Australian History*, NSW University Press, 1990, pp. 76–7; Clarke, F. G., *Australia. A Concise Political and Social History*, Melbourne, Oxford University Press, 1989, p. 114; Kingston, B., *Oxford History of Australia*, vol. III, pp. 104–5 and 198; Bell, R. in N. Meaney (ed.), *Under New Heavens: Cultural Transmission and the Making of Australia*, Heinemann, 1989, p. 331; Burgmann, V. and Lee, J., *Constructing a Culture. A People's History of Australia since 1788*, Ringwood, Penguin Books, 1988, pp. 262–3; Davison, G., McCarty, J. W. and McLeary, A. (eds), *Australians: 1888*, pp. 15 and 411; Jupp, J., *The Australian People*, p. 447; Birch, A. and Macmillan, D. S., *The Sydney Scene 1788–1960*, Melbourne University Press, 1962, p. 172. The most notable exceptions are McLachlan, N., *Waiting for the Revolution*, and Grassby, A., *The Australian Republic*.

14 Mansfield, B., 'The Background to Radical Republicanism in NSW in the 1880s'; McDonald, R. J., 'Republicanism in the Fifties'; Smith, S. M., 'Labor and the Monarchy' in G. Dutton (ed.), *Australia and the Monarchy*, pp. 152–70. Lawson, S., *The Archibald Paradox* is by far the best on the *Bulletin*'s republicanism. Since the contemporary republican debate began in 1991 there are signs that this narrow definition of republicanism is being challenged. See for example, Hudson, W. and Carter, D., *The Republicanism Debate*, especially pp. 7–8 and the chapter by Melleuish, G., 'Republicanism before nationalism'. Also see Atkinson, A., *The Muddle Headed Republic*, and Warden, J., 'The fettered republic: the Anglo–American Commonwealth and the traditions of Australian political thought'. Finally, see Hirst, J., *The Strange Birth of Colonial Democracy in NSW 1848–1884*.
15 Molony, J., *Penguin Bi-Centennial History of Australia*, p. 171.
16 McKenna, M., 'Tracking the republic', in D. Headon, et al., *Crown or Country*, pp. 5–7.
17 Ibid., pp. 25 and 27.
18 Fraser, A., *Spirit of the Laws: Republicanism and the Unfinished Project of Modernity*, pp. 79, 119–20 and 140.
19 Bell, R., in Meaney, N. (ed.), *Under New Heavens*, p. 331.
20 Lang, J. D., in Gilchrist, A. (ed.), *John Dunmore Lang. Chiefly Autobiographical: 1799–1878*, vol. II, p. 471; also *LE*, 3 February 1853.
21 Sheps, A., 'The American Revolution and the transformation of English republicanism', pp. 3–28, at pp. 18–19, and Springborg, P., 'An historical note on republicanism', in Hudson, W. and Carter, D. (eds), *The Republicanism Debate*, p. 204.
22 Belchem, J., 'Republicanism, popular constitutionalism and the radical reform platform in early nineteenth-century England', pp. 1–32, p. 6.
23 Ibid., p. 10.
24 Preece, A. A., in M. A. Stephenson and C. Turner (eds), *Australia: Republic or Monarchy*, pp. 135–6.
25 Pocock, J. G. A., *The Machiavellian Moment: Florentine Republican Thought and the Atlantic Republican Tradition*, pp. 361–5. Plato's *Republic* was not the origin of republicanism. The *Republic* was essentially a guide to the selection and education of the philosopher rulers of an ideal Greek city state.

26 Ibid. Also Warden, J., 'The Fettered Republic', pp. 84–5. It is important to remember, as Graham Maddox has observed, that the notion of a republic as a balance between monarchy, aristocracy and democracy was due, in large part, to the Greek historian, Polybius, who ascribed this quasi-Aristotelian taxonomy to Ancient Rome. The interpretation of Polybius influenced such writers as Machiavelli and Harrington. See Maddox, 'Republic for democracy', *AJPS*, vol. 28, 1993, p. 21.
27 Bagehot, W., *The English Constitution*, p. xviii.
28 Quoted in Winterton, G., 'Modern Republicanism', p. 24.
29 One exception is Keneally, T., *Our Republic*; see also Hirst, J., *A Republican Manifesto*, p. 106. Hirst denies that contemporary republicans have anything in common with republicans of the past.

1 THE PIRATICAL REPUBLIC 1788–1833

1 Tench, W., *Sydney's First Four Years*, Fitzhardinge, L. F. (ed.), Library of Australian History, Sydney, 1979, p. 273.
2 Parsons, T. G., 'Was John Boston's pig a political martyr?', pp. 165–6.
3 Eddy, J. J., *Britain and the Australian Colonies: 1818–1831*, p. 53. Also N. McLachlan, 'The future America', p. 368.
4 Merivale, H., *Lectures on Colonisation and Colonies*, p. 107. Neal, D., *The Rule of Law in a Penal Colony*, p. 22; also *SG*, 2 February 1833. Clark, C. M. H., *A History of Australia*, vol. I, p. 156.
5 On the martyrs, see Parsons, p. 165; (McLachlan, N., *Waiting for the Revolution*, pp. 38–45; and Rudé, George, *Protest and Punishment*, pp. 182–3). On Palmer's pamphlet, see Clark, vol. I, p. 100, also Rudé, p. 182. On Margarot, see McLachlan, pp. 40–1 and Clark, vol. I, p. 101.
6 Governor King to Under Secretary King, 14 August 1804, *HRNSW*, vol. 5, King 1803–1805, Bladen, F. M. (ed.), Government Printer, Sydney, 1897, pp. 446–7.
7 Margarot quote in McLachlan, p. 38. On the rebellion, see McQueen, H., 'Convicts and Rebels', pp. 3–30; Connell, R., 'The Convict Rebellion of 1804', pp. 27–37.
8 On the Irish convicts, see Clark, vol. I, p. 102 and Rudé, pp. 72–3. King to Earl Camden, 30 April 1805, *HRNSW*, vol. 5, King 1803–1805, Bladen, F. M. (ed.), Government Printer, Sydney, 1897, p. 598. Clark, vol. I, p. 155, notes Hunter's fears of the Irish. See also Hughes, R., *The Fatal Shore*, p. 190.
9 Smallsalts reported in *SG*, 30 March 1806; see also Clark, vol. I, p. 207. McKellar quoted in Parsons, p. 166.
10 For 'leveller', see Robbins, C. (ed.), *Two English Republican Tracts*, p. 42. For Boston's pig, see Parsons, p. 171.
11 On the Corps' legitimising attempts, see Neal, p. 193. Johnston quoted in Clark, vol. I, p. 223.
12 On Sydney's rejoicings, see McLachlan, p. 37. Johnston quoted in Clark, vol. I, p. 223.
13 For CO quote, see Eddy, p. 40. Ward, R., *The Australian Legend*, p. 15.
14 Darling to Hay, 20 April 1827, CO 323/149 (leaf 271).
15 Wentworth, W., *A Statistical, Historical, and Political Description of the Colony of NSW . . .*, p. 242.

16 Ibid., pp. 242–4.
17 Wentworth, p. 244. See also Clark, vol. II, pp. 44–5; McLachlan, p. 58 and Inglis, K., *The Australian Colonists*, p. 185.
18 Wentworth, p. 248.
19 Ibid., p. 246.
20 Ibid., pp. 247–8.
21 Ward, J. M., *James Macarthur—Colonial Conservative 1798–1867*, p. 16.
22 On John Macarthur's calls, see Eddy, p. 96. On Edward Macarthur, see Ward, *James Macarthur*, p. 35; also Inglis, pp. 185–6, McLachlan, p. 64, and Eddy, pp. 87, 94. On Wentworth, see *SG*, 23 January 1826.
23 Ibid.
24 The NSW Legislative Council first sat in 1824, in Tasmania the Legislative Council first sat in 1825. On *Australian*, see *ADB*, 1788–1850, vol. II, p. 585; also *Australian*, 14 October 1824.
25 *Australian*, 14 October 1824.
26 Wentworth to Murray enclosed in Darling to Murray, 28 May 1829, *HRA*, series I, vol. 14, Watson, F. (ed.), Library Committee of Australian Commonwealth, 1922, p. 835. Also *Monitor*, 8 December 1826. On Darling's bills, see Clark, vol. II, p. 75.
27 *Australian*, 27 January 1827.
28 Darling to Hay, 6 February 1827, *HRA*, January 1827 to February 1828, series I, vol. 13, Watson, F. (ed.), Library Committee of Australian Commonwealth, 1920, p. 82.
29 *SG*, 20 March 1827.
30 Darling to Hay, 20 April 1827, CO 323/149 (leaf number 260–280), Mitchell Library.
31 *Australian*, 25 May 1827 and Clark, vol. II, p. 79.
32 On Darling and the Stamp Act, see *SG*, 1 June 1827; *Australian*, 1 June 1827. Darling's comment in Darling to Murray, 8 November 1828, *HRA*, March 1828 to May 1829, series I, vol. 13, Watson, F. (ed.), Library Committee of Australian Commonwealth, 1922, p. 445.
33 Clark, vol. II, p. 108.
34 On vilification of Darling, see *SG*, 19 September 1827 (quoting *Monitor*). Americans comment in Darling to Murray, 8 November 1828, *HRA*, January 1827 to February 1828, series I, vol. 14, Watson, F. (ed.), Library Committee of Australian Commonwealth, 1922, p. 445.
35 *Monitor*, 25 February 1828 and 21 June 1827.
36 On republic as a second-class option, see Thompson, E., 'English institutions transplanted' in Jupp, J. (ed.), *The Australian People*, p. 442. On redress of grievances, see *Australian*, 1 June 1827 and *Monitor*, 21 June 1827.
37 On monarchy and early colony, see Atkinson, A., *The Muddle Headed Republic*, pp. 34–5 and 54–5. Eddy, p. 95.
38 Ferguson, J. A., 'E. S. Hall and the *Monitor*', p. 193.
39 Harpur quote from Ackland, M. (ed.), *Charles Harpur—Selected Poetry and Prose*, p. 69.
40 Compare Hall's editorial (Ferguson p. 186) to Wills' in *CL*, 24 November 1832.

41 On Wills' youth, see *ADB*, 1788–1850, vol. II, p. 605. Clark, vol. I, p. 329, vol. II, pp. 153, 155, 158.
42 See Inglis, p. 43 on *Currency Lad*. Wills quoted in *CL*, 25 August 1832.
43 *CL*, 8 September 1832.
44 On Wills' optimism, see *CL*, 13 October 1832. For Wills on future destiny, see *CL*, 20 October 1832. For Wills on reformers, see ibid.
45 *CL*, 24 November 1832.
46 On the numbers of native-born, see ibid. *SG*, 27 November 1832.
47 On meeting, see *SH*, 31 January 1833; McLachlan, p. 67. For report on Paine, see *SH*, 6 September 1832.
48 *SH*, 31 March 1833 and *SG*, 19 February 1833. On calibre of leadership, see McLachlan, p. 67.
49 Clark, vol. II, p. 158.
50 *CL*, 26 January 1833.
51 *SH*, 31 January 1833.
52 *Australian*, 1 February 1833.
53 *SG*, 19 February 1833 and *CL*, 2 February 1833.
54 *CL*, 26 January 1833.
55 Wills placed the circulation of *CL* at 525 per week, with subscribers on the increase (*Australian*, 31 May 1833).
56 *Australian*, 31 May 1833.
57 *CL*, 24 November 1832 for Wills' talk of cheap and democratic government. See *CL*, 20 October 1832 for his comments on monarchy.
58 *CL*, 5 January 1833.
59 *CL*, 23 February 1833. Also 2 February 1833.
60 McLachlan, pp. 68–9.

2 THE STOCKMEN'S REPUBLIC 1833–1848

1 Rudé G., *Protest and Punishment*, pp. 42–51, 96 and Ward, J., *James Macarthur . . .*, pp. 284–312. On Act of Union, see Melbourne, A. C. V. in Scott, E. (ed.), *Cambridge History of the British Empire*, vol. VII, Part 1, p. 272.
2 Davidson, A., *The Invisible State*, p. 164.
3 Tenniswood, W. Y., 'The policy of Great Britain regarding Australia: 1850–1900', p. 149.
4 Australian Patriotic Association, in Alomes, S. and Jones, C. (eds), *Australian Nationalism—A Documentary History*, p. 28.
5 *Atlas*, 28 December 1844, p. 49.
6 Clark, vol. III, p. 335.
7 Serle, G., *The Golden Age*, p. 195.
8 *SMH*, 2 May 1844.
9 Parkes quoted in Hirst, J., *The Strange Birth of Colonial Democracy in NSW 1848–1884*, p. 13. On the consent of people to laws, see Davidson, A., pp. 165 and 187. See also Charles Campbell speaking at a meeting in 1842 in Sydney to demand responsible government: *SH*, 17 February 1842 and Francis, M. F., *Governors and Settlers—Images of Authority in the British Colonies 1820–1860*, pp. 14–15.

10 *SMH*, 16 December 1843.
11 *Atlas*, 10 May 1845, p. 278. *Atlas*, 25 January 1845 and 8 February 1845.
12 On republican language, see *Atlas*, 4 January 1845, p. 62 and 18 January 1845, p. 88. On MacDermott, see *Australian*, 22 February 1842.
13 *SH*, 17 February 1842. *Australian*, 22 February 1842.
14 Gollan, R., 'Nationalism and politics before 1855', p. 42.
15 *SH*, 28 February 1842, has details of the second meeting.
16 On the new Constitution, see Ward, *James Macarthur*, p. 118; Clark, *A History of Australia*, vol. III, p. 195. For right to disallow, see Ward, *James Macarthur*, p. 119.
17 *Atlas*, 28 December 1844, p. 49.
18 *SMH*, 16 December 1843 and 22 December 1843.
19 Blair, D., 'John Dunmore Lang. A recollection', p. 489 and Baker, D. W., *Days of Wrath*, pp. 160–6. For revolutionary language, see *Atlas*, 19 July 1845, pp. 397–8.
20 *SH*, 30 January 1839.
21 Baker, p. 214.
22 Ward, *James Macarthur*, p. 145.
23 *SMH*, 10 April 1844, Burroughs, P., *Britain and Australia: 1831–1855*, p. 305. Also Clark, vol. III, p. 176.
24 *Morning Chronicle* quotes in Roberts, S. H., *The Squatting Age of Australia 1835–1847*, p. 247 and Burroughs, p. 305.
25 Roberts, *The Squatting Age*, p. 247. Also Roe, M., *The Quest for Authority in Eastern Australia: 1835–1851*, p. 64.
26 Wentworth's direction reported in *SMH*, 10 April 1844. On language of colonial press, see Roberts, *The Squatting Age*, p. 247; and Roe, p. 64. On Lowe's language, see *Atlas*, 26 July 1845, p. 411.
27 *Atlas*, 23 August 1845. *Atlas*, 25 January 1845, p. 97. *Atlas*, 8 February 1845, p. 121. Lowe's speech on British connection, *SMH*, 27 January 1846. Also Martin, A. W., *Henry Parkes*, p. 43.
28 *Atlas*, 19 July 1845, p. 398.
29 Ibid.
30 Ibid.
31 Baker, p. 217.
32 *Australian*, 29 July 1845. Curr's letter in *Australian*, 9 August 1845.
33 Hodgson, C. P., *Reminiscences of Australia, With Hints on the Squatter's Life*, pp. 91–2 and Ward, *James Macarthur*, p. 147.
34 Baker, p. 218.
35 Davidson, p. 165. Also Atkinson, A., *The Muddle Headed Republic*, pp. 37–8.
36 Gipps to Stanley, 29 April 1846, *HRA*, series I, vol. 25, April 1846–September 1847, Watson, F. (ed.), Library Committee of Commonwealth Parliament, 1925, p. 31.

3 THE LAST RESORT 1848–1856

1 Ackland, M. (ed.), *Charles Harpur—Selected Poetry and Prose*, p. 22.
2 Knight, R., *Illiberal Liberal: Robert Lowe in NSW 1842–1850*, p. 188.

3 Martin, A. W., *Henry Parkes*, p. 50.
4 On transportees and republican principles, see Rudé, G., *Protest and Punishment*, pp. 39, 99–100, 143–4. On German immigrants, see Sherington, G., *Australia's Immigrants—1788–1978*, p. 44; Clark, C. M. H., *A History of Australia*, vol. IV, p. 62 and McLachlan, N., *Waiting for the Revolution*, p. 80. Also Harmstorf, I. and Cigler, M., *The Germans in Australia*, Australasian Educational Press, 1985, p. 101; and Walker, R. B., 'German-language press and people in South Australia, 1848–1900', *RAHSJ*, vol. 58, pt 2, June 1972, pp. 121–40, at p. 122. Democratic and republican principles were espoused by two '1848-ers'—Otto Schomburgk and Carl Mücke, editors of the Adelaide-based *Süd-Australischer Zeitung* in the early 1850s.
5 *Atlas*, 30 September 1848, p. 473.
6 Blair, D., 'Henry Parkes in 1850', p. 617.
7 Martin, pp. 36–40.
8 Clark, *A History of Australia*, vol. III, pp. 396–8.
9 *PA*, 27 January 1849. Hirst, J., *The Strange Birth of Colonial Democracy in NSW 1848–1884*, p. 20.
10 *PA*, 2 December 1848, p. 1.
11 Hirst, *The Strange Birth* . . . , p. 4.
12 *PA*, 14 July 1849.
13 *Citizen*, 6 February 1847, pp. 185–6.
14 Harpur in Ackland (ed.), p. 25.
15 Hughes, R., *The Fatal Shore*, pp. 493, 497. On suspension of transportation, see ibid., p. 533.
16 Ibid., pp. 552–4.
17 Ibid.
18 Clark, vol. III, p. 416.
19 *PA*, 23 June 1849, p. 1 and *PA*, 14 April 1849.
20 Clark, vol. III, p. 418, also Hughes, p. 555 and Knight, pp. 218–22.
21 *PA*, 16 June 1849, p. 1, also Clark, vol. III, p. 418.
22 McLachlan, p. 74. Knight, p. 186 and Hughes, p. 556.
23 *PA*, 16 June 1849, p. 6.
24 Clark, vol. III, p. 419.
25 Parkes, H., *Speeches on Various Occasions Connected with the Public Affairs of NSW 1848–1874*, p. 7.
26 On Parkes' rejection of separation, see Martin, p. 31. For view of Australian character, see Parkes, p. 7.
27 *Argus*, 22 August 1849.
28 *Geelong Advertiser* on John Dunmore Lang's republicanism, 1850, quoted in Gilchrist, A. (ed.), *John Dunmore Lang. Chiefly Autobiographical: 1799–1878*, vol. II, p. 473.
29 Deniehy to Lang, 6 June 1854, Lang Papers, vol. VII, pp. 61–2.
30 *SMH*, 15 August 1850, letter from Terence Murray.
31 Baker, D. W., *Days of Wrath*, pp. 257–8.
32 *HTC*, 17 February 1853.
33 *SMH*, 17 April 1850.

34 For 'communities' quote, see Lang, J. D., *The Coming Event*, p. 5. For 'traditions' quote, see Baker, pp. 290–2.
35 Lang, p. 28. On Queen Victoria, see Lang, pp. 30–1.
36 Ibid., p. 4.
37 Ibid., p. 30.
38 Ibid., p. 31.
39 Parkes to Lang, 17 April 1850, Lang Papers, vol. XXII. Also quoted in Martin, p. 62.
40 *PA*, 20 April 1850, p. 8 and 11 May 1850, p. 8.
41 *SMH*, 30 April 1850; Martin, p. 62. For details on Blair, see *ADB*, vol. 3, 1851–1890, pp. 179–80, also *SMH*, 30 April 1850, p. 1.
42 *Argus*, 10 May 1850.
43 *PA*, 4 May 1850, p. 8.
44 On Lang and immigrants' grants, see Baker, chapter 14. On Lang as a candidate, see ibid., p. 299.
45 David Blair, 'John Dunmore Lang. A recollection', p. 489. *MH*, 8 June 1850 quoted in McDonald, R. J., 'Republicanism in the Fifties', p. 269, also Baker, p. 303. *SMH*, 30 April 1850, p. 1.
46 *Geelong Advertiser* quote in Gilchrist, vol. II, p. 473. Denison quote in ibid., p. 474.
47 Blair, 'John Dunmore Lang', p. 490.
48 *PA*, 27 July 1850.
49 Baker, pp. 306–8.
50 *Representative*, Saturday 20 July 1850, p. 1.
51 Blair, 'Henry Parkes', p. 619.
52 *SMH*, 15 August 1850.
53 *SMH*, 22 August 1850.
54 *SMH*, 15 August 1850. *PA*, 7 September 1850. Lang's lecture in *PA* of 31 August 1850 and Blair's lecture, *PA*, 7 September 1850.
55 Blair, D., 'Sydney in 1850. Morals and manners', pp. 686–7. Fitzroy's fears, for example, in a despatch to Grey: Fitzroy to Grey, 16 October 1851, Fitzroy quotes from one of his earlier despatches on 8 October 1850, CO, Piece 443, leaf no. 176.
56 Harpur, Charles, 'Lays for the Anti-Convict Association', September 1850, quoted in Evans, L. and Nicholls, P. (eds), *Convicts and Colonial Society 1788–1868*, p. 125.
57 Fitzroy on demonstrators, see Martin, p. 58. Protest meeting report in *PA*, 17 August 1850. Parkes' speech in ibid.
58 Ibid.
59 Ibid.
60 Wentworth on Canadian Constitution in Ward, J. M., *Colonial Self-Government and the British Experience 1759–1856*, p. 305.
61 *SMH*, 13 September 1850.
62 *SMH*, 18 September 1850 and 1 October 1850.
63 *PA*, 5 October 1850.
64 Clark, vol. III, p. 445. Martin, p. 66.

65 On Council and electoral boundaries, see Melbourne, A. C. V., in Scott, E. (ed.), *Cambridge History of the British Empire*, vol. VII, p. 278; Clark, vol. III, p. 447. Morrell, W. P., *British Colonial Policy in the Age of Peel and Russell*, p. 490.
66 Clarke, F. G., *The Land of Contrarities: British Attitudes to the Australian Colonies 1828–1855*, p. 64.
67 Martin, p. 70. The *Press* is held in the National Library, Canberra.
68 *Press*, 1 January 1851.
69 Martin, p. 101, also Parkes' speech in *PA*, 31 August 1850.
70 *PA*, 7 September 1850, p. 5.
71 *Press*, 12 February 1851. Also see *Empire*, 4 January 1851, and *SMH*, 18 January 1851 for *Morning Chronicle*. Also *Press*, 22 January 1851.
72 *SMH*, 18 January 1851.
73 *Empire*, 4 January 1851.
74 *Empire*, 13 February 1851, p. 20.
75 *Empire*, 11 April 1851.
76 The Australasian League did not include Western Australia and should not be confused with the Australian League.
77 *Press*, 6 August 1851, p. 367.
78 Parkes, H., *Fifty Years of Australian History*, vol. I, pp. 12, 17 and 18.
79 *Press*, 19 March 1851, p. 126.
80 *Empire*, 8 April 1851, p. 291.
81 Ibid.
82 Lang on *SMH* in *Press*, 16 April 1851, p. 1. *SMH* and League in Ward, *Earl Grey and the Australian Colonies*, p. 222.
83 'Tiberius Gracchus', *Empire*, 11 April 1851.
84 *Empire*, 31 March 1851, p. 259.Corbyn revealed his identity in *Empire*, 27 May 1851. *Empire*, 30 April 1851, p. 30, also 21 April 1851 ('Publicola'), 15 April 1851 ('Tiberius Gracchus'), 2 May 1851 ('Alonzo'), 7 May 1851 ('Alonzo'), 9 May 1851 ('Alonzo'), 18 May 1851 ('Tiberius Gracchus'), 5 May 1851 ('Alonzo').
85 On electoral boundaries, see Baker, p. 325. On public dissatisfaction, see Burroughs, P., *Britain and Australia: 1831–1855*, p. 377; Melbourne in Scott (ed.), *Cambridge History*, p. 279.
86 Clark, vol. IV, p. 5 (*SMH*, 1 May 1851). On Lang, see Clark, vol. IV, p. 8.
87 *Press*, 18 June 1851, also 11 June 1851.
88 *Press*, 2 July 1851, p. 309.
89 *Press*, 30 April 1851.
90 Evans, L. and Nicholls, P. (eds), *Convicts and Colonial Society 1788–1868*, p. 129.
91 Fitzroy to Grey, 31 July 1851, CO 201, Piece 441, leaf nos 458–462.
92 On the meeting, see *Press*, 9 July 1851, p. 319. Poem in *Press*, 30 July 1851, p. 357.
93 *LE*, 21 June 1851.
94 *PA*, 23 August 1851.
95 Weekes quote in *SMH*, 16 September 1851. Wentworth in ibid., and *Empire*, 16 September 1851.
96 *SMH*, 17 September 1851.
97 *SMH*, 18 September 1851.

98 Martin, p. 106.
99 Morrell, p. 380.
100 Ward, J. M., *James Macarthur—Colonial Conservative 1798–1867*, p. 184. On public meetings, see *SMH*, 29 December 1851.
101 *Press*, 6 August 1851.
102 Baker, pp. 342–4.
103 *SMH*, 8 April 1852.
104 Ibid. *SMH*, 13 April 1852. McEnroe quote in *SMH*, 8 April 1852.
105 Parkes, *Speeches on Various Occasions . . .*, pp. 14–15.
106 Lamb's plea in his speech; *SMH*, 8 April 1852.
107 Wright's speech, *SMH*, 1 July 1852. Supplement, p. 2. Deniehy's speech in ibid. and *SMH*, 1 July 1852 and Martin, pp. 107–8. Deniehy's visit to Ireland in Headon, D., 'God's aristocracy, Daniel Henry Deniehy's vision of a great Australian republic', pp. 137–8.
108 For details of Deniehy's library, see Blair, D., 'Daniel Deniehy. A recollection', p. 385.
109 *SMH*, 1 July 1852.
110 *HTC*, 4 September 1852 and 12 May 1852.
111 *SMH*, 17 April 1852. For details on Tasmanian petitions see Blackton, C. S., 'The Australasian League 1851–1854', p. 397, also Hughes, p. 569.
112 *SMH*, 20 April 1852.

4 A BUNYIP ARISTOCRACY

1 Also *Hobart Town Courier*, 31 January 1853.
2 House of Commons Debates in *Argus*, 31 January 1853.
3 On Lowe, see Clarke, F. G., *The Land of Contrarities: British Attitudes to the Australian Colonies 1828–1855*, pp. 68–71. Cobden's 1849 speech at Bradford, Morrell, W. P., *British Colonial Policy in the Age of Peel and Russell*, p. 488. Lord Stanley succeeded to the earldom (becoming the Earl of Derby) after his father's death on 21 February 1852.
4 Evans, L. and Nicholls P. (eds), *Convicts and Colonial Society 1788–1868*, p. 135.
5 Fitzroy to Pakington, 28 February 1853, CO 201/464, leaf no. 176. Also Ward, J. M., *Earl Grey and the Australian Colonies*, p. 223
6 *SMH*, 24 December 1853, p. 6. For further acknowledgment of the growing spirit of disloyalty, see *SMH*, 28 August 1852 and Blair, D., 'Henry Parkes in 1850', p. 620.
7 Clark, C. M. H., *A History of Australia*, vol. IV, p. 32.
8 Montefiore, J. L. and Piddington, W. R., secretary and treasurer of the NSW Constitution Committee, quoted in *SMH*, 23 August 1853.
9 Morrell, p. 383. Clarke, p. 71 and Loveday, P., 'Democracy in NSW. The Constitution Committee of 1853', p. 187.
10 Hirst, J., *The Strange Birth of Colonial Democracy in NSW 1848–1884*, pp. 38–9.
11 *PA*, 3 December 1853.
12 Fry, E. (ed.), *Rebels and Radicals*, pp. 60–1.
13 Martin, A. W., *Henry Parkes*, p. 112.

14 Parkes, H., *Speeches on Various Occasions Connected with the Public Affairs of NSW 1848–1874*, p. 35.
15 Parkes, *Speeches on Various Occasions . . .* , p. 35.
16 Silvester, E. K. (ed.), *NSW Constitution Bill—the Speeches of the Legislative Council of NSW*, p. 55.
17 Ibid., p. 71. Also pp. 55 and 82.
18 Ibid., pp. 145–6.
19 On Darvall's loyalty, see ibid., p. 105. Wentworth on Lang, see ibid., p. 106.
20 *SMH*, 5 September 1853.
21 *Empire*, 20 December 1853.
22 *PA*, 19 November 1853, p. 2.
23 Paine had also used the words 'Freedom and Independence' when writing *Common Sense*. (T. Paine, *Common Sense*, p. 122.)
24 Lang, J. D., *Freedom and Independence for the Golden Lands of Australia*, p. 120.
25 Ibid., pp. 52, 126 and 320–1. Lang stated in a letter to the *PA*, 19 November 1853 that he intended to publish a book called *The Future Australian Republic*—'A Socratic dialogue between an English gentleman and a colonist of 30 years standing'. Unfortunately no trace of this book, even in draft form, has been found.
26 Ibid., p. 93.
27 For Lang's admission of the colonists' apathy, see *Freedom and Independence*, p. 397.
28 *SMH* poem in Baker, D. W., *Days of Wrath*, pp. 356–7. *ISN*, 4 February 1854, pp. 137–8.
29 *Empire*, 5 December 1853, 12 December 1853 and 1 February 1854.
30 *Empire*, 19 November 1853.
31 *SMH*, 5 September 1853. Also 16 December 1853.
32 *Empire*, 19 November 1853.
33 *Empire*, 5 December 1853 and *Empire*, 12 December 1853.
34 *Empire*, 12 December 1853.
35 Ibid.
36 Robertson's criticism in Martin, p. 118. Lang's views in ibid., also *Empire*, 20 December 1853.
37 *Empire*, 12 December 1853.
38 *Empire*, 20 December 1853.
39 Ibid.
40 *PA*, 24 December 1853.
41 Lang, J.D., *Anatomical Lecture on the New Constitution*, p. 17.
42 *PA*, 27 January 1854.
43 Driver quote in *Empire*, 27 January 1854. Report of the meeting was carried in *Empire*, 27 January 1854. It contains the platform of the League which is also in the *PA*, 28 January 1854.
44 Lang 'citizenry' quote in *PA*, 28 January 1854. Lang and civic humanism in Hume, L. J., 'Foundations of populism and pluralism, Australian writings on politics to 1860', in Stokes, G. (ed.), *Australian Political Ideas*, UNSW Press, 1994, p. 61.

45 *PA*, 3 December 1853. Hawksely in *PA*, 13 February 1854, also 10 June 1854.
46 *PA*, 18 March 1854.
47 *Empire*, 1 February 1854.
48 Ibid.
49 *SMH*, 9 March 1854. *PA*, replied 11 March 1854.
50 *SMH*, 23 May 1854.
51 Ibid.
52 Ibid.
53 *SMH*, 23 May 1854.
54 Ibid.
55 Hirst, *The Strange Birth* . . . , pp. 62–4.
56 Baker, p. 373.
57 Lang Papers, A2242, vol. 7, pp. 61–2, Mitchell Library. Deniehy to Lang, 6 June 1854.
58 Hirst, *The Strange Birth* . . . , p. 66.
59 Wentworth's bill was passed minus the provisions for an hereditary upper house. Russell wisely left the way open for the first parliament to revise the amendment clause and it duly did so. Hirst, *The Strange Birth* . . . , pp. 40–5.
60 Clark, vol. IV, pp. 103 and 106.
61 *PA*, 17 June 1854.
62 *PA*, 6 October 1855, p. 8.
63 For Adelaide Ironside's 'Ode to Lang' see Poulton, J., *Adelaide Ironside—Pilgrim of Art*, pp. 22, 25, 33–4. In November 1860 she wrote to Lang from Rome 'Viva Garibaldi—I am with the republicans' (Poulton, p. 44). An interesting aspect about Lang's relationship with Ironside is that Lang was responsible for persuading the New South Wales government to award her a government stipend to enable her to further her studies in Rome. This was probably the first grant to an artist from an Australian government.
64 Deniehy to Ironside, 25 May 1854. Also *GH*, 20 October 1855 and 2 September 1855. My thanks to David Headon for these references.
65 Baker, chapter 25.
66 Tasmanian Governor Denison's letter of 1856 to Henry Du Pre Labouchere (the new Secretary of State for the colonies) in Gunn, J., *Along Parallel Lines. A History of the Railways of NSW*, Melbourne University Press, 1989, chapter 1, footnote 15.
67 *Empire*, 1 February 1854.

5 A VICTORIAN REPUBLIC

1 On Victoria's social change, see Serle, G., *The Golden Age*, pp. 10–11. On immigrants and possible dissent, see Bate, W., *Victorian Gold Rushes*, pp. 5 and 27–30, Serle, *The Golden Age*, p. 47.
2 *Argus*, 6 October 1852.
3 Blair, D., 'Sydney in 1850. Morals and Manners', pp. 688 and 491.
4 Ebbels, R. N. (ed.), *The Australian Labor Movement—A Documentary History*, p. 49.
5 On multicultural immigrants, see Serle, *The Golden Age*, p. 75. On population increase, see Bate, p. 8.

6 The phrase 'diggings community' belongs to Bate, p. 42. For the political loyalties of British immigrants, see Serle, *The Golden Age*, pp. 61 and 75. La Trobe to Newcastle, CO, 309, vol. 16, no. 2, 1 June 1853, Mitchell Library.
7 Webb, G. L. F., *The New Constitution Bill Debate in the Legislative Council of the Colony of Victoria*, p. 33.
8 Ibid, p. 130. The Constitution was considered so democratic by Governor Hotham that he referred to it as a 'design for a republic' (Blackton, C. S., 'The dawn of Australian national feeling 1850–1856', p. 129).
9 On Council's support see Gollan, R., *Radical and Working Class Politics. A Study of Eastern Australia 1850–1910*, p. 20. The 'pastoral wealth' quote from Macintyre, S., *A Colonial Liberalism*, p. 28.
10 McLachlan, N., *Waiting for the Revolution*, p. 86.
11 *Argus*, 24 October 1854, where these terms are employed by many speakers at the protest meeting. Crowd estimates in ibid.
12 McLachlan, p. 83.
13 *Argus*, 20 October 1852, also 4 October 1852. Also Macintyre, *A Colonial Liberalism*, p. 77.
14 La Trobe remarks on the popularity of the *Argus* (see note 6). Also Serle, *The Golden Age*, p. 143. Examples of the *Argus* editorials: 19 February 1852, 17 July 1852, 25 September 1852, 6 November 1852 and 31 March 1853. La Trobe (see note 6 La Trobe to Newcastle); and *Argus*, 17 July 1852.
15 *Argus*, 24 October 1854.
16 *Argus*, 17 July 1852. *LE* in *Argus*, 6 October 1852.
17 *Argus*, 24 October 1852.
18 *Argus*, 12 October 1854.
19 *Argus*, 24 October 1854.
20 Ibid. Also 23 October 1854.
21 Thomas McCombie held similar fears, see McLachlan, p. 87.
22 *Age*, 15 November 1854. Also 24 October 1854 and 1 November 1854.
23 *Age*, 7 December 1854.
24 Letter from 'An Australian', *Age*, 5 February 1855.
25 The phrase 'digger democracy' in Clark, C. M. H. (*A History of Australia*, vol. IV, p. 7). *Argus* quote in Blackton, 'Dawn of Australian National Feeling', p. 134. *Ballarat Times* quote in Daniel, E. and Potts, A., 'Republicanism and the disturbances on the Victorian goldfields', *HS*, vol. 13, no. 50, April 1968, p. 154.
26 Daniel and Potts, pp. 146 and 149. Also McKinlay, B. (ed.), *Australian Labor History In Documents*, vol. II, p. 7.
27 Quoted in Fitzroy to Pakington, 28 February 1853, CO 201/464, leaf no. 176, Mitchell Library.
28 La Trobe to Newcastle, CO 309, 1 June 1853, vol. 16, no. 2, Mitchell Library. Also Molony, J., *Eureka*, pp. 32–3.
29 Serle, *The Golden Age*, pp. 45–6.
30 *Argus* advertisement in Carboni, R., *The Eureka Stockade*, p. 3. *Age*, 17 October 1854; see also 23 October 1854.
31 *Age*, 15 November 1854.
32 Clark, vol. IV, p. 64.

33 Black quote in Daniel and Potts, p. 152. Carboni quote in Lynch, J., *The Story of the Eureka Stockade*, p. 13. McLachlan, p. 96.
34 Serle, *The Golden Age*, pp. 166–9.
35 Roberts, S., *Charles Hotham. A Biography*, pp. 122–3. Serle, *The Golden Age*, pp. 180–3. Bate, pp. 41–6.
36 Serle, *The Golden Age*, p. 181. Molony, J., *The Penguin Bi-Centennial History of Australia*, Viking, Penguin, 1987, p. 108. Molony, J., *Eureka*, pp. 154 and 202.
37 Serle, *The Golden Age*, p. 180.
38 Seekamp quote in McLachlan, p. 97 and *Age*, 23 November 1854. Platform from McKinlay (ed.), vol. 3, p. 6.
39 Gollan, p. 28.
40 For Chartist influence on diggers and their respect for British institutions see Serle, *The Golden Age*, pp. 61–2, 107, 109, 113, 164 and 380.
41 Black's 'declaration of independence' in Nicholls, H. R., 'Reminiscences of the Eureka Stockade', *CM*, November 1890, pp. 746–50, at p. 746. McLachlan, p. 92. Also see letter from digger in *Age*, 21 March 1855 which seems to confirm the existence of the declaration. Carboni, p. 88.
42 On Lalor and Irish diggers, see McLachlan, pp. 93–6. Nicholls, p. 746.
43 *Argus*, 10 April 1855.
44 Serle, *The Golden Age*, p. 182.
45 Lynch, p. 37. Nicholls, p. 746.
46 Carboni, p. 37. American digger's quote in Daniel and Potts, p. 152.
47 Serle, *The Golden Age*, pp. 43 and 180–1.
48 Daniel and Potts, p. 152 and Molony, *Eureka*, p. 154.
49 Carboni, p. 130.
50 Lynch, p. 26.
51 Clark, vol. IV, pp. 80–2.
52 *Age*, 10 January 1855, letter signed 'An Australian', from Bendigo. Also see letters also signed 'An Australian' in *Age*, 2 February and 5 February 1855.
53 *Age*, 10 January 1855. *Argus*, 5 January 1855.
54 *FJ*, 23 December 1854.
55 See the reproduction of the 'Wanted Sign' in Alomes, S. and Jones, C. (eds), *Australian Nationalism—A Documentary History*, p. 45 also Turner, H. G., *Our Own Little Rebellion*, p. 104.
56 *Age*, 7 December 1854.
57 *Age*, 5 December 1854. Turner, pp. 90 and 92.
58 Turner, p. 97.
59 *Age*, 7 December 1854. Serle, *The Golden Age*, pp. 169–71.
60 On speakers, see Turner, p. 100. Blackton, 'The dawn of Australian national feeling', p. 133.
61 *Age*, 23 January 1855.
62 Ibid.
63 *Age*, 19 March 1855.
64 McLachlan, p. 339 (footnotes), and Serle, *The Golden Age*, pp. 178–9.
65 *Age*, 17 May 1855. Editorial examples in ibid., also 16 May 1855.

66 *Age*, 21 March 1855.
67 *Age*, 15 May 1855, p. 4.
68 *Age*, 24 May 1855.
69 Lang's 'Declaration of Independence for Victoria' in Serle, *The Golden Age*, pp. 179 and 392–3.
70 *Age*, 13 August 1855. Also see 14 November 1854, 21 March 1855 and 16 and 17 May 1855. For a similar understanding of republicanism see the *Gold Digger's Advocate*, 1 April 1854 (Editorial).
71 Macintyre, *A Colonial Liberalism*, p. 77.

6 *QUIETA NON MOVERE* 1856–1880

1 Sherington, G., *Australia's Immigrants—1788–1978*, pp. 59–60; McLachlan, N., *Waiting for the Revolution*, p. 109.
2 McLachlan, p. 109.
3 Serle quoted in Shaw, A. G. L., 'Violent protests in Australian history', p. 556.
4 Macintyre, S., *A Colonial Liberalism*, pp. 31–2 and Shaw, 'Violent protests', p. 556.
5 Duffy in Alomes, S. and Jones, C. (eds), *Australian Nationalism—A Documentary History*, p. 40.
6 Ward, J. M., 'Charles Gavan Duffy and the Australian Federation Movement 1856–1870', pp. 1–33, at p. 1.
7 Ward, pp. 10 and 22, especially Duffy to Lang, May/June 1856 and his responses to Higinbotham's assertions of Victorian independence.
8 For equations of Federation with republicanism see Hall, H., *Australia and England—A Study in Imperial Relations*, p. 96; *Age*, 2 July 1870 and the report of the Colonial Conference in Melbourne—especially Cowper's equation of Federation and independence. For examples of the republic/independence/inevitability equation see Hall, pp. 92–3 and 100 (notes). Also, McLachlan, p. 107 and Thomas McCombie's speech in the Victorian Legislative Council, 11 December 1856, *VPD*, vol. I, pp. 108–11. Finally, *SMH*, 12 October 1869; *BC*, 12 June 1872 and 10 November 1869.
9 *SM*, 30 October 1869. Also see *FJ*, 30 October 1869.
10 Duffy to Lang, 16 June 1870 in Gilchrist, A. (ed.), *John Dunmore Lang. Chiefly Autobiographical: 1799–1878*, vol. II, p. 554. Also Macmillan, D. S., 'Australians in London 1857–1880', *RAHSJ*, vol. 44, pt. 3, 1958, pp. 155–81, especially p. 161. Also Hirst, J., *The Strange Birth of Colonial Democracy in NSW 1848–1884*, pp. 69–71.
11 The ex-colonists formed the Colonial Institute, formerly known as the Association for the Australian Colonies (1857–1862). On CO see Smith, G., *The Empire*, London, Henry and Parker, 1863, see pp. vii, 2, 24 and 36.
12 *SMH*, 21 May 1862. (See 23 May 1862 for 'experimental republic' and 31 May 1862 for 'where is the magic . . .'.). Also *BC*, 18 November 1864.
13 *SMH*, 12 October 1869. Also *BC*, 10 November 1869, *SM*, 30 October 1869, *FJ*, 30 October 1869 and 13 July 1872. The *FJ* was sympathetic to republicanism by the early 1870s. It frequently gave support to David Buchanan

MLC, Irish republican. See Buchanan's refusal to send condolences to the Queen on the death of her husband (*SMH*, 29 May 1862) and the *FJ*'s support of Buchanan, 10 August 1872. Also *Mercury*, 18 April 1873.
14 Hursthouse, C. F., *Australian Independence*, London, E. Stanford, 1870.
15 Martin, A. W., *Henry Parkes*, p. 232 and Inglis, K. S., *The Australian Colonists*, p. 97.
16 Inglis, p. 97.
17 Macpherson, in *SMH*, 16 March 1868.
18 *SMH*, 16 March 1868.
19 Inglis, p. 96.
20 *SMH*, 19 March 1868 (Parliamentary Debates on the Act).
21 *SMH*, 19 March 1868.
22 Ibid.
23 Ibid.
24 Ibid.
25 Amos, K., *Fenians in Australia: 1865–1880*, p. 68.
26 MacDonagh, O., 'Republicanism in modern Irish history', p. 41.
27 *SMH*, 7 September 1870, p. 17.
28 Michie, A. C., *Loyalty, Royalty and the Prince's Visits*, pp. 4, 12.
29 Ibid., pp. 11 and 16.
30 *SM*, 6 November 1869.
31 Shields, R. A, 'Australian opinion and defence of the Empire: a study in imperial relations 1880–1890, *AJPH*, vol. X, no. 1, April 1964, pp. 41–53; and Meaney, N. (ed.), *Australia and the World: A Documentary History 1870–1970*, pp. 50–2.
32 McCulloch in Meaney (ed.), p. 51. Duffy to Lang, 16 June 1870 quoted in Ward, p. 20.
33 *Age*, 2 July 1870.
34 McLachlan, p. 124.
35 *SMH*, 18 August 1870. Also the *Age*, 10 September 1870.
36 Quoted in abridged form by Somervell, D. C., *English Thought in the 19th Century*, David McKay, 1969 (first published 1929), p. 174.
37 Parkes, H., *Fifty Years of Australian History*, vol. I, p. 325.
38 *SMH*, 13 January 1877.
39 Macintyre, p. 65.
40 Serle, G. in Birrell, R., *A Nation of Our Own*, pp. 70 and 48.
41 For further details on Higinbotham, see Eggleston in Scott, E. (ed.), *Cambridge History of the British Empire*, vol. VII, pp. 522–30; also Bailey's chapter in the above, pp. 395–9; and Gollan, R., *Radical and Working Class Politics. A Study of Eastern Australia 1850–1910*, p. 54; or Ward, p. 21. Higinbotham is quoted by Bailey, p. 399. For Higinbotham's disavowal of separation, see Hall, H., *Australia and England*, p. 80. For Higinbotham and imperial connection, see Macintyre, p. 58.
42 *Age*, 8 September 1870.
43 In Parkes, H., *Speeches on Various Occasions Connected with the Public Affairs of New South Wales. 1848–1874*, pp. vi–vii. Also *Mercury*, 8 July 1875.

44 Blair in Parkes, *Speeches*, remarks on this absence of national feeling—see p. viii. Gladstone to Parkes, 30 June 1874, in Parkes, H., *Fifty Years of Australian History*, vol. I, p. 326.
45 Macintyre, pp. 57–8.
46 Cannadine, D., 'The context, performance and meaning of ritual. The British monarchy and the invention of tradition c.1820–1877', pp. 101–64.
47 Deniehy in an article entitled 'Forthcoming elections', *GH*, 20 October 1855.

7 A WHITE MAN'S REPUBLIC 1880–1887

1 Grassby, A., *The Australian Republic*, pp. 138–9.
2 Keneally, T., *Our Republic*, p. 155.
3 Cole, D., 'The crimson thread of kinship: ethnic ideas in Australia 1870–1914', p. 515.
4 I have included branches of the Australian Republican Union and the Australian Republican League in Sydney and the Australian Republican Association in Queensland.
5 Serle, G., *The Rush to be Rich. A History of the Colony of Victoria 1883–1889*, p. 227.
6 *DT*, Centennial Supplement, 23 January 1888. Victorian march in Alomes, S. and Jones, C. (eds), *Australian Nationalism: A Documentary History*, p. 80. On knighthood rejections, see Serle, *The Rush to be Rich*, p. 219.
7 Brown, M., *Australian Son, The Story of Ned Kelly*, pp. 279, 280.
8 Jones, I., *The Friendship that Destroyed Ned Kelly*, p. 155.
9 Brown, p. 276.
10 Vamplew, W. (ed.), *Australians: Historical Statistics*, Fairfax, Syme & Weldon, 1987, p. 26.
11 Blackton, C. S., 'Australian nationality and nativism: the Australian Natives Association 1885–1901', p. 37.
12 For example, see Aveling, M., 'A history of the Australian Natives Association'.
13 Blackton, 'Australian nationality and nativism', p. 39. Birrell, R., *A Nation of Our Own*, p. 96.
14 *DT*, 23 January 1888, p. 1. Meudell, G., 'Australia for the Australians', pp. 315–24.
15 Alomes, S. and Jones, C. (eds), pp. 48–9.
16 Ibid., pp. 46–73.
17 On imports and exports, see Davison, G., McCarty, J. W. and McLeary, A. (eds), *Australians: 1888*, pp. 415–16. *Bulletin*, 6 August 1881, p. 1.
18 Meaney, N. (ed.), *Australia and the World: A Documentary History 1870–1970*, pp. 60–2.
19 Ibid., p. 67.
20 Serle, *The Rush to be Rich*, p. 222.
21 *QPD*, vol. 44, 29 October 1884, p. 1189, also see p. 1577.
22 Eggleston, F. W., 'Australia and the Empire 1855–1921', in Scott, E. (ed.), *Cambridge History of the British Empire*, vol. VII, pt. 1, p. 529.
23 De Garis, B. K., 'The British influence on the federation of the Australian colonies', p. 41.

24 Service quote in ibid., p. 79. On British connection, see 'Northern Miner' in *Bulletin*, 7 July 1883, p. 11. On delegates' proposal, see Meaney, N. (ed.), p. 64.
25 *SMH*, 5 February 1885, p. 6 and 27 March 1885, p. 7 and Serle, *The Rush to be Rich*, pp. 222 and 236.
26 Parkes, H., 'Australia and the imperial connection', pp. 867–72.
27 *NSW PD*, vol. 16, 17–26 March 1885, pp. 5–9.
28 *SMH*, 4 March 1885.
29 I take the liberty of describing Suakin in these terms, having spent two weeks there in 1983. On British attitude to Australian assistance, see Inglis, K., *The Rehearsal: Australians at War in the Sudan 1885*, Rigby, 1985, p. 21; also pp. 52–61.
30 *NSW PD*, vol. 16, 17–26 March 1885, p. 29.
31 Ibid., p. 26.
32 Chorus reference from Meaney, N. (ed.), pp. 79–80. On meetings, see Fujikawa, T., 'Public meetings in NSW 1871–1901', p. 50. Barton in Shortus, S., 'Colonial nationalism. NSW Welsh identity in the mid 1880s', p. 47.
33 *NSW PD*, vol. 16, 17–26 March 1885, p. 13.
34 Ibid., p. 91.
35 Hall, H. L., *Australia and England—A Study in Imperial Relations*, p. 129.
36 Ibid., p. 128.
37 *Liberator*, 30 November 1889, p. 1268.
38 Hall, p. 131. Also *Bulletin* 29 September 1883 and 9 August 1884; *SMH*, 9 September 1891 and 3 February 1887.
39 *Democrat*, 29 March 1884.
40 *SMH*, 30 January 1884, p. 7.
41 McLachlan, N., *Waiting for the Revolution*, p. 164.
42 *Argus*, 11 December 1886.
43 *Age*, 14 December 1886 and Serle, *The Rush to be Rich*, p. 236.
44 *SMH*, 1 February 1886, p. 5. Froude, J. A., *Oceana: Or England and Her Colonies*, p. 158 on doubts about the imperial connection.
45 *Pioneer* (Adelaide), 28 May 1892, quoting an 1848 letter by the English novelist, George Eliot.
46 Docker, J., *The Nervous Nineties*, pp. 21, 105, 233. Public meetings in the Domain were revitalised in 1883. Fujikawa, p. 55. For details of the changes in the New South Wales parliament see Loveday, P. and Martin, A., *Parliament, Factions and Parties: the First 30 Years of Responsible Government in NSW 1856–1889*, p. 127. For the general climate also see Burgmann, V., *'In Our Time', Socialism and the Rise of Labor 1885–1905*, p. 2.
47 Statistics in Vamplew, W. (ed.), *Australians: Historical Statistics*, p. 41. For the shift to an industrial society see Markey, R., 'Populism and the formation of the Labor Party in NSW 1890–1900', pp. 40–1.
48 On clash between labour and capital, see Ebbels, R. N. (ed.), *The Australian Labor Movement—A Documentary History*, pp. 42, 45, 162. On alternative culture, see Davison, G., 'Sydney and the bush' in Russell, P. and White, R. (eds), p. 249. Also Connolly, C. N., 'Class, birthplace, loyalty', p. 231. Black quotes in Mansfield, B., 'The background to radical republicanism in NSW in the 1880s', p. 343.

49 On socialism interpretation, see Mansfield, B., 'The socialism of William Morris. England and Australia', *HS*, vol. 7, no. 27, November 1956, p. 288. On authoritarian and anti-authoritarian socialism, see *Honesty*, November 1988, p. 104 and William Lane, in Ebbels (ed.), p. 165. *Hummer*, 16 January 1892.
50 *Liberator*, 28 February 1891, pp. 2316–19.
51 The influence of these writers has been discussed at length, see Docker, J., pp. 73–81, 106–7, 110–11; Bell, P. and Bell, R., *Implicated: The United States in Australia*, pp. 30–3. Davidson, M., *The New Book of Kings*, pp. 10, 17, 21, 25, 30, 41, 42, 79.
52 *Bulletin*, 16 January 1892, p. 6.
53 For nationalist rhetoric, see *Bulletin*, 2 July 1887 and 19 March 1887. By 1887 the *Bulletin*'s circulation was approaching 20 000 weekly; Lawson, S., *The Archibald Paradox*, p. 122. Henry Lawson in Alomes, S. and Jones, C. (eds), pp. 94–7.
54 *Bulletin*, 27 August 1887 (letter from Cornstalk) and *Bulletin*, 19 March 1887, p. 4. On vilification of aristocracy, see *Bulletin*, 1 January 1887, p. 5.
55 *Liberator*, 17 July 1887, p. 1; and *Republican*, first edn 1887.
56 Darcy, F., 'Charles Bradlaugh and the English republican movement 1868–1878', pp. 367–83; also Royle, E., *Radicals Secularists and Republicans: Popular Freethought in Britain 1866–1915* and Robert Woodall, 'Republicanism in Victorian Britain', pp. 6–8. Regarding criticism of the monarchy in nineteenth-century England see Cannadine, D., in Hobsbawm, E. and Ranger, T. (eds), *The Invention of Tradition*, p. 111. For evidence of the influence of the *Reynolds News* on Archibald and the *Bulletin* see Lawson, S., p. 108. A good example of the *Bulletin*'s attitude to monarchy is the editorial on 9 April 1887, 'The same old Jubilee'.
57 For the derivative character of the Australian Socialist League see Mansfield, 'The socialism of William Morris. England and Australia', pp. 271–90. Membership of the League was initially only forty and was not to rise above 100. The most informed discussion of the League is in O'Farrell, P. 'The Australian Socialist League and the Labour Movement 1887–1891', pp. 152–65. The sectarian nature of Australian socialists is brought out by Nairn, N. B., *Civilising Capitalism, the Labor Movement in NSW 1870–1900*, pp. 36–9. Finally, essential reading is Burgmann, V., especially chapter 3. Burgmann stresses the ethnic diversity of the ASL's membership (predominantly European) and its various factions—such as State Socialism, Modern Socialism and Individualist Anarchism. A good example of the Anarchist attitude towards monarchy can be found in *Honesty*, June 1887, p. 33. Also *Honesty*, November 1888, p. 104.
58 Burgmann, p. 45.
59 Docker, p. 123.
60 Roderick, C. (ed.), *Henry Lawson: Autobiographical and Other Writings 1887–1922*, pp. 109–10.
61 Queen Victoria as matriarch, see Cannadine, D. in Hobsbawm, E. and Ranger, T. (eds), pp. 101–64; also *SMH*, 4 June 1887. Clark, C. M. H., *A History of Australia*, vol. IV, p. 395.

62 *SMH*, 4 June 1887.
63 Ibid. and *DT*, 4 June 1887.
64 *SMH*, 4 June 1887.
65 Ibid. and *DT*, 4 June 1887. Also Roderick, C., 'Henry Lawson', p. 109.
66 *DT*, 4 June 1887.
67 *SMH*, 4 June 1887.
68 *BC*, 6 June 1887, *DT*, 15 June 1887.
69 *DT*, 11 June 1887, p. 6.
70 *Bulletin*, 18 June 1887, p. 2.
71 *SMH*, 11 June 1887, p. 8.
72 *DT*, 11 June 1887, p. 6 and *FJ*, 11 June 1887. See Edward J. H. Knapps' letter (one of the organisers of the meeting), *SMH*, 15 June 1887, p. 5. Adjournment in *DT*, 11 June 1887, p. 6.
73 *DT*, 11 June 1887, also *Argus*, 11 June 1887, p. 10.
74 See especially *BC*, Monday 13 June. *Mercury*, 17 June 1887, p. 2 referred to the 'socialistic element' in Sydney. Also *Mercury*, 22 June 1887, p. 2 and 25 June 1887, p. 2 and *Argus*, 13 June 1887, p. 4. Also *NSW PD*, Legislative Council, vol. 27, 16 June 1887, p. 2110.
75 *BC*, 13 June 1887. Also *Argus*, 13 June 1887, p. 4 and *FJ*, 18 June 1887, p. 13.
76 *SMH*, 13 June 1887, p. 4. There were many who saw the conflict between Parkes and the demonstrators as more of a battle between Christendom and Godlessness than the Queen and republicans. See especially the letter of George Sutherland in *SMH*, 15 June 1887, p. 5. Walker's speech in *SMH*, 13 June 1887, p. 4.
77 *SMH*, 13 June 1887, p. 4.
78 Ibid. and *SMH*, 14 June 1887, p. 4.
79 *SMH*, 18 June 1887, p. 8.
80 *DT*, editorial, 14 June 1887.
81 *DT*, 13 June 1887, 14 June 1887 and 15 June 1887. On press consensus, see ibid. See also *SM*, 25 June 1887, p. 1316 and *SMH*, 13 July 1887. *NSW PD*, vol. 27, 16 June 1887, pp. 2140–3 and 24 June 1887, pp. 2269–71.
82 *DT*, 15 June 1887.
83 On fear of meeting disruption, see *SMH*, 16 June 1887, p. 6. On committee's action, see *DT*, editorial, 13 June 1887.
84 On committee's plans, see *SMH*, 16 June 1887, p. 5. *Bulletin*, 25 June 1887, p. 4. The Primrose League was an ultra-loyalist group.
85 *Bulletin*, 25 June 1887, p. 4.
86 *SMH*, 16 June 1887, p. 5.
87 For Norton at meeting, see *Bulletin*, 25 June 1887, p. 4. Description of meeting in *SMH*, 16 June 1887.
88 *NSW PD*, vol. 27, 16 June 1887, pp. 2170–1. Also the *Radical*, 25 June 1887, p. 107.
89 *SMH*, 16 June 1887, p. 5. *DT*, 16 June 1887 and 17 June 1887. *TCJ*, 18 June 1887, p. 1266.
90 *Bulletin*, 2 July 1887, p. 5; 'beats true' quote from *SM*, editorial, 18 June 1887. 'Dead Sea' quote from *ISN*, 15 July 1887, p. 2 and 'disloyal' quote from *SMH*, 16 June 1887, p. 6. Cable report in *Bulletin*, 2 July 1887, p. 5.

91 The figure is from *SMH*, 16 June 1887, p. 5 and *DT*, 16 June 1887, p. 5.
92 *SM*, editorial, 18 June 1887.
93 Fujikawa, T., pp. 56–7.
94 *NSW PD*, vol. 27, 16 June 1887, pp. 2163 and 2113.
95 Ibid., p. 2180.
96 Ibid., pp. 2164–9.
97 Ibid., 24 June 1887, p. 2269. This view of Parkes was widely held by many others, *SMH*, 15 June 1887, p. 8; *DT*, editorial, 18 June 1887; *FJ*, 25 June 1887 and *BC*, 14 June 1887, p. 4.
98 *SMH*, 16 June 1887, p. 8. Loyalist meeting at Parramatta or cables from rural towns in *SMH*, 17 June 1887, p. 4 and *SMH*, 23 June 1887, p. 4. Also see *SMH*, 24 June 1887.
99 *Advertiser*, 29 July 1887. *SMH*, 18 June 1887, p. 8. *ISN*, 15 June 1887, p. 2. *DT*, editorial, 13 June 1887 mentions the proposal for loyalist badges. See *SMH*, 20 June 1887, p. 3 for a report of church services in Sydney. *FJ*, 18 June 1887.
100 *FJ*, 25 June 1887. Also Birrell, R., p. 116.
101 Examples—*SMH*, 27 August 1887; *BC*, 22 June 1887, p. 4; *DT*, editorial, 22 June 1887; *SM*, editorial, 18 and 25 June 1887; *ISN*, 15 June 1887, p. 2; *NMH*, 30 July 1887, p. 4, 26 July 1887, p. 7, 28 July 1887, p. 7 and 3 August 1887, p. 5; *Radical*, 25 June 1887, p. 107, 2 July 1887, p. 116; *Mercury*, 22 June 1887, p. 2, 25 June 1887, p. 2; Perth *ICN*, 11 May 1887; *Advertiser*, 4 July 1887; *Age*, 28 June 1887, p. 4, 17 February 1887; *Argus*, editorial, 20 June 1887; *Liberator*, 26 June 1887, p. 67, 3 July 1887, p. 87; *Australian* [ANA Journal], June 1887, p. 17, December 1887, pp. 13–15.
102 *NMH*, 30 July 1887. *NSW PD*, Legislative Assembly, vol. 27, 16 June 1887, pp. 2173–4.
103 On lack of resistance, see Serle, *The Rush to be Rich*, p. 284. *Radical*, 18 June 1887, p. 98. On the cost of 'republicanism', see *Liberator*, 17 July 1887, p. 123. For similar juxtapositions see *Radical*, 18 June 1887, p. 98, 13 August 1887, p. 162 and 27 August 1887, p. 178. *Bulletin*, 9 April 1887. Debate on Republic versus Monarchy in the Newcastle Hall of Science reported in the *NH*, 26 July 1887. *Bulletin* on the Jubilee illuminations, 25 June 1887, p. 5 or Henry Lawson's poem 'The Statue Of Our Queen' (1890) or 'The English Queen' (1892). Also see Dawson, A., *Royalty*.
104 *NSW PD*, Legislative Council, vol. 27, 16 June 1887, pp. 2110–11.
105 Cheers for Bradlaugh and Besant reported in *SMH*, 16 June 1887 also in *NSW PD*, vol. 27, 16 June 1887, p. 2141 [Henson] Richard Jebb, in his *Studies in Colonial Nationalism*, p. 192, levelled similar criticisms at the *Bulletin*.
106 *NSW PD*, Legislative Council, vol. 27, 16 June 1887, pp. 2110–11.

8 NATION AND REPUBLIC   1887–1891

1 *Bulletin*, editorial, 2 July 1887, p. 4.
2 *Advertiser*, 4 July and 21 July 1887.
3 *SMH*, 5 July 1887, p. 11.
4 Roderick, C. (ed.), *Henry Lawson: Autobiographical and Other Writings 1887–1922*, p. 211.

5 *Republican*, October 1887, p. 4. Also *Bulletin*, 1 October 1887.
6 Black, G., in Pike, D. (gen. ed.), *ADB*, 26 October 1922, p. 14. Matthews, B., *Louisa*, pp. 157–63.
7 Roderick, C., *Henry Lawson: A Life*, pp. 34–5.
8 Roderick, C. (ed.), *Hentry Lawson: Autobiographical and Other Writings*, pp. 212–13.
9 *Republican*, July 1887, pp. 2, 6, August 1887, p. 1, April 1888, August 1887, October 1887.
10 *Republican*, August 1887, p. 4.
11 Ibid.
12 *SMH*, 13 and 20 August 1887.
13 *SMH*, 20 August 1887.
14 *SMH*, 23 August 1887.
15 'Sentimental loyalty' quote from *Republican*, October 1887, p. 2. There is a strong possibility that W. Foote was the son or brother of George William Foote who had been the secretary of the London Republican Club in the early 1870s. Interestingly, in 1873 George William Foote (like his namesake in Australia) also hoped for a republicanism which would 'exclude those vexed economic and social questions which so divide even avowed republicans'—Darcy, F., 'Charles Bradlaugh and the English Republican Movement 1868–1878', p. 378. Also *SMH* comments on the 'new chum' W. M. Foote, *SMH*, 24 August 1887, p. 5.
16 *SMH*, 24 August 1887, p. 5. Also *Bulletin*, 23 July 1887, letter from 'Native', p. 5.
17 *ISN*, September 1887.
18 *DT*, 24 August 1887; also *Age*, 26 August 1887. *Republican*, October 1887, p. 5.
19 *Republican*, January 1888, p. 1.
20 *NSW PD*, vol. 29, 24 November 1887, pp. 1529 and 1644. *Bulletin*, 7 May 1887. *Republican*, January 1888, p. 5 places the blame for the bill largely on Parkes. Also *Radical*, 10 December 1887, editorial. For allusions to the American War of Independence see *DT*, 18 and 21 November 1887. Thomas Walker's speech at a protest meeting in Sydney quoted in *SMH*, 3 February 1887, p. 11.
21 *Bulletin*, 24 November 1888.
22 Martin, A. W., *Henry Parkes*, pp. 368–9. *SMH*'s report from Victoria, 1 February 1888, p. 9 and for the lack of rural interest see the telegrams in *TCJ*, 4 February 1888, p. 228, or in *SMH*, 27 January 1888.
23 *Bulletin*, 21 January 1888.
24 *SMH*, 26 January and 3 February 1888. *SM*, 21 January 1888, p. 123. The denial in *ISN*, 26 January 1888.
25 Comments on Centennial Banquet from *DT*, 27 January 1888 and endorsed in *TCJ*, 4 February 1888, p. 220. The *DT* thought that the Labour Rally in Sydney on Saturday 28 January was 'the birthday of Australian nationality', a more fitting event than the State banquet. *SMH*, 13 January 1888, p. 6.
26 *Bulletin* on Queen's statue, 4 February 1888, p. 5. *SMH*, 13 January 1888, p. 6 and 25 January 1888.
27 *DT*, 7 January 1888, p. 9.

28 *TCJ*, 28 January 1888, p. 174. *SMH*, 13 January 1888, (As You Like It) and *TCJ*, 4 February 1888.
29 *AS*, 7 February 1890.
30 Parkes' speech at the Centennial Banquet in *DT*, 27 January 1888. Lord Carrington's speech at Parliament House in *DT*, 3 February 1888, p. 4. *SMH*'s defence of the connection and repudiation of republicanism, 24 January 1888, p. 9 and 28 January 1888, p. 13. *NMH*'s discussion of loyalty and royalty, 27 January 1888.
31 *DT*, 3 February 1888, p. 4.
32 *DT*, Centennial supplement, 23 January 1888 and *AS*, 5 July 1888. *Bulletin*, 21 January and 7 February 1888. Lawson, S. *The Archibald Paradox*, pp. 133–7.
33 Thomson, R., *Australian Nationalism*, p. 34 (also Hall, H. *Australia and England—A Study in Imperial Relations*, pp. 82–6). Anonymous, *A Plea for Separation*. *Bulletin*, 21 August 1886 (Phil May's cartoon). Also Lawson, S., pp. 145–7 and *Bulletin*, editorial, 2 August 1888. Hall, pp. 140–1, points out that republicans also feared that Imperial Federation would lead to a Chinese invasion, and Tregenza, J., *Professor of Democracy: The Life of Charles Henry Pearson 1830–1894*, pp. 218–19.
34 *Bulletin*, 24 March 1888, p. 5. Also *Bulletin* 18 February 1888 and *SMH*, 4 May 1888, p. 9; *Age*, 15 May 1888; *DT*, 5 May 1888, p. 5 and 15 June 1888, p. 4 and *Republican*, October 1887.
35 Davison, G., McCarty, J. W. and McLeary, A. (eds), *Australians: 1888*, p. 421. Also see the School of Arts Debating Club topic in *DT*, 19 May 1888, p. 9. 'Should Great Britain support the demands re Chinese Immigration ... Separation will be absolutely necessary'.
36 Divorce Laws, *Bulletin*, 31 March 1888, p. 80. Governors dispute in *DT*, 9 November 1888 and Bailey, K. H., 'Self government in Australia, 1860–1900', pp. 399, 401, 410–11, 416 and George Dibbs, in *NSWPD*, vol. 35, 21 November 1888, p. 556. Also see the Reverend R. Dale, 'Impressions of Australia', *Contemporary Review*, 1888 (Mitchell Library), and David Buchanan in Henry Parkes' *Fifty Years of Australian History*, pp. 251–2. Aveling, M., 'A History of the Australian Natives Association', p. 144. For ANA meetings see: *Argus*, 5 May 1888, p. 11, and 11 May 1888, *Age*, 5 April 1888. See also *Argus*, 1 May 1888 and *Age*, 9 April 1888. Blainey, G., *Our Side of the Country. The Story of Victoria*, p. 135 or Serle, G., *The Rush to be Rich*, pp. 309–11. Also Dilke, C., *Problems of Great Britain*, pp. 260–1, *Age*, 26 August 1887, *Argus*, 2 April 1888 and *DT*, 4 April and 4 May 1888. For loyalist attacks on the policy of the ANA in Victoria see *Argus*, editorial, 1 May 1888. Republican criticisms in *Age*, 28 April 1888 and 21 April 1888 (letter from 'Australian'). Also two letters in *DT*, 4 April 1888, p. 4. *Age*, 9 June 1888 (a letter from J. L. Dow, MLA) and the Orangeman celebration at the Protestant Hall in Melbourne in *Age*, 13 July 1888. *Bulletin*, 12 January 1889, p. 4. Finally, see Adelaide *Advertiser*, 11 April 1888, p. 4 and Perth *ICN*, 15 June 1888.
37 Deakin, A., *The Federal Story*, p. 9. Birrell, R., *A Nation of Our Own*, pp. 48 and 70.
38 *Liberator*, 14 June 1890.

39 Perth *ICN*, 15 June 1888. Debate on independence, *Argus*, 3 April 1888 and *Age*, 25 September 1888 and the *Australian* (ANA journal), December 1887, pp. 13–15.
40 Black, G., *A History of the NSW Labor Party from its Conception until 1917*, no. 1, p. 20.
41 Pike (gen. ed.), *ADB*, vol. 7, 1891–1939, pp. 302–3.
42 *Radical*, 14 January 1888, p. 7. *Radical*, 17 March and 14 April 1888. Also *Republican*, February 1888, p. 5 and *Radical*, 28 January 1888, p. 4. Black's Jubilee hymn in *Republican*, February 1888, p. 4.
43 *Republican*, February 1888, p. 5. Also *Liberator*, 19 February 1888, p. 196.
44 Black's letter to Queen Victoria, *Republican*, February 1888, p. 3. *Liberator*, 19 February 1888, p. 196.
45 *Radical*, 25 February 1888, p. 6; 18 February 1888, p. 6; 10 March 1888, p. 2 and 17 March 1888, p. 2.
46 Roderick, C., *Henry Lawson: A Life*, p. 43.
47 *Republican*, January 1888, pp. 1, 2, 5 and 7; February 1888, pp. 3, 4 and 5; April 1888. The *Republican* quoted the London *Commonwealth* (January 1888, p. 5). Poetry by William Morris (February 1888, p. 3). The April issue contained a pin-up centrefold of Garibaldi—'the Great Liberator of Italy'. On national anthem, see *Republican*, January 1888, p. 4. In February 1888 issue, p. 5 the *Republican* complained that children in public schools were being forced to sing the 'British' national anthem. Louisa Lawson's poem 'Australia' in *Republican*, April 1888, p. 4.
48 *Republican*, April 1888, p. 2.
49 *SAR*, 27 March 1888, p. 5, column 5 titled 'Botanic Park Address'. For details (however sketchy) of Black's speaking engagements in Adelaide see *Republican*, April 1888, p. 4.
50 *Advertiser*, 29 March 1888.
51 *Radical*, 3 May 1888, p. 5. *Argus* report in *Advertiser*, 25 April 1888, p. 4. Repression was not uncommon in Sydney as well. That 'dreadful republican paper' the (Newcastle) *Radical* was banned from Camperdown Library public reading room in 1888. See the letter from 'Australienne' Wagga Wagga in *Radical*, 4 August 1888, p. 5.
52 On disbandment, see Serle, *The Rush to be Rich*, p. 308. *Radical*, 25 February 1888, p. 6.
53 On Sunday afternoons, see *Radical*, 10 March 1888; at a meeting of the Republican League in March one anarchist accused modern republicanism of being opposed to true democracy. On Christianity and republicanism, see *Liberator*, 1 July 1888, p. 82. Joseph Symes' attack on the *Bulletin* in *Liberator*, 1 January 1888, p. 82.
54 *Bulletin*, 21 April 1888, p. 18.
55 *Radical*, 5 May 1888, p. 7 for a report of the School of Arts debating club meeting on Monday 30 April 1888 in Sydney. The meeting criticised the policy of the ANA with Foote and Black leading the way. Also reports in *DT*, 16 May 1888, p. 6 and 19 May 1888, p. 9 (letter from Davis, Vice President of the Debating Club who feared that republicans were infiltrating the Club). Foote's reply 21 May 1888, p. 7 defending republicans and their cause.

Republicans were in attendance for the visit of ANA President J. L. Purves to Sydney. As Purves spoke at the Town Hall, they cried out in support of a republic, yelling 'Yes! Yes!' when Purves asked the rhetorical question 'Did they [the ANA] mean to found a republic?' *DT,* 4 May 1888. Black's arguments in *Radical,* 12 May 1888, p. 3.

56 Roderick, C., *Henry Lawson: A Life,* pp. 47–8. Matthews, p. 259.
57 Black, G., *Why I am a Republican,* p. 22 and *Radical,* 11 August 1888, p. 3.
58 Roderick, C., *Henry Lawson: A Life,* p. 51. *Radical,* 12 May 1888, p. 3, and 14 July 1888, p. 5, *DT,* 16 May 1888, p. 6.
59 *Nationalist,* 8 August 1888, p. 3. Also *Radical,* 12 May 1888, p. 6 and 5 May 1888, p. 7, and *DT,* 5 July 1888.
60 McLachlan, N., *Waiting for the Revolution,* p. 158. McIlwraith's victory in ibid., also *Nationalist,* 8 August 1888; *Bulletin,* 21 April and 1 December 1888. On use of 'National', see McLachlan, p. 158.
61 Blackton, C., 'Australian nationality and nationalism 1850–1900', p. 362; *Nationalist,* 8 August 1888.
62 *Nationalist,* 8 August 1888.
63 Ibid.
64 Ibid.
65 Blackton, 'Australian nationality and nationalism 1850–1900', p. 363.
66 *Radical,* 21 July 1888, p. 4.
67 *Republican,* January 1888. Black's Botanic Park address in Adelaide, *SAR,* 27 March 1888, p. 5, column 5, as well as his speech at the Sydney School of Arts, *Radical,* 5 May 1888, p. 7. *Liberator,* 1 July 1888, p. 82; *Republican,* April 1888 and Blackton, 'Australian nationality and nationalism 1850–1900', pp. 363–4.
68 Despatches from US Consul-Generals in Sydney 1836–1906, 6 August 1889–18 May 1891, Sydney, 27 November 1889, p. 13, RAV FM626, Mitchell Library.
69 *DT,* 5 July 1888 and Dilke, C., *Problems of Great Britain,* p. 340. The *AS* did not like the *Telegraph*'s republicanism—*AS,* 5 July 1888, p. 4.
70 William Foote's letter to *SMH,* 5 November 1889, p. 4. *Bulletin,* 1 December 1888, p. 4. *DT,* 4 December 1888, p. 3; *AS,* 25 May 1889, p. 4. *SMH,* 4 September 1888. Gollan, R., in Greenwood, G. (ed.), *Australia: A Social and Political History,* p. 152. Also *Boomerang,* 3 March 1888 for the Intercolonial Trade Union Congress meeting which concluded with three cheers for the Federated Republic of Australia. For the 'transitional' stage of the connection, see Davison, McCarty and McLeary (eds), p. 422. The debates on the question of a republic can be found in *NSW PD,* vol. 35, 21 November 1888, pp. 563–601 and *NSW PD,* vol. 43, 4 December 1889, pp. 160, 161; and *AS,* 22 November 1888 and *SMH,* 19 June 1889, p. 4.
71 *SMH,* 4 September 1888 (meeting of ANA members in Sydney). *Republican,* February 1888, p. 5. *SAR,* 27 March 1888, p. 5. *AS,* 12 November 1888, p. 4. *Radical,* 12 May 1888, p. 6. William Foote also conceded that a 'considerable time would have to elapse' before a republic would be a realistic possibility, *SMH,* 5 November 1889, p. 4. Also Dilke, p. 344; and *Boomerang,* 13 February 1892, p. 5—poem 'The Coming Time'.

72 *DT*, 22 November 1888, p. 4. Fletcher and Lyne in *NSW PD*, vol. 35, 21 November 1888, pp. 565–6, 589. For 'good ship' quote, see Thomas Walker in ibid., p. 583.
73 Serle, *The Rush to be Rich*, p. 310. Also Mansfield, B., *Australian Democrat. The Career of E. W. O'Sullivan 1846–1890*, p. 264. Mansfield's analysis of O'Sullivan's republicanism is a fascinating case study of how the wider trends in the republican debate from the late 1880s to the early 1890s were mirrored in the attitudes of one man, also pp. 261–5.
74 Bolton, G., 'Labour Comes to Charters Towers', pp. 25–34. Buckley, K. and Wheelwright, T., *No Paradise for Workers: Capitalism and the Common People in Australia 1788–1914*, pp. 130–6. On Queensland and ALP, McMullin, R., *The Light on the Hill, the Australian Labor Party 1891–1991*, p. 1.
75 Dilke, p. 344. Also *QPD*, vol. 58, 8 August 1889, p. 1047 (Morehead).
76 Smith, A. B., 'Australian loyalty to the British Empire', pp. 369–77 (especially pp. 376–7). For an example of the reaction to McIlwraith's election, see Perth *ICN*, 15 June 1888.
77 *JBIA*, no. 26, October 1888, pt 15, vol. II, p. 567. *Bulletin*, 21 April and 1 December 1888, *DT*, 27 November 1888, p. 4, and *AS*, 25 May 1889, p. 4. On Governors, see *Age*, 20 November 1888.
78 On McIlwraith and CO, see Bailey, p. 401; *DT*, 4 December 1888 (also *QPD*, vol. 55, 13 November 1888, pp. 1113–15, where McIlwraith reveals to the House the exact nature of his correspondence with the CO). For examples of the Governors dispute as a sign of independence, see *DT*, 4 December 1888; *AS*, 10 September 1888, p. 4, 22 October 1888, p. 5 and 11 November 1888, p. 4. On Acts, see Bailey, p. 411.
79 *AS*, 10 September 1888, p. 4, 22 October 1888, p. 5 and 11 November 1888, p. 4. The phrase 'reciprocity of rights' comes from *BC*, quoted in *DT*, 19 May 1888. Dilke, p. 340 on duality of allegiance. For further evidence see *DT*, editorial, 4 December 1888. Also the debate on the Australian Naval Force bill in *QPD*, vol. 53, 22 and 24 November 1887, pp. 1700–1, 1710–11, 1782–3, and 1788–9.
80 Gollan, R. in Greenwood, G. (ed.), *Australia: A Social and Political History*, p. 152. *Boomerang*, 10 March 1888, p. 3. Other examples in Hinchcliffe, A., 'The Labor Party in Queensland', *CM*, June 1890, p. 867 and Spence, W. G., *Australia's Awakening*, The Worker Trustees, 1909, p. 275. Burgmann, V., *'In Our Time', Socialism and the Rise of Labor 1885–1905*, p. 19. Also Alomes, S. and Jones, C. (eds), *Australian Nationalism—A Documentary History*, p. 83 and Ross, L., *William Lane and the Australian Labour Movement*, Forward Press, 1937, pp. 64–6.
81 In Burgmann, p. 19. Also *Boomerang*, 28 January 1888, p. 6.
82 *Boomerang*, 24 March, 12 May and 2 June 1888. *Boomerang* cover, first issue, 1890.
83 *Boomerang*, 5 July 1890, p. 5. *Boomerang*'s references to the American Republic, 9 June 1888, p. 10, 25 January 1890, p. 6 and 1 February 1890.
84 Lane on McIlwraith and the liberalism of the *DT*. *Boomerang*, 28 April 1888, p. 3. The *Liberator* also thought McIlwraith's brand of nationalism unacceptable as well as the *Bulletin*'s: *Liberator*, 1 July 1888, p. 83.

85 *Boomerang*, 30 November 1889, also 19 November 1887; 14 August 1888. Editorials on 9 June 1888; 1 September 1888; 16, 23 March and 23 November 1889, p. 5.
86 *Boomerang*, 23 March 1889, 'The Coming Republic'.
87 *Charters Towers Times*, 4 February 1890, editorial.
88 Bolton, G., *A Thousand Miles Away. A History of North Queensland to 1920*, p. 186.
89 Bolton, 'Labour Comes to Charters Towers', p. 26. A good example of early republicanism in Charters Towers is Isaac Selby's lecture 'Monarchs of England' (a plea for republicanism) published in *Liberator*, 13 November 1887, p. 418.
90 Bolton, 'Labour Comes to Charters Towers', p. 30.
91 Buckley and Wheelwright, pp. 180–4. Gollan, R., *Radical and Working Class Politics. A Study of Eastern Australia 1850–1910*, p. 109. Burgmann, pp. 13–15, 23. McMullin, p. 1.
92 *Charters Towers Times*, 4 February 1890.
93 Ibid.
94 Ibid.
95 *AR*, 23 August 1890.
96 *Charters Towers Times*, 4 February 1890—or *AR*, 25 April 1891.
97 Davies, G., 'Atheistical and blasphemous notoriety seekers? The Australian Republican Association Charters Towers, 1890–1891', p. 104.
98 *AR*, 23 August 1890, p. 5 claimed 540 members in Charters Towers alone. Glenn Davies claims the peak membership of the ARA was 700, 10 per cent of eligible voters in Charters Towers, see Davies, G., 'The *Australian Republican*: a Charters Towers radical journal 1890–1891', p. 103. This issue of the *AR* is missing (as are many others). The first available number is vol. 1, no. 4, August 1890. Copies are held in the Australian National Library. Also, the Victorian State Library (Manuscripts) holds notes made from the *AR* by S. Merrifield. Merrifield did not have access to any copies which are not held by the Australian National Library.
99 *AR*, 17 August 1890, p. 8 and 18 October 1890, p. 5.
100 *AR*, 9 August 1890, p. 8. *AR*, 6 September 1890, p. 6.
101 *AR*, 6 September 1890, p. 6. See the letter signed 'Democrat' which deplored the absence of an honest labour paper. Also Albert Dawson's pamphlet *The Case Stated*, p. 1. *Charters Towers Times* supports the ARA, 29 September 1890.
102 *AR*, 25 April 1891.
103 *AR*, 23 August 1890, p. 1.
104 *AR*, 6 September 1890, p. 5. See also *Charters Towers Times*, 6, 7 and 8 May 1890.
105 Bolton, G., 'Labour Comes to Charters Towers', p. 32.
106 *AR*, 6 September 1890, p. 8.
107 *Boomerang*, 20 September 1890, p. 5.
108 *AR*, 18 October 1890, p. 4.
109 Ibid.

110 Bastin, J. and Stoodley, J., 'F.C.B. Vosper: an Australian radical', pp. 39–40. Descriptions of Vosper in Davies, G., 'The *Australian Republican*', p. 115.
111 Buckley and Wheelwright, p. 135.
112 Bastin and Stoodley, p. 41 and Bolton, *A Thousand Miles Away*, p. 197.
113 I am indebted to the work of Glenn A. Davies. See especially 'A time of perceived rebellion. A comparison of the Charters Towers and Rockhampton showcase trials of 1891', pp. 27–37 and pp. 29–31.
114 Bastin and Stoodley, p. 42.
115 *AR*, 20 June 1891, p. 1.
116 *AR*, 30 May 1891, p. 7. For similar sentiments, see *Pioneer* (Adelaide), 25 June 1892, p. 147, letter from Luke Gulson, Hay, NSW.
117 Sugar Bag Hoolan's claim that 'the republican spirit was premature' in *AR*, 23 August 1890, p. 5. 'Ballot or Bayonet' editorial, *AR*, 8 August 1891, p. 1.
118 Bastin and Stoodley, p. 43. *AR* was non-committal on the issue until Vosper's editorship in October 1890: *AR*, 20 September 1890. For Vosper's support of separation for north Queensland see *Charters Towers Times*, 5 September and 22 December 1890. The lack of unity among republicans was also acknowledged by the *Bulletin*, 30 January 1892, p. 6.
119 *AR*, 16 May 1891, Queen versus Vosper.
120 Dawson, *The Case Stated*, p. 1.

9 THE COMMON WEAL—REPUBLICANISM AND FEDERATION

1 Martin, A. W., *Henry Parkes*, p. 385. Good examples of early support for republican Federation in *Liberator*, 23 March 1889. *AS*, 22 November 1889. Anonymous, *A Plea for Separation*, pp. 2–5. W. Foote's letter to *SMH*, 5 November 1889, p. 4. Also R. Thomson's *Australian Nationalism*.
2 *YA*, December 1889, pp. 7–8, March 1890, pp. 51–2 and *USM*, March 1891, p. 547 and January 1891, p. 315.
3 *SMH* in *YA*, February 1891, p. 31.
4 Buchanan was a dedicated follower of Lang. See his defence of Lang in *YA*, March 1890, p. 52.
5 Smith, F. G., 'Danger Ahead. Anti-Imperial Federation'. Also Hogan, J. T., *The Australian in London*, London, Ward and Downey, 1889, p. 275.
6 *AS*, 22 November 1889. See the enthusiastic support of the *Star*'s editorial on the same day and *Boomerang*, 15 February 1889, p. 5. An interview with Lilley is also quoted in *SMH*, 28 January 1892, p. 7.
7 Justice Williams' remarks in *Age*, 14 September 1888, p. 6, *DT*, 31 October 1889, and Taylor, A. J., *Imperial Federation versus Australian Independence*. Speech of A. Brown, Member for Newcastle in *NSW PD*, vol. 44, p. 431, 14 May 1890, also E. W. O. Sullivan, p. 470, George Dibbs, p. 588, Gough, p. 672 and Traill, pp. 842 and 839. Also *Bulletin*, 16 January 1892. Sharwood, R., 'The Australasian Federation Conference of 1890' in Craven, G., *The Convention Debates 1891–1898. Commentaries Indices and Guide*, vol. VI, pp. 53 and 54.
8 Parkes' speech in *NSW PD*, vol. 44, 29 April 1890, p. 57. *Boomerang* (for betrayal), 15 February 1890, p. 6; also 25 January 1890, p. 6, 30 August 1890,

p. 5. The *Boomerang* paraphrasing Lang, 1 February 1890, p. 6, 5 July 1890, p. 5, 19 July 1890, p. 5, 30 August 1890, p. 5. *AS* (for 'contradiction'), 17 January 1890, p. 4; also 14 February 1890, p. 4, 4 February 1890, p. 4, 29 August 1890, p. 4. The *Bulletin* had been anti-Parkes' model of Federation for several years, 30 November 1888, p. 4. *AS*, 18 December 1890, p. 4.
9 *NSW PD*, vol. 44, 14 May 1890, p. 459. Also p. 462 (Seaver) and vol. 47, p. 3352 (McMillan). Parkes in *NSW PD*, Legislative Council, vol. 45, p. 1096. Dr Garran was one of the few who argued rationally that separation was not as inevitable as others believed, vol. 45, Legislative Council, 11 June 1890, p. 1230.
10 *NSW PD*, vol. 44, p. 840.
11 Ibid., vol. 44, pp. 494, 818 and 838–43.
12 McMillan in ibid., vol. 47, 28 August 1890, p. 3350.
13 See Smith in ibid., vol. 44, p. 885 for an example of the manner in which theoretical republicanism played into the hands of the anti-republicans. Also Dibbs, ibid., vol. 44, p. 588, Gough, ibid., vol. 44, pp. 672–4 and Walker, ibid., vol. 47, p. 3365.
14 Ibid., vol. 47, 10 September 1890, pp. 3644 and 3647; Nicoll, ibid., vol. 45, p. 1106 who suggested the phrase 'Union under the Crown' be left out.
15 In Queensland, the only other colony where one would expect to find a fair sprinkling of republican opposition to Parkes' proposal to federate under the Crown, MPs were largely supportive of Parkes, or inevitabilists: *QPD*, vol. 60, 23 July–6 August 1890, pp. 46, 47, 50, 56, 62, 70 and 73. Also *VPD*, vol. 66, 30 June 1891, pp.115, 118 and 14 July 1891, p. 377.
16 *NACD*, 1 April 1891, p. 551.
17 La Nauze, J. A., 'The name of the Commonwealth of Australia', p. 59 and p. 60. Also *VPD*, vol. 66, 30 June 1891, p. 105.
18 La Nauze, 'The name of the Commonwealth of Australia', p. 60.
19 *NACD*, 1891, pp. 551–2.
20 Ibid., pp. 550–7. Also *VPD*, vol. 66, 30 June 1891, p. 105, 9 July, p. 301, 14 July, p. 381 and 16 July, p. 391.
21 Wright in *NACD*, p. 554. For further reading on the etymology of the word 'Commonwealth', see Mehrotra, S., 'On the use of the term Commonwealth', pp. 1–16, and Hancock, W. K., 'A veray and true Comyn Wele', pp. 30–1. Also see first edn of the *CWA*, 18 August 1891, p. 1.
22 *VPD*, vol. 66, 30 June 1891, pp. 306, 307, 308, 14 July, pp. 341–7, 14 July, p. 381, 16 July, p. 391 and 4 August, pp. 716–19. *NSW PD*, vol. 66, 30 May 1893, p. 7619, vol. 89, Legislative Council, 17 August 1897, pp. 2988–94, and vol. 99, Legislative Council, 16 August 1899, pp. 738–9; *SAPD*, Legislative Council, Thirteenth Parliament, second session, 15 September 1891, pp. 1132–4, and 29 September 1891, p. 1310.
23 *CWA*, 18 August 1891, p. 1.
24 *NACD*, 13 March 1891, p. 323. Also *SMH*, 17 March 1891, p. 6, letter from T. Slattery.
25 See especially Parkes' speech, *One People One Destiny*. Barton in La Nauze, 'The name of the Commonwealth of Australia', p. 71.

26 Barton, G. B., *Draft Constitution of the Commonwealth*, p. 14. Naturally the term 'Commonwealth' was also a product of the Convention delegates' use of James Bryce's 'American Commonwealth' (see La Nauze, 'The name of the Commonwealth of Australia', p. 71). Also see the letters column *SMH*, 3 April 1891, 'The Commonwealth of Australia'. The word 'is the exact equivalent of the Roman Respublica—otherwise our modern republic'.

27 *NACD*, 1891, p. 875. Grey's proposal for an elected Governor-General, pp. 138–9 and 561–73 (Grey did not argue for separation). On Downer, see ibid., p. 572. Deakin argued that an elected Governor-General would have to derive his authority from the Australian people, not the sovereign of Great Britain, p. 571.

28 Abbott, *NACD*, p. 301.

29 *NACD*, 1891, pp. 186–8.

30 Neasy, J. M., 'Andrew Inglis Clark Senior and Australian Federation', *AJPH*, vol. 15, no. 2, August 1969, p. 15. And A. I. Clark, 'Australian Federation', confidential letter, Hobart, 6 February 1891.

31 Neasy, 'Andrew Inglis Clark Senior'.

32 *SAPD*, Legislative Council, Thirteenth Parliament, second session, 15 September 1891, pp. 1132–4, and Baker, R. C., *Australian Federation*, Adelaide, Burden & Bonython, 1891. Also *Advertiser*, 15 April 1891.

33 *Bulletin*, 16 January 1892, p. 6.

34 *Bulletin*, 14 March 1891, pp. 6–7. Also 27 June 1891, p. 6 and 8 August 1891, p. 7, Rolfe, P., *Journalistic Javelin*, pp. 140–1, Lawson, S., *The Archibald Paradox*, pp. 150–1 and Clark, M., *Sources of Australian History*, pp. 446–52.

35 *Mercury*, 9 March 1891, p. 2. For evidence of republican opposition to the bill see *AS*, 9 May 1891; 15 April 1891, p. 5; 20 May 1891, p. 5; 23 April 1891, p. 5; *Boomerang*, 28 February 1891, p. 3; 2 May 1891, p. 5; 14 March 1891, p. 4. *NA* (Bathurst), 3 March and 13 March 1891. Black, G., *Why I am a Republican*, p. 2. *AS*, 10 March 1891, p. 6, 16 March 1891, p. 4, 31 March 1891, p. 4; 1 April 1891, 2 April 1891, p. 4 and 15 April 1891, p. 5. Nairn, N. B., *Civilising Capitalism, the Labor Movement in NSW 1870–1900*, p. 57. *AR*, 2 May 1891, p. 1. In South Australia the German democrat, T. Scherk, member for East Adelaide, campaigned against the Commonwealth bill, see Burgmann, V. *'In OurTime'*, p. 150.

36 Interview with Lilley, *SMH*, 28 January 1892 and *Truth*, 27 December 1891, p. 7. Also Drake, J. G., *Federation, Imperial or Democratic*, p. 20.

37 *Truth*, 12 July 1891, p. 4, also 2 August 1891, p. 4, 8 February 1890, 12 March 1891, p. 2, 23 November 1890, p. 2; 9 November 1890, 19 October 1890, p. 2 and 14 September 1890, p. 2.

38 *Truth*, 12 July 1891, p. 4. Bernard O'Dowd's Melbourne *Tocsin* also kept republicanism alive. McLachlan, N., *Waiting for the Revolution*, p. 165. Correspondence in *Truth*, 9 November 1890, p. 2.

39 Walker, R. B., 'German language press and people in South Australia 1848–1900, *RAHSJ*, vol. 58, pt 2, June 1972, pp. 121–40; and *Pioneer*, 24 January 1891, pp. 65–6, 3 October 1891, pp. 92–3, and 25 June 1892, pp. 146–7; also Burgmann, V. *'In Our Time'*, pp. 149–51.

40 McMullin, R., *The Light on the Hill, the Australian Labor Party 1891-1991*, p. 12. On League's platform, see Clark, *Sources of Australian History*, pp. 410-11.
41 *QPD*, vol. 70, 18 July 1893, p. 234.
42 Hirst, J., *A Republican Manifesto*, pp. 33-41.
43 Ibid., p. 35. Calls for a republic were also defeated at the People's Federal Convention in Bathurst in 1896. The final report of the Convention stated that no concessions were made to untimely and ill-advised republicanism (Clark, C. M. H. (ed.), *Select Documents in Australian History*, vol. 2, pp. 504-7).
44 Macintyre, S., 'Corowa and the voice of the people', *CHJ*, no. 33, March 1994, pp. 4-5.
45 *SMH*, 4 July 1893 and 5 July 1893.
46 Macintyre, S., 'Corowa and the voice of the people', p. 6.
47 *VPD*, vol. 66, 8 July 1891, p. 275.
48 *AS*, 22 November 1889. Also Thomas Walker in *NSW PD*, vol. 61, 7 December 1892, p. 2528, and *Truth*, 29 March 1891, p. 3.
49 *Hummer*, 13 February 1892, p. 1. *Hummer*, 6 February 1892, and 13 February 1892, p. 1 and 19 March 1892, p. 1. Also McLachlan, p. 156 and Markey, R., *The Making of the Australian Labor Party*, p. 209. Also see Birrell, R., *A Nation of Our Own*, p. 111.
50 *Bulletin*, 25 August 1894, p. 4. For the fate of Henry Lawson's republicanism in the 1890s, see Roderick, *Henry Lawson: A Life*, pp. 60-5, 73, 77 and 81.
51 Lawson, p. 151. Lawson claims the *Bulletin* hauled down its republican flag on 25 August 1894, but only three months later its platform explicitly stated that it favoured 'a Republican form of Government' (see Docker, J., *The Nervous Nineties*, pp. 33-4 and *Bulletin*, 17 November 1894, p. 2). Also *Bulletin* calling for separation on 27 April 1895, p. 6.
52 *Bulletin*, 14 November 1896.
53 *Truth*, 26 July 1891, p. 1.
54 *AW*, 13 June 1896 and 23 May 1896. Quote from *AW*, 12 June 1897, p. 2.
55 Roderick, C., *Henry Lawson, A Life*, pp. 61-2.
56 Cheryl Saunders' chapter on Financial Settlement, in Craven, G., *The Convention Debates 1891-1898. Commentaries Indices and Guide*, vol. VI, p. 149.
57 *SMH*, 5 January 1891, p. 4. *AS*, 7 May 1889, p. 4. For republican complaints regarding the apathy of the general public see *AS*, 14 June 1889, p. 4; *Bulletin*, 14 November 1896; and Lawson, p. 151. For comments on the duality of allegiance see the speech of E. Coombes, *NSW PD*, Legislative Council, vol. 66, 30 May 1893, p. 7620; also Hall, H., *Australia and England—A Study in Imperial Relations*, pp. 143-4; and Dilke, C., *Problems of Great Britain*, p. 340; and Jebb, R., *Studies in Colonial Nationalism*, pp. 198-9. For a good example of the importance of communication technology in bringing Australia and Britain closer together, see *AS*, 21 February 1891, p. 5.
58 *Truth*, 12 October 1890, p. 2.
59 *Bulletin*, 13 March 1897, p. 7.
60 'Federation and Democracy', an article by Robert Thomson in *Truth*, 22 March 1891, p. 1.

61 *AS*, 'Forcing a republic', 3 April 1891. Also *QPD*, vol. 70, 18 July 1893, pp. 231–5; *NSW PD*, vol. 61, 23 November 1892, pp. 2092, 2169, 2494–9, 2517–20, 3000, and vol. 66, 30 May 1893, pp. 7626, 7620, and vol. 81, 7 November 1895, p. 2452. There were exceptions, of course. Walker, Buchanan until his death in April 1891, Rae, Brown and Hutchison, who argued convincingly for a plebiscite on the question of Federation under the Crown, *NSW PD*, 11 January 1893, vol. 61, p. 3042 and 7 November 1895, vol. 81, pp. 2450–3; Brown, Legislative Council, 23 May 1893, vol. 66, pp. 7401–4; Walker, 7 December 1892, vol. 61, p. 2528. Black in *NSW PD*, vol. 61, 7 December 1892, p. 2532.

62 *NSW PD*, vol. 61, 24 November 1892, p. 2159.

63 *VPD* (McIntyre), vol. 66, 27 August 1891, p. 1112.

64 For Bruce Mansfield's excellent investigation of the change in E. W. O'Sullivan's republicanism as a reflection of general trends see Mansfield, B. E., *Australian Democrat. The Career of E. W. O'Sullivan 1846–1890*, pp. 256–65.

65 Barton, E., in *NSW PD*, vol. 61, 23 November 1892, pp. 2092 and 2386. 'Despotic' was used by Arthur Rae, see *NSW PD*, 12 October 1893, vol. 67, p. 412; lack of liberty by J. Fitzgerald, see vol. 61, p. 2521.

66 *NO*, 7 July 1894, p. 5. *Bulletin* quoted in *Liberator*, November 1888, p. 104. *Hummer*, 16 January 1892, p. 3, and 30 January 1892, p. 6.

67 Black, George, Papers 1874–1933, MLMSS 256 Box 5. Also see Black, G., *Draft Federation Bill* 1897 (Mitchell Library).

10 THE IMPERIAL MARDI GRAS 1901–1963

1 Roderick, C., *Henry Lawson. A Life*, pp. 314–17 and Grimshaw, C., 'Australian nationalism and the imperial connection 1900–1914', p. 167.

2 On parade, see Clark, C. M. H., *A History of Australia*, vol. V, p. 177. On Constitution, see Grimshaw, p. 162. *Australian Constitution*, p. 5. On boundaries, see Ward, R., *A Nation for a Continent, A History of Australia 1901–1975*, Heinemann, 1985, p. 12. Alomes, S., *A Nation at Last. The Changing Character of Australian Nationalism*, p. 39.

3 Cunneen, C., *King's Men: Australia's Governors-General from Hopetoun to Isaacs*, pp. 188–90. On lack of independence in Constitution, see Clark, vol. V, pp. 177–80.

4 *SMH*, 21 March 1932, p. 10.

5 Cannadine, D., 'The context, performance and meaning of ritual. The British monarchy and the invention of tradition c.1820–1877', in Hobsbawm, E. and Ranger, T. (eds), *The Invention of Tradition*, pp. 101–64; Inglis, K., 'The imperial connection, telegraphic communication between England and Australia 1872–1902', in Madden, A. F. and Morris-Jones, W. H. (eds), *Australia and Britain: Studies in a Changing Relationship*, pp. 21–38; and Alomes, pp. 23–4.

6 Souter, *Lion and Kangaroo*, ch. 6; also Firth, S. and Hoorn, Jeanette, 'From Empire Day to Cracker Night', in Arnold, J., Spearritt, P. and Walker, D. (eds), *Out of Empire. The British Dominion of Australia*, pp. 127–48. Fewster, K.,

'Politics, pageantry and purpose—the 1920 tour of Australia by the Prince of Wales', p. 63. The Labor member's for Riverina (Robertson's) speech in the House of Representatives before the royal tour in 1954 emphasised the bipartisan nature of loyalty to the throne: *CAPD*, H of R, 12 November 1953, pp. 146–7.

7 For the excessive loyalty displayed during the 1920 tour by the Prince of Wales see Fewster. The 1954 royal tour is best covered by Spearritt, P., 'Royal progress: the Queen and her Australian subjects', pp. 75–94. For a good example of Menzies' loyalist rhetoric, see his introduction to Davis, R., *Elizabeth our Queen*, p. 9, or Brett, J., *Robert Menzies' Forgotten People*, pp. 129–55.

8 *The Royal Visit and You*, 1954. For an appreciation of loyalist philosophy see Ingamells, R., *Royalty and Australia*, pp. 84 and 88–9, especially Menzies' introduction.

9 My thanks to Jane Connors for this reference. The article by Chiplin can be found in *CR*, June 1953, pp. 177–9. A more extensive discussion is in Maher, L. 'Dissent, disloyalty and disaffection', pp. 1–78.

10 Kwan, E., 'The Australian flag, ambiguous symbol of nationality in Melbourne and Sydney 1920–21', *AHS*, vol. 26, October 1994, pp. 280–303, at p. 297.

11 Souter, p. 281.

12 *CAPD*, vol. S. 25, 27 February 1964, p. 93.

13 Alomes, S., 'Australian nationalism in the eras of imperialism and internationalism', in Arnold, Spearritt and Walker (eds), p. 181.

14 Clark, vol. V, p. 178.

15 Duffy quoted in Meaney, N. (ed.), *Australia and the World: A Documentary History 1870–1970*, p. 222. O'Farrell, P., *Vanished Kingdoms*, UNSW Press, 1990, pp. 225 and 248 and MacDonagh, O., et al., *Irish Culture and Nationalism 1750–1950*, Macmillan, 1983, p. 80. Mannix declaring his loyalty to Australia 'first' in Souter, p. 262. For a good analysis of the Irish Catholic rejection of Empire Day see Firth and Hoorn, in Arnold, Spearrit and Walker (eds), pp. 127–48. Implication statement, see Kwan, p. 292.

16 Crowley, F. (ed.), *Modern Australia*, vol. IV, 1901–1939, Nelson, 1978, p. 342.

17 *CAPD*, House of Representatives, vol. 94, 11 November 1920, pp. 6384, 6385, 6387, 6400–1, 6440–1 and 6470–1. See especially J. H. Catts quoting Joseph Cook's pro-republican speech in New South Wales Parliament some thirty years earlier, p. 6401.

18 *VPD*, vol. 97, 25 June 1901, pp. 109–25. Ibid., p. 125 (Pendergast).

19 For O'Dowd's *Tocsin* see McLachlan, N., *Waiting for the Revolution*, p. 178 and McKinlay, B. (ed.), *Australian Labor History in Documents*, vol. II, pp. 25–7. A good example of the Hobart *Clipper* can be found in Alomes, S. and Jones, C. (eds), *Australian Nationalism—A Documentary History*, pp. 141–2. Also Booker, M., *A Republic of Australia. What Would It Mean?*, pp. 15–16 for Broken Hill *Flame*.

20 *Labor Call* debated the republican question in 1920, see Fewster, p. 62. Also Labor Senator J. C. Stewart speaking in the Senate in 1910, in Meaney (ed.),

p. 195. Stewart hoped for an Australian republic by 2001. On left wing, see McKinlay (ed.), vol. III, p. 41.
21 Alomes and Jones (eds), p. 162.
22 Amos, K., *The New Guard Movement 1931–1935*, pp. 24, 26, 64, 74 and *SMH* 13 May 1932, p. 8. Communists were reported as being behind a proposal to abolish Empire Day in State schools in 1932: *SMH*, 11 May 1932, p. 11.
23 Communist Party of Australia. Statement of Aims. Also see Spearritt, p. 81.
24 In the 1950s the CPA did use some language reminiscent of more mainstream republicanism. In the report from the 18th Congress in April 1958 entitled 'Australia's Path to Socialism' (Current Books, 1958, p. 18) the people's programme spoke of asserting Australian independence by proclaiming a democratic republic and putting an end to the interference of imported Governors-General and Governors representing the Crown. See Meaney (ed.), *Australia and the World*, p. 300 for *DT* report of a Labor Council meeting at the Domain in 1921 where the Union Jack was torn to shreds by men wishing to fly the red flag instead. Also, the mandatory loyalty meeting that followed, pp. 302–5. See Lang's 1936 speech in Alomes and Jones (eds), p. 206.
25 Stephensen, P. R., *The Foundations of Culture in Australia*, p. 142, also pp. 18, 19, 66, 67 and 145–8; and Ward, R., pp. 211–313. And for the article that provoked Stephensen and his reply see Alomes and Jones (eds), pp. 254–6, and McLachlan, p. 233. Finally, see Muirden, B., *The Puzzled Patriots. The Story of the Australia First Movement*, pp. 1–4, 12–14, 152–63.
26 Stephensen, p. 66.
27 Hudson, W. J. and Sharp, M. P., *Australian Independence*, p. 138. For the adoption of the statute by Federal parliament in 1942 see Meaney (ed.), *Australia and the World*, pp. 476–8.
28 Crisp, L. F., 'The appointment of Sir Isaac Isaacs as Governor-General of Australia, 1930. J. H. Scullin's account of the Buckingham Palace interviews', p. 257; also Cowen, Z., *Isaac Isaacs*, pp. 192–205.
29 Cunneen, pp. 188, 192 and 193.
30 McLachlan, p. 214 and Hudson and Sharp, p. 54. Telegram in Meaney (ed.), *Australia and the World*, pp. 273–4.
31 Hudson and Sharp, pp. 86 and 87.
32 Ibid, pp. 75–6, 90 and 122.
33 Ibid., pp. 129, 130 and 133. Winterton, G., 'The evolution of a separate Australian Crown', *MULR*, vol. 19, no. 1, 1993, pp. 1–22, at p. 21.
34 Hudson and Sharp, p. 133. Also see Bruce in Meaney (ed.), *Australia and the World*, insisting on legislative independence on the one hand and closer links with Empire and 'British nationality', pp. 358–9.
35 Menzies, R., 'The function of the Crown', in Davis, R.; Ingamells, R., pp. 14 and 17; E. J. Harrison's introduction to *The Royal Visit and You*; and Harrison in *CAPD*, House of Representatives, vol. 213, 20 June 1951, pp. 142–3.
36 Hancock, W. K., *Argument of Empire*, p. 12.
37 Firth and Hoorn in Arnold, Spearritt and Walker (eds), pp. 127–47. Gavin Souter uses the word 'tempered' in *Lion and Kangaroo*, p. 307.
38 Alomes and Jones (eds), pp. 215–19.

39 Ward, R., p. 191.
40 Meaney (ed.), *Australia and the World*, p. 549.
41 Spearritt, 'The British Dominion of Australia', in Arnold, Spearritt and Walker (eds), pp. 10–11.
42 Alomes and Jones (eds), p. 160.
43 Eddy, J. and Schreuder, D. (eds), *The Rise of Colonial Nationalism 1880–1914*, pp. 46–9.
44 McKinlay (ed.), vol. II, p. 72.
45 Eddy and Schreuder (eds), p. 135.

11 THE END OF THE AFFAIR 1963–1995

1 Miller, T., 'Anglo–Australian partnership in defence of the Malaysian area', in Madden and Morris-Jones (eds), *Australia and Britain: Studies in a Changing Relationship*, pp. 85–9. On EEC, see Perkins, J. O., 'Changing Economic Relations', in Madden and Morris-Jones (eds), p. 181.
2 Perkins, p. 191. An early example of this loyalty shift can be seen in the article on the royal tour of 1963 in *Bulletin*, 9 March 1963, p. 11; also Horne, D., *The Lucky Country Revisited*, Dent, 1987, pp. 92–3 and 114–17.
3 Meaney, N. (ed.), *Australia and the World: A Documentary History 1870–1970*, p. 705. Fortress Australia in Borne, H. D., 'British immigration to Australia', in Ibid., p. 114.
4 Sherington, G., *Australia's Immigrants—1788–1978*, pp. 150 and 151.
5 Meaney (ed.), pp. 635–7.
6 Dutton, G., 'British subject', *Nation*, 6 April 1963, pp. 15–16; also Horne, D., et. al., *The Coming Republic*, pp. 6–9.
7 Dutton, 'British subject', p. 16. Also Dutton, *Out in the Open*, pp. 281–2.
8 Dutton G. (ed.), *Australia and the Monarchy*. Also *Bulletin* editorial, 'A Republican Australia', 30 October 1965, p. 13 and Dutton, *Out in the Open*, pp. 329–30.
9 Dutton (ed.), p. 169.
10 Ibid., pp. 7–8.
11 Horne, *The Coming Republic*, p. 9; also Alomes, S. and Jones, C. (eds), *Australian Nationalism—A Documentary History*, pp. 128–9.
12 Horne, *The Coming Republic*, p. 9. On Horne, see *Bulletin*, 8 April 1967, pp. 22–5, and *Bulletin*, 27 November 1971, p. 27. See Horne, 'British and us', *Quadrant*, vol. 9, no. 1, January–February 1965, pp. 9–13. On Dutton and Horne, see Alomes and Jones (eds), pp. 348–50.
14 Australian Republican Party, Platform and Policy 1964, Victorian State Library (and election platform from which the quote comes). Also ARP Platform for Federal election 1969. See *Nation*, 20 April 1963, p. 15 for the letter of R. Mullins, Federal President of the ARP. Mullins wrote in reply to Dutton's article in *Nation*, 6 April 1963. Also Margaret Jones' article on the ARP in *SMH*, 27 June 1970, p. 18.
15 *Bulletin*, 20 November 1965, p. 30.
16 *OZ*, October 1965, p. 1. *OZ*, December 1963–January 1964, p. 1.
17 Walsh in Dutton (ed.), *Australia and the Monarchy*, p. 135.
18 Ibid., pp. 174–5.

19 *SMH*, 27 June 1970, p. 18.
20 Gough Whitlam, addressing National Press Club in Washington, August 1973, quoted in Meaney (ed.) *Australia and the World*, p. 750.
21 Horne, D., *Time of Hope, Australia 1966–72*, Angus & Robertson, 1980, pp. 154–5; and Crowley, F., *Tough Times: Australia in the Seventies*, pp. 30–4 and ch. 17.
22 Alomes, S., *A Nation at Last. The Changing Character of Australian Nationalism*, pp. 3 and 321. Also Crowley, pp. 262–6. Whitlam, G., *The Whitlam Government 1972–1975*, p. 130.
23 Alomes and Jones (eds), p. 355.
24 Whitlam, *The Whitlam Government*, pp. 130–52.
25 Bjelke-Petersen in Crowley, p. 341. *CAPD*, House of Representatives, vol. 82, 8 March 1973, pp. 407–8, vol. 86, 24 October 1973, p. 2626, vol. 85, 29 August 1973, pp. 533–40.
26 *CAPD*, H of R, vol. 83, 12 April 1973, pp. 1373–4.
27 Whitlam denied his government was republican in federal parliament, *CAPD*, H of R, vol. 83, 12 April 1973, p. 1374 and *The Whitlam Government*, p. 131.
28 *CAPD*, H of R, vol. 86, 24 October 1973, pp. 2626–9 (James and Morris); and vol. 82, H of R, 8 March 1973, p. 407. Whitlam, *The Whitlam Government*, p. 131.
29 *CAPD*, H of R, vol. 85, 23 August 1973, p. 359.
30 Goot, M., 'The Queen in the polls' in Arnold, J., Spearritt, P. and Walker, D., *Out of Empire. The British Dominion of Australia*, p. 298.
31 *Australian*, 17 November 1975, p. 7.
32 Ashbolt, A., 'It's Queen's move in Australia', *New Statesman*, 26 June 1976, p. 842. Bruce Petty's cartoons depicted Kerr with a crown on his head, see Gollan, M. (ed.), *Kerr and the Consequences*, p. 63.
33 *Australian*, 17 November 1975; also Detmold, M. J., *The Australian Commonwealth*, p. 226; *SMH*, 25 November 1975, p. 3; *Nation Review*, 14 November 1975; *SMH*, 24 January 1976, p. 2.
34 Myfanwy Gollan's introduction to Gollan (ed.), pp. 12–13.
35 Donald Horne, speaking at a Constitutional Conference in September 1977 in Melbourne. Donald Horne papers, Mitchell Library, Horne, MLMSS 3525, Add on 1871 Box 18.
36 Horne, D., *Death of the Lucky Country*, Penguin, 1976, pp. 44, 95–6.
37 Gollan (ed.), p. 14.
38 Ibid, pp. 12, 16–17, 38–9 and 65.
39 Ibid, pp. 52–3. On 'trustworthy constitution', see ibid, p. 76, and *CM*, 12 November 1976.
40 Claude Forell in Crowley, p. 338.
41 *C-M*, 16 November 1976 reported on a Remembrance Day meeting with the headline '1,000 voices call for a republic'. For results of polls: Gallup poll in *Sun*, 26 November 1976; Herald survey, *SMH*, 11 December 1976, p. 1; Age poll, *Age*, 11 December 1976. Also see *Sun Herald*, 19 December 1976. For Kerr speaking against republicanism see *SMH*, 28 October 1976. Whitlam, *DT*, 2 November 1976. *Australian*, Wednesday, 20 October 1976. Also see *Australian*, 1 December 1976 (Sir Mark Oliphant). Copies of *Eureka*

published by People for Australian Independence can be found in the Mitchell Library. *Eureka* relied more heavily on traditional left-wing rhetoric complaining about US and colonial imperialism, unemployment and foreign ownership (*Eureka*, November 1976). 'Independence' movements also emerged on university campuses, see for example 'Students for Australian independence', La Trobe University, 1977–1979. In addition, there were republican organisations such as the more left-wing 'People for Australian Independence' which included the journalist and historian Humphrey McQueen. Also *Sun Herald*, 19 December 1976.
42 *Australian*, 1 December and 25 November 1976.
43 *Australian*, 23 July 1976.
44 Rallies were held in other capitals: *C-M*, 4 March 1977. Donald Horne addressed the National Press Club luncheon in Canberra on 7 March 1977, transcript of tape recording, Commonwealth of Australia, Parliamentary Library, Canberra, p. 2. Also *Australian*, 8 March 1977; *Age*, 8 March 1977 and *SMH*, 8 March 1977.
45 *Mercury*, 10 March 1977; *SMH*, 14 March 1977; *SMH*, 14 March 1977; *Australian*, 18 March 1977; *CT*, 11 March 1977 and *NT*, 24 September 1977. CAPD, H of R, vol. 104, 1977, pp. 65, 68, 113, 291–2 and 507.
46 On Horne, see ibid. CAPD, Senate, vol. 572, 16 March 1977, p. 215. *Heritage*, March–May 1977, p. 17.
47 Details of Meetings and the Constitutional Conference can be found in Donald Horne Papers, MLMSS 3525, Add on 1871 Box 18. Exhibition details in Donald Horne Papers, MLMSS 3525, Add on 1871 35 (38).
48 Donald Horne Papers, MLMSS 3525, Add on 1871 35 (38).
49 Dutton, G. (ed.), *Republican Australia*. Also *Age*, 19 August 1977 and 23 July 1977; *Bulletin*, 20 August 1977.
50 Horne, D. in Dutton, *Republican Australia*, p. 13.
51 Polls quoted in Goot, M., 'Contingent inevitability' in Winterton, G. (ed.), *We the People*, p. 66. Also *SMH*, 10 June 1995, p. 1.
52 Goot in Winterton (ed.), pp. 80–5.
53 Horne, National Press Club Address, 7 March 1977, p. 4. Also see Horne, D., *Power from the People*, p. 17.
54 Australian Republican Movement, Platform, 1991.
55 Monday Conference 177 and 237. Transcripts held at Parliamentary Library, Canberra.
56 Donald Horne Papers, MLMSS 3525, Add on 1871 Box 18.
57 White reported in *C-M*, 7 March 1977. Dutton (ed.), *Republican Australia*, p. vii. Also Hume, L. J., 'Another look at the cultural cringe', *PTN*, vol. 3, no. 1, April 1991, pp. 1–36. Hume claims the cultural cringe was an invention of left intellectuals who needed it to advance their own nationalist agenda.
58 See note 41 for *C-M* report.
59 For editorials during the Queen's visit which were largely critical of republicanism, see *Mercury*, 10 March 1977; *SMH*, 14 March 1977 and 7 March 1977; *Advertiser*, 10 March 1977. Malcolm Fraser declared that an Australian republic would be a 'tragedy', *SMH*, 4 April 1977. There was also discussion about Prince Charles becoming Governor-General which was

quashed by the palace: *Age*, 10 March 1977 and *SMH*, 9 February 1979. The Australian Heritage Society's response to the republican debate can be found in *Heritage*, March 1977–May 1977 and December 1977–February 1978.
60 Lionel Bowen, *Australian*, 6 April 1977; *LE*, 5 April 1977; *SMH*, 5 April 1977 and *Sun-Pictorial*, 26 September 1977. Whitlam published *On Australia's Constitution* in 1977 and came out strongly in support of a republic, see pp. 8–12 especially. His position had hardened since 1976, see *Australian*, 20 October 1976, p. 9; *SMH*, 14 May 1977, 13 November 1978 and 17 October 1978.
61 CFD report in *DT*, 12 November 1979. Whitlam, G., *The Truth of the Matter*, p. 181.
62 Whitlam, G., *On Australia's Constitution*, p. 12.
63 *Sun Herald*, 24 April 1977: '64% against a Republic'.
64 *C-M*, 7 February 1979. Also *NT*, 14–19 March 1979, p. 26. Kerr, J., *Matters for Judgment*, p. 391. CFD continued under the leadership of Bill and Joan Symonds, who continued the push for a republic. They named 11 November 1979 as 'Republic Day' and continued to hold republican gatherings on the anniversary of the dismissal into the 1980s (CFD *Newsletters*, Mitchell Library).
65 Clark, M. (1979), *Occasional Writings and Speeches*, Fontana Collins, 1980, p. 216.
66 Bennett, T., Buckridge, P., Carter, D. and Mercer, C. (eds), *Celebrating the Nation: A Critical Study of Australia's Bicentenary*, Allen & Unwin, 1992, see Carter's chapter 'Manning Clark's hat: public and national intellectuals', p. 88.
67 Ibid., pp. 98 and 102–3.
68 Bridge, C. (ed.), *Manning Clark: Essays on his Place in History*, Melbourne University Press, 1994, see John Warhurst's chapter 'In the public arena, p. 156. Atkinson, A., 'A great historian?' in ibid., p. 122.
69 Warhurst in Bridge, C. (ed.), pp. 154–5 and Miriam Dixson, 'Clark and national identity', in ibid., p. 191.
70 Warhurst in Bridge, C. (ed.), pp. 157–61, pp. 156 and 162, and Clark, *Occasional Writings*, p. 230.
71 Grassby, A. in Dutton (ed.), *Republican Australia*, p. 190 and Kalantzis, M. *et al.*, 'Mistaken identity' in Whitlock, G. and Carter, D., *Images of Australia*, University of Queensland Press, 1992, pp. 129–41.
72 Turner, G., *Making it National*, Allen & Unwin, 1994, pp. 92 and 66. Bennett, Buckridge, Carter and Mercer (eds), pp. 188–9. Also *Australian Historical Studies*, vol. 23, no. 91, October 1988.
73 Turner, pp. 7 and 119.
74 Dixson and Clarke in Bridge (ed.), p. 194.
75 Tony Palfreeman, 1990. Palfreeman lectures in the Department of Political Science at the University of New South Wales. This remark was made in a private conversation with the author.
76 *Age*, 28 July 1981. The Young Liberals voted against a republic (24:20) in the following month, *Australian*, 3 August 1981.
77 On 8 December 1983 Andrew Peacock and Doug Anthony issued a press release which warned of the Labor Party's enthusiasm for a republic. Federal

parliamentary debates on the Citizenship Amendment bill and Flag's Amendment bill reveal a wealth of debate on the republic, allegiance and identity. Most of it is extremely repetitive. For Hawke's non-committal statements on republic see *Age*, 22 October 1987 and *C-M*, 10 October 1987. For republican debate associated with the election of the Hawke government see: *Sunday Times*, 3 April 1983, p. 11; *AFR*, 10 May 1983; *SMH*, 26 March 1983; *DT*, 28 January 1985.

78 Advertisements in *Australian*, 19 November 1984, 24 November 1984 and 10 October 1983. Snedden in *C-M*, 15 September 1983.
79 *CAPD*, H of R, vol. 145, 25 November 1985, pp. 3596–7.
80 *Heritage*, September–November 1986, p. 5.
81 Australian Republican Party, Platform 1982 (State Library of Victoria). For more on fringe republican elements such as Peter Consandine and Brian Buckley see *SM* (Brisbane), 12 July 1987 and *WA*, 3 September 1988. See Consandine's arguments in Giles, R. (ed.), *For and Against. Public Issues in Australia*, Brooks Waterloo, 1989, pp. 259–67. See also *SMH* Good Weekend Magazine, 25 July 1992, pp. 16–21.
82 McMillan, J., Evans, G. and Storey, H., *Australia's Constitution, Time for Change?* and G. Evans and G. Reid, Counterpoint Forum, 'God Save the Queen? Australia as a Republic', 29 September 1982, University of Western Australia.
83 Dutton in *Bulletin*, 14 April 1981 and *Australian Playboy*, January 1982. In 1987 former New South Wales Premier Neville Wran called for an Australian republic by 2001: *DT*, 8 October 1987, 9 October 1987 and 10 October 1987.
84 *SMH*, 22 August 1987, p. 44.
85 *SMH*, 15 July 1985.
86 The dilemma is identifiable in Australia Day editorials especially *Age*, 26 January 1988 and *SMH*, 26 January 1988 (and 31 December 1988), also *Mercury*, 26 January 1988. Spearritt, P., 'Celebration of a nation: the triumph of spectacle', *Australian Historical Studies*, vol. 23, no. 91, October 1988, p. 20.
87 Murphy, J., 'Conscripting the past: the Bicentenary and everyday life', in ibid., p. 54. *SMH*, 15 July 1985.
88 *NT*, 8 March 1987. Kirk also withdrew funds for a film on republicanism, *SMH*, 9 March 1987.
89 Early 1980s editorials seem to reflect the view that Australia was not yet ready for a republic: *Australian*, 21 March 1983; *CT*, 7 May 1984; *Age*, 31 March 1986; *Mercury*, 13 December 1985. Hayden's appointment did cause a stir: P. P. McGuinness in *AFR*, 13 July 1988; *Sun Herald*, 29 January 1989; *SMH*, 13 January. For the debate that did exist in the Press in 1988 see: *SMH*, 24 January 1988; *ST*, 10 January 1988; *SMH*, 29 April 1988; *Age*, 9 May 1988; *SMH*, 10 February 1988; *Quadrant*, June 1988; *LIJ*, vol. 62, no. 12, December 1988; *Airways*, November/December 1987, pp. 53–4; *Australian*, 31 December 1988.
90 Final Report of the Constitutional Commission 1988, vol. 1, pp. 314–15. See I. G. Cunliffe's (secretary of the Commission) letter to *ST*, 17 January 1988,

'We'll stay a monarchy'. Debate on Constitutional Change and Republic in *AJFS*, vol. 20, no. 4, July 1988, pp. 267–72 (Sir Maurice Byers).
91 Details of referendum in *CBPA*, no. 55, 8 June 1988, pp. 12–17. For details on Australia Act see Final Report of Constitutional Commission, 1988, vol. 1, pp. 76–8. *CAPD*, H of R, vol. 145, 25 November 1985, p. 3583 (Nehl).
92 *SMH*, 30 September 1993, 26 October 1995, 14 September 1993.
93 Prime Minister Bob Hawke, 6 April 1990, quoted in CFD, *Newsletter*, June/July 1990, p. 8.
94 *SMH*, 20 July 1990.
95 *SMH*, 6 April 1991, 4 April 1991, p. 3. *SMH*, 26 March 1991. Astronaut cartoon in *DTM*, 8 July 1991, p. 10.
96 *SMH*, 26 June 1991, p. 7 and 25 June 1991, p. 1. *CM*, 26 June 1991, p. 1; Bannon in *CT*, 27 July 1991; also Jim McLelland, *SMH*, 17 July 1991, p. 14.
97 Hewson in *SMH*, 26 June 1991; Ruxton in *CM*, 26 June 1991.
98 See all major dailies on 8 July 1991. ARM pamphlet 'Australian Republican Movement'.
99 Arena, Franca, 'Lead up to the launch of the Australian republic', unpublished document.
100 Keneally, T., *Our Republic*, p. 77; elitist allegations in *Australian*, 9 and 11 October 1995.
101 *TA*, 22 July 1991; *Sun Herald*, 7 July 1991; *Age*, 25 July 1991; *Mercury*, 10 July 1991. *AFR*, 10 July 1991; *DTM*, 8 July 1991, p. 10 (2001).
102 *Australian*, 19 August 1995.
103 Keating's speech in Horne, *The Coming Republic*, p. 27. For Keating's statements on Britain and Singapore, see *Australian*, 29 February 1992, p. 1. On changing the flag, *SMH*, 1 February 1992, p. 3. Republic as part of the election campaign, *SMH*, 25 February 1993, p. 1.
104 *Australian*, 29 April 1993, also 27–28 March 1993 and 6 October 1993. Kelly's personal views on a republic can be found in *Quadrant*, vol. 37, no. 11, November 1993, pp. 10–15. Keating continued the Republic–Asia link during his 1994 visit to France, *Australian*, 9 June 1994, p. 1.
105 ARM preamble to platform, 1991. Keneally's speech to the National Press Club, 15 July 1992, pp. 5 and 11 (available from ARM); and Keating's speaking of the need for a 'singularly Australian identity to replace the old imperial one', in *SMH*, 27 June 1992, p. 1.
106 *TA*, 26 April 1993. Fahey in *SMH*, 29 April 1993.
107 *SMH*, 27 January 1994, p., 1.
108 Academic debate best observed in *AJPS*, vol. 28, 1993, special issue 'Republicanism'; *LS*, vol. 6, no. 2, 1992; Hudson, W. and Carter, D. (eds), *The Republicanism Debate*; Headon, D., Warden, J. and Gammage, B. (eds), *Crown or Country*; Winterton (ed.); Atkinson, A., *The Muddle Headed Republic*. For Women and the Republic, see *Vox Republicae*, J. Hoorn and D. Goodman (eds), special issue of *JAS*, no. 47, 1996.
109 *CAPD*, House of Representatives, 27 February 1992, p. 374.
110 *SMH*, 8 June 1995 (Keating's speech) and 12 July 1995, p. 1 (Howard) and *Republic*, Winter, 1995, no. 2, vol. 3, p. 3.

111 *Australian*, 30 August 1995, p. 9; also Robert Manne in *Quadrant*, April 1995, pp. 2–4.
112 Keneally in *Australian*, 16 July 1992. Horne in *Sun Herald*, 2 February 1992. Malcolm Turnbull, Speech to the National Press Club, 18 March 1992 (available from ACM).
113 *Australian*, 28 June 1991 (John Paul); *Bulletin*, 27 October 1992 (D. McNicoll).
114 Quoted in *An Australian Republic, the Options, the Report*, vol. 1, pp. 39–40. This view is also reflected in 'Leadership beyond politics', Australians for Constitutional Monarchy, charter for the defence of the Australian Constitution (available from ACM).
115 *Quadrant*, July–August 1993, p. 38.
116 *SMH*, 23 April 1992, p. 15.
117 *Australian*, 23 September 1991. Winterton's Constitution can be found in Winterton, G. (ed.). Saunders in *Australian*, 30 April 1993, p. 19.
118 Keating, P. J., *An Australian Republic: The Way Forward*, p. 3; also subsequent parliamentary debates, *CAPD*, vol. House of Representatives, 29 June 1995, pp. 2639–78.
119 *SMH*, 26 June 1994. Also *IM*, June 1993, p. 22 and Republic Advisory Committee, *The Options—An Overview*, p. 22. This theme continued in June 1995 after Paul Keating's speech. The broadsheet press described Keating's republic as 'modest': *CM*, 8 June 1995, *Australian*, 8 June 1995.
120 *Australian*, 29–30 January 1994, p. 18.
121 Examples of maximimalists in O'Brien, P., 'We the People', *IM*, June 1993, pp. 20–3; Fraser, A., 'Strong republicanism and a citizens' constitution' in Hudson and Carter (eds), pp. 36–60; Walker, G. de Q., Ratnapala, S. and Kasper, W., *Restoring the True Republic*; and Thompson, E., 'Giving ourselves better government' in Horne, *The Coming Republic*.
122 Watson, D., 'A toast to the post-modern republic', *Island*, issue 55, Winter 1993, p. 5.
123 *SMH*, 28 January 1994, p. 11.
124 On Mabo, see *DTM*, 29 February 1992, and speech of Justice Meagher in *SMH*, 20 November 1992. Prince Charles in *SMH*, 28 January 1994, p. 10. For the crisis in 'identity' see the front cover of *TA*, 6 April 1992; *Australian*, 9–10 October 1993, p. 34.
125 Keating's 'tugging the forelock', *CM*, 29 February 1992, p. 1; 'licking the British bootstraps', *DTM*, 28 February 1992, p. 1. 'Bog Irish', *Herald Sun*, 6 March 1992, p. 3; Blainey in *Sunday Herald Sun*, 1 March 1992, p. 16.
126 *AFR*, 26 February 1992, p. 5; *DTM*, 29 February 1992.
127 *SMH*, 26 February 1992.
128 *DTM*, 28 February 1992, p. 11.
129 *Age*, 26 February 1992. Response of British press to Keating: *CM*, 29 February 1992; *AFR*, 26 February 1992; also *Australian*, 28 February 1992.
130 Speech by Prime Minister Paul Keating, Corowa, 31 July 1993, pp. 5–7; also *DTM*, 29 February 1992, and Keating's H. V. Evatt lecture, 28 April 1993.

EPILOGUE

1. See, for example, Smith, D., 'The Australian Constitution and the monarchy/republic debate' in Grainger, G. and Jones, K. (eds), *The Australian Constitutional Monarchy*, pp. 71–86 at p. 85. Also Kirby, M., 'Reflections on constitutional monarchy' in Hudson, W. and Carter, D. (eds), *The Republicanism Debate*, pp. 61–76 at p. 75, and Galligan, B., *A Federal Republic*, pp. 12–15. See Maddox arguing against the disguised republic: Maddox, G., 'The possible impact of republicanism on Australian government in Winterton, G. (ed.), *We the People*, pp. 125–38 at p. 126.
2. See, for example, early Labor Party platforms in McKinlay, B. (ed.), *Australian Labor History in Documents*, vol. 2, The Labor Party, pp. 10, 28, 31–2, 38 and 72 where the republic is either omitted or implicitly referred to under the euphemisms 'national sentiment' or 'national basis'.
3. For 'failure' see *SMH*, 4 May 1996, Spectrum, p. 4.
4. For Keating's speech see *SMH* and *Australian*, June 1995.
5. See, for example, Horne, D. in *Australian*, 29 March 1996, special liftout, 'The Constitution, Towards 2001' p. 7. Also Horne in *Australian*, 17–18 February 1996, p. 27. See McKenna, M. in *SMH*, 26 January 1995, p. 17, 27 March 1995, p. 13, 4 July 1995, p. 13, 25 January 1996, p. 17. For Constitutional Centenary Foundation see *SMH* 1 January 1996, p. 3. For Women and the Republic see Hoorn, J. and Goodman, D. (eds), *Vox Republicae: Feminism and the Republic*.
6. The most recent and impressive analysis of the monarchist position is Brett, J., 'From monarchy to republic: into the symbolic void?' in Hoorn, J. and Goodman, D. (eds), ibid., pp. 17–32.

Select Bibliography

NEWSPAPERS

Sydney
Atlas (1844–49)
Australian (1824–48 and 1964 to present)
Australian Financial Review (1951 to present)
Australian Star (1887–1910)
Australian Town and Country Journal (1870–1919)
Australian Workman (1890–97)
Bulletin (1880 to present)
Catholic Freeman's Journal (1850–1942)
Citizen (1846–47)
Communist Review (1941–43)
Currency Lad (1832–33)
Daily Mirror (1941–90)
Daily Telegraph (1879–1990)
Daily Telegraph Mirror (1990 to present)
Democrat (1884)
Empire (1850–75)
Illustrated Sydney News (1853–94)
Independently Monthly (July 1989–September 1993); as *Independent* (October 1993 to present)
Land (1911 to present)
Monitor (1826–41) (after 16 August 1828 as *Sydney Monitor*)
National Times (1971–86)
Nationalist (1888)
New Order (1884–1901)
People's Advocate (1848–56)
Press (1851)
Republican (1887–88)
Sun (1910–88)
Sun Herald (1953 to present)
Sunday Telegraph (1961 to present)
Sydney Gazette (1803–42)
Sydney Herald (1831–42)

Sydney Mail (1860–1938)
Sydney Morning Herald (1842 to present)
Time Australia (July 1986 to present)
Truth (1890–1958)

Outside Sydney:
Advertiser (1858 to present—Adelaide)
Age (1854 to present—Melbourne)
Argus (1846–1957—Melbourne)
Australian Republican (1890–91—Charters Towers)
Boomerang (1887–92—Brisbane)
Brisbane Courier (1846–1933)
Canberra Times (1926 to present)
Charters Towers Times (1888–91)
Courier-Mail (1933 to present)
Goulburn Herald (1848–1927)
Herald (1840 to present—Melbourne)
Hobart Town Daily Courier (1827–59)
Hummer (1891–92—Wagga Wagga)
Inquirer and Commercial News (1840–1901—Perth)
Launceston Examiner and Commercial and Agricultural Advertiser (1842–1900)
Liberator (1884–1904—Melbourne)
Mercury (1854 to present—Hobart)
National Advocate (1889–1963—Bathurst)
Newcastle Herald (1861 to present)
Newcastle Morning Herald and *Miner's Advocate* (1858–1980)
Pioneer (1890–92—Adelaide)
Radical (1887–90—Newcastle)
South Australian Register (1839–1900—Adelaide)
Sunday Mail (1923 to present—Brisbane)
West Australian (1833 to present)
Worker (1890–1905—Brisbane)

PAPERS – OFFICIAL CORRESPONDENCE

Black, George, Papers, MLMSS 256
Colonial Office Papers—*see notes for volumes used*
Despatches from US Consul-Generals in Sydney, 1836–1906, Mitchell Library, RAV FM4496
Historical Records of Australia—*see notes for volumes used*
Historical Records of New South Wales—*see notes for volumes used*
Horne, Donald, Papers, MLMSS 3525, Mitchell Library
Lang Papers, vols I, VII and XXII 1843–55, MLMSS A2221–A2249, Mitchell Library
Parkes Papers, MLMSS 4312, Mitchell Library

DEBATES/GOVERNMENT PUBLICATIONS

An Australian Republic, the Options, the Report. Australian Government Publishing Service, Canberra, 1993

Australasian Federal Convention, *Official Record of the Proceedings and Debates of the Australasian Federation Conference held in the Parliament House Melbourne*, Government Printer, Melbourne, 1890
Australian Constitution, Government Publishing Service, 1986
Australian Federal Convention, Melbourne 1897, *Official Record of the Debates*, Government Printer, Melbourne, 1897
Australian Federal Convention, Sydney 1897, *Official Report of the Debates*, Government Printer, Sydney, 1897
Barton, G. B., *Draft Constitution of the Commonwealth*, Government Press, 1891.
Commonwealth of Australia Parliamentary Debates—*see notes for specific references*
Evans, H., *Essays on Republicanism: small r republicanism*, Papers on Parliament, no. 24, Department of the Senate, Parliament House, Canberra, September 1994
Final Report of the Constitutional Commission 1988, vols 1 and 2, Australian Government Publishing Service, Canberra, 1988
Keating, P. J., *An Australian Republic: The Way Forward*, Australian Government Publishing Service, 1995
National Australasian Convention, Adelaide 1891, *Official Record of Proceedings and Debates*, Government Printer, Adelaide, 1891
National Australasian Convention, Sydney 1891, *Official Record of Proceedings and Debates*, Government Printer, Sydney, 1891
New South Wales Parliamentary Debates—*see notes for specific references*
Queensland Parliamentary Debates—*see notes for specific references*
The Royal Visit and You, Government Publishing Service, 1954
South Australian Parliamentary Debates—*see notes for specific references*
Victorian Parliamentary Debates—*see notes for specific references*
Votes and Proceedings of the Legislative Council of NSW 1843–55

THESES

Aveling, M., 'A history of the Australian Natives Association', PhD, Monash University, 1970.
Davies, G., 'The *Australian Republican*: a Charters Towers radical journal 1890–1891', BA Hons, James Cook University of North Queensland, 1988.
De Garis, B. K., 'The British influence on the federation of the Australian colonies', PhD, Oxford University, 1965.
McKenna, M., 'A history of republicanism in Australia, 1788–1880', PhD, University of New South Wales, 1995.
Mansfield, B., 'Australian nationalism and the growth of the labour movement in the 1880s', MA, Sydney University, 1951.
Tenniswood, W. Y., 'The policy of Great Britain regarding Australia: 1850–1900', PhD, Edinburgh University, 1936.

JOURNAL ARTICLES, PAMPHLETS AND BOOK CHAPTERS

Abbott, T., 'This taxing republic', *Quadrant*, vol. 37, no. 11, November 1993, pp. 16–17.

Ackland, M., 'Charles Harpur's republicanism', *Westerly*, vol. 29, October 1984, pp. 75–88.
Adams, W. P., 'Republicanism in political rhetoric before 1776', *American Speech*, vol. 85, no. 3, September 1970, pp. 397–421.
Anonymous, *A Plea for Separation*, George Robertson, 1888.
Atkinson, A., 'The Australian monarchy: imperfect but important', *Australian Journal of Political Science*, vol. 28, 1993, pp. 67–82.
Atkinson, A., 'Time, place and paternalism: early conservative thinking in NSW', *Australian Historical Studies*, vol. 23, no. 90, April 1988, pp. 1–18.
Atkinson, A., 'Towards independence: recipes for self-government in colonial NSW', in Russell P. and White R. (eds), *Pastiche I. Reflections on Nineteenth-Century Australia*, Allen & Unwin, Sydney, 1994, pp. 85–99.
Bailey, K. H., 'Self-government in Australia, 1860–1900', *Cambridge History of the British Empire*, vol. 7, pt. I, 1988 (First published 1933), pp. 395–424.
Banning, L., 'Jeffersonian ideology revisited', *William and Mary Quarterly*, vol. 43, January 1986, pp. 3–19.
Bastin, J. and Stoodley, J., 'F.C.B. Vosper: an Australian radical', *University Studies Journal*, vol. 5, no. 1, 1967, pp. 38–53.
Belchem, J., 'Republicanism, popular constitutionalism and the radical reform platform in early nineteenth-century England', *Social History*, vol. 6, no. 1, 1981, pp. 1–32.
Black, G., *Draft Federation Bill*, 1897 (Mitchell Library).
Blackton, C. S., 'Australian Nationality and Nationalism 1850–1900', *Historical Studies*, 9, May 1961, pp. 351–65.
Blackton, C. S., 'Australian Nationality and Nationalism: The Imperial Federationist Interlude', *Historical Studies*, 7, November 1955, pp. 1–16.
Blackton, C. S., 'Australian Nationality and Nativism. The Australian Natives Association, 1885–1901', *Journal of Modern History*, vol. 30, March 1958, pp. 37–46.
Blackton, C. S., 'The Australasian League 1851–1854', *Pacific Historical Review*, vol. 8, no. 4, December 1939, pp. 385–400.
Blackton, C. S., 'The Dawn of Australian National Feeling 1850–1856', *Pacific Historical Review*, vol. 24, no. 2, May 1955, pp. 121–37.
Blair, D., 'Daniel Deniehy. A recollection', *Centennial Magazine*, vol. 1, 1888, pp. 384–7, Mitchell Library.
Blair, D., 'Henry Parkes in 1850', *Centennial Magazine*, vol. 1, 1888, pp. 616–21, Mitchell Library.
Blair, D., 'John Dunmore Lang. A recollection', *Centennial Magazine*, vol. 1, 1888, pp. 488–92, Mitchell Library.
Blair, D., 'Sydney in 1850. Morals and manners', *Centennial Magazine*, vol. 1, 1888, pp. 685–9, Mitchell Library.
Bolton, G., 'Labour comes to Charters Towers', *Australian Society for the Study of Labour History*, no. 1, January 1962, pp. 25–34.
Cannadine, D., 'The context, performance and meaning of ritual. The British monarchy and the invention of tradition', *c*.1820–1877, in Hobsbawm E. and Ranger T. (eds), *The Invention of Tradition*, Cambridge University Press, Canto, 1992, pp. 101–64.

Churchward, L. G., 'The American influence on the Australian Labour Movement', *Historical Studies*, vol. 5, no. 19, November 1952, p. 258.

Cole, D., 'The crimson thread of kinship: ethnic ideas in Australia 1870–1914', *Historical Studies*, vol. 4, no. 56, April 1971, pp. 511–26.

Communist Party of Australia. *Statement of Aims*, Wright & Baker, 1931.

Condren, C., 'The Australian Commonwealth, a republic and republican virtue', *Legislative Studies*, vol. 6, no. 2, Summer 1992, pp. 31–4.

Connell, R. W., 'The convict rebellion of 1804', *Melbourne Historical Journal*, vol. 5, 1965, pp. 27–37.

Connolly, C. N., 'Class, birthplace, loyalty', *Historical Studies*, vol. 18, no. 71, pp. 210–32.

Cowen, Z., 'Governor-Generalship in the Commonwealth', *Journal of Royal Society of the Arts*, 13 August 1985, pp. 650–61.

Cowen, Z., 'The Australian head of state', *Quadrant*, April 1992, vol. 36, no. 4, pp. 63–73.

Cowen, Z., 'The legal implications of Australia's becoming a republic', *Australian Law Journal*, vol. 68, August 1994, pp. 587–92.

Craven, G. J., 'The constitutional minefield of Australian republicanism', *Policy* (St Leonards, NSW), vol. 8, no. 3, Spring 1992, pp. 33–6.

Crisp, L. F., 'The appointment of Sir Isaac Isaacs as Governor-General of Australia, 1930. J. H. Scullin's account of the Buckingham Palace interviews', *Historical Studies*, vol. 2, no. 42, April 1964, pp. 253–7.

Cristaudo, W., 'Republic of Australia?: the political philosophy of republicanism', *Current Affairs Bulletin*, vol. 69, no. 11, April 1993, pp. 4–9.

Daniel, E. and Potts, A., 'American republicanism and the disturbances on the Victorian Goldfields', *Historical Studies*, vol. 13, no. 50, April 1968, pp. 145–64.

Darcy, F., 'Charles Bradlaugh and the English republican movement 1868–1878', *Historical Journal*, vol. 25, no. 2, 1982, pp. 367–83.

Davies, G., 'A time of perceived rebellion. A comparison of the Charters Towers and Rockhampton showcase trials of 1891', *Australian Journal of Politics and History*, vol. 38, no. 1, 1992, pp. 27–37.

Davies, G., 'Atheistical and blasphemous notoriety seekers? The Australian Republican Association Charters Towers, 1890–1891', *Royal Historical Society of Queensland Journal*, vol. XIV, no. 3, August 1990, pp. 99–112.

Davison, G., 'Sydney and the bush', in Russell P. and White R. (eds), *Pastiche 1*, Allen & Unwin, 1994, pp. 241–59.

Dawson, A., *Royalty*, Sydney, 1887.

Dawson, A., *The Case Stated*, J. Brice, 1890.

Drake, J. G., *Federation, Imperial or Democratic*, Benjamin Woodcock, 1896.

Dutton, G., 'British subject', *Nation*, 6 April 1963, pp. 15–16.

Eggleston, F. W., 'Australia and the Empire 1855–1921', *Cambridge History of the British Empire*, vol. 7, pt I, 1988 (First published 1933), pp. 521–45.

Elford, K., 'J. D. Lang, a prophet without honour. The political ideas of J. D. Lang', *Journal of the Royal Australian Historical Society*, vol. 54, pt 2, 1968, pp. 161–75.

Else-Mitchell, R., 'American influences on Australian nationhood', *Journal of the Royal Australian Historical Society*, vol. 62, pt 1, June 1976, pp. 1–19.

Eureka Centenary Supplement, *Historical Studies, Australia and New Zealand*, December 1954, pp. 1–96.

Evans, G. and Reid, G., 'God Save the Queen? Australia as a Republic', Counterpoint Forum, University of Western Australia, 1982.

Evans, H., 'A note on the meaning of republic', *Legislative Studies*, vol. 6, no. 2, 1992, pp. 21–3.

Ferguson, J. A., 'E. S. Hall and the *Monitor*', *Journal of the Royal Australian Historical Society*, vol. 17, 1931, pp. 163–200.

Fewster, K., 'Politics, pageantry and purpose—the 1920 tour of Australia by the Prince of Wales', *Labour History*, no. 38, May 1980, pp. 59–66.

Fujikawa, T., 'Public meetings in NSW 1871–1901', *Journal of the Royal Australian Historical Society*, vol. 76, pt 1, June 1990, pp. 42–61.

Gollan, R., 'American populism and Australian utopianism', *Labour History*, no. 9, November 1965, pp. 15–21.

Gollan, R., 'Nationalism and politics in Australia before 1855', *Australian Journal of Politics and History*, vol. 1, no. 1, November 1955, pp. 38–48.

Gossman, N. J., 'Republicanism in nineteenth century England', *International Review of Social History*, vol. VII, 1962, pp. 47–60.

Grimshaw, C., 'Australian nationalism and the imperial connection. 1900–1914', *Australian Journal of Politics and History*, vol. 3, May 1958, pp. 161–82.

Hancock, W. K., 'A Veray and True Comyn Wele', *Australian Rhodes Review*, March 1934, pp. 20–31.

Headon, D., 'God's aristocracy: Daniel Henry Deniehy's vision of a great Australian republic', *Australian Journal of Political Science*, vol. 28, 1993, pp. 136–45.

Headon, D., 'Going for the whole hog—John Dunmore Lang's radical republicanism and the American connection', *Westerly*, no. 1, March 1984, pp. 25–33.

Hirst, J., 'The conservative case for an Australian republic', *Quadrant*, September 1991, pp. 9–11.

Hoorn, J. and Goodman, D. (eds), *Vox Republicae: Feminism and the Republic*, special issue of the *Journal of Australian Studies*, no. 47, La Trobe University Press, 1996.

Horne, D., *Power from the People*, Victorian Fabian Society, 1977.

Irving, H., 'Boy's own republic', *Arena*, December 1993–January 1994, pp. 24–6.

Irving, J. H., 'Some aspects of the radical politics in NSW before 1856', *Labour History*, no. 5, November 1963, pp. 18–25.

Kelly, P., 'A case for the republic', *Quadrant*, vol. 37, no. 11, November 1993, pp. 10–15.

Kiek, L. and Henderson, J., 'Collection of two articles on the question of whether Australia should become a republic', *Australian Marxist Review*, no. 30, September 1993, pp. 5–13.

Kirby, M. D., 'A defence of the constitutional monarchy—address to Australian Society of Labor Lawyers (1993: Adelaide)', *Quadrant* (Sydney), vol. 37, no. 9, September 1993, pp. 30–5.

Lang, J. D., *Anatomical Lecture on the New Constitution*, F. Cunninghame, 1854.
La Nauze, J. A., 'The name of the Commonwealth of Australia', *Historical Studies*, 15, no. 57, October 1971, pp. 59–71.
La Nauze, J. A., 'The gold rushes and Australian politics', *Australian Journal of Politics and History*, vol. 13, no. 1, April 1967, pp. 90–4.
Loveday, P., 'Democracy in NSW. The Constitution Committee of 1853', *Journal of the Royal Australian Historical Society*, vol. 42, 1956, pp. 187–200.
MacDonagh, O., 'Republicanism in modern Irish history', *Legislative Studies*, vol. 6, no. 2, Summer 1992, pp. 41–2.
Macintyre, S., 'Corowa and the voice of the people', *Canberra Historical Journal*, no. 33, March 1994, pp. 2–8.
McDonald, R. J., 'Republicanism in the fifties', *Journal of the Royal Australian Historical Society*, vol. 50, pt 4, October 1964, pp. 262–76.
McKenna, M., 'A history of the inevitable republic' in M. Stephenson (ed.), *Australia, Republic or Monarchy*, University of Queensland Press, 1994, pp. 50–71.
McKenna, M., 'Tracking the republic' in D. Headon *et al.*, *Crown or Country*, Allen & Unwin, 1994, pp. 3–56.
McLachlan, N., 'The future America', *Historical Studies*, vol. 7, no. 68, April 1977, pp. 361–83.
McQueen, H., 'Convicts and rebels', *Labour History*, no. 15, November 1968, pp. 3–30.
Maddox, G., 'The origins of republicanism', *Legislative Studies*, vol. 7, no. 1, Spring 1992, pp. 35–8.
Maher, L., 'Dissent, disloyalty and disaffection', *Adelaide Law Review*, vol. 16, no. 1, 1994, pp. 1–78.
Mansfield, B., 'The background to radical republicanism in NSW in the 1880s', *Historical Studies*, vol. 5, no. 20, May 1953, pp. 338–48.
Markey, R., 'Populism and the formation of the Labor Party in NSW 1890–1900', *Journal of Australian Studies*, no. 20, May 1987, pp. 38–48.
Mehrotra, S. R., 'On the use of the term Commonwealth', *Journal of Commonwealth Political Studies*, vol. 2, 1963–1964, pp. 1–16.
Melbourne, A. C. V., 'The establishment of responsible government', *Cambridge History of the British Empire*, vol. VII, pt 1 (first published 1933), pp. 272–95.
Meudell, G., 'Australia for the Australians', *Melbourne Review*, vol. 7, January–October 1882, pp. 315–24.
Michie, A., *Loyalty, Royalty and the Prince's Visits, A lecture delivered at Princess Theatre Melbourne, 12 July 1869*, Still & Knight, 1869.
Nicholls, H. R., 'Reminiscences of the Eureka Stockade', *Centennial Magazine*, November 1890, pp. 746–50.
O'Farrell, P., 'The Australian Socialist League and the Labour Movement 1887–1891', *Historical Studies*, vol. 8, no. 30, May 1958, pp. 152–65.
Parkes, H., 'Australia and the imperial connection', *Nineteenth Century*, May 1884, pp. 867–82.
Parkes, H., *One People One Destiny. Speech at the Gaiety Theatre in Sydney on Saturday, 13 June 1891*, Turner and Henderson, 1891 (Mitchell Library).

Parsons, T. G., 'Was John Boston's pig a political martyr?', *Journal of the Royal Australian Historical Society*, vol. 71, 1985, pp. 163–77.
Paul, J., 'An Australian republic? But why?', *Quadrant*, vol. 35, no. 9, September 1991, pp. 11–13.
Perkins, E., 'Rhetoric and the man, Charles Harpur and the call to armed rebellion', *Age Monthly Review*, vol. 6, no. 5, 1986, pp. 7–14.
Petit, P., 'Liberty in the republic', John Curtin Memorial Lecture, Australian National University, 1989.
Pocock, J., 'Republicanism and ideology Americana', *History of Ideas*, vol. 48, no. 2, April–June 1987, pp. 325–46.
'The Republic: four points of the compass', *Quadrant*, vol. 37, nos 7–8, July–August 1993, pp. 28–39.
'The republic we have to have', *Independent Monthly*, June 1993, pp. 20–3 (includes George Winterton's 'Draft Republican Constitution').
Republican Party of Australia, *The Regional Co-operative Government Plan for Australia*, 1990, RPA.
Roderick, C., 'Henry Lawson', *Journal of the Royal Australian Historical Society*, vol. 45, pt 3, 1959, pp. 105–38.
Ross, L., 'Left Ideas in the Eighties', *Labor Digest*, no. 5, August 1946, pp. 41–4.
Schacht, C., 'The case for a republic', *Executive Action*, February 1992, pp. 10–12.
Sharman, C., 'Australia as a compound republic', *Politics*, no. 25(i), May 1990, pp. 1–5.
Shaw, A. G. L., 'Violent protests in Australian history', *Historical Studies*, vol. 15, no. 60, April 1968, pp. 545–61.
Sheps, A., 'The American revolution and the transformation of English republicanism', *Historical Reflections*, vol. 2, issue 1, 1975, pp. 3–28.
Shoemaker, R. W., 'Democracy and republic as understood in late eighteenth century America', *American Speech*, vol. 41, 1966, pp. 83–95.
Shortus, S., 'Colonial nationalism. NSW Welsh identity in the mid 1880s', *Journal of the Royal Australian Historical Society*, vol. 51, pt 1, March 1973, pp. 31–51.
Smith, A. B., 'Australian loyalty to the British Empire', *Sydney Quarterly Magazine*, 1888, pp. 369–77.
Smith, D., 'A toast to Australia', *Quadrant*, May 1991, pp. 11–17.
Smith, F. G., 'Danger Ahead. Anti-Imperial Federation', Melbourne 1889.
Spearritt, P., 'Royal progress: the Queen and her Australian subjects', *Australian Cultural History*, no. 5, 1986, pp. 75–94.
Taylor, A. J., *Imperial Federation versus Australian Independence*, Mercury, 1889 (Tasmanian State Library).
Walker, R. B., 'David Buchanan, Chartist radical and republican', *Journal of the Royal Australian Historical Society*, vol. 53, pt 2, June 1967, pp. 122–38.
Ward, J. M., 'Charles Gavan Duffy and the Australian Federation Movement 1856–1870', *Journal of the Royal Australian Historical Society*, vol. 47, pt 1, 1961, pp. 1–33.
Warden, J., 'The fettered republic. The Anglo–American Commonwealth and the traditions of Australian political thought', *Australian Journal of Political Science*, vol. 28, 1993, pp. 83–99.

Watson, D., 'A toast to the post-modern republic', *Island*, issue 55, Winter 1993, pp. 3–5.
Western, C., 'The theory of mixed monarchy under Charles I and after', *English Historical Review*, July 1960, pp. 426–43.
Westgarth, W., 'The relations of the colonies to the mother country', *Proceedings of the Royal Colonial Institute*, vol. I, 1869.
Wiener, J., 'Richard Carlile and the republican', *Victorian Periodicals Review*, vol. 13, no. 3, 1980, pp. 78–85.
Winterton, G., 'A Constitution for an Australian republic', *Independent Monthly*, March 1992 (insert).
Winterton, G., 'Modern republicanism', *Legislative Studies*, vol. 6, no. 2, Summer 1992, pp. 24–6.
Woodall, R., 'Republicanism in Victorian Britain', *Historian*, vol. 13, 1986–87, pp. 6–8.

BOOKS

Ackland, M. (ed.), *Charles Harpur—Selected Poetry and Prose*, Penguin, 1986.
Alomes, S., *A Nation at Last. The Changing Character of Australian Nationalism*, Angus & Robertson, 1988.
Alomes, S. and Jones, C. (eds), *Australian Nationalism—A Documentary History*, Angus & Robertson, 1991.
Amos, K., *Fenians in Australia: 1865–1880*, NSW University Press, 1988.
Amos, K., *The New Guard Movement 1931–1935*, Melbourne University Press, 1976.
Arnold, J., Spearritt, P. and Walker, D. (eds), *Out of Empire. The British Dominion of Australia*, Mandarin Press, 1993.
Atkinson, A., *The Muddle Headed Republic*, Oxford University Press, 1993.
Bagehot, W., *The English Constitution*, Oxford University Press, 1955 (first published 1867).
Bailyn, B., *The Ideological Origins of the American Revolution*, Harvard University Press, 1967.
Baker, D. W., *Days of Wrath*, Melbourne University Press, 1985.
Bate, W., *Victorian Gold Rushes*, Penguin, 1988.
Beaumont, J. (ed.), *Where to Now?, Australia's Identity in the Nineties*, Federation Press, 1993.
Bell, P. and Bell, R., *Implicated: The United States in Australia*, Oxford University Press, 1993.
Birrell, R., *A Nation of Our Own*, Longman, 1995.
Black, G., *A History of the NSW Political Labor Party from its Conception until 1917*, nos 1–7, George A. Jones, 1926–29 (Mitchell Library).
Black, G., *Why I am a Republican*, Robert Bear, 1891 (first published 1888).
Blainey, G., *Our Side of the Country. The Story of Victoria*, Sun Books, 1991.
Bolton, G., *A Thousand Miles Away. A History of North Queensland to 1920*, Australian National University, 1962.
Bolton, G., *The Oxford History of Australia, vol. V, 1942–1988*, Oxford University Press, 1990.
Booker, M., *A Republic of Australia. What Would It Mean?*, Left Book Club, 1992.

Brett, J., *Robert Menzies' Forgotten People*, Macmillan, 1992.
Brown, M., *Australian Son, The Story of Ned Kelly*, Georgian House, 1948.
Buckley, K. and Wheelwright, T., *No Paradise for Workers: Capitalism and the Common People in Australia: 1788–1914*, Oxford University Press, 1988.
Burgmann, V., *'In Our Time', Socialism and the Rise of Labor 1885–1905*, Allen & Unwin, 1985.
Burroughs, P., *Britain and Australia: 1831–1855*, Clarendon Press, 1967.
Carboni, R., *The Eureka Stockade*, Atkinson, 1855.
Churchward, L. G., *Australia and America 1788–1972*, Alternative Publishing Co-op., 1974.
Clark, C. M. H. (ed.), *Select Documents in Australian History*, vol. 1 (1788–1850) and vol. 2 (1851–1900), Angus & Robertson, 1950 and 1955.
Clark, C. M. H., *A History of Australia I: From the Earliest Times to the Age of Macquarie*, Melbourne University Press, 1985 (first published 1962).
Clark, C. M. H., *A History of Australia II: NSW and Van Diemen's Land 1822–1838*, Melbourne University Press, 1985 (first published 1968).
Clark, C. M. H., *A History of Australia III: The Beginning of an Australian Civilisation 1824–1851*, Melbourne University Press, 1985 (first published 1973).
Clark, C. M. H., *A History of Australia IV: The Earth Abideth Forever 1851–1888*, Melbourne University Press, 1985 (first published 1978).
Clark, C. M. H., *A History of Australia V: The People Make Laws 1888–1915*, Melbourne University Press, 1981.
Clark, C. M. H., *A History of Australia VI: The Old Dead Tree and the Young Tree Green 1915–1935*, Melbourne University Press, 1987.
Clark, M., *Sources of Australian History*, Oxford University Press, 1971.
Clarke, F. G., *The Land of Contrarities: British Attitudes to the Australian Colonies 1828–1855*, Melbourne University Press, 1977.
Cowen, Z., *Isaac Isaacs*, Oxford University Press, 1967.
Craven, G., *The Convention Debates 1891–1898. Commentaries Indices and Guide*, vol. VI, Legal Books, 1986.
Crowley, F. (ed.), *A New History of Australia*, Heinemann, 1990 (first published 1974).
Crowley, F., *Tough Times: Australia in the Seventies*, Heinemann, 1986.
Cunneen, C., *King's Men: Australia's Governors-General from Hopetoun to Isaacs*, Allen & Unwin, 1983.
Davidson, A., *The Invisible State*, Cambridge University Press, 1991.
Davidson, M., *The New Book of Kings*, Socialist Labour Party of Australia, 1925.
Davis, R., *Elizabeth our Queen*, Collins, 1976.
Davison, G., McCarty, J. W. and McLeary, A. (eds), *Australians: 1888*, Fairfax, Syme & Weldon Associates, 1987.
Deakin, A., *The Federal Story*, J. A. La Nauze (ed.), Melbourne University Press, 1963.
Detmold, M. J., *The Australian Commonwealth*, Law Book Co., 1985.
Dilke, C., *Problems of Great Britain*, Macmillan, 1890.
Dixon, R., *The Course of Empire—Neo-Classical Culture in NSW 1788–1860*, Oxford University Press, 1986.

Docker, J., *The Nervous Nineties*, Oxford University Press, 1991.
Dutton, G. (ed.), *Australia and the Monarchy*, Sun Books, 1966.
Dutton, G. (ed.), *Republican Australia*, Sun Books, 1977.
Dutton, G., *Out in the Open: An Autobiography*, University of Queensland Press, 1994.
Ebbels, R. N. (ed.), *The Australian Labor Movement—A Documentary History*, Australian Book Society, 1960.
Eddy, J., *Britain and the Australian Colonies: 1818–1831*, Clarendon Press, 1969.
Eddy, J. and Schreuder, D., *The Rise of Colonial Nationalism 1880–1914*, Allen & Unwin, 1988.
Encel, S., Horne, D. and Thompson, E., *Change the Rules: Towards a Democratic Constitution*, Penguin, 1977.
Evans, L. and Nicholls, P. (eds), *Convicts and Colonial Society 1788–1868*, Macmillan, 1984.
Everdell, W. R., *The End of Kings*, Collier-Macmillan, 1983.
Ferguson, C. D., *Experiences of a 49er in Australia and New Zealand*, Gaston Renard, 1979 (first published 1888).
Fitzpatrick, B., *The British Empire in Australia: An Economic History 1834–1939*, Macmillan, 1969.
Fontana, B. (ed.), *The Invention of the Modern Republic*, Cambridge University Press, 1994.
Francis, M. F., *Governors and Settlers—Images of Authority in the British Colonies 1820–1860*, Canterbury University Press, 1992.
Fraser, A., *Spirit of the Laws: Republicanism and the Unfinished Project of Modernity*, University of Toronto Press, 1990.
Froude, J. A., *Oceana: Or England and Her Colonies*, Longmans Green, 1886.
Fry, E. (ed.), *Rebels and Radicals*, Allen & Unwin, 1985.
Galligan, B., *A Federal Republic*, Cambridge University Press, 1995.
Gilchrist, A. (ed.), *John Dunmore Lang. Chiefly Autobiographical: 1799–1878*, vols I and II, Jedgarm Publishers, 1951.
Gollan, M. (ed.), *Kerr and the Consequences*, Widescope, 1976.
Gollan, R., *Radical and Working Class Politics. A Study of Eastern Australia 1850–1910*, Melbourne University Press, 1976.
Grainger, G. and Jones, K. (eds), *The Australian Constitutional Monarchy*, ACM Publishing, 1994.
Grassby, A. L., *The Australian Republic*, Pluto, 1993.
Greenwood, G. (ed.), *Australia: A Social and Political History*, Angus & Robertson, 1955.
Hall, H. L., *Australia and England—A Study in Imperial Relations*, Longmans Green & Co., 1934.
Hancock, W. K., *Argument of Empire*, Penguin, 1943.
Hancock, W. K., *Australia*, Jacaranda, 1961 (first published 1930).
Hayden, B., *Hayden. An Autobiography*, Angus & Robertson, 1996.
Headon, D., Warden, J. and Gammage, B. (eds), *Crown or Country*, Allen & Unwin, 1994.
Higonett, P., *Sister Republics, the Origins of French and American Republicanism*, Cambridge University Press, 1988.

Hirst, J., *A Republican Manifesto*, Oxford University Press, 1994.
Hirst, J., *The Strange Birth of Colonial Democracy in NSW 1848–1884*, Allen & Unwin, 1988.
Hobsbawm, E. and Ranger, T. (eds), *The Invention of Tradition*, Cambridge University Press, Canto edn, 1992.
Hobsbawm, E., *Nations and Nationalism since 1780, Programme, Myth, Reality*, Cambridge University Press, Canto edn, 1991.
Hodgson, C., *Reminiscences of Australia, with Hints on the Squatter's Life*, W. N. Wright, 1846.
Horne, D., *The Lucky Country*, Penguin, 1986 (first published 1964).
Horne, D. and others, *The Coming Republic*, Sun Books, 1993.
Hudson, W. and Carter, D. (eds), *The Republicanism Debate*, New South Wales University Press, 1993.
Hudson, W. J. and Sharp, M. P., *Australian Independence*, Melbourne University Press, 1988.
Hughes, R., *The Fatal Shore*, Pan Books, 1988 (first published 1987).
Ingamells, R., *Royalty and Australia*, Hallcraft, 1954.
Inglis, K. S., *The Australian Colonists*, Melbourne University Press, 1974.
Jebb, R., *Studies in Colonial Nationalism*, Edward Arnold, 1905.
Jones, I., *The Friendship that Destroyed Ned Kelly*, Lothian, 1992.
Jones, I., *Ned Kelly. A Short Life*, Lothian, 1995.
Jupp, J. (ed.), *The Australian People*, Angus & Robertson, 1988.
Keneally, T., *Our Republic*, Heinemann, 1993.
Kerr, J., *Matters for Judgment*, Sun Books, 1988 (first published, Macmillan, 1978).
Kingston, B., *The Oxford History of Australia*, vol. III, 1860–1900, Oxford University Press, 1988.
Knight, R., *Illiberal Liberal: Robert Lowe in NSW 1842–1850*, Melbourne University Press, 1966.
Kociumbas, J., *The Oxford History of Australia*, vol. II, 1770–1860, Oxford University Press, 1992.
Lang, J. D., *Freedom and Independence for the Golden Lands of Australia*, F. Cunninghame, 1857 (first published 1852).
Lang, J. D., *Historical and Statistical Account of the Colony of NSW*, 1870 (first published 1834).
Lang, J. D., *The Coming Event*, D. L. Welch, 1850.
Lawson, S., *The Archibald Paradox*, Penguin, 1987.
Lewis, C., *On the Use and Abuse of Political Terms*, London, 1837.
Loveday, P. and Martin, A., *Parliament, Factions, Parties: the First 30 Years of Responsible Government in NSW 1856–1889*, Melbourne University Press, 1966.
Lynch, J., *The Story of the Eureka Stockade*, Australian Catholic Truth Society, 1949 (first published 1893).
MacDonagh, O. and Mandle, W. (eds), *Ireland and Irish–Australia: Studies in Cultural and Political History*, Croom Helm, 1986.
MacDonagh, O. and Mandle, W. (eds), *Irish–Australian Studies*, Australian National University, 1989.
Macintyre, S., *The Oxford History of Australia*, vol. IV, 1901–1942, Oxford University Press, 1986.

Macintyre, S., *A Colonial Liberalism*, Oxford University Press, 1991.
McCombie, T., *A History of Victoria*, Sands & Kenny, 1888.
McGinn, W. G., *Nationalism and Federalism in Australia*, Oxford University Press, 1994.
McKinlay, B. (ed.), *Australian Labor History in Documents*, vols I–III, Collins Dove, 1990.
McLachlan, N., *Waiting for the Revolution*, Penguin, 1989.
McMillan, J., Evans, G. and Storey, H., *Australia's Constitution, Time for Change?*, Law Foundation of NSW and Allen & Unwin, 1986.
McMullin, R., *The Light on the Hill, the Australian Labor Party 1891–1991*, Oxford University Press, 1991.
McQueen, H., *A New Britannia*, Penguin, 1980 (first published 1970).
Madden, A. F. and Morris-Jones, W. H. (eds), *Australia and Britain, Studies in a Changing Relationship*, Sydney University Press, 1980.
Mansfield, B., *Australian Democrat. The Career of E. W. O'Sullivan 1846–1890*, Sydney University Press, 1965.
Markey, R., *The Making of the Australian Labor Party*, New South Wales University Press, 1988.
Martin, A. W., *Henry Parkes*, Melbourne University Press, 1980.
Matthews, B., *Louisa*, Penguin, 1987.
Meaney, N. (ed.), *Under New Heavens: Cultural Transmission and the Making of Australia*, Heinemann, 1989.
Meaney, N. (ed.), *Australia and the World: A Documentary History 1870–1970*, Longman Cheshire, 1985.
Merivale, H., *Lectures on Colonisation and Colonies*, Longman Green & Roberts, 1861.
Molony, J., *Eureka*, Penguin, 1984.
Morrell, W. P., *British Colonial Policy in the Age of Peel and Russell*, Clarendon Press, 1930.
Muirden, B., *The Puzzled Patriots. The Story of the Australia First Movement*, Melbourne University Press, 1968.
Nairn, N. B. (gen. ed.), Serle, G. and Ward, R. (section eds), *Australian Dictionary of Biography 1851–1890*, vol. 6, Melbourne University Press, 1976.
Nairn, N. B., *Civilising Capitalism, the Labor Movement in NSW 1870–1900*, Australian National University, 1973.
Neal, D., *The Rule of Law in a Penal Colony*, Cambridge University Press, 1991.
O'Farrell, P., *The Irish in Australia*, New South Wales University Press, 1993.
Oldfield, A., *Citizenship and Community: Civic Republicanism and the Modern World*, Routledge, 1990.
Paine, T., *Common Sense*, Kramnick, I. (ed.), Penguin, 1986 (first published 1776).
Paine, T., *Rights of Man*, Collins, H. (ed.), Penguin, 1976 (first published 1791).
Parkes, H., *Fifty Years of Australian History*, vols I and II, Longmans Green & Co., 1892.
Parkes, H., *Speeches on Various Occasions Connected with the Public Affairs of NSW 1848–1874*, Blair, D. (ed.), George Robertson, 1876.
Partington, G., *The Australian Nation. Its British and Irish Roots*, Australian Scholarly Publishing, 1994.

Perkins, E. (ed.), *The Poetical Works of Charles Harpur*, Angus & Robertson, 1984.
Pike, D. (gen. ed.), Nairn, N. B., Serle, G. and Ward, R. (section eds), *Australian Dictionary of Biography 1851–1890*, vols III, IV and V, Melbourne University Press, 1969, 1972 and 1974.
Pike, D. (gen. ed.), Shaw, A. G. L. and Clark, C. M. H. (section eds), *Australian Dictionary of Biography 1788–1850*, vols I and II, Melbourne University Press, 1966 and 1967.
Pocock, J. G. A., *The Machiavellian Moment: Florentine Republican Thought and the Atlantic Republican Tradition*, Princeton University Press, 1975.
Poulton, J., *Adelaide Ironside—Pilgrim of Art*, Hale & Iremonger, 1987.
Rahe, P. A., *Republics Ancient and Modern—Classical Republicanism and the American Revolution*, University of North Carolina Press, 1992.
Robbins, C. (ed.), *Two English Republican Tracts*, Cambridge University Press, 1969.
Roberts, S., *Charles Hotham. A Biography*, Melbourne University Press, 1985.
Roberts, S. H., *The Squatting Age of Australia 1835–1847*, Melbourne University Press, 1964.
Roderick, C. (ed.), *Henry Lawson: Autobiographical and Other Writings 1887–1922*, Angus & Robertson, 1972.
Roderick, C., *Henry Lawson. The Master Story Teller*, Angus & Robertson, 1972.
Roderick, C., *Henry Lawson: A Life*, Angus & Robertson, 1991.
Roe, M., *The Quest for Authority in Eastern Australia: 1835–1851*, Melbourne University Press, 1965.
Rolfe, P., *Journalistic Javelin*, Wildcat Press, 1979.
Royle, E., *Radicals, Secularists and Republicans: Popular Free Thought in Britain 1866–1915*, Manchester University Press, 1980.
Rudé, G., *Protest and Punishment—The Story of the Social and Political Protesters Transported to Australia: 1788–1868*, Oxford University Press, 1978.
Ryan, M. (ed.), *Advancing Australia. The Speeches of Paul Keating*, Tower Books, 1995.
Scott, E. (ed.), *Cambridge History of the British Empire, Australia*, vol. VII, pt I, Cambridge University Press, Australia 1988 (first published 1933).
Serle, G., *The Golden Age*, Melbourne University Press, 1963.
Serle, G., *The Rush to be Rich: A History of the Colony of Victoria 1883–1889*, Melbourne University Press, 1971.
Shaw, G. (ed.), *1988 and All That. New Views of Australia's Past*, University of Queensland Press, 1988.
Sherington, G., *Australia's Immigrants—1788–1978*, Allen & Unwin, 1985 (first published 1980).
Silvester, E. K. (ed.), *NSW Constitution Bill—The Speeches of the Legislative Council of NSW*, Thomas Daniel, 1853.
Solomon, D., *Elect the Governor-General*, Nelson, 1976.
Souter, G., *Lion and Kangaroo*, Fontana, 1976.
Springborg, P., *Western Republicanism and the Oriental Prince*, Polity, 1992.
Stephensen, P. R., *The Foundations of Culture in Australia*, Allen & Unwin, 1986 (first published 1936).
Stephenson, M. A. and Turner, C. (eds), *Australia: Republic or Monarchy*, University of Queensland Press, 1994.

Thomson, R., *Australian Nationalism*, Moss Brothers, 1888.
Train, G. F., *My Life in Many States and in Foreign Lands*, Heinemann, 1902.
Trainor, L., *British Imperialism and Australian Nationalism*, Cambridge University Press, 1994.
Tregenza, J. T., *Professor of Democracy: The Life of Charles Henry Pearson 1830–1894*, Melbourne University Press, 1968.
Turnbull, M., *The Reluctant Republic*, Heinemann, 1993.
Turner, H. G., *Our Own Little Rebellion*, Whitcombe & Tombs, 1913.
Vetterli, R. and Bryner, G., *In Search of the Republic*, Roman and Littlefield, 1987.
Walker, G. de Q., Ratnapala, S. and Kasper, W., *Restoring the True Republic*, Centre for Independent Studies, 1993.
Ward, J. M., *Colonial Self-Government and the British Experience 1759–1856*, Macmillan, 1976.
Ward, J. M., *Earl Grey and the Australian Colonies*, Melbourne University Press, 1958.
Ward, J. M., *James Macarthur—Colonial Conservative 1798–1867*, Sydney University Press, 1981.
Ward, R., *The Australian Legend*, Oxford University Press, 1985 (first published 1958).
Webb, G. H. (ed.), *The New Constitution Bill Debate in the Legislative Council of the Colony of Victoria*, Melbourne, 1854.
Wentworth, W., *A Statistical, Historical, and Political Description of the Colony of NSW and its Dependent Settlements in Van Diemen's Land. . .*, G. & W. B. Whittaker, 1819.
Whitlam, G., *On Australia's Constitution*, Widescope, 1977.
Whitlam, G., *The Truth of the Matter*, Penguin, 1979.
Whitlam, G., *The Whitlam Government 1972–1975*, Viking Press, 1985.
Winterton, G. (ed.), *We the People*, Allen & Unwin, 1994.
Winterton, G., *Monarchy to Republic*, Oxford University Press, 1986.
Wood, G. S., *The Creation of the American Republic 1776–1787*, University of North Carolina Press, 1969.

Index

This is a book about political and social ideas and how these have been used for rhetorical and eristic purposes; none of which have been straightforward, either in intention or in execution. The language is therefore full of synonyms and tropes. To have indexed all of these would have been to rewrite the book, they have therefore been indexed in clusters.

For example: there is no reference to England; instead there is an entry for 'Mother England' which also subsumes 'mother land' and 'parent state'. There are no subentries for America – which is a very long entry – because all those who referred to America made use of the country and its history as a paradigm of 'what might happen if ...'. Finally there is no entry for revolution – which wasn't ever an issue, although the word was used; 'separation/severance' was what was really at stake.

Because most of the terms used are rhetorical concepts it has in many cases not been possible to subdivide the entries. If this is irritating to some readers it at least has the merit of being shorter than a word-list type index and I hope more useful to those who are interested in the underlying structure and development of the arguments described.

Illustrations are given in italic, but are not separately indexed where there is already a main entry. There is a separate index of prominent persons and also of the newspapers – the primary evidence for the debate.

AVERIL CONDREN

INDEX OF IDEAS, ORGANISATIONS, PLACES AND EVENTS

Aboriginal Australians/Aboriginal rights
   152, 188, 234, 240, 245, 254, 263
Acts of Parliament 175, 215
   Act for the Sale of Waste land (1842) 34
   Act of Union for Canada (1840) 29, 30
   Australia Act (1986) 215, 246, 256, 258
   Australian Colonies Government Act (1850) 59
   Bill of Rights (1689) 7, 8, 34
   Commonwealth of Australia Constitution Act (1900) 205, 216, 248; Constitution of NSW (1842) 33–4, 40, 65
   Convict Prevention Act (1852) 94, 98
   Crimes Act (1914) 210
   Draft Bill for Australian Federation (1891) 192–5, 197, 200, 204
   Immigration Restriction Acts 164
   Nationality and Citizenship Act (1949) 217
   Naval Defence Force Bill (1887) 160
   Reform Act (1832) 18, 23, 24; Reform Bill (1854) 15; 2nd Reform Bill (1867) 46
   Royal Style and Titles Act (1973) 228
   Statute of Westminister (1931) 214, 215, 258
   Treason Felony Act (1868) 112–13, 147
   (Wentworth's) Constitution of NSW Bill (1853) 75–9, 81, 82, 83, 89, 93–4
Adelaide 147–8, 153, 168, 173, 174, 196, 223, 233
alcohol 15, 25, 85, 104, 113, 201
Allegemeiner Deutscher Verein 196–7
America/American War of Independence
   'a warning and ... model for change' (p. 7) 12, 15, 16, 17, 19, 20–2, 25, 29, 30, 32, 34, 36, 39, 44, 47, 57, 64, 68, 72, 79, 92, 96, 103, 105, 108, 110, 111, 114, 123, 129, 150, 153, 157, 193–4,

326   Index

America/American War of Independence (cont.)
  196, 203, 206, 219, 221, 237, 249
  as disguised monarchy 81–2
  influence of American nationals in Australia 73–4, 97–8, 101
  see also constitution, democracy
Anti-Transportation Movement 56, 58, 64, 71–2; *see also* Australasian League
Anzac (Aust & NZ Army Corps) 38
Asia 219, 221, 252, 254, 260
associations *see* by name
Australasian Federation League 198
Australasian League 50, 51–3, 61, 64–6, 69, 70, 82, 84–6, 94, 127
Australia – relationship with Britain *see* Mother Country
Australia – Federated Commonwealth of 205–7, 211, 214, 215, 216, 258
Australia First movement 213
Australian Heritage Society 228, 234, 244
Australian National Association 171–2
Australian National Union 153
Australian Natives Association 124, 153, 164, 171, 197
Australian Labor Party (Federal) 166, 174, 196, 217, 219–21, 226, 228, 243, 246, 249, 253; *see also* Labor Electoral League
Australian Labour Federation 179, 183, 186
Australian Republican Association 178–83, 186, 187
Australian Republican League 166–71, 172
Australian Republican Movement 236, 247, 250–1, 253, 254, 257, 258, 261
Australian Republican Party 224
Australian Republican Union 151, 157–60, 163, 166, 172
Australian Socialist League 133, 135, 166, 167, 172
Australians for Constitutional Monarchy 260

Balfour Declaration (1926) 214
Ballarat Reform League 99–100
'bastard' *see* cricket
Bathurst People's Convention (1896) 199
beer *see* alcohol
Bendigo 94, 97, 101, 130–31, 178
Bicentenary of Settlement 239, 240, 241, 243, 245–6
birthrights – as free-born Britains 15, 24, 30–1, 33, 36, 39, 43, 58, 62, 71, 72, 74, 78, 105, 114, 122, 206, 260
blood sacrifice *see* Eureka/Imperial wars

Blue Mountains 15–17, 22
Boston's republican/levelling pig 14, 263
Brisbane 122, 141, 149, 181, 183, 190, 233, 236

Canada 29–30, 33, 35, 78, 110, 203
capital-capitalism 132, 135, 151, 174, 175, 189, 203, 210
Catholicism *see* Roman Catholic Church
Centenary – 1888: 134, 160–3, 166
Centennial Park (Sydney) 161, 205, 211
Charters Towers 122, 178–82
Chartists/chartism 33, 42–3, 49, 50, 61, 68, 80, 92, 99–100, 102, 128
China/Chinese 92, 135, *152*, 163–4, 167, 171, 172, 188–9; *see also* racial purity
Citizens for Democracy 231, 237–9, 240
colonial aristocracy 75–6, 84, 170; *see also* squatters
Colonial Conference (1870) 115; (1883) 126; (1888) 163
Colonial Governors, powers of 118–9, 164, 175–6
colonial grievances 18, 24, 30, 34, 40, 57, 58, 65–6, 68, 69, 74, 83, 88, 93, 103, 109–10, 126; *see also* franchise, land, taxation, transportation
Colonial Office 15–16, 22, 24, 29–30, 31, 33, 34, 36–9, 43, 47, 59, 64, 66, 67, 71, 73–4, 89, 108
  as encouraging separation 111, 117
  see also colonial grievances
colonial public culture *see* political culture
committees *see* by name
Commonwealth – as term 191–4
Commonwealth – British – family of nations 122, 211, 216
Commonwealth of Australia *see* federation
communism/Communist Party 210, 213; *see also* socialism
conferences *see* under name
consent (of people to government) *see* sovereignty
Constitution, British – true spirit of/faith in 15, 17, 19, 28, 32, 34, 35, 36, 43–4, 57, 70, 71, 74, 76–9, 82, 83, 99, 100, 101–2, 104, 105, 108, 119, 142, 182, 193, 194, 203–4, 214, 216, 257
Constitutional Association 42, 45, 49, 51
Constitutional Commission (1988) 246
Constitutional Convention (1991) 248–9
constitutional monarchy *see* sovereignty
conventions *see* under name
convict stain/convict heritage 15, 19, 30, 31, 45–6, 52, 57–8, 63, 64, 72, 86, 94,

109, 126, 140–1, 161–2, 171, 245, 261; *see also* colonial grievances, racial purity, transportation
Corowa Conference/Federal Convention (1893) 197–8, 262
cost of government/crown 24, 27, 34, 37, 134, 135, 149, 151, 157, 170
Country Party 227
Cracker Night *see* Empire Day
cricket 27, 28, 216–7; *see also* alcohol
Crown, authority of 32, 38, 43, 62, 64, 80, 82, 95, 118–9, 164, 228–31, 237, 246, 256, 263
cultural cringe 213, 223, 236–7, 240, 261

Declaration of Rights (Lang's) 64–5
defence *see* isolation, invasion, Imperial war
democracy 17, 18, 27, 28, 30, 42–4, 54, 62, 65, 75, 76, 78, 80, 89, 108, 114, 120, 137, 169, 170, 178, 196, 198, 229–33, 236, 238, 240
Democratic Alliance 129
distribution of wealth *see* socialism, capitalism
Domain *see* Sydney
Dominion status *see* Australia

education 52, 85, 177, 180, 196
egalitarian, Australian society as 40, 122, 124, 151–2, 173–4, 226
electoral reform *see* franchise
emancipist movement/emancipation 16–17, 18, 21, 22, 46
Empire *see* Mother England
Empire Day 207, 211, 216
English Civil War and Settlement 14, 28, 33, 56, 71, 72, 107, 110, 150, 192–3, 195
Eureka 97–105, 108, 158,189, 234
European Economic Community *see* trade

Federal Convention (1891) 190, 192, 194, 195, 197; (1897) 197–200
Federal Council 188, 190
Federation (Federated Republic of Australia) 3, 9, 10, 40, 49, 64, 110–11, 116, 117–18, 124–5, 126, 129, 134, 158, 164, 166, 170, 171, 174, 175, 188–204, 256
fin de siècle 131, 134, 253
France/French Revolution(s) 12, 13, 15, 17, 32–3, 40–1, 42–3, 44, 56, 64, 68, 71, 80, 103, 110, 114, 194, 196, 250
French activities in Pacific: New Caledonia 116; New Hebrides 126, 128; *see also* America
franchise 16–19, 24, 25, 26, 31–3, 42–3, 54, 93, 177, 180, 234; *see also* colonial grievances, responsible government

Germany 125–6, 128, 207, 253
Papua New Guinea 125–6; *see also* Imperial war
Glorious Revolution 1688, 7–8, 81, 82, 95–6, 100; *see also* English Civil War
gold/gold rush/goldfields 40, 65, 68, 69, 73, 92–4, 97–102, 178, 186
Governor-General – office of/nominal royalty 110, 194, 204, 206, 214, 215, 228, 229–31, 235–6, 244, 246, 258
Great Depression *see* trade
Greece *see* Rome

Hobart 69, 72, 131, 149, 249; *see also* Tasmania
Houses of Assembly rights to, *see* franchise, Legislative Assembly/Council
humanism *see* secularism

immigration 22, 31, 34, 41, 49, 50, 52, 64, 66, 92, 109, 116, 125, 130, *152*, 174, 211, 221, 224; *see also* racial purity
Imperial Conference (1926) 214
Imperial Federation League 129
Imperial foreign policy *see* Imperial war
Imperial war, involvement in/threat of 51, 86–9, 116, 125–9, 157, 170, 188–9, 206, 219, 221
independence/maturity/growth 24–5, 31, 37, 46, 47, 50, 52, 55, 59–60, 65, 68, 71, 74, 76, 80, 82, 84, 89–90, 92, 97, 100, 105, 107, 108, 111, 118–19, 121, 124, 126, 134, 151, 156, 171–2, 173, 175, 182, 190, 195, 196, 205, 214, 215, 217, 228, 232, 236–7, 254, 262; *see also* nationhood
independence – types of – when achieved: diplomatic (1923); executive (1926); legislative (1931) 215
industrial action *see* trade unions
invasion (of Australia) 50–1, 87, 116, 129, 157, 189, 200, 207, 215; *see also* Imperial war
Irish, as threat to colonial stability, 13, 41, 71–2, 98, 100, 101, 112–3, 123, 148, 173, 210, 211–12, 260–1; *see also* sectarianism
isolation *see* Imperial war

Jubilee year (1887) 134, 136–49, 151, 156, 158, 160, 162–3, 232; *see also* loyalism

Labor Electoral League 166, 197, 198, 199, 205, 212–13; *see also* Australian Labor Party
labour movement *see* trade unions
land 25, 33, 34–5, 38, 53, 109–10, 177, 180, 196; *see also* squatters, taxation
Land Convention (Victoria) 109–10
larrikin *see* mob
law 16–19, 23, 180; *see also* colonial grievances
leagues *see* by name
Legislative Council/Legislative Assembly – *see* under state; *see also* responsible government
levelling/levellers *see* English Civil War
Liberal Party (Federal) 221, 227, 251, 253–6
loyalism/loyalists 14, 17, 32, 33, 37, 47, 50, 58, 63, 65, 67, 70–1, 78, 88–9, 95, 103, 107, 112–17, 122, 124, 127, 128–30, 131, 132, 139–40, 142–8, 151, 158, 162–5, 191, 192–3, 197, 200, 205–13, 215–16, *220*, 226, 234, 235, 243, 262; *see also* Constitution, monarch, petitions

Melbourne 45, 47, 92–3, 115, 129, 141, 164, 168–9, 173, 234
 anti-transportation attitudes of 56, 69, 72, 94–5
 Centenary exhibition 130
 Jubilee year 136
 Melbourne Anarchists (association) 135
 response to Eureka in 103–4, 105
Military/military presence 14–15, 37, 57, 99, 101, 102, 116–17, 215
mob/larrikins/rabble (convict rabble) 12, 32–3, 46, 56, 57, 66, 68, 138, 140–1, 149, 217, 227, 234
monarch as symbol/royal visits 14, 32, 43, 50, 95–6, 103, 107, 112–15, 118, 120, 122, 130, 206–9, 142, 148, 153, 162, 178, 194, 205, 206–7, *208 & 9*, 211, 212, 216, 219, 221, 228–9, 234, 256–7, 262
monarchy as burden/collection of degenerates 131–5, 149, 151, 170, 173, 177, 195, 203, 207, 224–5, *247*; *see also* cost
Moreton Bay *see* Queensland
mother country *see* 'Mother England'
'Mother England' 15–16, 22, 49, 55, 57, 59, 62, 63, 68, 72, 73, 80, 83, 86–88, 91, 93, 95, 99, 105, 109, 111, 116–17, 122, 128, 146, 160, 165, 176, 190, 201, 222, 256; *see also* separation
multiculturalism 93, *230*, 240–1, 245, 254, 260, 262

national anthem 168, 206, 227, 228, 235, 243
National Australasian Convention (1891) *see* Federal Convention
national flag 168, 206, 235, 243, 253
national mythology/new dreaming 158, 162, 168, 226, 240, 245
National Party (Q'ld) 171, 175–6, 243, 261
nationhood/nationalism/national identity 1, 29–30, 65, 88, 97, 107–8, 116–17, 120, 121, 122–3, 127, 135, 151, 157, 158, 162, 166, 171, 197, 205–6, 213–14, 217, 221, 222–3, 226–7, 229, 236, 237, 239–41, 244, 248–63; *see also* independence
native-born (non-Aboriginal) 15, 21, 22–7, 46, 50, 56, 86, 123–5, 130, 151, 171, 173, 174, 211
New South Wales
 as 'Australia' 15, 17, 18, 20–2, 24–5, 29, 30, 31, 36, 37, 47, 51, 56, 62, 65, 69, 72, 74, 86, 89–91, 161
 as state 92, 93, 115, 127–8, 133, 149, 151, 153, 157, 161, 164, 171, 188, 195, 224, 262
 Constitution Committee 75, 83–4
 Legislative Council of NSW 19, 33, 35, 45, 53–5, 57, 58, 59, 65, 67–8, 69, 74–9, 81, 88, 89, 90–1, 109, 112–13, 127, 128, 131, 140–9, 164, 174, 191, 195, 200, 201; *see also* Sydney
newspapers *see* Index of Newspapers

oath of allegiance 227, 228, 235, 243, 253; *see also* loyalism
Orangemen *see* loyalism

parent state *see* 'Mother England'
Parliament – State – *see* Legislative Council
Parliament Federal 212, 214–5, 228, 232, 243
people, by name *see* Index of Personal Names
petitions to the Crown 17, 19, 25–6, 33, 47, 62, 66, 69, 72, 84, 95, 101, 142
political apathy 52, 80, 85, 137, 157, 159, 164, 171–2, 199, 238
political culture 10, 18, 31, 52, 69, 88, 114, 121, 215, 223
political parties, development of 131, 242–31

Port Phillip 37, 47, 53
Presbytarianism 34, 49, 53
president *see* Governor-General
press
  American 69
  Australian (colonial/independent) 18, 22–8, 35, 53, 65, 80, 114, 122, 142, 145–6, 147–8, 158–9, 234, 254, 261
  British 49, 61–2, 64, 65, 73, 120, 261
  see also Index of Newspapers
Primrose League *see* loyalism
Privy Council 215, 228, 246

Queensland 69, 88, 125–6, 133, 171, 174–87, 188, 195, 224, 233
  Legislative Council 171, 181, 233

racial purity – White Australia policy 50, 52, 66, 117, 120, 122, 124–5, 151–3, 163–4, 172, 176–7, 180, 188–9, 203, 206, 211, 217–18, 219–21, *230*, 260
referenda – (1897–8) 198–9; (1988) 246 (republic) 226, 246
representative *see* responsible government
republic: as
  abandoned joey 21
  alternative to direct monarchy: 24, 44, 81, 119, 194
  bogey-man/source of moral decay 78–9, 80–1, 113
  coming by stealth 244, 246
  constitutional development/evolving 28, 182, 186, 216, 246
  disguised ('substance without the shadow of the name') 81, 82, 86, 91, 108, 111, 119, 159, 163, 190, 194, 203–4, 216, 229, 257
  emotional and sexy 239
  inevitable/future 10, 43, 49, 62, 78, 82, 110, 111–12, 129–31, 159, 173–4, 178, 186–7, 188, 190–1, *202*, 222, 233, 234, 243, 245, 253, 256
  nationalist/anti-loyalist backlash 148–9, 156, 162–3
  masculine/manly 63, 124, 153, 182, 196, 222
  minimalist 210, 223, 235–6, 254, 256, 257–8
  racist/sexist 121–2, *152*, 153, 188,
  reunification of divided soul 253
  socialist utopia 133–4, 167, 176–7, 180, 213
  young man about to set up shop 84
Republic Advisory Committee 253, 257, 258

republican riots *see* Jubilee
R(eturned) S(ervices) L(eague) 223, 249
responsible government 19, 29–31, 34, 40, 44, 59, 62, 67, 73, 89–90, 93–4, 98, 102, 108, 109–10, 114, 151, 158, 214; *see also* colonial grievances, franchise, rhetoric 18, 34, 35, 41, 44, 47, 81, 87, 110, 111, 119, 123, 135, 157, 158, 159, 168, 234
revolution *see* separation
rights of man *see* Paine, Thomas in Index of Personal Names
Roman Catholic Church 114, 148, 210–11; *see also* Irish
Rome as example of classical republicanism 8, 65, 78, 80, 81, 129, 194
Royal Prerogative *see* Crown
rum *see* alcohol

Scotland/Scottish radicals 13, 41
sectarianism 112, 114, 116, 210, 261; *see also* Irish
secularism/free thought 10, 138, 141, 154, 156, 165, 167, 169
sedition *see* loyalism
self government *see* responsible government
Senate *see* Parliament – Federal
separation/severance 16, 17, 18, 21, 22, 29, 30, 32, 39, 40, 43, 47, 49–51, 54, 55–6, 65–7, 68–71, 72, 73–4, 78, 80, 83–4, 87–8, 91, 93–5, 96, 98–100, 103, 105, 107–8, 109, 112, 116–17, 120, 122, 126–9, 131, 139, 142, 146, 149, 153, 156, 157, 163, 164, 173, 174, 175, 186, 190, 192–5, 199, 213–15, 234
Sesquicentenary (1938) 206
shearers *see* trade unons
slavery/slaves 24, 31, 46, 95, 196
Social Darwinism 124
socialism 10, 62, 120, 131–6, 149, 151, 156–7, 159, 166–7, 170, 178, 182, 212–13, *see also* republic as socialist utopia
societies *see* by name
South Australia 115, 164; *see also* Adelaide
sovereignty of the people 31–2, 36, 64, 81–2, 95–6, 102, 118, 164, 195, 205, 230, 256–7; *see also* Crown
squatters 33, 34–39, 45, 56, 65, 80, 109; *see also* land
Sydney 19, 23, 41, 52, 65, 66, 67, 69, 87, 92, 111, 133, 164, 171, 198, 236, 249, 263

anti-transportation attitudes of 45, 46, 47, 57, 66, 72
Centenary 161, 162, 166
Domain 10, 121, 131, 148, 164, 166, 167, 169, 173
Federation celebrations in 205
Harbour Bridge 206
Jubilee public meetings 136–46, 148
response to the election of Lang 53–4, 68
royal visit (1977) 231–4
Sydney republican movements 166–74, 177, 186, 181, 198; *see also* Australian Republican League

Tasmania, 3, 45, 53, 67, 69, 72, 73, 96, 115, 131
taxation 20, 21, 31, 34, 36, 37, 38, 93, 97, 99–100, 170; *see also* colonial grievances, America
trade/economic prosperity 109, 111, 116, 125, 130, 131, 157, 213, 219–22, 252–3
trade unions 122, 156, 157, 174, 178–81, 200–1, 212–13
 Maritime Strike (1890) 179, 181
 Shearers' Strike (1891) 179, 181, 183, 185–6

transportation 40 44–7, 51, 54, 56–8, 59, 64, 65, 66, 69, 73–4, 93, 95, 126, 164; *see also* colonial grievances; convict stain
treason *see* loyalism
tyranny – arbitrary rule: British Government's behaviour as 15, 21, 34, 38, 41, 46, 71, 72, 96, 99, 102, 107, 150

universal suffrage *see* franchise

Van Diemen's Land *see* Tasmania
Victoria 59, 65, 69, 92–108, 109, 115, 120, 122–3, 124, 130, 133, 137, 153, 164–5
 Legislative Council 72, 93, 101, 108, 109, 118–19, 130, 198, 199, 212–3; *see also* Melbourne
Vietnam 221, 224, 237

Western Australia 3, 164, 186, 233
women/women's rights 154, 170, 177, 234; *see also* franchise
World War I & II 211, 213, 214, 215, 251, 261

INDEX OF NEWSPAPERS

Advertiser (Adelaide) 147, 168
Age 96, 97, 98, 102, 1038, 109, 119, 1301, 159, 169
Albury Banner 114
Argus 47, 52, 92, 94–5, 97, 98, 100, 103, 107–8, 140, 169, 188
Atlas 30, 32, 34, 35, 36, 46
Australian 18, 2, 21, 26, 37
Australian (Murdoch) 227, 251, 252, 253
Australian Republican 181–4, 185, 186
Australian Star 162, 175
Australian Worker 178, 179
Australian Workman 200
Australischer Zeitung 196

Ballarat Times 197, 99
Bowen Observer 181
Brisbane Boomerang 121, 135, 176, 177–8, 180, 183
Brisbane Courier 137–8, 140, 201
British Banner 49, 52
Bulletin 121–3, 124, 134–6, 158, 195, 202, 203, 238
 account of Jubilee Riots 138, 144, 146
 attitude to Federation 195, 199, 201

 definition of nationalism 151, *152*, 153, 156, 160–180
 post-1960 222, 223, 226

Charters Towers Times 180, 185
Citizen 43
Clipper (Hobart) 212
Commonwealth and Workers Advocate 193
Courier-Mail (Brisbane) 239
Currency Lad 23–8

Daily News (London) 62, 111
Daily Telegraph 122, 124, 137, 142, 146, 159, 163, 171, 173, 174, 175,
Dawn 170, 171
Democrat 129

Economist 229
Empire 59, 61, 63, 65, 76, 81, 83, 86, 104

Flame (Broken Hill) 212
Freeman's Journal 103, 148

Geelong Advertiser 53

Index 331

Goulburn Herald 90

Herald (Melbourne) 53, 169
Hobart Town Courier 49, 73
Hummer (Riverina) 133, 199, 203

Illustrated Sydney News 80, 148, 159
Inquirer & Commercial News (Perth) 151, 165

Launceston Examiner 67, 95
Liberator 129, 135, 147, 165

Mercury 195
Monitor 18, 19, 20, 21
Moreton Bay Courier 89
Morning Chronicle (London) 35, 36, 37, 62

Nationalist 171–2
Newcastle Morning Herald 149
News (Adelaide) 222
Northern Miner 178

Oz 220, 224–5

People's Advocate 42–4, 51, 52, 58, 68, 76, 85, 90
Pioneer 196
Post (Cairns) 181

Press 59, 65, 67

Radical 134, 135, 149, 166, 168
Representative 55, 61
Republican 134, 154–7, 158–60, 167, 168, 170, 174, 181
Reynolds News 135, 172

San Francisco Herald 69
Sydney Gazette 19, 23, 25, 27
Sydney Herald 18, 25, 26, 32, 33, 34
Sydney Mail 111, 146
Sydney Morning Herald
  pre-1900 31, 40, 53, 54, 62, 64–5, 70, 72, 74, 78, 80, 127, 158
  post-1900 206, 217, 245, 258, 261
  attitude to Federation 189, 200
  definition of loyalty/republicanism 81, 82, 86, 111, 112, 114, 117
  report of Centenary 161, 162
  report of Jubilee riots 136, 137, 139, 144, 145, 146, 148

The Times 73
Tocsin 212
Town & Country Journal 146, 151
Truth 137, 195–6

Worker (Sydney) 213

INDEX OF PERSONAL NAMES

Aaron, Dr Isaac 42–3
Abbot, Tony 260
Alfred, HRH Prince 112–15
Alomes, Stephen 211
Archibald, J. F. 23, 121, 135–6, 151, 153, 172, 238, 259
Arena, Franca 235, 245, 246

Bailes, A. S. 130–1, 137
Baker, Sir Richard 195
Bannon, John 249
Barton, Edmund 128, 193
Barton, G. B. 193–4
Basedow, Friedrich, 196
Berry, Sir Charles 122
Besant, Annie 156–7
Bjelke-Petersen, Lady (Florence) 233
Bjelke-Petersen, Sir Johannes 228, 233, 244
Black, Alfred 100, 101, 103
Black, George 99, 133, 154–6, 159, 160, 165, 166–71, 172–4, 194, 195, 197, 198, 201, 204, 238

Blackton, Charles 124
Blainey, Geoffrey 261
Blair, David 41, 42, 52, 53–6, 61, 72, 92, 94–6, 105–8, 119
Bligh, William (Governor of NSW) 14–15, 36
Bowen, Lionel 237, 246
Boyd, Arthur 251
Bradlaugh, Charles 135, 156, 157, 165, 172
Bruce, Stanley Melbourne (Australian Prime Minister) 88
Buchanan, David 127, 128, 173, 174
Byrne, J(oe) H. 123, 171, 174

Campbell, Charles 64
Carboni, Rafaello 99–101
Carr, Bob 232
Carrington, Lord, Charles Robert Wynne Lincolnshire, 1st Marquess of (Governor of NSW) 144, 145, 188
Charles, HRH Prince of Wales 246, 260
Chifley, Ben 217

Chiplin, Rex 210
Clark, Andrew Inglis 192, 194–5
Clark, Charles Manning Hope 25, 227, 232, 234, 239–41
Clarke, Marcus 124–5
Cobden, Richard 73, 111
Cockburn, Sir John Alexander 192
Coleman, Peter 226
Consadine, Peter 244
Corbyn, Charles Adam 63, 65
Cowper, Charles 58, 61, 70, 116
Cromwell, Oliver *see* English Civil War in Index of Ideas
Cunningham, Francis 43
Curr, Edward (MLC) 37

Dalley, William Bede 127–8, 153
Darley, Sir Frederick 138–9, 140
Darling, Ralph (Governor of NSW) 18–21
Darvall, John 78, 87
Davidson, Morrison (*Book of Kings*) 134, 135, 170
Dawkins, John 249
Dawson, Andrew 181–2, 187
Deakin, Alfred 122, 164–5, 191–2, 194
Deas-Thompson, Edward 53
Deniehy, Daniel 42, 49, 71–2, 76, 77, 85, 89–91, 110, 120, 124, 256, 258
Denison, Sir William Thomas (Governor of Tasmania and Governor-General) 53, 103
Derby, Lord Edward Henry Stanley, Earl of 73, 125
Dibbs, George 145–6, 194
Dilke, Sir Charles 175
Disraeli, Benjamin, Earl of Beaconsfield, 117
Downer, Sir John 192, 194
Drewe, Robert 227
Driver, Richard 85
Duffy, Charles Gavan 110–11, 116
Duffy, John Gavan 211
Dunsford, John 178–81
Dunstan, Don 219
Durham, Lord John George Lambton, 1st Earl of 29–30
Dutton, Geoffrey 214, 221, 222–6, 235, 236–7, 238, 245, 259

Edward VIII (as Prince of Wales) 213
Elizabeth II 178, 207, 211, 219, 228, 233–4, 236–7, 246, 261–2
Encel, Sol 235
Evans, Gareth 229, 245
Evatt, Joan 232

Fahey, John 253

Findley, Edward 212
Fitzgerald, Jack D 157, 187
Fitzroy, Sir Charles Augustus (Governor of NSW and Governor-General) 46, 56, 58, 65, 66, 67, 69, 74, 75, 97, 98
Foote, William M. 157–8
Forbes, Justice Francis 20
Forster ,W. E. 113
Fraser, Sir Malcolm 233, 243, 245, 251, 256
Fulton, John 25–6

Gaden, John 232
George V 214
Gipps, George (Governor of NSW) 33, 35–9
Gladstone, William Ewart 45, 55, 58, 73, 117, 120
Gollan, Myfanwy 231, 232, 234, 238
Gordon, General Charles of Khartoum 127
Goss, Wayne 249
Grey, Henry George 3rd Earl (Colonial Secretary) 44, 45, 47, 49, 56–9, 67, 69, 70, 72, 73, 74
Grey, Sir George 94, 95, 96, 194
Griffin, G. W. 173
Griffith, Sir Samuel 192, 194

Hall, E. S. 18–23
Hancock, Keith 216
Harpur, Charles 40, 42, 44, 72, 76, 90, 177
Harris, Max 222
Hawke, R. J. 'Bob' (Australian Prime Minister) 130, 243–5, 248–9, 251
Hawksely, E. J. 42, 43, 51, 56, 64, 83, 91
Hay, Robert William (Permanent Under-Secretary – Colonial Office) 19
Hayden, Bill (Governor-General) 243, 246
Her Majesty the Queen of Australia *see* Elizabeth II
Hewson, Dr John 249, 261
Higinbotham, George 118–19, 122, 164–5, 176
Hirst, John 257
Hodgman, Michael 244
Hodgson, Christopher 37
Horne, Donald 80, 214, 221, 222–6, 231–2, 233–9, 245, 250, 256, 259
Horne, Myfanwy *see* Gollan
Hotham, Charles (Governor of Victoria) 94–7, 101, 102, 103, 107
Howard, John 256, 260
Howe, George 23, 27
Hughes, Billy 88, 212, 214–15
Humffray, J. Basson 101
Hunter, John (Governor of NSW) 13

Hutchinson, Alexander 191

Ironside, Adelaide 42, 90
Isaacs, Isaac (Governor-General) 214

Jardine, Douglas 216–17
Jebb, Richard 218
Jones, Charles 157

Keating, Paul (Australian Prime Minister) 240, 251–6, 257, 258, 260–3
Keating, Annita 261
Keep, William 154–6, 160, 166, 167, 170, 171, 172, 173
Kelly, Ned 123, 234
Kelly, Paul 251
Keneally, Thomas 49, 80, 85, 249–50, 253, 256
Kerr, Sir John (Governor-General) 10, 216, 229–31, 233, 235, 236, 237, 240, 249
Killen, Jim 228
King, John Charles 70
King, Philip Gidley (Governor of NSW) 13
Kirby, Justice Michael 246
Kirk, Jim 246

La Trobe, Charles (Governor of Victoria) 47, 66, 74, 93, 94, 95, 97, 98
Lalor, Peter 100–1, 103
Lamb, John 68, 70
Lane, William 173, 176–8, 179
Lang, John Dunmore 34–8, 74, 110, 113, 116, 173, 189, 256, 259
  Coming republic/Coming Event lectures 28, 47–53
  as candidate for election 54–6, 67–72, 79–91
  in anti-transportation campaign 56–67
  parts company with Parkes 59–63
  Freedom & Independence 79–85
  see also Deniehy, Daniel; Parkes, Henry
Lang, Jack 213
Lawson Henry 121, 136, 137, 153–6, 158, 160, 166, 167–8, 171–4, 200, 256, 259; *see also Bulletin, Republican*
Lawson, Louisa 137, 153–4, 155, 160, 166, 167–8, 171, 172, 173
Lilley, Sir Charles 190, 195
Lowe, Robert 9, 30, 32, 35, 36, 38, 41, 42, 44, 45, 46, 73,

Macarthur, Edward 17
Macarthur, James 32, 33, 69, 78
Macarthur, John 17
MacDermott, Henry 32, 33

Maddison, James 4
Mahon, Hugh 212
Maloney, William 198
Martin, James 112, 113
McQuaker, James 185
McCulloch, Sir James 116
McDonald, Charles 181–2
McEnroe, Archdeacon John (Catholic Archdeacon of Melbourne) 70–1
McIlwraith, Thomas 125–7, 171, 173, 175–7
McKay, Angus 41–2
McKellar, Ensign Neil 12, 14
McLelland, (Diamond) Jim 232
McMillan, Wiliam 191
McNamara, William 166
Menzies, Sir Robert 88, 107, 207–10, 217, 219, 221, 226, 227, 231, 237, 259
Merivale, Herman 30, 39
Meudell, G. W. 124, 127
Michie, A. C. 115
Michie, Thomas 96
Mitchell, Major Thomas 87
Moorhouse Rev. Dr James (2nd Anglican Bishop of Melbourne) 129
Moran, Cardinal Patrick 148, 211
Mort, Thomas 58
Muche, Dr Carl 196
Muggeridge, Malcolm 222–3
Mundey, Jack 232
Murdoch, Rupert 222, 251
Murphy, John 245
Murray, Les 236–7
Murray, Terence 55
Murray-Smith, Stephen 222

Newcastle, 5th Duke of 73, 75
Nicholls, H. R. 100–1
Nilhols, C. F. 101
Nordau, Max (*Conventional Lies*) 134, 170
Norton, John 138, 139, 141, 145, 146, 157, 170, 195–6, 198, 200–1

O'Brien, Patrick 257
O'Dowd, Bernard 168, 212
O'Farrell, Henry James 112, 113, 115
O'Kane, Thadeus 178
O'Shane, Pat 232
O'Sullivan, E. W. 198, 201

Paine, Thomas (*The Rights of Man*), 6, 14, 25, 27, 32, 33, 79, 102, 114, 134, 258
Pakington, Sir John 73–4
Parkes, Henry 31, 41–7, 64, 72, 76, 107, 112, 117, 127, 162, 192–6, 256
  as Colonial Secretary 112

as advocate of Federation 188, 190, 192–6
  role in Jubilee riots 140–5, 147, 156
  relations with Lang 51–63, 79–84, 86, 88–91
Passey, Fred 183
Pearson, Charles 118
Peek, Richard 56–7
Peter, William 98
Petty, Bruce 232
Phillip, Capt. Arthur 262
Pooley, Tony 250

Rasmussen, Hans 167, 172
Reith Peter 246
Riley, Alban Joseph (Mayor of Sydney) 137, 139–40
Rivett, Rohan 222
Robinson, Sir Hercules 117
Russell, Lord John 1st Earl 59, 73, 75, 89
Ruxton, Bruce 249

Saunders, Cheryl 257
Scullin, James Henry (Australian Prime Minister) 214
Seekamp, Henry 99
Service, James 126
Sheehan, Sarah 232
Sinclair, Ian 229–30
Smallsalts, Joseph 14
Smith, James 92
Smith, Goldwin, 111
Snedden, Sir Billy 244
Stanley of Bickerstaffe, Lord Edward George Geoffrey Smith, 14th Earl of Derby (Colonial Secretary) 30, 34, 36, 38
Stephen, Sir Alfred 138, 149–50, 153
Stephen, Sir Ninian (Governor-General) 243

Stephensen, P. R. 213–14
Sudds, Joseph 19
Syme, David 118
Syme, Ebenezer 94, 105, 107, 108
Symes, Joseph 129, 165, 169, 173

Tench, Watkin 12
Thompson, Elaine 235
Thomson, Robert 163, 171, 201
Tiberius Gracchus *see* Corbyn, Charles
Timmann, A. A. 196
Traill, W. H. 171, 190, 201
Turnbull, Malcolm 201, 250, 256, 258
Turner, Graeme 240

Vern, Frederick 99
Victoria – Queen *see* Monarch
Vosper, Frederick Charles Burleigh 183–7, 259

Walker, Thomas 136, 137, 141–2, 154–6, 159, 160, 166, 169, 173, 191
Walsh, Richard 222, 224
Wardell, Robert 18–19
Watson, Don 251, 259, 262
Weekes, John 68
Wentworth's bill *see* Index of Ideas: Acts
Wentworth, William, 15–22, 23, 26, 35, 36, 57, 68, 74–9, 92, 194
West, John 64, 67
White, Patrick 232, 236
Whitlam, Gough 221, 226–9, 233, 235, 236–8, 239–40, 245, 259
Wills, Horatio 22–8, 38, 124, 259
Wiltshire, James 52
Windemeyer, William 38
Winterton, George 214, 244, 257
Woodfull, Bill 216–17
Wran, Neville 245, 250
Wright, Gilbert 64, 67, 70, 71